Mister Brownrigg's Boys

Magdalen College School and The Great War

Mister Brownrigg's Boys

Magdalen College School and The Great War

The story of the fifty boys from MCS who lost their lives during the conflict

David Bebbington

Foreword by
Professor Sir Hew Strachan

Pen & Sword
MILITARY

First published in Great Britain in 2014 by
PEN & SWORD MILITARY
an imprint of
Pen & Sword Books Ltd
47 Church Street
Barnsley
South Yorkshire
S70 2AS

ISBN 978-1-78346-299-5

A CIP catalogue record for this book is available from the British Library.

Typeset by Concept, Huddersfield, West Yorkshire, HD4 5JL.
Printed and bound in England by CPI Group (UK) Ltd, Croydon CR0 4YY.

Pen & Sword Books Ltd incorporates the imprints of Pen & Sword Archaeology, Atlas, Aviation, Battleground, Discovery, Family History, History, Maritime, Military, Naval, Politics, Railways, Select, Social History, Transport, True Crime, and Claymore Press, Frontline Books, Leo Cooper, Praetorian Press, Remember When, Seaforth Publishing and Wharncliffe.

For a complete list of Pen & Sword titles please contact
PEN & SWORD BOOKS LIMITED
47 Church Street, Barnsley, South Yorkshire, S70 2AS, England
E-mail: enquiries@pen-and-sword.co.uk
Website: www.pen-and-sword.co.uk

Contents

Foreword

by Professor Sir Hew Strachan

The centenary of the First World War has prompted a paradox, a local response on a European and even global scale. In Britain, as elsewhere, communities are establishing links with their predecessors who in 1914 went forth to fight, from villages and towns, from farms and factories. Schools are at the heart of these acts of commemoration. Today many still bear one obvious manifestation of the war, a roll of honour listing those who died. Some others continue to benefit in less obvious ways from the determination of interlocking groups to remember their losses. In the war's immediate aftermath, memorials could take more 'useful' guises, from scholarships to chapels, from libraries to assembly halls. These were investments in the future, as much as manifestations of who had been lost. Today we are urged once again to 'remember them'. But nobody does: not because of neglect, but because of the passage of time. None of us were alive (or very few of us were) when they were, or when the debates about how best to commemorate them raged back and forth, from mourning to triumphalism.

So, for any old boy, teacher, parent or pupil of Magdalen College School, what the centenary promises is not remembrance but discovery. David Bebbington's book will ensure that that is possible. His determination to uncover the lives of those who were at the school before 1914, and who died in the war or as a consequence of it, is a labour of love: a war memorial in its own right.

One of those young men, Noel Chavasse, has not been forgotten, and is still venerated far beyond his old school. But most of the fifty recorded here will be unfamiliar. Roughly half of the boys who entered the school between 1888 and 1916 joined up, and 20 per cent of them died. That is a loss rate higher than the national average (which was 12 per cent of all who served), and comparable with that of the college which is the school's parent institution. For those who left major public schools or matriculated at Oxford or Cambridge colleges in the three or so years before the war's outbreak the chances of not surviving until 1918 rose to about one in three.

In this respect Magdalen College School is typical of comparable educational establishments, but in others it is not. None of the fifty named here came from a military family. Their fathers were academics, clergymen and local businessmen, and most of their sons probably planned to follow in their parents' footsteps. That presumption is reinforced by another striking difference between the school and most others. In 1908 Richard Burdon Haldane had overseen the creation of the Territorial Army and established as part of it the Officers Training Corps, with a Senior Division in universities and a Junior in schools. Magdalen College School was exceptional in not having an OTC in 1914. The notion, that young middle-class men joined up because they had been 'militarised' before the war, does not look sustainable in the case of Mr Brownrigg's boys.

All those from the school who died served in the Army (and the Royal Flying Corps, which was part of it), none in the Royal Navy, and thirty-nine were killed on the western front in France and Flanders. Only five fell in theatres further afield, at Gallipoli, in Mesopotamia and Palestine. Four died at home, two of them after the armistice. Magdalen College School therefore captures – probably more than most – the archetypical experience of the infantry subaltern's war. How true that generalisation is depends on the career profiles not only of those who did not come back but also of those who did, who were, after all, at 80 per cent the overwhelming majority.

David Bebbington has written about a cohort whose experience fits into a broader national narrative, but its power lies in its recounting of individual stories. Here is the pathos: promise denied and parents bereaved. In recognising the wastefulness of this war, we need to remember that that does not – sadly – necessarily distinguish it from other wars. What makes it different is that the pupils of Magdalen College School, and of many other schools, responded as they did. They thought that Britain was fighting a necessary war, a conviction that those they left behind clung to, not least in pursuit of consolation.

Hew Strachan
June 2014

Preface

The Preface below was written well before any other word was penned for the book and before the book was properly planned and its content decided. It was written at the beginning of the idea, with emotive meaning about why the book should be written and what it would stand for. With the book now complete the preface still holds true, so it is included below untouched.

All the boys in this book have two things in common: they attended Magdalen College School, Oxford (some for eight years, others for only a few terms) and they are commemorated each year on or close to 11 November.

Every current MCS pupil sees and hears these names each year during a twenty-minute Remembrance Service in Big School (the School Chapel), but who were these boys that we continue to celebrate 100 years on? What was their character? What did they do whilst at school? What did they do after they left school? What were their aspirations?

Many of the MCS boys who died in the First World War knew each other, were friends, played for the same sporting teams; some even fought together. Seven of the boys were aviation pioneers, the first young men in history to fly into battle. Others were medics trying to mend wounds and minds and save lives. Many were infantrymen.

Each boy has a story to tell. Each mother chose a name for her son, to hopefully be used throughout a kind and prosperous life of seventy or more years; but their lives were cut short by a war that was on a different scale to all other wars before it. Their names would not be used and enjoyed by their families beyond their innocent years of school, college or their early adult life. However, through memorialization and commemoration their names are still used today, for even longer than their mothers or fathers could have wished. They are not forgotten. Their names deserve to be heard and re-heard and their life stories told and cherished. Anyone who reads this book will find a story or part of the book they can relate to; it will bring to life the characters that we acknowledge each year and help us to understand what they sacrificed when they lost their lives during the period of the First World War.

The book is not filled with 'going over the top' heroism, but brings the real lives of these boys back into focus. Through painstaking research the story of each boy has been uncovered and is recorded here for future MCS communities to read, connect to, cherish and be proud of.

David Bebbington
28 May 2012

Post-completion of the book, with all the added extras of maps, images and appendices that were crucial if the story of the boys and the school was to be fully understood, it is hoped the book is still versatile enough to be read in many different styles. Hopefully it will suit both the 'cover to cover' reader who wants to better appreciate the school immediately before and at the time of the Great War and the sacrifice made by the boys, and the 'reference book' reader who wants to dip into the book to occasionally refer to one aspect of the school or read an individual boy's story. Whatever the style, it is hoped that the reader, whether directly connected with the school or not, will appreciate the sacrifice that was made by these Old Waynfletes and nearly one million other British service personnel during the period of the Great War.

> Greater love hath no man than this, that a
> man lay down his life for his friends.
>
> *John 15.13*

Acknowledgements

I would like to express my gratitude to all those people and organizations that have helped with contributions of information, photographs and advice towards the writing of this book. It is with trepidation that I start the list of thanks, for fear of leaving anyone out who has helped me along at some stage during the past three years. For those people who do feel they have not been acknowledged, please accept my apologies, but rest assured that in your own way you helped contribute to what turned out to be more than the booklet it was initially envisaged to be. I hope that I have done justice and paid respect to the fifty boys by writing a comprehensive, sensitive and informative account of their lives and the story of the school and Mr Brownrigg during an era that profoundly shaped the school that we know today.

Finding descendants or relatives of any of the fifty boys was always going to be difficult, not only because 100 years had passed since the events took place but because most of the boys died young and had no offspring themselves. Only six of the boys married and only four had children. The search for relatives was therefore never going to be easy. However, with adversity comes good fortune, and early on in the project I made contact with Pauline Boase, the granddaughter of Charles Brownrigg, the central character in this book. I am indebted to her for her family anecdotes of 'Brigger' and the loan of family photographs of him for use in the book.

The other central character to the book was always going to be the celebrated Noel Chavasse, so often written about before but never from the viewpoint of his early school days in Oxford. When a long-time friend of my wife's, who had agreed to do some cartographer work for the book, coolly told me that he had known John Chavasse and sung at Christopher Chavasse's (Noel's twin brother) memorial service at St Peter's some years ago, and that his son was still in touch with Peter Chavasse, I knew fortune was on my side. It is therefore Peter Chavasse (great-nephew of Noel Chavasse) that I thank for giving me his blessing for the book and the consent to use his father's family photographs of Noel.

None of the boys on the War Memorial have relatives currently attending or living close by the school, but when along the journey of researching for the book I discovered three more boys who have been missed off the original school memorial it was to my great surprise and delight to find that one of them had a great-nephew who was a parent of a current boy at the school. This I discovered from the mutual use of a First World War internet forum. I am therefore very grateful to Edwin Richards for allowing me access to photographs and information to add to my story of his great-uncle Joseph Morton, someone who turned out to be more of a crucial figure in the evolution and modernization of the 'Public School' system and workings of MCS than any other boy.

Leaving a written tribute on a small cross of each grave of all thirty-nine MCS Western Front victims in the summer of 2013 (thank you, Sam) also brought about another chance connection, when David Yaw, who had knowledge of a relation of Leslie Yeo, spotted one of the crosses on his grave and contacted me directly. I am indebted to him for his forethought and to the relation of Leslie Yeo, who wishes to remain anonymous, for access to information and pictures of Yeo.

Boswell's, one of Oxford's best known companies and landmarks, still remains in the ownership of the family of Wilfrid Pearson, and I am very appreciative of Jonathan Pearson for putting me in touch with the grandson of Wilfrid Pearson, James Waite, and for James allowing access to some fascinating archives and permission to use photographs of his grandfather.

I am also very grateful to three other relatives for providing information, photographs and stories of a further trio of 'Brownrigg Boys'. These are David Baillie (grandson of L.D. Cane) for information and picture of Leonard Cane, Roger Bellamy for information on John Bellamy and for permission to use his photograph, and Nick Crews for information relating to Percy Lees.

During the search for material connected to the fifty boys I have discovered that it is not only family members that have thoughtfully preserved photographs, letters and medals of the MCS boys. To the following people and organizations I am very grateful for allowing me access to, and use of, their varied collections of memorabilia: Martyn Lovell for his information, letters and photographs relating to C.P. Sells; Jonathan Saunders for his information on C.E. Hemmerde; Ian Hembrow and Cumnor Cricket Club for information on, and the team photograph including, F.D. Wilkinson; Steve John for information and the picture of T. Thomas; Brian Collins for kind permission to reproduce the photographs of John Fox Russell; Scouts Wales for the kind permission to reproduce the photograph of the 1st Wolf Patrol, Holyhead Boy Scouts in 1909 (including John Fox Russell); Archie Connell (Burns Monument Centre) for information on A.D. Darbishire; and Tim Edwards for his mother's picture of the 1881 Wales Rugby Team, which included R.D. Garnons Williams. I would like to give a special thank-you to Stephanie Jenkins, a prolific local historian for Oxford, for her responses to my sporadic bombardments of questions and requests and for permission to use selected photographs for the book.

As in any era, many boys of the school in the late nineteenth and early twentieth centuries not only attended MCS but often came from other schools to join MCS or left MCS to finish their schooling elsewhere. I am therefore indebted to the following people and schools for their willingness to open up their records and find any piece of information they could about the boys in question, and for permission to reproduce photographs from their archives: Sarah Wearne (Abingdon School) for information and pictures of H.S. Cannon and K.V. King; Jane Kirby (Bedales School) for information on R.C. Christie; Lesley Koulouris (Berkhamsted School) for information on J.L.M. Morton;

Tony Chew and Louise Smith (Clayesmore School) for information on R.C. Christie and the picture of 'Christie's chapel window'; Charles Knighton (Clifton College) for information and the tug-of-war photograph of C.M. Dyer; Fiona Atkinson (Denstone College) for information on F.M.C. Houghton; Calista Lucy (Dulwich College) for information on N. Henderson, and the Governors of Dulwich College for kind permission to reproduce the photograph of Neil Henderson; Chris Nathan (St Edward's School) for information and pictures of B.H. Carter and for information on J.L.M. Morton; Christopher Dawkins (Felsted School) for information on E.W. Hanby; John Hamblin (Lancing College) for information on K.V. King; John Harding (The Leys School) for information on W.H. Pearson and the picture of the Rugby XV; Alexandra Aslett (St Paul's School) for information on H. Brereton; and Lindy Clegg (Perse School) for information on J.L.M. Morton.

Several of the boys went on to study at University and I am grateful to the following people for help with information about the boys' University lives: Julian Reid (Merton College) for information on C.P. Sells; Adam Green (Trinity College) for information on R.D. Garnons Williams and L.F. Yeo; Vanessa King and Richard Robertson (Victoria University of Wellington) for information on and the photograph of G.G. Matheson; Emma Goodrum (Worcester College) for information and copies of documents relating to C.R.C. Maltby.

Other people and organizations, big and small, have been most generous with information and permission to use photographs. I would especially like to thank Peter Hooper and John Carpenter for information and the picture of Francis B. Pitts; Pam and Ken Linge (The Missing of the Somme project) for information and photographs of J.W. Jenner-Clarke, G. Bradley and E.R.L. Andrews, and information on G.S. Gadney; English Heritage for kind permission to reproduce the photographs of Andrew's Saddle Shop and The Plain; Oxford Heritage Centre (especially Helen Drury) and Oxfordshire County Council for kind permission to reproduce the photograph of the view of 'the island', now School Field, from Milham Ford, the South African War Memorial and images from the *Oxford Journal Illustrated*.

The school has of course always had a special relationship with Magdalen College. Its relationship has evolved over the years, but much of their histories are inseparable. The choristers have always provided and still provide a link between the school and the college that is mutually beneficial to both institutions. The work of this book has coincided with the research by Richard Sheppard (Emeritus Professor of Magdalen College) and others towards a book commemorating the sacrifice made by the men of the college during the Great War (*The Slow Dusk*). Thirteen of 'Mr Brownrigg's Boys' were choristers, and as such were part of the 'College Foundation', effectively members of the college. After independent research on the thirteen choristers, we have been able to communicate and corroborate many pieces of information and stories about the choristers, helping each other with missing links. It has truly worked well, and I thank Richard for all his help and support. The common origins of the two institutions mean that much vital information about the school in the years of interest, 1870–1920, is located in the College archive. I am very appreciative of Robin Darwall-Smith (Magdalen College Archivist) for allowing me access to the archive and for many useful suggestions.

If it is through the photographs that this book brings the boys alive, it is through its maps that you orientate yourself to the location of the events. I am indebted to Alan Whitaker (Awa Graphics) for the production of the maps, with an attention to detail and accuracy that makes each of them a work of art. Living in Newbury, I did not know of Alan's connection to Oxford, but his enthusiasm for the task as soon as he knew he was working on a project about the place he grew up in and about people he had an association with made the process of developing the cartography an adventure on its own. Alan, you have my sincerest thanks.

I also wish to thank the MCS Governors and Tim Hands for their support with the project and for allowing me sabbatical leave in May and June of 2013 to forge ahead with the work on the book, for permission to use the school archive to its full potential and for permission to reproduce photographs belonging to the school. The MCS Development Department (Bella Raeburn, Sian Rees-Evans, Ruth Harvey-Powell and OW Kate Apley) have also been a great source of enthusiasm and support, and I thank them for helping to promote the project so enthusiastically and professionally. The response to the project from The Old Waynfletes' Club, especially from the chairman Bill Morris, has been heart-warming. I thank them for their show of support and encouragement for the book at the OW lunch in November 2013.

For a project like this to have, from an early stage, the agreement of a world-renowned publisher to publish and market the book is a massive incentive. I would therefore like to thank Henry Wilson of Pen & Sword for his enthusiasm and encouragement for the project.

Rebecca Roseff (MCS Archivist) has been a constant source of information and a sounding board for my ideas. The school is not rich in photographs from the past but she has managed to unearth some gems of images that add so much to this book. Her work at the Imperial War Museum on the Noel Chavasse collection added much to our knowledge of this already iconic figure. Rebecca's eye for spotting consistency errors proved invaluable in proofreading the book.

Peter McDonald is the 'proofreader extraordinaire', correcting grammatical errors and spellings in the manuscript to make it appear as if the book was written by a person who achieved a better grade at O-Level English than I actually did.

Alan Cooper (teacher, House Master, Director of Alumini Relations and general oracle of MCS) provided many leads that have become small treasures within the book. He knows more about the history of the school than anyone and has been an inspirational figure in initially getting me addicted to the annals of the school. Working all hours of each day for the school, he still found time to proofread the entire book. It was Alan and Rebecca who insisted I meet Michael

Hickey (OW, 1939–1947), with whom the final link to the First World War era at MCS was truly made. Michael had been filled with so many stories of his father's, as well as his grandfather's, school days at MCS stretching the years of this book, only to eventually become a chorister himself following the same rituals in the same boarding house, that talking to him was like taking a step back in time and experiencing the happiness and hardship of school at MCS during the days of 'Mr Brownrigg's boys'. Michael read the first draft of the manuscript in the later part of his fight with illness, providing much guidance and confidence-boosting feedback. For him and his wife, Bridget, to find this time for me at such a point in their lives was very special. Many thanks for all the cups of tea and biscuits Bridget, rest in peace Michael.

In addition to the above quartet of proof readers I am grateful to Professor Laurence Brockliss (Magdalen College, Oxford) for reading an early first draft of the book and providing much positive and constructive feedback.

To visit the battlefields of France and Belgium is a great learning and often an emotional experience. I would recommend to anyone who has even the slightest interest in history or has a distant relative who fought in the war to go on a battlefields trip. You may find you return more than once! To take a pilgrimage and make a trail to visit every one of the boys' graves and memorials buried in France, Belgium or England was an incredible and unforgettable adventure. This I did in the summer of 2013, clocking up over 900 miles with the company and assistance of my son, Sam. I am indebted to him for his support, for writing a tribute to each boy on a small cross at each grave and for the photography of every boy's burial or memorial site, from every angle, close-up and distant, and of their resting place's view. I am also very fortunate to have had a patient and considerate daughter, Aggie, who has shown interest in the project, supplied me with endless cups of tea and pieces of cake and helped out with all the chores to allow me to continue working on the book undisturbed. Finally, the vast majority of research towards the book, including many weeks spent at the the National Archive in Kew and at the Oxford History Centre, plus many months on a computer late at night, has been done by my wife, Debbie. She has a magnificent eye for detail and a love of solving mysteries and uncovering stories, the perfect chief researcher and book critic. It would not have been possible without her. We have shared incredible moments of discovery about the boys, their families and the school during the three years of producing this book and we have both come to know each and every one of the boys as if we knew them and their families personally.

It has truly been an emotional, enlightening journey, and an incredibly privileged way to learn in detail the true nature of the Great War and its effects. The tragic stories of these fascinating and gifted boys can sometimes make for sad reading, but there is not one of the boys I would not have loved to have known in real life. They include ground-breaking academics, international sportsmen, motor racing pioneers, dedicated surgeons, the first pilots in history, local business men and vicars. After such an intense and focussed three years researching and writing about the boys and the school, I feel as if know each of them personally. It is my hope that the book leaves the reader with the same feeling, a knowledge of who these 'names on the memorial' were, and an appreciation of the ultimate sacrifice made by the fifty boys and the toll it took on their immediate families and communities, most notably on Mr Brownrigg.

David Bebbington
April 2014

CHAPTER ONE

The School

The fifty Magdalen College School, Oxford, boys who died during the First World War attended MCS over a period that stretches almost fifty years (1870–1916). The school during this time was to change little on the surface, although numbers attending the school fluctuated from as few as 36 to a peak of 101 boys at any one time.[1] The 1870 Education Act had made elementary schooling compulsory for children under the age of 13, with MCS educating boys between the ages of 9 and 18 it was mainly providing a second tier of education for the small proportion of teenagers who did not enter the workforce immediately upon reaching teenage years. Five Masters (Headmasters) were to serve the school during this time, with Charles Edward Brownrigg being the stable and guiding character before, during and after the war years.

The school was a mixed boarding and day school for boys, totalling on average seventy to eighty boys including sixteen boarding choristers at any one time. The level of fees meant that the majority of the boys came from reasonably prosperous backgrounds and were more often sons of professional men rather than tradesmen. It meant a rivalry developed between MCS and Oxford High School[2] (school to Thomas Edward Lawrence, 'Lawrence of Arabia', in the years 1896–1907) due to their much lower fees and hence greater ability to attract day boys; and between MCS and St Edward's, who because of their location in Summertown were better able to attract boys from fashionable North Oxford than MCS, who had the poorer East Oxford area on its doorstep. In addition, no boy was admitted to MCS unless he satisfied the Master in an examination or had been admitted as a chorister. An entrance examination for the school comprised

Day fees at MCS during the period 1883 to 1914 were £18.18s annual instruction fee, and £3.3s a year for subscription to the Library, Cricket Club, Boat Club, Football, Athletic Sports and for use of the Bathing Place. Hence a total payment was £22.1s a year for a day boy. Boarders' fees from 1888 to 1895 were 51 guineas a year for board and subscriptions and 18 guineas for tuition.[3] Hence a total payment of 69 Guineas (£72.9s) a year for a boarder (apart from choristers).[4] The cost for board was reduced in 1895 to £42 per annum,[5] making the inclusive fee with tuition of £64.1s per annum. If music was studied this was £2 a term extra. Boys reading the 'higher branches' of the natural sciences, by special arrangement, would be liable to an additional fee for laboratory expenses. Also charged per year was 8s for stationery, 3s for *The Lily* and 1s.6d for drawing materials.

writing from dictation, easy questions in English Grammar and questions using the first four rules of Arithmetic.

The work of the school was mainly arranged with the idea of preparing the boys for entry into 'the' University (i.e. Oxford). The school was annually examined by the Oxford and Cambridge Universities Schools' Examination Board. Boys in the Upper Fifth and Sixth Forms (age 16 to 18) were being examined for Higher Certificates; those in the Lower Fifth Form for Lower Certificates (age 14 to 15). For each boy one overall Certificate result was given either as a Pass or Fail, with each subject also assigned a Distinction, Pass or Fail on the Higher Certificate and Class 1, 2 or Failed on the Lower Certificate. Subjects taught included Latin, Greek, French, Mathematics, Science (only Physics- and Chemistry-related topics, but theoretical and practical classes in both),[6] Divinity/Scripture, History, English Grammar, Literature, Composition, and Drawing.[7]

The Masters

The teaching staff at the school was made up of the Master (headmaster), Usher (deputy headmaster), chaplain, and between three and nine assistant masters (usually subject specialised teachers), depending upon pupil numbers. R.H. Hill was the Master of the school when Richard Garnons Williams was a schoolboy, the oldest of the boys to die. None of the boys who died were at the school during the era of the next two Masters, H.C. Ogle and E.R. Christie. It was the following two Masters, W.E. Sherwood and C.E. Brownrigg (who led the school for forty-two years between them) that knew the other forty-nine boys' characters, having taught some of them for up to eight years.[8]

W.E. Sherwood was the Master when Cane, Chavasse, Darbishire, Dawes, Gadney, Roberts, Steward and Morris were at the school. The remaining forty-one boys would all know C.E. Brownrigg as their only Master. Sherwood and Brownrigg were appointed Master and Usher together after a disastrous year of Christie as Master, and Brownrigg remained at MCS for a further forty-two years. Brownrigg's knowledge, closeness and connection to all the boys, bar

Table 1. Masters of Magdalen College School, 1864–1930.

Master	Dates (years in office)	Usher	Dates (years in office)
R.H. Hill	1864–76 (12)	H.E.F. Garnsey	1861–66 (5)
		H.C. Ogle	1866–67 (1)
		H.E.F. Garnsey†	1867–76 (9)
H.C. Ogle*	1876–87 (11)	J.H. Audland	1876–87 (11)
E.R. Christie	1887 (1)	O. Seaman	1887 (1)
W.E. Sherwood	1888–1900 (12)	C.E. Brownrigg	1888–1900 (12)
C.E. Brownrigg*	1900–30 (30)	P.D. Pullan	1901–35 (34)

* Previously Usher † Reappointed

Charles E. Brownrigg, 'Brigger'.
Magdalen College School Usher (1888–1900) and Master (1900–1930).
Outside the old chapel on the Longwall site.

Garnons Williams, was unparalleled, and the loss he was to feel can only be imagined. He was affectionately known as 'Brigger' by the boys.

As well as being Usher then ultimately Master of the school, Irish-born Brownrigg taught classics throughout the school. Latin was compulsory at MCS for all boys, including the Sixth Form, and 50 per cent of the preps set would be for Latin. No boy whom 'Brigger' taught would 'ever forget the zest and twinkling Irish humour' of the man who devoted forty-two years to the service of the school. Whenever he heard the national anthem played he would stand to attention for its duration, no matter where he was or what he was doing.[9] He set high standards of respect for his students to follow and his eye for detail in his teaching necessitated nothing but the best in return when written work was submitted for marking.

Corporal punishment was an established part of schooling in this era. Although Brownrigg rarely resorted to such punishment, boys reported to him for gross misbehaviour did receive four or six strokes with a special horse whip. True to Brigger's sporting prowess, he is said to have delivered these from the wrist as if late-cutting a cricket ball through the slips! Minor infringements were dealt with by the prefects of the school and, given the Master's consent, were allowed to request lines from boys and to carry out canings on behalf of the Master.[10] In 1910 abuse of this system resulted in a senior prefect appearing before Oxford City Magistrates Court accused of assault.[11] The senior prefect involved was found guilty of using excessive force and employing the inappropriate punishment of face-slapping a boy. The court concluded that the slapping punishment had been inflicted without the knowledge of the Master and that on its advice the prefectorial system at MCS was to be more closely monitored. The senior prefect was fined 20s plus 14s costs, or a calendar month's imprisonment. The incident caused the school and the college serious embarrassment. The professional community of Oxford, who usually looked upon MCS to educate its boys, was unsurprisingly alarmed by the episode. At the start of the following academic year, Michaelmas 1910, no new day boys joined the school and the total number in the school fell from a consistent eighty-plus boys to sixty-seven. As the war years approached the numbers attending the school that Brownrigg had built up had still not recovered.

Charles Brownrigg was recognized nationally as one of the top headmasters in the country and was given the honour of being the chairman and host of the annual meeting of the Headmasters' Conference in 1907.[12] Brownrigg was the only Master of MCS to have had this honour until the present day Master, Dr Tim R. Hands, became Chairperson 106 years later in 2013/14.

Charles Brownrigg married Adolphine Mary Arbuthnot, known as Mary, in 1897 and had a son (who died before his first birthday) and two daughters. Sadly, Mary died on 18 December 1904 not long after the birth of their second daughter. Brownrigg married his second wife, Valerie Margaret Elizabeth Akerman in 1908 and had two further sons (John Herbert Leslie in 1909 and Philip Henry Akerman in 1911). Cruelly, Brownrigg was to lose his second wife in 1929, one year before his retirement as Master of MCS. Charles Brownrigg himself died in 1942, aged 77. Two years after his death, his son John (an Old Waynflete who, like his father, represented Oxfordshire at cricket) was killed in action in Italy on 18 February 1944.

Location and Buildings

In September 1894 the current School House on Cowley Place was completed as the new boarding house.[13] Until this time the school existed solely on the Longwall site, now part of Magdalen College. On the Longwall site the school had been using a purpose built school house (the original *Big School*, now Magdalen College library), playground and fives court since 1851. A red-brick school chapel had been built in 1856/7 attached to the boarding house on Longwall Street.[14] Indeed, the Master's residence and boarding house on the corner of the High Street and Longwall had been improved several times during J.E. Millard's reign (1846–64), the school buying the house next door (called 'Fifty Seven') and adding a dining room, kitchen and, in 1863, a school laboratory.

In 1871 a classroom was added to the eastern end of the original Big School on the Longwall site, running north at right angles to it. The fives court was rebuilt farther up the playground to accommodate this and the science laboratory was also improved at this time to allow ventilation suitable for practical chemistry work. The school also seems to have had a science laboratory in the old glass bottle factory on Merton Street, but when in 1889 the school refurbished the laboratory for analytical chemistry teaching, the teaching of what would now be called physical chemistry and physics was carried out in the college's Daubeny Laboratories. Across the High Street from Magdalen College, and facing the college buildings, were (and still are) the Daubeny Laboratories (first built in 1848) and the Botanic Gardens (in existence since 1621). For thirty years (from 1888 to 1918) all the science at MCS was taught by John J. Manley (the Daubeny Curator). Indeed, it is this teacher's class notebooks, containing set lists and end of term exam grades, which are the closest thing to an MCS register that survives from this period.[15]

It was during Sherwood's Mastership that the school was to create its two most visible links with current times by building what is now known as School House (now home to the Junior School) and obtaining a lease for the playing field (School Field, an island in the middle of the River Cherwell) in 1893 from Christ Church.

The demise of the old boarding house together with its Chapel on the corner of Longwall Street and High Street was accelerated by an outbreak of scarlet fever in 1891, revealing deficiencies in its drainage system. Work on the new School House was started soon after 1891 and this new boarding house by The Plain, designed to accommodate fifty boarders, was completed and occupied in 1894.[16] A new Chapel (made of stone) was built on the north side of the Longwall playground and opened in 1895. In the winter of 1894 the first game of football

View of the island (now School Field) from Milham Ford, with Magdalen College behind (c.1870).

was played on School Field. The island required significant levelling, and it was another ten years before the whole area was fit for purpose. Until the white bridges were built (November 1894) the boys were punted across to the semi-levelled field which was (and remains) liable to occasional flooding. Today the cricket ground is considered one of the most picturesque grounds in England, with the backdrop of punts on the Cherwell, the Botanic Gardens, Magdalen tower and the dreaming spires beyond.

During the 1890s the bicycle had become popular amongst the middle classes and in 1901 the first MCS bicycle shed was constructed in the playground. It is understood that Brownrigg's bicycle was made by William Morris (later 1st Viscount Nuffield and the founder of Morris Motors Ltd) whose family lived on James Street close to the modern school.[9] Two new, but temporary and hastily constructed classrooms were also built in 1905 in the playground to help accommodate the consistently higher number of boys now attending the school (approximately ninety, compared to around seventy a decade earlier). The greater emphasis on games necessitated that the remainder of School Field be levelled in 1907, and in 1913 the School Field Pavilion was built.[17]

At the beginning of Brownrigg's reign as Master, the school ran seven forms (I, II, III, IV, Vα, Vβ, VI). Form Vα, Vβ, and VI occupied the first floor and Forms III and IV used the ground floor of Big School on the Longwall site, the forms being separated by curtains. Forms I and II were taught in the library of

The School Pavilion (c.1914).

the new School House on Cowley Place. Specialist groups preparing for other examinations or entry into the army were taken in the School House coat lobby.

Pupil Numbers

The MCS boys who died during the First World War attended the school between the years 1870 and 1916, a period of forty-six years. However, forty-nine of the fifty boys attended during just a twenty-eight-year period from 1888 to 1916. As stated earlier, the Master to the oldest MCS boy to be killed in action was R.H. Hill. Only two other Masters, W.E. Sherwood and C.E. Brownrigg, were to educate the other boys who died as a result of the war. During this time, 1888 to 1916, the numbers attending the school fluctuated from as few as 36 to a peak of 101 boys. In common with all Public Schools during this era, the school year was less rigid, with boys arriving and leaving in all three terms. In addition, some boys remained at school until 18 (a few even longer to 19), but the majority left school at younger ages. Only a small percentage went on to University. On the eve of the outbreak of war it is estimated that the number of boys at the school was approximately seventy, ranging from age 9 to 18 across five forms.

The school's Roll of Service (MCS men known to have served their country during the war) numbers 248, of whom eight were staff (see Appendix 1A).[18] Although it is not possible to know exactly the total number of boys to have attended the school during the period 1888–1916, it is confidently calculated that the number is between 450 and 500. Approximately half of those attending

Table 2. Pupil numbers at Magdalen College School between 1864–1917.

Master	Years	Year	Number of boys		
R.H. Hill	1864–1876	1864		91[$]	
H.C. Ogle	1876–1886	1886		<80[#]	
E.R. Christie	1887–1888	1888		36[&]	
			Easter	Summer	Christmas
W.E. Sherwood	1888–1900	1888		41	46
		1889	55	55	55[*]
		1890	62	59	71
		1891	71	72	63
		1892	63	70	72
		1893	78	84	80
		1894	74	76	75
		1895	72	71	78
		1896	81	84	96
		1897	92	89	96[+]
		1898	92	97	95
		1899	95	101	96
C.E. Brownrigg	1900–1930	1900	92	88	
		1905			83
		1906	86	91	88
		1907	88	91	81
		1908	80		81
		1909	84	81	78
		1910		77	67
		1917		70[£]	

Formal MCS Registers for this time no longer exist. The numbers given in this table were therefore compiled and corroborated using five alternative sources. Where numbers were found for individual terms these are given separately as Easter, Summer and Christmas.

[$] The number had risen from 18 to more than 80 during J.E. Millard's mastership (1846–64). The number reported (91) here is the number for 1864 and consisted of 63 boarders and 28 day boys. During Hill's time this number neared the 100 mark for a short period.

[#] Numbers showed a tendency to decline during Ogle's mastership, and for most of the time were below 80.

[&] Despite bringing 20 new boys with him, Christie's short reign reduced the school number to 36 by the time his tenure was abruptly ended.

[*] 16 choristers, 20 other borders (of which 5 were ex-choristers), 19 day boys (of which 2 were ex-choristers).

[+] Stanier reports that the number in 1897 was 100 and that the proportion of boarders to day-boys was now approximately 50:50.

[£] In 1917, the year before the war ended, the number of boys at the school was 70 (50 of whom were boarders and 5 prefects). A similar roll number is quoted by C.G. Hey for December 1917 in his Diary (61 total, 32 ordinary boarders, 16 choristers and 21 day boys). This roll number was to more than double within four years of the war ending until in 1922, with the number of boys at 150, it was necessary to arbitrarily divide the school by establishing a six-house system.

between these years therefore served, with one in five of these boys losing their lives as a direct result of the war.

During Hill's time as Master (1864–76), MCS boys won fifty open scholarships and exhibitions. University teachers were employed as part-time masters and access to University lectures was obtained for the boys. It was even possible for boys to proceed to examinations of the University. Complaints began to be heard in the town that MCS was now unduly difficult to get into! Towards the end of Hill's reign it was rumoured that there was talk of abolition of the school or its reduction to a choir school ('The 1875 Crisis'). Greater clarity in the school's future was needed and regulations for the conduct of the school drawn up. Although not overly favourable for the future development of the school it was at least 'retained as a first-grade classical school'.[19]

In Ogle's first few years as Master (1876 onwards), the school hours were changed to suit the day boys, and compulsory games and chapel for day boys was abolished.[20] This appears initially to have had the effect of increasing numbers, but by 1884 the numbers had reduced to their previous level.[21] In 1887 Ogle was replaced by E.R. Christie, who brought twenty boys from his previous school in Kent.[22] To reduce the bullying and abuse of authority by older boys that appears to have developed during Ogle's time, the old prefects were degraded and the Kent boys made prefects. Bitter hostility developed between the two factions, and Christie was feared and hated by most. Even *The Lily*, the MCS magazine, had its name changed by the Brockley boys.[23] After only one year in charge the College took decisive action and Christie left.

W.E. Sherwood, a former pupil of the school,[24] was appointed as the new Master in 1888 and the school, at the time reduced to only thirty-six boys, immediately began to recover. Numbers increased and within ten years the school was 100 strong. The school results of certificate examinations improved and numbers of scholarships and exhibitions won by the school became very healthy.[25] Crucially, Sherwood appointed C.E. Brownrigg (in 1888) and P.D. Pullan[26] (in 1897), who between them would give the school eighty years of service, culminating in a thirty-year Master and Usher double act. Sherwood, an Oxford Blue in rowing, also brought about a greater keenness and efficiency in the playing of games (cricket, football and hockey) and broadened boys' interests by increasing the number of extracurricular societies. During Sherwood's twelve-year reign as Master boys gained 101 senior certificates.

In 1900 the charge of the revitalized school was transferred from Sherwood[27] to the Usher, C.E. Brownrigg. Continuity was maintained since during the first twelve years of Brownrigg's tenure as Master boys gained 118 senior certificates. Given the school's small size and together with the twenty-six scholarships and exhibitions to Oxbridge during this time, this was considered an achievement the school and its community should be proud of. In 1906 Brownrigg initiated the school's long tradition of a Commemoration Service (in Magdalen College chapel initially), ensuring a proud link with the past and an appreciation for all the benefactors of the school. It immediately captured the imagination of the

Magdalen College School Football XI, 1891.
Standing, left to right: H. Badcock, R.H. Ankstell, H.M. Parham, G.S.A Jones, W.B. Green, J.S. Williams, W.H. Ferguson.
Seated, left to right: W.D. Coddington, C.E. Brownrigg, E.C. Sherwood,[28] A.W.T. Perowne.[29]

school community with old boys and their families returning for the celebration, which included lunch and sports. More than 100 years on, 'Commem', as it is affectionately called by the school today, is still a thriving whole-day celebration, with the service conducted in the University Church of St Mary the Virgin, followed by festivities including a leavers' lunch and School versus Old Waynfletes cricket and tennis matches on School Field.

An excellent all round sportsman, Brownrigg was a big advocate of the importance of games, playing in the school teams himself, alongside the boys, as many of the fixtures of this time were against mature college sides.[30] He played football, hockey and cricket for the school sides, first appearing in school fixtures when Usher in 1888 and still turning out for the boys' sides when Master until 1908, aged 43. During the early 1900s the games captains made their own fixture lists, managed the discipline, picked the teams and were responsible for all the arrangements for away matches. Indeed, it is written that 'No master ever went

Magdalen College School Cricket XI, 1890.
Standing, left to right: A.W.T. Perowne, C.E. Brownrigg, W.H. Ferguson.
Seated, left to right: R.H. Ankstell, C.H. Tollit, W.H.C. Weippert, H.C.S. Gmelin,[31] J.F.G. Little, J.M. Bridgman, C. Hayes, H.B. Parsons.

away with a team to keep order; it was unnecessary.' The philosophy of the school appears to have been not only to give the boys an appreciation of academic values but also to prepare them for responsibility in future life. Up to the end of the First World War the proportion of boarders to day boys tended to increase, necessitating a prefectorial system that suited such a small school and developed a great sense of loyalty and unity.

The School Day

Punctuating the boys' school days were the bells of Magdalen tower, chiming every quarter hour then as they do today, but significantly more prominent because of the school's proximity before it moved (in 1928) across the river to its current position by The Plain.

During Sherwood's and Brownrigg's time, it is known that the boys dressed in dark coats and wore black or dark blue ties. Either a straw hat with a school ribbon or a school cap was worn. Choristers were required to wear traditional Eton jackets (known to the boys as 'bum-freezers') with shirt collars falling outside the jacket, and straw boater hats. The choristers, as they do today, dressed in cap and gown, walked in line each day to chapel. Since 1894, when the boarders moved into the new school house by The Plain, the sight of the 'crocodile of choristers' crossing Magdalen Bridge to get to the college chapel has changed little.

Thirteen of the MCS boys to die as a result of the war were ex-choristers. All were taught by the legendary organist, choir master Dr John Varley Roberts

Magdalen College Choir, 1907.
The MCS boys:
Third row, ***left*** to right: J.V. Haseler[32], **D.H. Webb**, D.I. Davies, E.R. Hicks.
Third row, ***right*** to left: B.A. Carter, T.A. Scattergood, **J. Fox Russell**.
Front row, ***left*** to right: E.V. Richardson, **J.C. Callender**, K.L. Dams, W. Moulding, F.B. Luget, **H. Brereton**, **C.E. Hemmerde**, B.G.L. Hickey, G.C. Carter.
Central to the photo, seated is T.H. Warren (President of the College). To the right is J.V. Roberts (College Organist 1882–1918), to the left is J.M. Thompson (Dean of Divinity).

Ivor Novello.
The dark-haired boy, third from the left on the third row of the choir photograph (opposite), holding his jacket with his left hand is David Ivor Davies, later to change his name to Ivor Novello. Novello was the writer of the enormously popular First World War song 'Keep the Home Fires Burning' and the wartime hit musical 'Theodore & Co'. The photo on the left was signed by Novello and given to Colonel S.M. Hickey, the son of fellow Chorister B.G.L. Hickey.

(whose name still adorns a chorister prize each year at Prize Giving); he was fondly referred to as 'Bob' by the boys he taught and was regarded as one of the great choir masters of his age.

From 1894, it would have been a regular sight to see all the boarders crossing Magdalen Bridge to attend classes, which usually took place in Big School on the Longwall Street site. During the early 1900s a usual morning routine for those boarding in School House would be to rise at 6.30am, wash, dress, then eagerly gulp down hot cocoa received from the serving hatch in the hall. Between 7.10 and 7.50am, and following morning prayers, prep from the night before would be completed. Finally breakfast was taken. At 8.45am the boarders would cross Magdalen Bridge and assemble with the day boys in the school chapel for a brief morning service. By 9.15am the boys headed to their respective form rooms. Classes were taken for three hours in the morning and two hours in the afternoon.

Choristers were members of the three youngest forms and at 9.45am left their classes to sing choral matins in the College Chapel.[33] This finished at 10.40am, but practice took over and the choristers would eventually return to class at 11.45am. The 'remnants' of the class would have continued lessons with semi-recreational work.

The boarders received tea at 5.00pm back in School House, but at 5.45pm the choristers would be off again to sing the evening service in the college chapel.

Prep was from 7.15pm until 8.15pm in the dining hall. At 8.30pm supper was taken, followed by Prayers. The choristers also sang at Sunday service, which other boarders, but not day boys, would be expected to attend.

The scene on The Plain for the MCS boys from the early 1900s would not be an unfamiliar picture to us today in 2014. A grocery shop, Underhill's, existed on the other side of The Plain from where the boys supplemented their diet (especially during the period when the school patriotically voluntary rationed bread during the war years), and the octagonal Victoria Fountain (a drinking fountain) became a main feature outside the School House when it was built in 1899 to commemorate Queen Victoria's Diamond Jubilee.[34] The roundabout area was still the former St Clement's Church Yard, and horse-drawn trams posed the greatest threat to boys crossing The Plain.

School was six days a week for all pupils, with half-day holidays on Wednesdays and Saturday afternoons during the two winter terms, Michaelmas and Hilary. During the summer term, Trinity, there were two half-day holidays on Thursday and Saturday afternoons, plus a third half-day holiday on Tuesday afternoons for

The Plain, with School House on the right (c.1905).

The occasion of the unveiling of the South African War Memorial (sheeted, left), at The Plain, 19 September 1903.
Dedicated to the 142 men of the 1st Battalion, Oxfordshire and Buckinghamshire Light Infantry.[35]

cricket, but only for those boys whose work during the previous week had been satisfactory. Holidays were seven weeks in the summer, four weeks at Christmas and at least a fortnight at Easter.

During the late nineteenth and early twentieth centuries the boys would have been surrounded by imperialistic teaching and nationalistic pride. Memorialization and commemoration of heroic battles, wars and fallen old boys were on the school's door step and within its walls. On 19 September 1903 a South African War Memorial, dedicated to the 142 men of the 1st Battalion, Oxfordshire and Buckinghamshire Light Infantry who died in the South African (Boer) War of 1899 to 1902, was unveiled on the site of The Plain roundabout (the former churchyard of St Clement's Church). Approximately 5,000 people gathered to watch the ceremony, which started with a procession from School House in Cowley Place. The memorial (a bronze statue of an OBLI soldier atop a 9-feet high Portland stone plinth) stood on the site until the 1950s and can now be seen at the entrance to Dalton Barracks in Abingdon. This statue would have been the dominant feature seen by the boys from School House at Cowley Place.

The South African War Memorial, The Plain, Oxford in 1907.

A year later, the memorial to Frank G. Twiss was unveiled at the school. Twiss, a contemporary of Noel Chavasse, had been at the school for three years when he was one of three boys who volunteered to join the Imperial Yeomanry (Private 8143, 59th Company, 15th Battalion) and fight for his country in the Boer War. He died on 30 May 1900 of enteric disease while participating in the western advance towards Hoopstadt. Aged only 16, he was probably the youngest

The Magdalen College School Memorial to Frank Twiss.

trooper to die in the campaign. Amongst old boys at the time serving in the Boer War was Arthur A. Steward, who was later killed during the Great War.

Even Sports Day (the afternoon of the Commemoration Service post-1906) had a military occasion to it, with the band of the 4th Battalion, Oxford and Buckinghamshire Light Infantry being a regular feature to entertain the crowd.

The War Years

As 1914 approached many in Britain were predicting an imminent war with Germany, and numerous organizations made plans in order to be ready for its eventualities. The writer May Wedderburn Cannan (1893–1973), who had grown up at Magdalen Gate House[36] on the corner of Rose Lane and across the road from the school's Longwall site, took first aid and nursing classes and became a member of the Oxford Voluntary Aid Detachment in the run-up to the war. The VAD was approached by the War Office to set up voluntary Red Cross hospitals in the event of troop mobilization. In her autobiography Cannan states that in 1913, when aged only 20, she was charged with having to find a building for the Oxford VAD hospital. She went to see Brownrigg in the winter of 1913 at his accommodation in School House on Cowley Place. Cannan says the building at the time had only recently been completed with a new wing and she proposed this as a location for a sixty-bed VAD hospital, should war be declared. Brownrigg advised that she must speak to the President of the College. No official record has been found of any subsequent meeting between May Cannan and the President, nor are there any College meeting minutes referencing the proposal. However, in her autobiography May Cannan tells the story that MCS did become a war hospital, if only very briefly. She writes that on the declaration of war the VAD was mobilized and two days later, by the evening of 6 August 1914, they had an equipped hospital of sixty beds in School House. At the same time the Examination School in the High Street was being turned into a Military Base Hospital under the orders of the Army Medical Corps. The Red Cross VAD waited through August and were then told that no Red Cross VAD hospitals would be needed. The VAD nurses were told they could work in the military hospitals if they wanted. May Cannan herself accepted the offer of work at the military hospital and arrived in the Examination School at the same time as the Colonel had received a telegram telling him he must have sixty beds ready immediately. The Examination School was not ready, so with relief the Colonel took up the offer of temporary use of the VAD Hospital already set up at MCS. It is likely that the first consignment of wounded men to return to Oxford, sixty of them, went initially to convalesce in MCS School House on Cowley Place.

The Editorial section of the November 1914 *Lily* reports that the sick wards and the little dormitory of School House were used to provide for wounded soldiers during the holiday. However, as soon as the Army Medical Authorities had the Base Hospital at the Examination Schools operational, the sick wards and dormitory in School House were restored for the use of the school. MCS continued doggedly during the war years but the school community 'could not escape the grim undertones of war'. Nurses and soldiers became common sights along the High Street. It was not long before the first news of deaths of old boys reached the school. News of each old boy death was mourned with pride, but the real horrors of the trenches, the ordeals at sea and the short life expectancy of members the Royal Flying Corps were concealed from the young boys at the school. Brigger, as Brownrigg was affectionately known by the boys, was to hold the school community together during this time, welcoming back its heroes and memorializing the lost boys who had only recently graced the class rooms, playing field and river. In 1916 the school, like the whole nation, was stunned by the death of the iconic Lord Kitchener while en route to Russia aboard HMS *Hampshire*.

In the early part of the First World War, female teachers[37] taught at the school to help fill the gaps left by those that left to join the army.[38] A Cadet Corps was also formed in 1914 with Brownrigg as the Commanding Officer. Much of the boys' spare time was given over to doing drill and manoeuvres (see Chapter Two, The School Cadet Corps). Colin Hey's diary records that Cadet training was a dominant feature for the MCS boys and even bombing classes were taken in 1917, for which the Master purchased a number of bombs![39] Any spare time not taken up by cadet drill was used to dig for victory, growing vegetables on previously unexploited land to supplement the diet during the strict food rationing. While food rationing was in force, day boys had to bring their ration books into school with them. Book and paper shortages also hindered teaching, making drill and gardening even more useful to fill the boys' time. In 1916 six Serbian refugees (all older than 16) were housed by the school and took lessons with the other boys, their places being sponsored by the Oxford Community for Serbian Relief. The charitable spirit saw the school and the boys donate money continuously to purchase war loans and to special money-raising targets for 'Destroyer Week'. Boys donated money deducted from the value of their prize day gifts to the Red Cross Hospital, and weekly egg collections, under the National Egg Collection for the wounded soldiers scheme, were carried out by the boys.[40] This charitable spirit at MCS continues today, with weekly collections for good causes in Friday chapel and a Community Service Organization that provides more than 4,000 student volunteer hours to the community every year.

The city of Oxford had aid raid warnings, but was never attacked by the Zeppelins that caused so much destruction in and around London and the east coast. Whenever an alert was sounded warning of approaching Zeppelins, the boarders were taken down to the library in the semi-basement of School House until the 'all clear' sounded. Prefects and older boys who were members of the Oxford Volunteer Training Corps were allowed to patrol the streets as a precaution, to look out for possible incendiary devices dropped from passing Zeppelins. Thankfully, of the fifty plus indiscriminate and haphazard Zeppelin bombing and incendiary raids on Britain during the war, none troubled the 'Dreaming Spires'.

During the war the boarders would regularly route their Sunday walk via Port Meadow, where they could watch at close quarters aeroplanes landing and taking off. The Royal Flying Corps aerodrome at Port Meadow was an obvious attraction for the young boys, many of whom would dream of flying the glamorous machines. One of the boys, H.S.H. Read (nicknamed 'Piggy' and son of D.S. Read who was a teacher at MCS from 1901 to 1919), who left the school in 1916 and went on to train at Port Meadow, pre-arranged a fly-past in 1917 with some of his friends who were still prefects at the school. On 27 September while the Cadet Corps was on parade near the second white bridge on School Field, Read in an SE5 fighter plane hurtled over their heads at a height of only 100 feet, going in the direction of Magdalen Tower. He narrowly avoided the tower and was fortunate enough, despite his schoolboy antics during training, to survive the war.

On Friday, 4 May 1917 it was widely reported in Oxford that the sound of gigantic artillery bombardments could be heard at 1.00am. This was part of the major offensive known as the Battle of Arras, that was to take the life of Donovan Leicester the following Tuesday. Four years earlier, Leicester had been at MCS about to embark on his studies at Hertford College. The sounds of war reaching Oxford and the mounting losses from the school suddenly made the conflict seem much closer for the MCS community.

Brownrigg kept the boys informed about the progress of the war, especially during the dramatic final months during 1918. On 17 October 1918 Brownrigg gave a talk to the whole school, but because of the rapid developments at that stage of the war he returned after prep to update the school that the allies had recaptured Lille and Ostend. On 11 November the armistice came into effect at 11.00am and school therefore finished at 12.00 noon. Flags were hung everywhere and all the City's bells could be heard ringing. Suddenly, from the cupola on top of School House a few volleys were fired from a twelve bore shot gun by some of the prefects. It was hard not to show the joy and relief that the end of hostilities brought. Sadly, in the two years following the war MCS was to lose two further old boys as a direct result of the effects of the war, C.P. Sells in 1919 and F.D. Wilkinson in 1920.[41]

Communication with the Boys at War

Old boys and their families kept the school well informed of the service and fate of old boys during and after the war. The school responded by recording those 'serving with the Colours' and detailed their Regiments with pride in the termly *Lily* magazine. Honours, promotions and deaths were all reported meticulously. Finally, obituaries were added, usually by Brownrigg, who had a personal knowledge of and attachment to each and every one of them. Thus the news about old boys was reported to the wider school community. *The Lily* was even sent out to old boys at the front, so they could catch up on the school news from home. On one occasion J.M. Thompson, Dean of Divinity of Magdalen College, supplied Lieutenant S.C.W. Disney with a copy of *The Lily* when he came across him recovering from wounds in a hospital in Boulogne, France in 1915.

Letters from old boys serving in the armed forces describing the conditions at the front and the progress of the war were also regularly received by the school. Some of these letters were even worthy of publication in *The Lily*. Two in particular capture the imagination.

The first, giving an appreciation and importance of trench construction (by the end of 1914, and for the next four years, the War on the Western Front became a war of the trenches) by Captain R.H. Clapperton was printed in *The Lily* of June 1915:[42]

> Dear Sir,
> I have just come from the Musketry School, where we were shown the very latest type of trenches, as used in France today, and I thought there might be some readers of *The Lily*, who would like to know how they are made, and what they are like.
>
> When the rifle was not deadly at much more than 100 yards and there was no shrapnel shells, 'cover' was not necessary; but the improvement of the rifle very soon taught men to take advantage of all 'natural cover' – folds in the ground, rocks, etc. – over, or round which they could get a clear view of the target they wished to hit; while bright coloured uniforms had to be

discarded, in favour of the now universal 'khaki'. The control of rifle fire – men being directed to the targets by section and squad commanders using field-glasses – together with the introduction of high-explosive and shrapnel shells, necessitated more secure cover than nature provided, and men were forced to imitate rabbits and to dig holes to hide in.

These holes developed into long trenches, about 3 feet or more in width, and 4 or 5 feet in depth, and the earth, which was taken out of them, was thrown forward 4 or 5 feet to stop bullets which would hit the men in the head or shoulders, when they stood up to fire. During a long battle, these were deepened and made more habitable, and had loop-holes for each rifle, and drains to take off water if they became flooded; till, finally, the trenches today, in which the men have had to stay for weeks at a time, are quite comfortable, when there is a lull in the fighting, and when they aren't full of water. The process of modification and elaboration has gone on continuously since last August, to meet new conditions – to protect men from shells exploded by time fuses (instead of by contact with the ground), which, if properly timed, burst above, or a little behind the trench, so as to hit the defenders with their bullets and fragments in the back, and also in order to protect them against observation from above. The earth was heaped up behind the trench, as well as in front, and, where sufficient time was available, roofs were constructed – 'props' being fixed, and timbers laid across, to support the branches, straw, earth and sods, of which the roof was made.

These roofs are not 'bomb-proof', but are merely intended to conceal the trench from the observation of hostile aeroplanes, which would signal the position to their own gunners. The chances of dropping a bomb in a trench from an aeroplane are not 1 in a 1,000.

The stages in the construction of trenches are best explained by diagram. The first stage consists in digging small trenches about 4 feet deep and 6 yards long, at intervals of about 2 yards (Cp. Diagram A.). About half the men dig, while the others use their rifles, if they are under fire at the time; otherwise, the men are told off in relays, to dig and rest alternately. These trenches are called 'fire trenches', and as soon as they are finished, they are widened and connected up (Cp. Diagram B) in such a way as to leave traverses, to prevent a bursting shrapnel or an enfilade fire from doing damage in more than one portion of the trench; they are also deepened, and earth is heaped up behind as well as in front, and on top of the traverses. (The connecting trenches must admit the passing of a stretcher at the corners.) To give shelter, if the trench is not covered, or before material can be obtained to cover it, 'dug outs' are made in the front of the trench (Cp. Diagram C.), in which a man can sit in comparative safety. These are, of course, made singly, and not in continuous line, or the trench would collapse.

If the trench is intended for protracted use, it is made still wider, more elaborately drained, timbered, roofed and loop-holed; there is a platform to stand on when shooting, and an elbow rest, and holes are cut in the face of

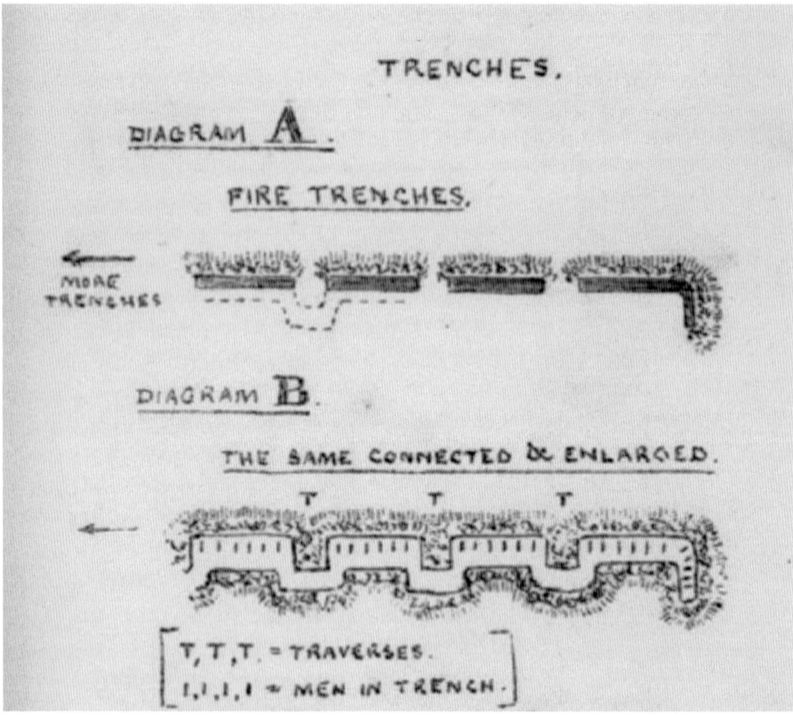
TRENCHES.
DIAGRAM A.
FIRE TRENCHES.
MORE TRENCHES
DIAGRAM B.
THE SAME CONNECTED & ENLARGED.
T
T
T
T, T, T. = TRAVERSES.
1,1,1,1 = MEN IN TRENCH.

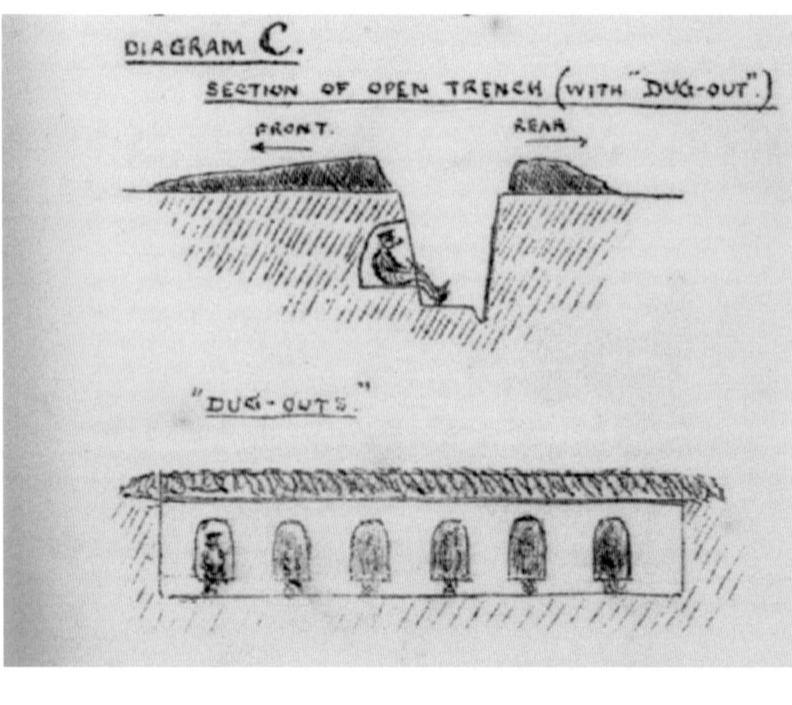
DIAGRAM C.
SECTION OF OPEN TRENCH (WITH "DUG-OUT".)
FRONT.
REAR
"DUG-OUTS."

the trench, at a convenient height, to hold ammunition. (Cp. Diagrams D & E).

When the trench has been completed, or during the process, the supports, who are in other trenches behind, not so elaborate, dig their way up to the fire trenches by tunnels, or by zig-zag trenches, throwing out the earth on

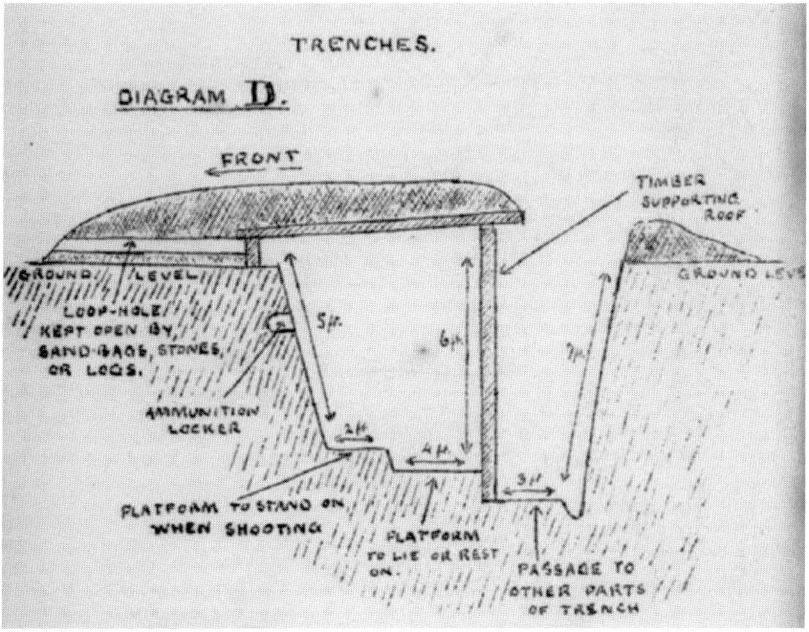

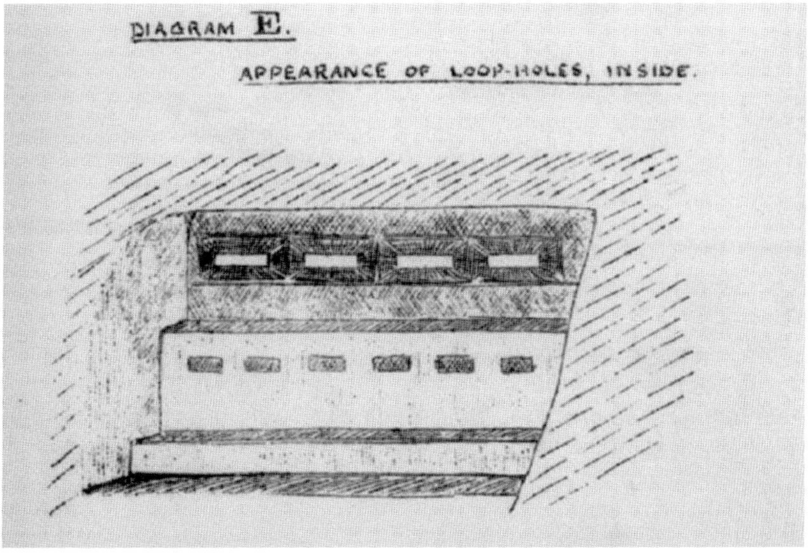

the side from which the bullets are likely to come; and it is through these 'communication trenches' that fresh men and ammunition are sent to the firing line, and the wounded are carried back to the big covered pits, which serve as kitchens and resting places, at some convenient place in the rear, capable of accommodating anything up to fifty men.

I hope that this will not be quite unintelligible to everyone. I could explain it much more clearly on a black-board. Please excuse the diagrams.

R.H. Clapperton

The second, a letter from S.C.W. Disney, printed in *The Lily* of November 1915, indicates the unpredictability and sad fortunes of war:[43]

Dear Sir,

I received the last number of The Lily while lying in No. 7 Stationary Hospital, Boulogne, from the hands of the Dean of Magdalen, who was an unexpected visitor, and I thought your readers might like a few lines from the front.

My regiment took over the line of so-called trenches in March, and held them until the night after the Boches 'scuppered' me with a rifle grenade [19 June 1915]. They are now enjoying the air on the tip of the Ypres salient. The above mentioned trenches more nearly resembled mud-heaps than the trenches so ably described by 'Bertie' [R.H. Clapperton] in the June number, and there was very little cover and not a vestige of shelter, while the approach was over miles of exposed, bullet-swept fields. However, months of steady work altered affairs, and the division had the pleasure of being congratulated upon inhabiting the most comfortable trenches on the line, shortly before they were moved. We had all the usual excitements, including trenches blown up, and I managed to collect a large and varied assortment of souvenirs, including two Prussian helmets. 'Punch' has recorded the doings of our division in a series of articles entitled 'The Watch-dogs', which are essentially founded on facts.

I was eventually 'laid out' one night by a stray rifle grenade, which burst between my feet and killed and wounded 14 in all. This seemed rather unfair as two hand grenades previously, bowled directly at my head, had failed to explode, and a German sniper had preferred to perforate my clothing in several places, rather than touch my body; but that's the fortune of war. I am sorry to say that Eric Fairburn, the well-known Cambridge oar, was killed by the same grenade; he was in our trench for instruction.

I did some work in early March in the 'Plug Street' trenches, and was delighted to meet **H.W. Canton** there. We had a long talk over old days, and it was a sad blow to hear of his death later [Canton was killed in action on 13 May], as he had been through everything up to date, including the retreat, and had done remarkably well. Poor old Herbert! One of the best oars who ever rowed for the school, and a splendid soldier; he was much beloved by his men, and absolutely fearless. He took me out 'wiring'[44] one night, and insisted on crawling almost to the German trenches, to try to catch what they were saying; unfortunately, we were stopped by the presence of an enemy patrol.

I expect to get out again in a few months, but have an ugly elbow at present.

It would be interesting if you could compile a table of the actual number of Old Boys serving.

I am, Sir,
Yours faithfully,
S.C.W. Disney, Lieut.
1st/5th Lincoln Regt.

Post War

After the outpouring of euphoria and relief that the war was over, the country attempted to move on and forget the life-shattering happenings of the previous four years. Institutions and communities were, however, determined to honour the sacrifice made by their friends and family. In 1919 Charles Brownrigg donated £50 of his own money to the cost of the MCS War Memorial. This was a significant sum in those days and it is estimated in 2014 terms to be the equivalent of £2,000; a reflection of the loss Brownrigg felt and his desire for the boys not to be forgotten. Many more contributed, including teachers, parents and relatives. The memorial, unveiled on 16 February 1920 by the President of Magdalen, Sir Herbert Warren, consisted of a memorial window[45] in the old chapel on the Longwall site, plus two large brass plaques, one listing the names of the fallen and the other listing the honours received by MCS boys during the war. The two brass plaques now hang in Big School.

As well as the dead, many young men had been physically and mentally scarred by their experiences, and families suffered in silence in their determination to survive and forget. Many longed to return to their pre-war normality, but the world had changed. Jobs for returning soldiers were hard to find and the newly-found freedom experienced by many women, to work and speak up for themselves, appeared to some to have vanished overnight as the men came back from the front. Many of the young partied, determined to enjoy their youth as if to make up for those that had lost theirs.

On 8 February 1921, the newly erected Memorial Cross in St John's Quadrangle of the College was dedicated in the presence of the Prince of Wales. The whole school attended the ceremony and was given an extra half-day holiday. Ultimately, there seems to have been little desire from the fellows and students to see the cross every time they entered the College, and the symbol appears to have been a step too far for the now shaken faith of the survivors. Normality was longed for and a new, different world had replaced the old. Like all communities, Magdalen had changed for ever, and the focus of its rising generation was on the new and changing political climate and the world outside the bounds of the

The Magdalen College School Great War Memorial Window.

school and college. Seen as a prescriptive symbol of Christian loss, the Memorial Cross was finally removed from the Quadrangle in the early part of the Second World War and eventually re-sited at Wheatley in 1971.

Boys at the school in the years following the war were privileged to receive visits from three eminent but very different wartime characters. In the June of 1919, the great French Leader Marshal Joseph J.C. Joffre was visiting Oxford to receive an honorary degree, and President Warren brought him along to the chorister practice rooms so that the choristers could meet him. Colin Hey tells the story of Joffre asking how many of them were ambitious to follow a military career when they left school. The boys felt 'a little uneasy and possibly ashamed', for none had an appetite for the Military after hearing the stories of the previous four years of war and seeing its results and effects on their communities. On 18 November 1921, Brownrigg organized for the legendary army chaplain Reverend P.T.B. Clayton (better known as 'Tubby Clayton') to come and give a talk to the MCS boys. He told them about the conditions on the Western Front and about the founding of Talbot House (or Toc H), a rest house for soldiers at Poperinge in Belgium. His story made an instant connection and lasting impression with the boys. Little did they imagine that the majority of them were

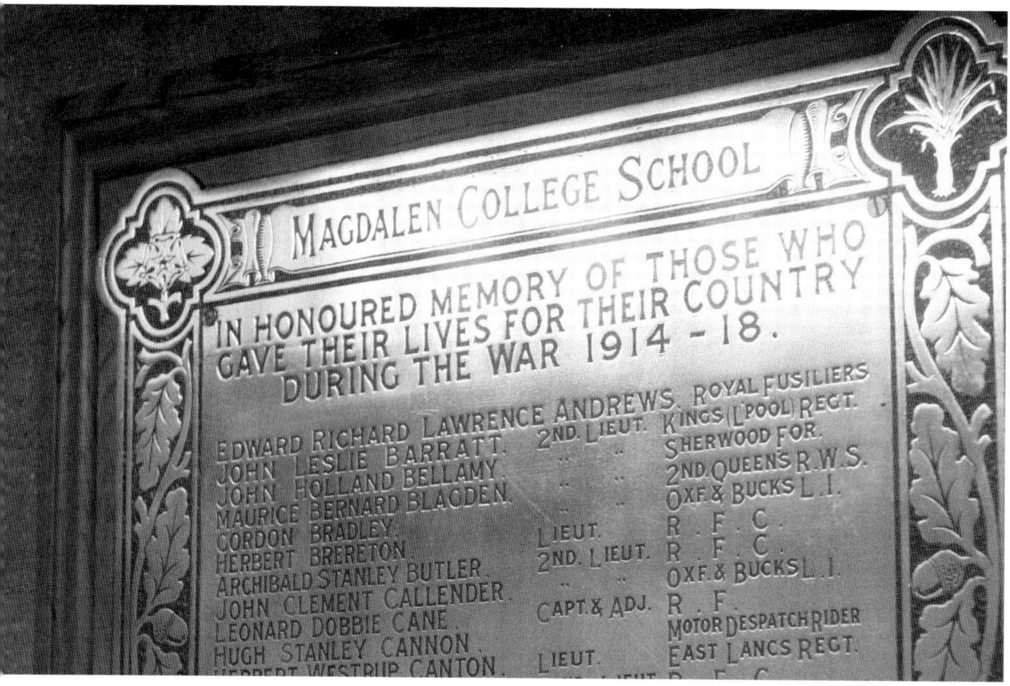

Brass plaque recording the MCS boys who lost their lives in the Great War.

Brass plaque listing the honours won by MCS boys in the Great War.

destined to be in uniform themselves within twenty years. No doubt their observations of and exposure to memorialization and the stories of The Great War were still fresh in their minds. Finally, a name that has come to symbolize and highlight the sacrifice made by MCS and other Public School boys during the Great War is that of double VC winner Noel Chavasse. After the war Noel's twin brother Christopher settled back in Oxford, where in 1929 he became the first Master of St Peter's Hall, and eventually became Bishop of Rochester. Christopher was himself decorated with an MC in 1917 and revisited the school he and Noel had loved on several occasions after the war, giving talks and attending the Commem services. Christopher Chavasse's story reminds us that beyond the accounts in this book of the boys who lost their lives, there are unwritten stories of the survivors of the war, each character having made their own contribution and sacrifice, then having to readjust and make their way in a very different world post-armistice.

Evolution of the House System

Prior to and during the Great War, a house system did not exist at MCS because the small number of boys did not demand it. However, because the house system is now such a fundamental part of the school and because the house names honour several of the boys that died during the First World War it is important to touch upon its formation and evolution.[46] The house system at MCS came about after the war mainly due to necessity as the school grew rapidly in number from 70 in 1917 to 150 in 1922. In the summer of 1922 six 'houses' were created on an alphabetical surname basis to help with pastoral organization and sporting competitions. The Houses were imaginatively called Boarders A to G; Boarders H to L; Boarders M to Z; Day boys A to L; Day boys M to Z; and Lanercost.[47]

In the December 1923 edition of *The Lily* a letter to the Editor suggested that proper names should be given to the 'Houses', the writer claiming that it was difficult to cheer 'Come on A to G' during a fast-moving sports event. Subsequently on 25 June 1924, R.A.V. Prendergast (MCS 1915–24) during a games committee meeting proposed that the houses should be named after three honoured old boys who fell during the war: Callender, Chavasse and Leicester. The motion was passed and these three names were given to the boarders' houses, with the day boys' houses retaining their alphabetical nomenclature. Sometime later, three additional old boy names were proposed to identify the remaining day boy houses and the Lanercost boarding House; Blagden and Maltby (in operation by 1925) and Wilkinson (by 1932). In 1938 the six Houses were paired up to be: Chavasse-Leicester, Maltby-Callender and Wilkinson-Blagden, with the first name of the amalgamated Houses being for the senior boys and the second name for the junior boys. Walker-Dunn House was added in 1945, after the Second World War, and commemorates two boys (Geoffrey Walker and Bruce Dunn) who fell during the 1939–45 World War. In the same year, house prefects were instituted for the first time to help carry out prefectorial duties within each house.

Table 3. The Evolution of the Magdalen College School House System.†

1922	1925	1930	1938	1945	1955	1972
Boarders A–G*	Callender*	Callender*	Chavasse-	Chavasse-	Chavasse-	Chavasse*[48]
Boarders H–L*	Chavasse*	Chavasse*	Leicester*	Leicester*	(Leicester)*	Leicester
Boarders M–Z*	Leicester*	Leicester*	Maltby-	Maltby-	Maltby	Maltby
Day-boys A–L	Day-boys A–L	Blagden	Callender	Callender	Callender	Callender
Day-boys M–Z	Day-boys M–Z	Maltby	Wilkinson-	Wilkinson-	Wilkinson-	Wilkinson-
Lanercost*	Lanercost*	Wilkinson	Blagden	Blagden	(Blagden)	Blagden
				Walker-Dunn	Walker-Dunn	Walker-Dunn

† The year dates are intended to indicate approximate timings only; *Boarders; ( ) indicates the second name fell into disuse during this time.

Junior houses disappeared to be replaced by 'houserooms' within each house. In 1955 Maltby-Callender was split to become two separate houses. Finally, in 1972 Leicester and Chavasse were parted to become two separate houses and reveal the six-house system that the school still has today: Callender, Chavasse, Leicester, Maltby, Walker-Dunn and Wilkinson-Blagden.[49]

Tributes to Brownrigg

Before his retirement Brownrigg oversaw the final transfer of the school from the College site in 1928 to its new home and buildings on Cowley Place (now known as the '1928 Buildings'), across the way from School House. In the same year, and

The Charles Brownrigg Memorial Window.

Panoramic photograph of MCS CCF on School Field in 1928, with Botanical Gardens, Magdalen Tower, School House and St Hilda's in the background.

MCS 1930. At the centre is C.E. Brownrigg. In the background are the 1928 buildings.

Charles E. Brownrigg, 1930.

some ten years after the end of the First World War, a photograph captured the pride and readied state that Brigger had instilled in the school's CCF since its inception in 1914.

As 1930 dawned, Brownrigg approached completing his forty-second year at MCS. Over four decades of service to the school, its boys and staff, through all the stressful war years, had taken their toll on this most loyal Magdalen servant. In the school photo of 1930, just prior to his retirement, the strain of the previous four decades, plus the sadness of losing his wife the year before, could be seen on his face.

After his retirement in 1930 Brigger continued to live close by in Iffley and kept in contact with the school that had been his life for the previous forty-two years. He returned each year to attend Sports Day at the Iffley Road Track, firing the starting pistol for the races. This he did for fifty consecutive years until his

Charles E. Brownrigg.
This Portrait that hangs in the school Dining Hall.

death in 1942. Fittingly, a portrait of Brownrigg was commissioned by the old boys and has hung in a central place in the school ever since.[50]

In addition, a memorial window in the old school chapel, designed by Lawrence Lee, was dedicated to Brownrigg on 3 July 1955.[51] The window consists of his coat of arms and crest boldly displayed on a background of antique glass sprinkled with fleurs-de-lis. The specially chosen inscription on the coat of arms reads 'VIRESCIT VULNERE VIRTUS' (courage becomes greater through a wound).

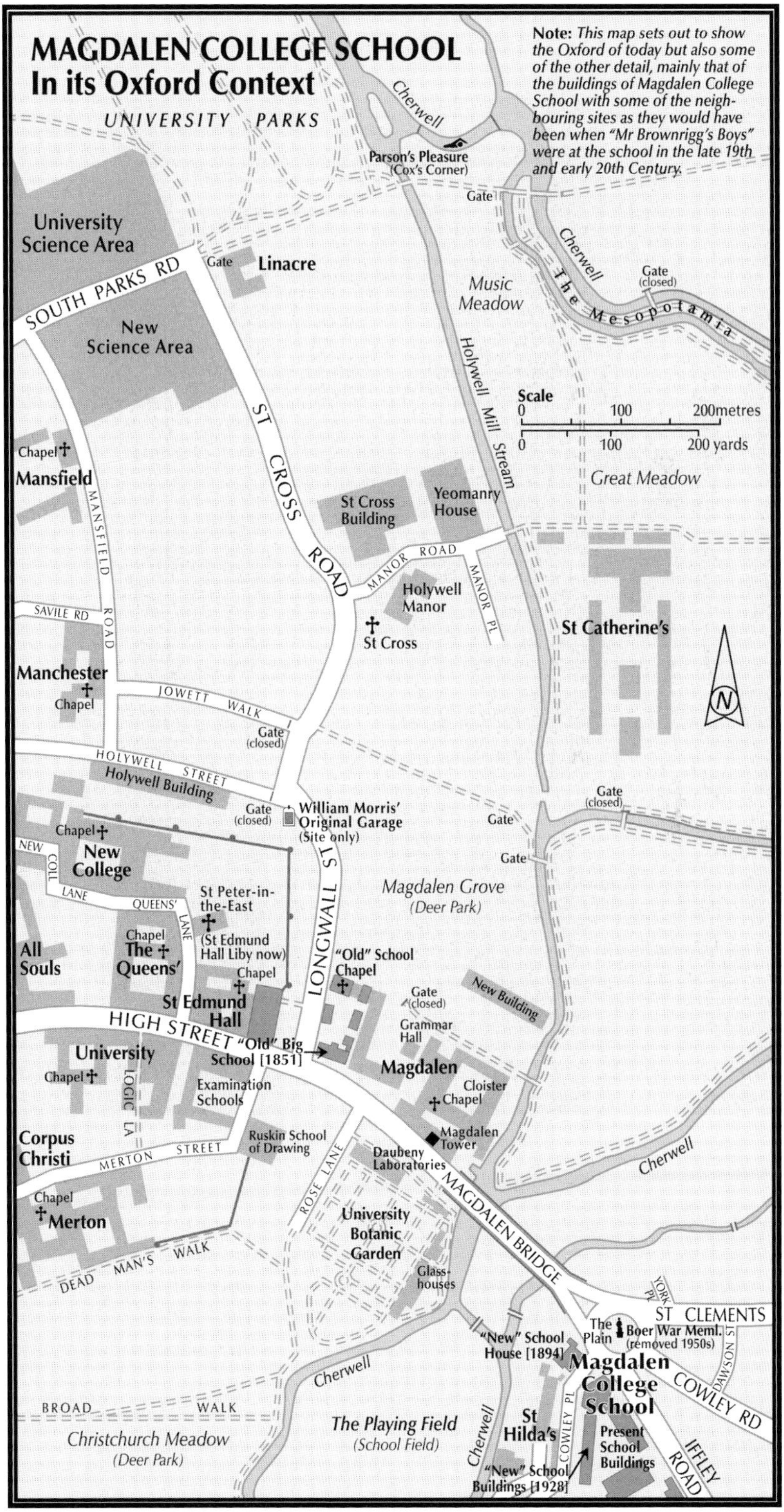
MAGDALEN COLLEGE SCHOOL
In its Oxford Context
Note: This map sets out to show the Oxford of today but also some of the other detail, mainly that of the buildings of Magdalen College School with some of the neighbouring sites as they would have been when "Mr Brownrigg's Boys" were at the school in the late 19th and early 20th Century.
UNIVERSITY PARKS
Cherwell
Parson's Pleasure
(Cox's Corner)
Gate
University Science Area
Gate
Linacre
Music Meadow
Cherwell
The Mesopotamia
Gate
(closed)
SOUTH PARKS RD
New Science Area
Holywell Mill Stream
Scale
0 100 200metres
0 100 200 yards
Great Meadow
ST CROSS ROAD
Chapel
Mansfield
MANSFIELD ROAD
St Cross Building
Yeomanry House
MANOR ROAD
MANOR PL
Holywell Manor
St Cross
St Catherine's
SAVILE RD
Manchester
Chapel
JOWETT WALK
Gate
(closed)
N
HOLYWELL STREET
Holywell Building
Gate
(closed)
William Morris' Original Garage
(Site only)
Gate
(closed)
Gate
Gate
Chapel
New College
NEW COLL LANE
QUEENS' LANE
St Peter-in-the-East
(St Edmund Hall Liby now)
Magdalen Grove
(Deer Park)
LONGWALL ST
All Souls
Chapel
The Queens'
Chapel
St Edmund Hall
"Old" School Chapel
Gate
(closed)
New Building
Grammar Hall
HIGH STREET
"Old" Big School [1851]
University
Chapel
Magdalen
Cloister
Chapel
LOGIC LA
Examination Schools
Magdalen Tower
Corpus Christi
MERTON STREET
Ruskin School of Drawing
ROSE LANE
Daubeny Laboratories
Cherwell
Chapel
Merton
University Botanic Garden
MAGDALEN BRIDGE
DEAD MAN'S WALK
Glass-houses
YORK PL
ST CLEMENTS
The Plain
Boer War Meml.
(removed 1950s)
"New" School House [1894]
Magdalen College School
DAWSON ST
Cherwell
COWLEY RD
BROAD WALK
The Playing Field
(School Field)
Cherwell
St Hilda's
COWLEY PL
Present School Buildings
IFFLEY ROAD
Christchurch Meadow
(Deer Park)
"New" School Buildings [1928]

Notes

1. The School's connections and relationship with the College were under constant debate and modification during this time and afterwards. For discussions on the evolution of the relationship of the College with MCS (and its other two schools at Waynflete, Lincolnshire and Brackley, Northamptonshire) and their eventual separation see Brockliss, L.W.; *Magdalen College Oxford. A History*, Magdalen College, 2008.
2. The City of Oxford High School for Boys was established in 1881 as a day school and was maintained by Oxford City Council.
3. 1 guinea = £1.1s (1 pound and 1 shilling, or 21 shillings), £1.05 in today's money.
4. The College covered the sixteen choristers' board and lodgings, and paid all their tuition fees before 1903 (only a subscription fee of 3 guineas a year was paid by chorister parents) and half their tuition fees after 1903.
5. In the early 1900s this boarder's fee seems to have been raised to £48 per annum.
6. The Science subjects covered are recorded in detail in the John J. Manley Science Register/Notebooks, three volumes dating from Lent 1888 to Michaelmas 1918.
7. Prior to 1895 German was taught occasionally and Geography and English literature seem to have had limited instruction, for they were either not examined or received poor reports from examiners about the quality of candidates. Brownrigg appears to have introduced more emphasis into the teaching of German when he became Master in 1900.
8. Upon the retirement of Reverend W.E. Sherwood as Master, the School employed a separate Chaplain.
9. Email correspondence with C.E. Brownrigg's granddaughter, Pauline V. Boase (née Brownrigg), May 2013.
10. Prefectorial systems of managing discipline and administering punishment was common to the majority of Public Schools of the day.
11. For a full account of this infamous episode in Oxford's history and its central characters see the chapter on J.L.M. Morton.
12. Never one to miss an opportunity to include sport in all areas of his profession, it was typical of Brownrigg that a golf match was arranged during the Headmasters' conference (20–21 December 1907). Brownrigg captained the Headmasters' team versus Senior Members of the Oxford University Club. Played at the Oxford University Supplementary course at Cowley on 21 December, the match, which included the Headmasters of Eton (Edward Lyttelton), Malvern (Rev. Sydney R. James) and Rugby (Herbert A. James) amongst others, was tied at 5½ points each. Reported in *The Times*, 23 December 1907.
13. Designed by Sir Arthur Blomfield, it then had 'large and airy dormitories and studies for the boys, with dining hall, library, and music and changing rooms. It is fitted with all modern sanitary arrangements, and is lighted throughout with electric light.' This was a real step into the modern world, as electric lighting had only started to be introduced into some homes in the 1880s. Bloomfield was also the architect for St Barnabas and All Saints Churches in Oxford.
14. The funding for the chapel had primarily come from old boys and parents. The quality of the building was however questioned; the *Oxford Herald* of 10 January 1857 reported the walls 'will be found to be of insufficient strength'.
15. School registers only survive for the period 1879 to 1886 then from 1916 onwards.
16. School House at Cowley Place stands on the site of The Willows, previously called Turrell House, that was owned by Christ Church and rented by Thomas Fisher, a farmer.
17. The total cost of the build was £362 (approx. £20,000 in today's money), of which ninety percent was met by contributions from the MCS community (old boys, Parents and Friends of the School). The list of contributors to the Pavilion fund can be found in *The Lily* of March 1914. Interestingly, the Prince of Wales (later to become King Edward VIII), who was a student at Magdalen College from 1912 to 1914, contributed five guineas by 'his own wish, and with no request on our [the school's] part'. An arson attack in 1990 resulted in extensive roof and internal

damage to the Pavilion, but reconstruction and extension work to the rear saw the iconic building restored to its former understated glory without delay, with the added benefit of toilets.

18. The MCS Roll of Service published in *The Lily* in 1917 listed 228 men. The actual number is undoubtedly higher than this, indeed research for this book found a further twenty MCS men served during the war. *The Lily* records relied upon old boys or their families contacting the school to inform them they were serving. It is thought that the school simply lost contact with many old boys. Indeed, in December 1918 the school makes a plea in *The Lily* magazine for any old boys not already recorded in the published lists (or if they know of any others not in the list) to send details about themselves or others. The idea was to publish a complete and accurate Roll of Service in 1919. This was never done.
19. One of the Regulations drawn up in the Scheme of 1875 put a limit to the number of boarders at forty (not including choristers). In the following ten years Ogle's efforts during his leadership (1877–1886) were largely directed to making the School more suitable for day boys, something that the local community hoped for, as the local paper put it, 'the freer introduction of a good industrious stamp of day-boys will benefit not only the boarders (for boarders are still to be a marked feature of the school) but also the citizens and residents of Oxford.'
20. Prior to Ogle, the school hours were 8.00am–10.00am; Chapel at 10.00am; 11.00am–1.00pm; 3.00pm–4.00pm; 6.30pm–8.00pm.
21. Contributing factors included having to reduce the number of boarders; the school losing its ability to allow boys to stay at the school once they had matriculated at the University; competition from newly established schools like Summerfields; a continued impression of exclusiveness that existed because of the school's admission procedure and generally a widespread depression during these years.
22. West Kent Grammer School, Brockley.
23. '*The Magdalen College School Journal*', was founded in 1870. The familiar name of '*The Lily*' was adopted in 1880, but in 1887 the Brockley boys changed its name to '*The Magdalen Magazine*'. It has been *The Lily* ever since 1888.
24. The term Old Waynflete (OW) to signify a former pupil of MCS was not used until after the First World War. The first appearance of the term is in a *Lily* of 1935.
25. Twenty-three scholarships and exhibitions to Oxbridge were won during Sherwood's twelve-year Mastership.
26. P.D. Pullan's name is remembered each year at Prize Giving, The Pullan Prize for English is presented to the top English student in the 5th Form.
27. W.E. Sherwood lived in Oxford for another twenty-seven years, occasionally coaching the school rowing until 1913 and becoming the first President of the Old Boys' Club (later to become the 'Old Waynfletes' in 1935). He became the Mayor of Oxford in 1913, serving for two terms.
28. E.C. Sherwood, captain of the team, was the son of the then Headmaster, W.E. Sherwood.
29. A.W.T. Perowne was an Assistant Master (January 1890–July 1892).
30. Brownrigg had himself played cricket against MCS while a student at Magdalen College in 1885 and 1886.
31. In 1896, at the first modern Olympiad in Athens, Charles Gmelin became Britain's first ever competing Olympic athlete (100m) and Britain's first ever Olympic medal winner (finishing third in the 400m final).
32. J.V. Haselor stuck his tongue out and pulled a 'funny face' while this photograph was taken, at the time the college therefore blurred his image in the original photo.
33. The morning service in chapel was continued until 1926.
34. The Victoria Fountain, built on the site of the former St Clement's Toll House, was inaugurated on 25 May 1899 by the Queen's daughter, Princess Louise.
35. The memorial was unveiled by the Bishop of Oxford while still unfinished, without the statue, so that the 1/OBLI could be present at the ceremony before departing for duty in India.
36. Magdalen Gate House had been the home of the Darbishire family from 1882 to 1887. See section on Arthur D. Darbishire.

37. The first female assistant 'master' recorded at MCS is a Miss Baker, who in 1899 and 1900 was the teacher for Form I in the new classroom set up in the library.
38. Also two Fellows of the College, P.V.M. Benecke and A.L. Pedder, helped with teaching at the school during the war.
39. In 1926 the efficiency of the Cadet Corps was recognised by the War Office and it became a contingent of the OTC.
40. The egg collections were a vivid memory for Colin Hey. The eggs collected went to the Oxford Military Hospitals, including the main hospital at the Examination Schools.
41. In addition to this it is known that F.B. Luget tragically died by taking his own life a few years after the war (1921), possibly as a result of his war experiences.
42. R.H. Clapperton (MCS 1905–12) coxed the Oxford University boat in 1913, and then stroked the Oxford University 2nd boat in 1914. He survived the war.
43. S.C.W. Disney (MCS 1906–11) survived the war. He later served with distinction in the Second World War, becoming a Lieutenant Colonel and winning an MC, TD and OBE. His name is remembered each year at Prize Giving when the Disney Prize for History is awarded to the top History student in the 5th Form.
44. Wiring was the name for the job of laying, repairing and strengthening the barbed wire barriers in no-man's land, usually during the night by a team of men.
45. The memorial window was moved to a new school chapel on the Cowley Place site in 1928, but since its demolition in 2005 the window has been in storage. The window consists of five panels, the centre one being adapted from Holman Hunt's *Light of the World*, the other four being the four national patron Saints, St George, St Andrew, St Patrick and St David, as among the MCS losses were boys from all four countries; beneath the window was a brass plaque which reads 'Erected in memory of the members of this school who gave their lives in the Great War'.
46. The evolution of the house system is only approximately summarised, as detailed discussion of its many intricate modifications over these years detract from the focus of this book.
47. Lanercost was an additional boarding house opened in about 1921. Lanercost was on the Iffley Road and was managed by Mr Shepherd, who had previously looked after a few boarders at a house further up the Iffley Road. Lanercost closed in 1933 when the temporary boom in boarders subsided.
48. Boarding at MCS ceased in 1996 and all six houses became day houses serving different geographical areas.
49. The name of Leicester and Blagden fell into disuse by the late 1950s, but in 1972, when the name of Leicester was reintroduced as a separate house, the full name of Wilkinson-Blagden came back into common usage.
50. The portrait by Hayward now hangs in the new dining hall.
51. The old chapel on the Cowley Place site was demolished in 2007 and the Brownrigg window is currently in storage awaiting installation into a future new building.

CHAPTER TWO

The School Cadet Corps

A Cadet Corps of sorts was evident at MCS during the second half of the nineteenth century. In 1871, approximately half way through R.H. Hill's twelve-year headship, a Cadet Company was added to the extracurricular activities laid on for the boys.[1] This Cadet Company is shown in the Army Lists and was affiliated to the 1st University of Oxford Rifle Volunteer Corps. Described by R.P. Colomb, an assistant master under R.H. Hill and H.C. Ogle, as 'A Rifle Corps we also had, a Cadet Company, attached to the 1st Oxford (University) RVC, a gallant band of some fifty boys, mostly small, who were ready to go anywhere and do anything . . . We wore a uniform of very dark blue, laced across the chest with black mohair braid, a busby of imitation astrakhan, with a blue and black plume, carbines, and the long sword-bayonets in black belts and frogs, and we fancied ourselves in this uniform quite a lot, though, looking back on things, it was a ridiculous dress and particularly ugly.'

After the Corps' first public parade, *Magdalen College School Journal* ironically gives the following advice to boys who do not belong to the Corps, 'but who are led by patriotic feelings to accompany [the Corps] it in its parades, to preserve a respectful distance, and on no account to attract the attention of those in the ranks.' The attraction of boys not in the CCF to imitate their mates, when parading, from a distance is still evident on Tuesday afternoons today.

This form of the Cadet Corps appears to have only survived for about ten years before it was allowed to drop about half way through Ogle's Headship.

The modern form of the Officer Training Corps was founded during the Haldane reforms in 1908 to remedy a critical shortage of officers that had been encountered during the South African War (1899–1902), with senior sections in eight universities and junior sections in public schools. During the First World War, the senior OTCs became officer-producing units and some 30,000 officers passed through, but after the war they reverted to their basic military training role.

When war came in 1914 the Army called upon Lieutenant Colonel A.D. Godley (originally a student at Balliol, later a fellow and tutor at Magdalen College) to raise, equip and command a new unit called the Oxfordshire Volunteer Training Corps (OVTC). Some of the older senior boys of the school and a number of the staff immediately joined the OVTC, affectionately known as 'Godley's Own'. It was the formation of this Corps and the close friendship between Godley and Brownrigg (both dedicated classicists and both Irish) that made the beginnings of cadet training at MCS possible. Brownrigg instigated drill squads which continued through 1914 and 1915 until the formation of an official Cadet Corps in 1916.

The senior boys and masters who attended the OVTC were able to provide elementary infantry training to the other senior boys and eventually to the younger boys in the school. In 1915 groups of the school's older cadets went over to the Army Ordnance Depot at Didcot to assist the proper troops.[2] More enjoyable for the cadets were night exercises in replica front line trenches at Cumnor with the Oxford Volunteer Regiment.

In 1916 the MCS Cadet Corps was formally established and recognized, with Brownrigg initially given the rank of Second Lieutenant and established as its commanding officer. In May of 1916, despite the lack of uniforms, its first official parade took place, consisting of two platoons, each of two sections. The Corps did not actually receive uniform for another two years, but this did not stop progress and on 15 June 1916 the two platoons participated in company drill on School Field with the rest of the OVTC.[3] In addition, 'A' platoon were allowed to attend military training lectures with the OVTC in Oxford.

As well as frequent half-hour drills before afternoon lessons or games, formal weekly parades lasting an hour were held each Wednesday at 09.00am on School Field. Drill and manoeuvres took up all the boys' spare time, but Brownrigg also seemed determined to give the cadets as much preparation for the battlefield as possible. It was reported in 1917 that he 'purchased a number of bombs to add to the Cadet Corps' arsenal, and that bombing classes would soon be in full swing.'

In the Autumn of 1916 the Corps was provided with dummy rifles[4] for arms drill and mock weapon training. It was hoped that practice and drill with these rifles would allow accurate 'slope' and 'presentation' of arms when next visited by the recent head prefect John Callender, because it was his mother that contributed to the cost of nearly all the rifles. Sadly, Lieutenant Callender, who had been 'A' platoon Commander of the OTC in 1916, was killed in action in 1917 and was never able to receive this honour.

Sometime during 1917 the OVTC appears to have become a regiment of its own, the Oxfordshire Volunteer Regiment (OVR).

Of the other boys to die in the First World War, Maurice Blagden and John Leslie Barratt were also members of the MCS Cadet Corps, with Barratt being the Sergeant for 'B' platoon in 1916. As well as Brownrigg commanding the Corps, seven other masters were part of the OVR: J.H.H. Allen, G.R. Brewis, Lance Corporal Rev G.L. Deuchar, Lieutenant J.L. Etty (later Oxfordshire and Buckinghamshire Light Infantry), C.L. Freeman, P.D. Pullan, G.R. Wood (later OBLI).

The MCS Cadet Corps continued its close association with the new regiment and the commitment to its functioning took its toll on the school's academic work.[5] Brownrigg was promoted to Captain in the Spring of 1918 and as the war entered its last month the school's commitment to the Cadet Corps was as true as ever, for on the 10 October 1918 the 'A' platoon went to Bicester with the 1/OBLI for an open range shooting competition. A final procession during the

Top Row—F. K. Hussey. C. A. Plaxton. G. V. Jacks. F. E. Barratt. R. C. Kelly.

Second Row—C. A. Webb. E. R. S. Johnston. E. N. Knowles. L. Borlée. R. C. Webb. B. M. Kovandgitch. H. A. Vesty. K. B. G. Allen.

Sitting — Cpl. G H. H. Cockram. Sgt. J. H. G. Paton. C.S.M. Rev. G. L. Deuchar (1st Vol. Bn. Oxf. & Bucks L.I.). Cadet Officer A. E. M. Gale. Capt. C. E. Brownrigg Cadet Officer G. D. Clapperton. C.S.M. A. H. L. Masson. Sgt. C. E. Tidswell. Cpl. G. E. Bushell.

Magdalen College School 'A' Platoon with its new uniform in 1918.

war took place on 24 October 1918 when the school gave a half-day holiday so that several members of the Cadet Corps could march with the 1/OBLI to publicize the Oxford War Savings effort.

After the Armistice in November 1918, the OVR was gradually run down and eventually disbanded, with the MCS Cadet Corps becoming officially attached to the Oxfordshire Territorial Force Association.[6] The Corps continued to thrive, increasing its number and expanding to four platoons. Sixty old cavalry carbines were received and the Corps drilled with these even after it received a substantial batch of obsolete Lee Enfield rifles. On 26 June 1919, the Corps was given the honour of forming part of the Guard of Honour for Admiral Beatty and Field Marshal Sir Douglas Haig when they both received the freedom of the City of Oxford.

On 22 September 1926, the efficiency of the MCS Cadet Corp was officially recognized by the War Office and it became a contingent of the OTC (Junior Division) under the supervision of the Depot of the OBLI. Brownrigg chose to hand over command at this poignant moment to Major C.H.B. Shepherd MC (late Manchester Regiment and Machine Gun Corps).

Sometime after the First World War, the OTC (Junior Division) was renamed the Junior Training Corps, and it was in this guise that the MCS Corps played

Oxfordshire Volunteer Regiment cap badge depicting an Ox and Ford.

Magdalen College School Cadet Corps cap badge.

its part in the defence of Oxford against possible enemy parachutists and fifth columnists, as well as taking its turn to do fire-watching duties during the Second World War. It was from the Junior Training Corps that the current-day Combined Cadet Force organization was created in 1948 by the amalgamation of the Junior Training Corps and the school contingents of the Sea Cadet Corps and Air Training Corps.

Notes

1. Rossall School (Lancashire) is acknowledged as the first public school to enrol volunteers into a Cadet Force and have them sworn in under the provisions of the Volunteer Act on 1 February 1860.
2. According to *The Lily*, this example was later followed by Eton and other big public schools. Tasks included heavy and horrible work unloading and stacking materials and equipment from trains during the hot summer days.
3. The Cadet Corps' first uniform parade took place on 10 July 1918, over two years since the Corps was established.
4. These rifles were made of solid wood and had been specially designed and constructed for the school.
5. In September 1917 the 'A' platoon marched to Cumnor Hill with the OVR to carry out field operations. On 26 November 1917 a half-day holiday was granted to allow the Cadet Corps to practise 'offensive operations'. On 5 December the Corps demonstrated a 'Platoon in the attack' in front of Colonel Godley and other officers of the OVR. On the 18 March 1918 the Corps paraded with the 1/OVR.
6. The OTFA was part of the OBLI.

CHAPTER THREE

The Theatres of War

Timeline of the War

Many people view the First World War as a giant battle and struggle between the German army and Allied armies of France and Britain, across trenches that stretched the length of France. Names such as the Somme and Ypres conjure up images of large battles with intense shell barrages and masses of troops going over the top, only to be mown down by machine-gun fire from enemy trenches. Any person who reads more will discover that for Britain the war that became known as 'The Great War' was not only fought on the 'Western Front' in France, but in essentially nine 'theatres' in all: China (1914 only), Turkey (the Gallipoli peninsula), Italy, Mesopotamia (now known as Iraq), Egypt and Palestine, Macedonia (Salonica), Africa and Russia. Add to this the battle of the skies with the emerging Air Forces and the battle of the seas with the established Navies and it can be seen that it was truly a war that affected the entire globe. Its effects have shaped the world for the last 100 years and it holds a fascination today that has never been greater.

Of the fifty MCS boys to die as a result of the First World War, thirty-nine died at the Western Front, two at Gallipoli, one in Mesopotamia, two in Palestine and four in England. Two boys died as a result of the effects of their injuries shortly after the war was over.

The following summary is not intended in any way to be a complete history of the war years, but is intended to give the reader an appreciation of the regions of the world to which Brownrigg's boys were posted and the historic battles and struggles in which they found themselves involved. It will give a timeline to the stages of the war in which the boys lost their lives. The individual biographies of the boys can then be read in context.

The War on the Western Front officially began on 4 August 1914 when German soldiers violated Belgian territory. Britain immediately sent an army (the British Expeditionary Force) to France, with the first men arriving on 7 August. The BEF concentrated itself close to the Belgian border approximately 12 miles south of Mons and on 21 August moved forwards into Belgium. The first skirmishes happened in the following two days, but on 23 August the full might of the German First Army was encountered. Although Field Marshal John French contemplated standing his ground, he was ordered to retreat. The fighting retreat lasted until 5 September 1914, before the BEF crossed the River Aisne and then the River Marne. Here the retreat halted, 20 miles from Paris. The Germans, despite crossing the two rivers, found themselves too far advanced to enable resupply. The brief but bloody Battle of the Marne followed (5–10 September),

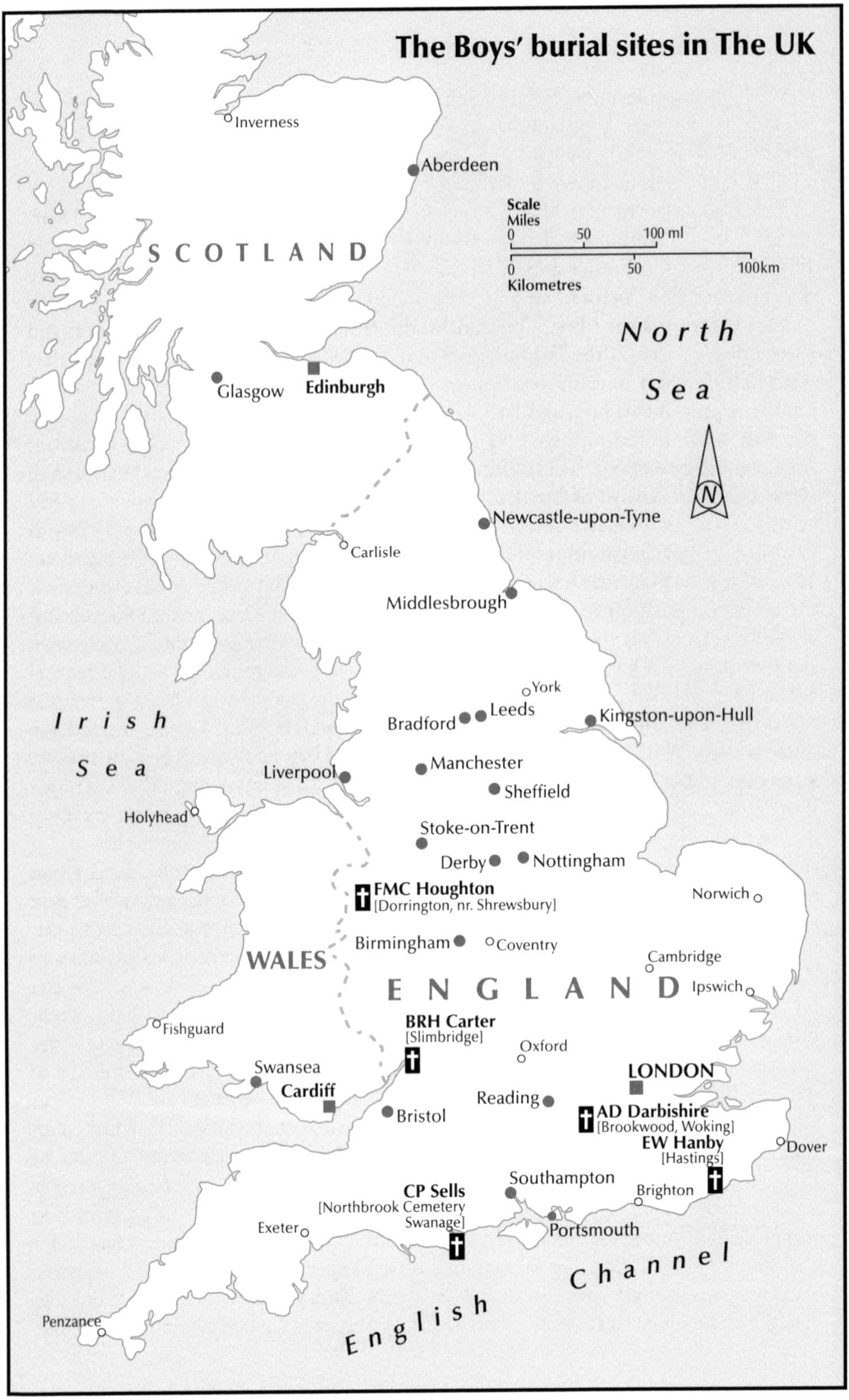
The Boys' burial sites in The UK
Scale
Miles
0
50
100 ml
0
50
100km
Kilometres
North
Sea
N
Irish
Sea
English Channel
SCOTLAND
WALES
ENGLAND
Inverness
Aberdeen
Glasgow
Edinburgh
Newcastle-upon-Tyne
Carlisle
Middlesbrough
York
Bradford
Leeds
Kingston-upon-Hull
Liverpool
Manchester
Sheffield
Holyhead
Stoke-on-Trent
Derby
Nottingham
FMC Houghton
[Dorrington, nr. Shrewsbury]
Norwich
Birmingham
Coventry
Cambridge
Ipswich
Fishguard
BRH Carter
[Slimbridge]
Oxford
Swansea
Cardiff
LONDON
Bristol
Reading
AD Darbishire
[Brookwood, Woking]
EW Hanby
[Hastings]
Dover
Southampton
CP Sells
[Northbrook Cemetery
Swanage]
Brighton
Exeter
Portsmouth
Penzance

resulting in the Germans falling back to the north bank of the River Aisne. The French Army were then left to stop any further German progress from this advanced point, while the British[1] were redeployed further north to Belgium to what would become known as the Ypres Salient. The British redeployment north was essentially a 'race to the sea', to stop the Germans outflanking the Allied armies. After a number of battles, the lines eventually solidified and the mobile stage of the war in France and Belgium was almost over; what followed was a busy period creating a fortified system of trenches.

The Western Front line, denoted by the trench system, eventually zigzagged from Nieuwpoort on the Belgium coast to the Swiss mountains, some 450 miles. The British were initially only responsible for approximately 25 miles of the northern part of this line, and by 1918 for about 125 miles. The war now entered the well documented 'trench warfare' stage, with the desperate struggle to exploit weaknesses in an enemy's entrenched positions to capture advantageous land with the eventual objective of breaking through enemy fortified lines.

Late October saw the last major offensive by the Germans on the Western Front in 1914. After holding the town of Ypres for ten days in early October, on 15 October the Germans attempted one last push to recapture Ypres, to cut off the BEF and push on to the Channel ports. During this First Battle of Ypres the British first lost but retook the now infamous Menin Road (the main route into the town) on 31 October. The battle was such a close-run thing that the British contemplated abandoning Ypres in early November, but they held out and due to exhaustion on both sides and worsening weather the battle ceased on 22 November. News reached the school that it had lost its first old boy during the struggle to save Ypres. Corporal **Hugh Cannon** of the 6th Signal Troop, Royal Engineers was killed on 30 October whilst on his motor bicycle carrying despatches. He would be the only MCS boy to die in 1914.

In the spring of 1915, a policy of constant aggressive pressure on the German lines was employed, with a series of offensive operations along the front. The first of these operations took place in March 1915 and was designed to remove the German bulge into the line (the Ypres Salient) that was threatening supply lines to this crucial area. The tactics employed would be the same as those used for the following two years on the Western Front: a methodical bombardment of enemy positions followed by a charge to take the first and second lines (and a repeat of the process to take the reserve trenches and hopefully form a breakthrough). In the early hours of 10 March, the heaviest British bombardment of the war so far opened up. Some thirty-five minutes later, British troops, including Lieutenant **Leslie Yeo**, 2nd Battalion, South Staffordshire Regiment, 'went over the top' in the first British set-piece attack on the Western Front. Some 2 miles of enemy front were attacked and in British hands by nightfall. Later that day, Leslie Yeo would die of wounds received in the initial attack. Fierce fighting continued for the next two days, after the Germans had worked throughout the first night to create a new trench line. Second Lieutenant **Percy Lees**, 2nd Battalion, the Northamptonshire Regiment, was killed in action on 11 March during this Battle

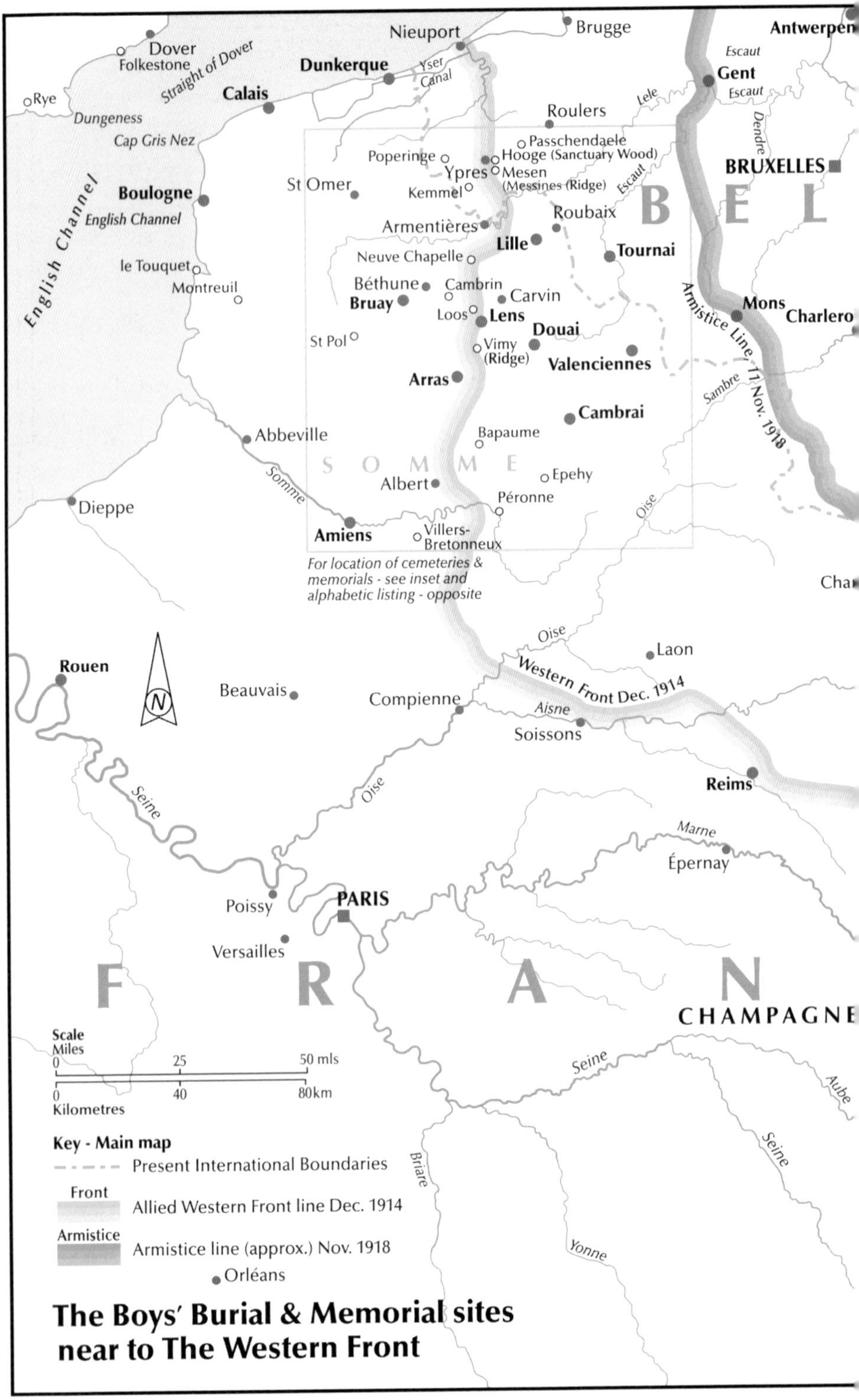

The Boys' Burial & Memorial sites near to The Western Front

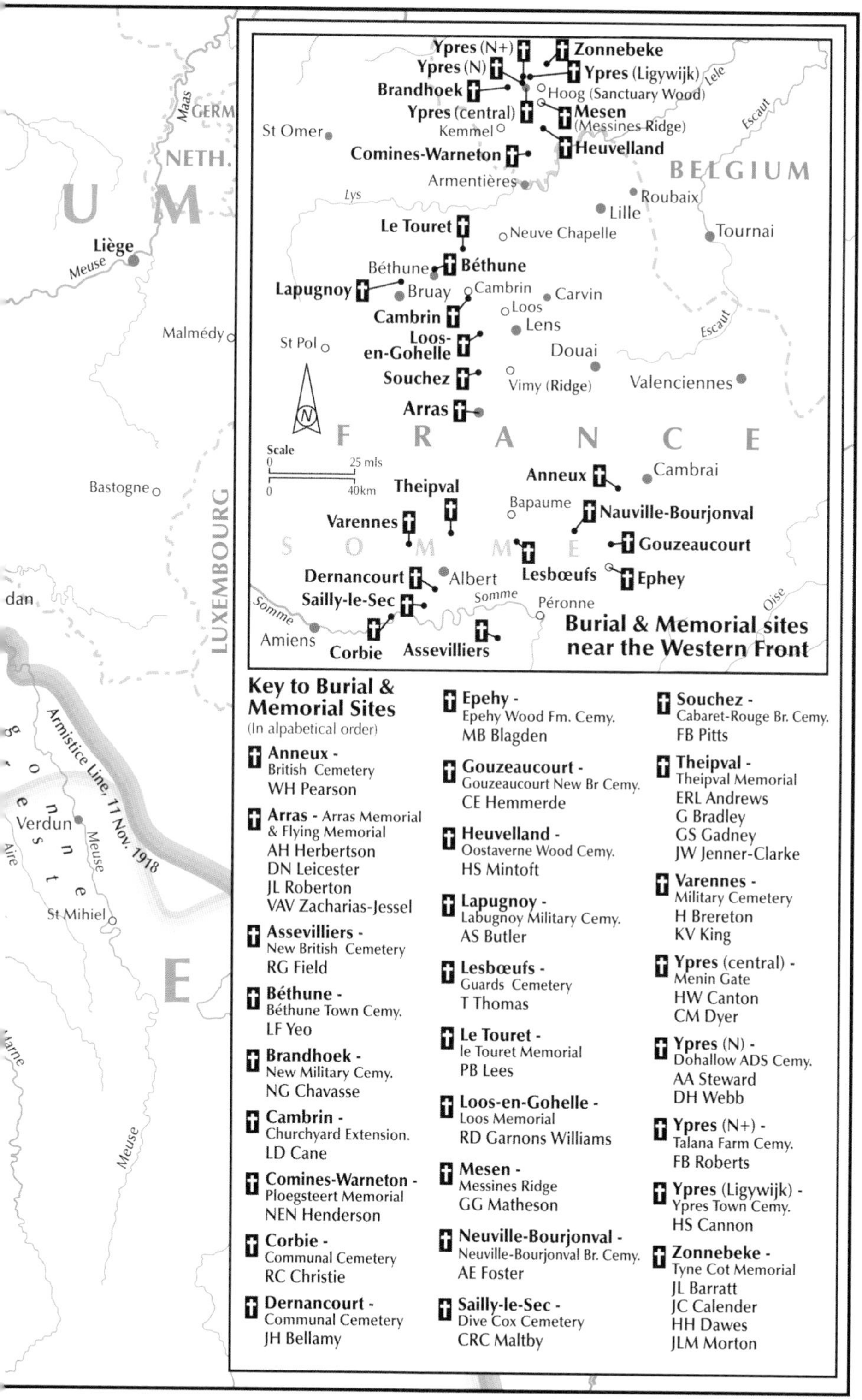

Key to Burial & Memorial Sites

(In alpabetical order)

Anneux - British Cemetery
WH Pearson

Arras - Arras Memorial & Flying Memorial
AH Herbertson
DN Leicester
JL Roberton
VAV Zacharias-Jessel

Assevilliers - New British Cemetery
RG Field

Béthune - Béthune Town Cemy.
LF Yeo

Brandhoek - New Military Cemy.
NG Chavasse

Cambrin - Churchyard Extension.
LD Cane

Comines-Warneton - Ploegsteert Memorial
NEN Henderson

Corbie - Communal Cemetery
RC Christie

Dernancourt - Communal Cemetery
JH Bellamy

Epehy - Epehy Wood Fm. Cemy.
MB Blagden

Gouzeaucourt - Gouzeaucourt New Br Cemy.
CE Hemmerde

Heuvelland - Oostaverne Wood Cemy.
HS Mintoft

Lapugnoy - Labugnoy Military Cemy.
AS Butler

Lesbœufs - Guards Cemetery
T Thomas

Le Touret - le Touret Memorial
PB Lees

Loos-en-Gohelle - Loos Memorial
RD Garnons Williams

Mesen - Messines Ridge
GG Matheson

Neuville-Bourjonval - Neuville-Bourjonval Br. Cemy.
AE Foster

Sailly-le-Sec - Dive Cox Cemetery
CRC Maltby

Souchez - Cabaret-Rouge Br. Cemy.
FB Pitts

Theipval - Theipval Memorial
ERL Andrews
G Bradley
GS Gadney
JW Jenner-Clarke

Varennes - Military Cemetery
H Brereton
KV King

Ypres (central) - Menin Gate
HW Canton
CM Dyer

Ypres (N) - Dohallow ADS Cemy.
AA Steward
DH Webb

Ypres (N+) - Talana Farm Cemy.
FB Roberts

Ypres (Ligywijk) - Ypres Town Cemy.
HS Cannon

Zonnebeke - Tyne Cot Memorial
JL Barratt
JC Calender
HH Dawes
JLM Morton

of Neuve Chapelle, which resulted in the British capturing the village, but without any full penetration of the German trench system. The offensive was called off on 12 March.

Over 12,000 British men had been killed, wounded or were missing in action from the three days of the battle. It highlighted the need for heavier and longer bombardments and more men to take advantage of an initial breakthrough.

During the remainder of March and start of April 1915 both sides consolidated and prepared for the next big engagement. The Germans were planning a major offensive around Ypres, to creep closer to the town and establish a stranglehold and an increased disruptive influence on supply lines. On 9 April, during the build-up to the Second Battle of Ypres, Second Lieutenant **Cecil Dyer**, 6th Rifle Brigade (The Prince Consort's Own) was killed. The battle began on the morning of 22 April and started with the first significant deployment of gas by the Germans.[2] The French fell back in disarray, leaving the Canadian left flank exposed. The following day's counter-attack, led by the Canadians, precipitated a second gas attack by the Germans. A fighting retreat by the Canadians and redeployment of the Northumberland Division re-formed the defensive line and the Germans were stopped. The battle, along just 9 miles of front, continued for a whole month. It was during this time of extended bombardment and sniping that Captain **Herbert Canton**, 1st Battalion, East Lancashire Regiment, was killed on 13 May while in the trenches.

The Ypres Salient had been reduced in size by the Germans, the Canadian Division had suffered the loss of one quarter of its strength (approximately 4,200 killed or wounded) and the Northumberland Division, who had landed in France only a week before the battle, had lost almost half its 4,000 total strength. In total there had been 60,000 British casualties,[3] there was a shortage of shells and the Government back home was under growing pressure.[4]

The second Battle of Ypres was over, but the fighting around this area would never cease. On 16 June 1915 a reduced-strength Liverpool Scottish[5] attacked German positions 3 miles east of Ypres at Hooge. Twenty-one of the twenty-three officers and almost a fifth of the 519 other ranks were killed. Lieutenant **Noel Chavasse**, Royal Army Medical Corps attached to the 10th Battalion, The King's had established a Regimental Aid post in Sanctuary Wood adjacent to Hooge. Despite its name, the wood became a target for the Germans knowing that retreating soldiers and stragglers would find shelter and treatment there. It was here that Noel Chavasse won his Military Cross for his work and treatment of the wounded while under fire.

The stalemate that was becoming evident on the Western Front in early 1915 forced the Allies to consider other options to achieve an advantage in the war. The chosen strategy was to try to knock Turkey[6] out of the war by firstly forcing a passage through the narrow straits of the Dardanelles and threatening the Turkish capital of Constantinople from the sea. Simultaneously, an invasion would be carried out in Western Turkey to take control of the capital.[7] After two failed attempts to break through the Dardenelles by sea it was decided to raise a

Mediterranean Expeditionary Force to land on the Aegean side of the Gallipoli peninsula. The force was made up of a British regular army division, a Royal Navy division, the French Oriental Expeditionary Force and the Australian and New Zealand Army Corps. The invasion started on 25 April 1915, but the Turkish troops were well prepared. The landings by the British in the south of the peninsula and the ANZACS further north were ultimately a disaster. Many soldiers surviving the bullets and shells would ultimately die of disease during the hot Turkish summer. On 6 August Lieutenant **Michael Morris**, 2nd Battalion, Hampshire Regiment, and on 21 August Second Lieutenant **Edmund Tarbet**, 1st Battalion, Royal Inniskilling Fusiliers, were killed during the struggle to break-out of British beachhead positions. By late August the attempt to take Turkey was all but over. On 13 November 1915 Lord Kitchener himself visited the troops, who were essentially unable to push inland or advance north further than approximately 3 miles. He persuaded the War Office to evacuate the peninsula. In total over 44,000 British and ANZAC troops had been killed, and twice this number seriously wounded in the campaign. Remarkably, the evacuation of over 40,000 troops was undertaken (in December 1915) and completed (on 8 January 1916) without a single loss of life from enemy action. To this day, both Australia and New Zealand have a public holiday on 25 April to commemorate the sacrifice made by the ANZAC troops during the Gallipoli campaign.

Back in France, a British offensive against the town of Loos timed to coincide with the French offensive in Champagne got underway on 25 September. The British used gas for the first time, eventually over an 8-mile front. However, like the supply of shells, the supply of gas was insufficient to be effective; some blew back into British trenches where troops were ready to go 'over the top'. Despite this, Loos was captured on the opening day, only for a strong German counter-attack to push back any gains during the following three days.[8] During the opening day of the Battle of Loos, MCS was to lose its oldest and most senior officer to die during the war, Lieutenant Colonel **Richard Garnons Williams**, 12th Battalion, Royal Fusiliers while leading his men in a charge on enemy positions. The Loos offensive was called off on 8 October.

As 1915 drew to a close the war of attrition continued with occasional action up and down the front line, but without any more major offensives. By the end of year the Western Front had hardly moved, but two more MCS boys had lost their lives: Lieutenant **Richard Christie**, 80th Field Company, Royal Engineers, killed by a sniper on 15 December while out of his trench and Second Lieutenant **Arthur Darbishire**, Royal Garrison Artillery, on 26 December, of meningitis in Scotland before seeing active service. Early in 1916 a further two boys lost their lives at the front: Captain and Adjutant **Leonard Cane**, 20th Battalion, Royal Fusiliers was killed by a sniper while in the trenches near Cambrin on 24 January and Captain **Francis Roberts**, 9th Battalion, Rifle Brigade was killed near Ypres on 8 February.

By 1916 the British had raised their 'New Volunteer Armies' to replace the initial small army it had at the start of the war.[9] A giant joint Anglo-French

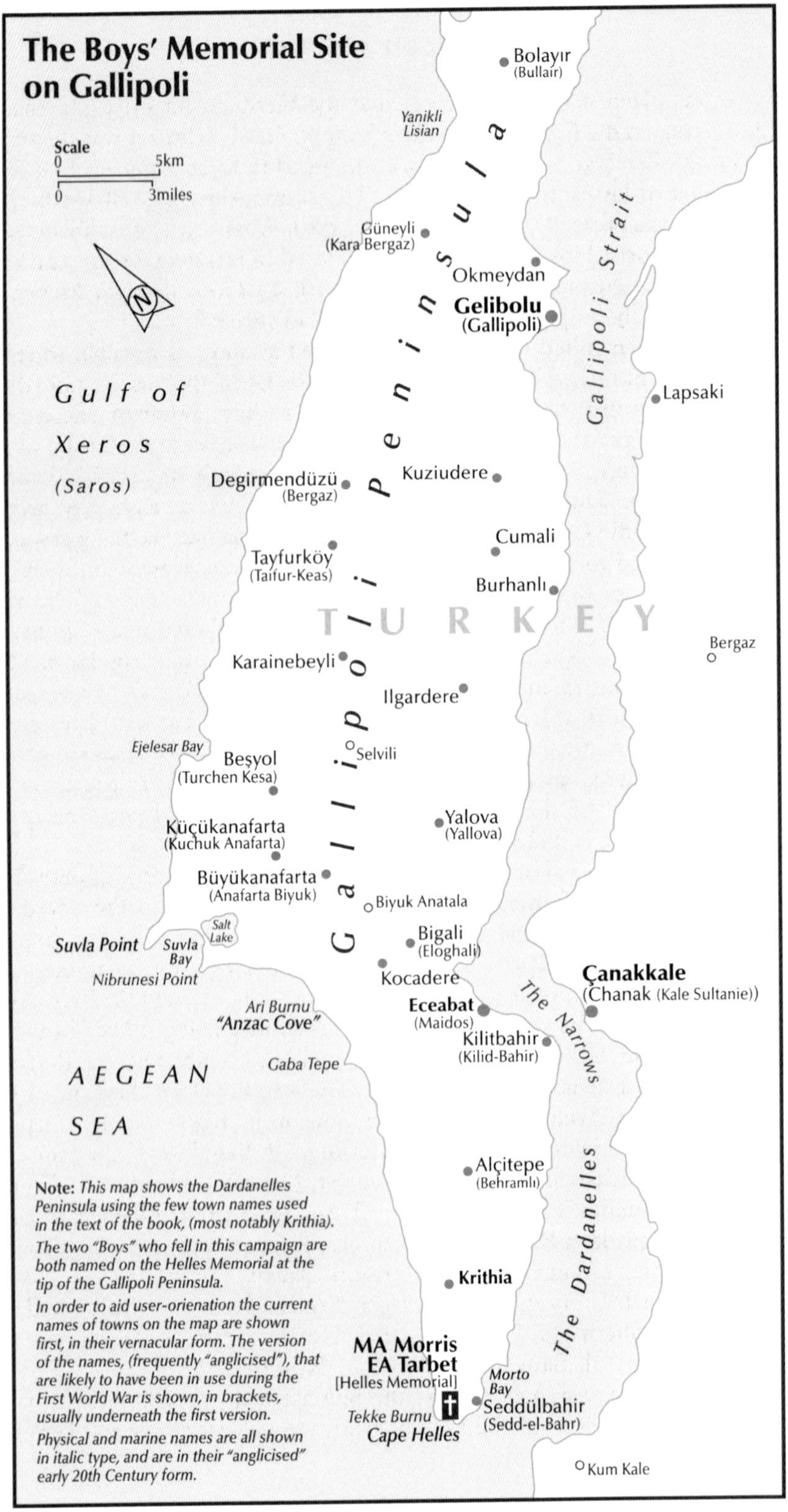
The Boys' Memorial Site on Gallipoli
Scale
0 5km
0 3miles
N
Bolayır
(Bullair)
Yanikli Lisian
Gallipoli Peninsula
Güneyli
(Kara Bergaz)
Okmeydan
Gelibolu
(Gallipoli)
Gallipoli Strait
Lapsaki
Gulf of Xeros
(Saros)
Degirmendüzü
(Bergaz)
Kuziudere
Cumali
Tayfurköy
(Taifur-Keas)
Burhanlı
TURKEY
Bergaz
Karainebeyli
Ilgardere
Ejelesar Bay
Beşyol
(Turchen Kesa)
Selvili
Küçükanafarta
(Kuchuk Anafarta)
Yalova
(Yallova)
Büyükanafarta
(Anafarta Biyuk)
Biyuk Anatala
Salt Lake
Suvla Point
Suvla Bay
Bigali
(Eloghali)
Nibrunesi Point
Kocadere
Çanakkale
(Chanak (Kale Sultanie))
The Narrows
Ari Burnu
"Anzac Cove"
Eceabat
(Maidos)
Kilitbahir
(Kilid-Bahir)
Gaba Tepe
AEGEAN SEA
Alçitepe
(Behramlı)
The Dardanelles
Note: This map shows the Dardanelles Peninsula using the few town names used in the text of the book, (most notably Krithia).
The two "Boys" who fell in this campaign are both named on the Helles Memorial at the tip of the Gallipoli Peninsula.
In order to aid user-orientation the current names of towns on the map are shown first, in their vernacular form. The version of the names, (frequently "anglicised"), that are likely to have been in use during the First World War is shown, in brackets, usually underneath the first version.
Physical and marine names are all shown in italic type, and are in their "anglicised" early 20th Century form.
Krithia
MA Morris
EA Tarbet
[Helles Memorial]
Morto Bay
Seddülbahir
(Sedd-el-Bahr)
Tekke Burnu
Cape Helles
Kum Kale

offensive was planned for the summer, but the Germans hit first. The massive German attack on the French held city of Verdun on 21 February was the start of a ten-month relentless offensive that was designed to force the French, through sheer number of losses, to sue for peace. The action, the Battle of Verdun, was the longest battle of the war and initially saw the Germans take ground and some well-defended forts. However, both sides suffered horrendous losses, and eventually the initiative turned in favour of the French. By December, the French had retaken most of the important positions they had earlier lost.

During 1916, an Allied offensive was required as soon as possible to relieve pressure on the French at Verdun by requiring the Germans to divert and divide their effort. This new offensive was now to be mainly, although not entirely, British, as a result of the French commitment to defend Verdun. On 1 July, the first day of the battle, 19,240 British died, the worst single day in the history of the British Army. The prelude to the battle had been an eight-day artillery bombardment of the German trenches, then on the opening morning seventeen giant underground mines were exploded. The Germans, incredibly, were prepared, and many of the objectives for day one were not achieved. The bitter struggle continued for four and a half months and included twelve individual battles in the Somme *département*. The whole offensive, termed the Battle of the Somme, petered out in mid-November 1916 with the British having gained approximately 5 miles of land across a 12-mile front. The battle had resulted in 420,000 British and 200,000 French casualties compared to Germany's 427,000 casualties. Considered an Allied victory, the arguments still continue, but the battle was the start of the progressive exhaustion of the German army that resulted in its defeat in 1918.

It was during the period of the Battle of the Somme that the now Captain **Noel Chavasse** MC had performed deeds in August that resulted in the award of a Victoria Cross. The world had also been introduced to the tank for the first time in September (during the Battle of Flers-Courcelette). The now infamous Battle of the Somme, with its atrocious muddy conditions, had claimed the lives of nine MCS boys, including its youngest casualty and its first flying officer casualties: Second Lieutenant **Gilbert Gadney**, 8th Battalion, Gloucestershire Regiment on 3 July; Private **Edward Andrews**, 20th Battalion, Royal Fusiliers on 16 July; Second Lieutenant **Archibald Butler**, 25 Squadron, Royal Flying Corps on 16 August; Second Lieutenant **Gordon Bradley**, 5th Battalion, Oxfordshire and Buckinghamshire Light Infantry on 24 August; Captain and Adjutant **Charles Maltby**, 12th Battalion Rifle Brigade on 27 August; Second Lieutenant **James Roberton**, 25 Squadron RFC on 6 September; eighteen-year-old, and youngest MCS boy to die, Lieutenant **John Jenner-Clarke**, 6th Battalion, Duke of Cornwall's Light Infantry on 16 September; Second Lieutenant **John Bellamy**, 11th Battalion, Sherwood Foresters on 4 October; and Second Lieutenant **Thomas Thomas**, 9th Battalion, OBLI on 3 November.

By the end of the year, Verdun and the Somme had put such a drain on the German war machine it would be 1918 before it was able to launch another major offensive in the West. In fact, it induced the Germans into building a further defensive system 20 miles behind the front, the Hindenburg Line.

Before the end of 1916 two further MCS boys were to die: Private **Roger Field**, 20th Battalion, Royal Fusiliers on 20 December; and MCS's third flying officer victim Lieutenant **Herbert Brereton**, 15 Squadron, Royal Flying Corps on 21 December.

The following year provided no respite from the horrors of the war; indeed, 1917 was the worst year for MCS casualties. The year saw the French Army mutiny (a fact that was kept quiet from the Germans until the French had reorganized themselves); Canadian and British troops win a notable success with the attack on Vimy Ridge during the Battle of Arras; American entry into the war (although they declared war on Germany on 6 April 1917 they did not enter action on a significant scale until May 1918); and an armistice agreement between Russia and Germany in December 1917.

Lieutenant **Victor Zacharias Jessel**, 15th Battalion, Durham Light Infantry was killed on 6 April during the preliminary bombardment that led up to the Arras Offensive (during April and May 1917 nine individual battles made up this offensive). Second Lieutenant **Arthur Foster**, 7th Battalion, Kings Own Yorkshire Light Infantry, was killed on the opening day of the offensive on 9 April. Second Lieutenant **Edward Hanby**, 6th Battalion, Middlesex Regiment, died on 30 April in hospital in England after returning from France. Three further boys were to die at the front during this period: Second Lieutenant **Donovan Leicester**, 12th Battalion, Gloucestershire Regiment was killed on 8 May; Lieutenant **Andrew Herbertson**, 7th Battalion, Kings Royal Rifle Corps was killed on 16 May; Second Lieutenant **Francis Pitts**, 8th Battalion, Leicestershire Regiment was killed on 17 May.

In preparation for a British breakout from the Ypres Salient, the Germans' formidable defences on the southern end of the long low ridge south of Ypres had to be cleared. In the ten days leading up to 7 June 1917, the area known as the Messines Ridge was bombarded constantly by 2,250 artillery pieces. Then, at 03.10 on 7 June, seventeen mines that had been dug under the ridge the previous year were detonated (a total of twenty-four mines were prepared under the Messines Ridge; two were destroyed by German counter-mining operations; three were saved for firing later in the assault but were eventually not needed and dismantled; two did not detonate. Of the two that did not detonate one did so without warning in 1955, one whose exact location is not known still remains). Former MCS pupil, T.W. Edgeworth David (MCS 1870–76) was the chief military geologist behind the plan and the construction of Messines Ridge tunnels.[10] Eventually becoming a Lieutenant Colonel, David was himself badly injured by a fall down a shaft near Vimy Ridge in France in 1916. He was mentioned in dispatches three times, received the DSO and was knighted for his services during the war. A total of 420 tons of high explosive immediately reconfigured the landscape, 10,000 German soldiers were instantly killed and the noise was so loud that people in London were woken from their sleep. The ridge was then charged by the infantry, and by midday the 9-mile-wide ridge objective had been taken by the British and Empire forces. Private **Graham Matheson**, 1st Battalion, Auckland Regiment died on the morning of 7 June in the charge to take the ridge.

The British then delayed before pressing ahead with the next phase of the offensive, which became eleven separate battles and is now referred to as the Third Battle of Ypres. The intermediate period between the Messines success and the start of the new offensive on 31 July had been exceptionally dry. However, with the new offensive came unrelenting rain. The Flanders landscape was turned to mud on a scale and depth that enveloped any man, horse or machine that was unlucky enough to fall from the rapidly constructed duckboard road and walkways. The planned breakout from Ypres through to Roulers and to the Belgian coast was no longer a possibility.

The British had suffered 300,000 casualties during the 1917 summer campaigns and were effectively unlikely to meet even reduced objectives as September approached. In desperation, Field Marshal Sir Douglas Haig requested the Canadian Corps help to take the remaining ridges of the Ypres Salient and relieve the pressure on the town so as to provide a strong position from which to launch an offensive when the weather improved in the following year. The final assault of the offensive on the ruined village of Passchendaele started on 26 October 1917 and took two weeks, with the Canadians suffering 15,633 casualties. The British casualties were as heavy as the German casualties, but the high ground around Ypres had been taken and the town for the first time since 1914 was not in the front line.

Going forward at the start of the Ypres offensive of 31 July were the Liverpool Scottish accompanied by Captain **Noel Chavasse** MC VC. They successfully crossed the German front line and pressed onto the second line. Chavasse set up his Regimental Aid Post between the two lines in a small German bunker. During the morning he was hit by shrapnel. After having the injury dressed and being told to await evacuation he returned to the RAP to continue his work at the front. He continued to work throughout the rest of the day and into the evening. The next day he continued, this time right through the day and all night, working to locate and treat desperate men while in full view of the firing line. On the third day his struggle in the horrendous conditions of war and rain was ended. A German shell directly entered the RAP, killing or rendering all inside unconscious apart from Chavasse. He now had to fight for his own life, walking back towards Ypres to find surgical help. He found it in the shape of the surgeon and coincidentally double VC winner, Lieutenant Colonel Martin-Leake, RAMC. However, despite Martin-Leake's expertise Chavasse died two days later at a hospital near Ypres on 4 August 1917, on the third anniversary of the start of the War. Later that month it was announced that Noel Chavasse had been awarded a second posthumous Victoria Cross.[11]

Also killed during the Flanders/Ypres offensive of 1917 were Lieutenant **John Callender**, 2nd Battalion, OBLI on 21 August; Second Lieutenant **John Barratt**, 13th Battalion, The King's on 27 September at the Battle of Polygon Wood;

Second Lieutenant **Henry Mintoft**, 1st Battalion, East Yorkshire Regiment on 4 October; Lieutenant **Arthur Steward**, 11th Balloon Company, RFC on 6 October; Captain **Joseph Morton**, 23rd Battalion, Manchester Regiment on 22 October; Private **Harold Dawes**, 28th Battalion, Artists Rifles on 30 October; and Lieutenant **Dennis Webb**, 2nd Company, Machine Gun Corps on 10 November, the final day of the Battle of Ypres.

Meanwhile, the campaign in Mesopotamia against the Turks had been hampered by incompetence and lack of planning since 1914, with British and Indian troops initially capturing Basra before advancing towards Baghdad. However, the British force, being too small to fight effectively and leave good supply and communication lines over such a large distance, were soon in trouble. The British and Indian troops retreated to the city of Kut where the Turks lay siege to the city for nearly five months. Despite two expeditions to break the siege which were repulsed by the Turks, and the first air supply operation in history by the RFC, the 13,000 British and Indian troops eventually surrendered on 29 April 1916. At one stage, a delegation, which included T.E. Lawrence (of Arabia), attempted to negotiate a secret deal with the Turkish leaders for the release of the troops, but even Lawrence's powers of persuasion were rejected. The captured British and Indian troops were marched over a gruelling 700 miles to Aleppo, Syria and beyond to Anatolia, Turkey. During the march and subsequent captivity 70 per cent of the British and 50 per cent of the Indian troops died of disease or at the hands of their guards. One of those taken prisoner was Captain **Leslie Hoyne-Fox**, 120th Rajputana Infantry. Hoyne-Fox survived the march and the ordeal of captivity but died of pneumonia shortly after release on 13 October 1918. He is buried in Baghdad. In December of 1916 a stronger more organized force was sent to Mesopotamia, advancing from Basra along both sides of the Tigris, to capture Baghdad. Firstly Kut was recaptured in February 1917, and finally in March Baghdad fell to the Anglo-Indian Force. The British had control of the oil fields, but they had suffered almost 100,000 casualties in the process. Battles for Ramadi and Tikrit were later fought against the Turks, city names which are familiar from more recent conflicts. The campaign took a further year to complete and it was only when the British, advancing from Palestine, had captured the Syrian city of Aleppo in October 1918 and effectively cut off the Turkish retreat, that an armistice with the Turks was signed on 31 October 1918.

The Palestine campaign had been in progress since January 1915, with the British initially protecting the Suez Canal, their major supply route to India, from Turkish attacks launched from Palestine. The British eventually decided to push the Turkish army out of the Sinai Peninsula in late 1917, and it was during this offensive at the Battle for Beersheba that Captain **John Fox Russell** MC, RAMC, attached to the 1/6th Battalion, Royal Welsh Fusiliers, repeatedly went out to attend the wounded under murderous fire from snipers and machine guns. Although exhausted and with no other means at hand, he carried the wounded back to safety himself. He was eventually killed on 6 November 1917 and posthumously awarded the Victoria Cross in January 1918.

For most of 1918 the British had scaled down the force in Palestine to help out on the Western Front. It was during this period that Britain benefited from the Arab irregular army, aided by the leadership skills of T.E. Lawrence (an Oxford High School boy), to harry important Turkish positions in Palestine. Supporting this disruptive role was Captain **William Williams**, 142 Squadron RFC, who was killed while flying in Palestine on 3 May 1918. In October, Damascus and Beirut were captured by Australian and Arab, and Indian Forces, respectively. The Palestine and Mesopotamia campaigns ultimately met and cornered the Turks at Aleppo, effectively bringing hostilities in the Middle East to an end.

During this period, Second Lieutenant **Bernard Carter**, 19 Squadron RFC died in a flying accident in Wales, en route to Ireland, on 7 November 1917.

As 1918 dawned, Germany's allies Austria-Hungary and the Ottoman Empire were fast becoming ineffective in the war. Germany knew that to stand any chance of winning the war they had to launch a series of massive offensives and force the French and British into submission before the Americans were ready to take military action. The German Offensive codenamed Michael began on 21 March 1918, and despite Allied intelligence knowing the plan and start date they could do nothing to stop the German advance and their new tactic, the *Feuerwalze* (Fire Waltz). Within two weeks the Germans had pushed the British and French Armies back 30 miles, even capturing the never before held town of Albert with all its British Army infrastructure. Before Michael finally ran out of steam on its northern flank at Aveluy Wood on 28 March and on its southern flank at the long ridge just above Villers-Bretonneux on 24 April, the second offensive, Georgette, was launched further north on 9 April. Georgette made such rapid progress that the Messine and Passchendaele ridges around Ypres, taken with such loss the previous year, had to be abandoned by the British. The front line eventually stopped west of Ypres, and although the town itself was never captured the highest point in the region, Mont Kemmel, was taken by the advancing Germans for the first time since 1914. Mont Kemmel is now the site of the hostel used for recent MCS visits to the battlefields.

Second Lieutenant **Neil Henderson**, 1st Battalion, King's Own Scottish Borderers was killed during the German offensive on 11 April. Lieutenant **Frank Houghton**, 73 Squadron, Royal Air Force, after serving for eighteen months as an observer in the RFC and in 1917 receiving his pilot's 'wings', was killed in a flying accident in the UK on 6 May.

Further, more southerly offensives (Blucher/Yorck, Gneisenau and Reims) launched in late April through to July brought the Germans close enough to Paris that the French capital itself came under fire from the German's 'Paris Gun'. However, the German offensives (overall codename *Kaiserschlacht*) never succeeded in making a break out to the channel ports or taking critical strategic points that were in their original plans. The German high command, having used all their resources and run out of steam in this last throw of the dice, recognized the war was essentially lost.

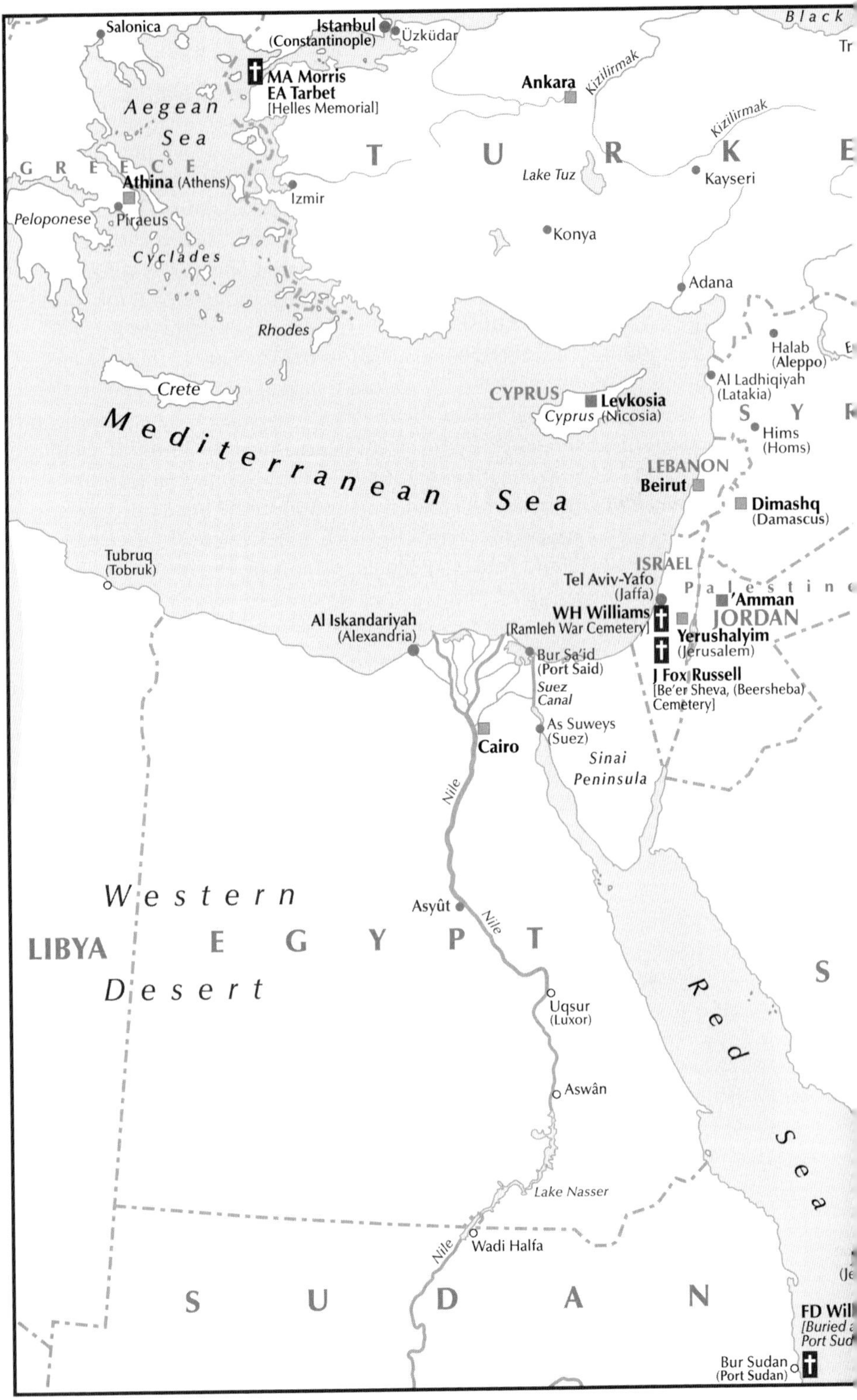

Salonica
Istanbul
(Constantinople)
Üzküdar
Black
MA Morris
EA Tarbet
[Helles Memorial]
Ankara
Kizilirmak
Kizilirmak
Aegean
Sea
T U R K E
GREECE
Athina (Athens)
Izmir
Lake Tuz
Kayseri
Peloponese
Piraeus
Konya
Cyclades
Adana
Rhodes
Halab
(Aleppo)
Crete
Al Ladhiqiyah
(Latakia)
CYPRUS
Levkosia
Cyprus
(Nicosia)
Mediterranean Sea
Hims
(Homs)
LEBANON
Beirut
Dimashq
(Damascus)
ISRAEL
Tubruq
(Tobruk)
Tel Aviv-Yafo
(Jaffa)
Palestine
'Amman
JORDAN
WH Williams
[Ramleh War Cemetery]
Al Iskandariyah
(Alexandria)
Yerushalyim
(Jerusalem)
Bur Sa'id
(Port Said)
J Fox Russell
[Be'er Sheva, (Beersheba) Cemetery]
Suez
Canal
As Suweys
(Suez)
Cairo
Sinai
Peninsula
Nile
Western
Desert
LIBYA
E G Y P T
Asyût
Nile
Uqsur
(Luxor)
Red Sea
Aswân
Lake Nasser
Wadi Halfa
Nile
S U D A N
Bur Sudan
(Port Sudan)

The Boys' Burial and Memorial sites in The Middle East

The Allied armies initially hit back on 18 July in a three-pronged attack that removed the Germans' salient from Soissons to Reims and pushed the front line back to the river Aisne, where they had started in late April before Blucher/Yorck. Lieutenant **Kenneth King**, 52 Squadron, RAF was killed in aerial combat during this offensive, on 30 July 1918 while attacking the German divisional headquarters south-west of Albert. After a three-week planning period, on 8 August British, ANZAC and Canadian forces succeeded in pushing the Germans as far as 8 miles from Amien. They inflicted 27,000 casualties on the Germans and whole units now started to surrender. On 12 September the Americans, in their first major engagement of the war, removed the German salient at St Mihiel, south of Verdun.

The next American involvement, the offensive in the Argonne Forest, started on 26 September and lasted until the final day of the war. It was not considered a success, the Germans' lines of communication were kept intact and the Americans lost 26,000 killed and 96,000 wounded. Meanwhile, the next British offensive in late September made rapid progress, recapturing the villages of the Somme and breaking the Hindenburg Line. The British were now behind the German lines, but it was costing further MCS lives. Second Lieutenant **Maurice Blagden**, 1st Battalion, The Queen's was killed on 21 September while retaking the village of Epéhy. On the same day Lieutenant **Francis Wilkinson**, 10th Battalion, East Kent Regiment was severely wounded and taken prisoner by the Germans. Captain **Charles Hemmerde**, 1st Battalion, The Queen's Own was killed on 27 September and Second Lieutenant **Wilfrid Pearson**, 57th Battalion, MGC was killed on 29 September.

Finally, on 28 September the British launched a further offensive to clear the Belgium coast and the northern area around Ypres. Within three weeks the coast up to the Dutch border was in British hands and even Lille and Bruges had been liberated. During the German retreat, Lieutenant **Francis Wilkinson**, 10/EKR was discovered alive but in a poor state of health, having been held captive by the Germans in a cellar for several weeks.

On 29 October the German Navy mutinied in refusal to undertake a last attempt to defeat the British in the North Sea. Kaiser Wilhelm II abdicated on 9 November and the newly empowered German parliament entered into discussion with the Allied powers. No compromise for the Germans was allowed, an unconditional surrender agreement was signed and the armistice was set for eleven o'clock in the morning, on 11 November.

In the coming years many men were to suffer and die as a result of physical and mental wounds they had received or diseases they had caught during their service to king and country. One would be Captain **Clement Sells**, RAMC, attached to the RAF, who after being invalided home from France in January 1919, died of endocarditis on 4 July 1919. The final MCS victim was Lieutenant **Francis Wilkinson**, who after suffering and struggling to recover from horrendous injuries, finally died on 19 August 1920 while on his way to convalesce and build a new life in a better climate at a disabled officers' colony in British East Africa.

This brought the number of Brownrigg's boys to die as a result of the war to fifty. Fittingly, Wilkinson had returned to visit his old Master and school on two occasions during his recovery in 1919. His affection and loyalty for the school and Brownrigg was as strong as any of the boys'. But one last piece of sad news was still to be received and disseminated by Brownrigg. During the Master's annual prize giving speech of Michaelmas 1920, saying for the last time 'I regret to have to add to our heavy tale of losses two more boys', he closed the chapter on the Great War losses suffered by the school. At last the list was complete, no more MCS boys would die as a result of the First World War, and Brownrigg could refocus on the remaining ten years of his headship.

Notes

1. The term British is used at many points throughout the book when the person of interest was part of a British regiment. However, at the forefront or in support in many of the actions were the Imperial Forces of Canada, Newfoundland, Australia, New Zealand, Undivided India, South Africa, and the other Colonies. Additionally, many of the British actions on the Western Front were joint operations with the French Army.
2. Chlorine, released from thousands of cylinders, was employed. The gas cloud was blown by a northerly wind down the slopes from the Germans' higher ground and into French and Algerian trench systems.
3. The term 'casualties' signifies soldiers killed, missing, wounded or captured.
4. On 17 May 1915 the Liberal leader and Prime Minister, Herbert Asquith invited the Conservatives into a coalition. This marked the end of the last all-Liberal government. David Lloyd George was appointed Minister of Munitions and given the responsibility of sorting out the shortage of shells and ammunition. The coalition lasted until the end of 1916 when the Conservatives withdrew their support from Asquith and gave it to Lloyd George instead. Lloyd George became Prime Minister at the head of a coalition government largely made up of Conservatives.
5. The 10th (Scottish) Battalion, The King's (Liverpool Regiment) were known as the Liverpool Scottish.
6. Turkey, initially unsure whether to side with the Central Powers (Germany and Austria-Hungary) or the Triple Entente group (France, Russia and Great Britain), entered the war on 1 November 1914 on the side of the Central Powers after Britain had made several diplomatic blunders that offended Turkey, whilst at the same time Turkey was wooed by Germany who supplied her with arms and naval supplies. Germany hoped Turkey would make things difficult for British interests in the Mediterranean and Mesopotamia and be able to protect against any expansion of Russia southwards beyond the Black Sea. Turkey was also seeking the best opportunity to regain territories previously part of the Ottoman Empire.
7. Control of the Dardanelles would allow access to the Sea of Marmara and the Black Sea from the Mediterranean and Aegean Seas, opening up a southern supply route to Russia. In addition, control of Turkey would allow Germany and its European allies to be surrounded.
8. Sir John French was relieved of his command of the BEF at this point and Sir Douglas Haig took over.
9. In mid-December 1915 the BEF numbered approximately 270,000 officers and men. The strength of the British Army at the end of the war, November 1918, had been increased to approximately 3.5 million with the creation of the new armies.
10. Edgeworth David was originally commissioned major in the Australia Imperial Force, Australian Mining Corps in October 1915 and was eventually attached to the inspector of mines at General Headquarters, British Expeditionary Force in June 1917.
11. At the time Noel Chavasse and Arthur Martin-Leake were the only people to have been awarded a second Victoria Cross. Martin-Leake survived the war. Since then only one other person has been awarded two VCs, Captain Charles Upham during the Second World War.

CHAPTER FOUR

The Fifty Boys

Edward Richard Lawrence ANDREWS

27 September 1894 – 16 July 1916

Rank and regiment: Private (9684), 20th (Service) Battalion (3rd Public Schools), Royal Fusiliers (City of London Regiment).
Medals awarded: Victory, British War. **Theatre of War:** Western Front.
Memorial: Thiepval Memorial, France.

Lawrence Andrews was born at 93 Kingston Road, Oxford on 27 September 1894. His father (Edward Andrews), uncle (Henry Andrews) and grandfather (Henry Andrews) were all saddlers by profession. His mother, Martha Ellen Andrews (*née* Lawrence), was a farmer's daughter from Wiltshire. The family saddlers occupied 141 High Street, Oxford, between 1861 and 1918, which was only a short walk from Magdalen College School. The original building at 141 High Street was replaced in the mid-1930s and the site is now occupied by Edinburgh Woollen Mill.

Lawrence was the youngest of the family and had three older sisters: Marion Ellen Doreen, Annie Muriel and Irene May. He was baptized at SS Philip and James (known locally as Phil and Jim's) Church, Oxford, on 11 November 1894, and the family moved to 6 Chalfont Road some time around the turn of the century. Lawrence was confirmed in Magdalen College School chapel on Thursday, 10 March 1910. Sharing the service was James Leslie Roberton, who was to die in France only two months after Andrews.

Life at Magdalen College School (1906–1911) and beyond

Andrews joined MCS aged 11 years as a day boy in the Michaelmas term 1906 and steadily worked his way up to the Ushers', Mr P.D. Pullan's form.

Andrews was a keen sportsman, playing cricket (batsman), hockey (half) and football (goalkeeper) whilst at MCS. In 1910 he played for both the U15 and the 2nd XI cricket side. Playing alongside Andrews in these teams were Victor A.V.Z. Jessel (U15, 2nd XI) and John Callender (U15). In this year's 2nd XI close-fought victory over Abingdon School Andrews was the top run scorer (21). The following year saw Andrews play cricket for the 1st XI, while continuing to play for the U15, where he was joined by Roger G. Field.

Andrews was one of the mainstays of the 1910/1911 MCS hockey side. His character as a hockey player was reported in *The Lily* as 'neat and stick-clever as a forward and should be good later on: too slow at present and does not pass the ball hard enough'. Both the Master, Brownrigg and the Chaplain, Rev. Deuchbar, played as forwards in the team and so it is perhaps unsurprising that Andrews'

Exterior view of Andrews shop front (1909).

skill as a hockey player would be specifically mentioned when his obituary was published in *The Lily*.

According to the notebooks kept by Manley, the stalwart teacher of chemistry during the years leading up to the Great War, Andrews studied science throughout his time at MCS and was joined in most of his science lessons by John Callender. In fact, in their very first term's examination (Christmas 1906) they were in joint fourth place in their set, only one position behind Donovan Leicester, who came third.

However, of all the subjects studied at MCS, mathematics was clearly his strength, which was perhaps to serve him well in his choice of career, as he joined Barclays Bank in Ascot immediately after completing his time at MCS in 1911, aged 17.

Andrews' War

Edward Andrews gave up his position in Barclays Bank and enlisted in the 29th (Reserve) Battalion, Royal Fusiliers on 9 December 1915 while they were based in Oxford.[1] In March 1916, after completing his basic training, the battalion relocated to Edinburgh, while Andrews transferred to the 20th Battalion, Royal Fusiliers and went out to France, joining the battalion that Leonard Cane had until recently been Adjutant to.

The battalion was located at the front line near Béthune, occupying the trenches of Le Quesnoy, Annequin, Cuinchy, Beuvry and Auchy, and periodically

Lawrence Andrews.

falling back to reserve billets in and around Béthune. Andrews was immediately exposed to all forms of warfare, experiencing mine explosions, heavy artillery guns, sniper fire, bomb attacks and frontal attacks by the Germans in his first month. On 27 April a gas attack was launched by the Germans approximately 7 miles north of the 20/RF, but by the time it reached them about one hour later the gas was thankfully mild and caused no casualties.

On 10 July 1916 the battalion entrained at Annezin near Béthune and travelled 50 miles south to Longueau, near Amien. The battalion had arrived on the Somme. After detraining the battalion marched to billets at Poulainville (7 miles). Over the next five days they marched east via Vecquemont (8 miles), Buire-sur-l'Ancre (9 miles), Méaulte, Bécordel-Bécourt (5 miles) and beyond Albert, eventually arriving at Mametz Wood (4 miles) on 15 July. Here they bivouacked on ground just below the wood. The next day at 03.00 the battalion moved forwards to relieve the 16th battalion, Kings Royal Rifles who were acting as support to the firing line, in preparation for the 19 Brigade attack on High Wood. As Andrews' platoon was moving up to the trenches they were hit by a shell, killing and wounding twenty-one men. Edward Andrews was one of those killed, aged 21, and he was buried close by at the roadside at Bazenten-Le-Grand, about 1½ miles from Montauban-de-Picardie. Over the following two years his resting place was lost due to the repeated fighting over this ground. His name appears as one of 'the missing on the Somme' on the Thiepval Memorial, a few miles further along the Pozières ridge. The officer commanding his company wrote that Andrews was 'a good and keen soldier, and his loss was a great one to his comrades and officers.' By 20 July the battalion had helped to capture High Wood, receiving 480 casualties, including nineteen officers.

1. Andrews enlisted as a private, unusual given his education, but the Royal Fusiliers were famous for being 'raised from upper and middle classes only'.

John Leslie BARRATT

23 August 1898 – 27 September 1917

Rank and regiment: Private (762497), 28th Battalion (Artists Rifles) The London Regiment; Second Lieutenant, 13th (Service) Battalion, The King's (Liverpool Regiment). **Medals awarded:** Victory, British War. **Theatre of War:** Western Front. **Memorial:** Tyne Cot Memorial, Belgium.

John Leslie Barratt was born on 23 August 1898 in Warwickshire, the eldest of two sons of John William Barratt and his second wife, Rose Laura Harrison Barratt (*née* Denza). He also had a half-brother, Herbert William Barratt (b. *c.*1888). His father and his half-brother were chartered accountants, Herbert working in the Birmingham branch of his father's firm after the war. The family moved to London and are recorded in the 1911 census as living at 16 Greville Road, Maida Vale. Both he and his younger brother Frank Edmund Barratt (born 1 December 1902) were choristers at MCS. Frank Edmund was still at MCS when the news of his brother's death in Belgium reached the school on 4 October 1917. He went home the next day.

Life at Magdalen College School (1909–1916)

Barratt was a boarder at the school and known by his second name, Leslie. He was a chorister between 1909 and 1910.

In 1915 Leslie Barratt played for the Football XI at full back, playing in the 2–2 draw with Abingdon and the 1–1 draw with the 3/4th Battalion, Oxfordshire and Buckinghamshire Light Infantry. In this later game against the soldiers it is said that the school did well against a much stronger team, with the halves and backs playing particularly well. After the game Barratt was presented with his half colours and Mrs Brownrigg entertained the teams to tea. Sadly, before October was out, Barratt suffered an accident to his knee, producing the condition described as 'water on the knee', so he missed the subsequent victory against Cuddesdon College. The Rev. G.L. Deuchar took Barratt's place in the side.

John Leslie Barratt.

Rowing for the coxed 2nd IV in 1914, Barratt at 9st 7lb rowed at no. 2 in the head-to-head race versus annual rivals, King's Worcester. MCS won by over six lengths and Barratt's character description in *The Lily* that year read: 'The most important oar in the boat. Works hard and keeps his swing when tired. Has quite a good swing, which could be improved by steadying it a little more during the last part forward. Is fairly firm on his feet. Must remember to keep his eyes in the boat.' He was awarded his 2nd IV colours for his efforts. By the time we reach the rowing season of 1916 Barratt has gained a stone in weight and is now 10st 6lbs rowing at stroke for the coxed 1st IV. He was the Captain of rowing in his final year at the school and is described in *The Lily* as having 'a future' and 'Does things quite right in a way, save for a sad hang over the stretcher. A week or two behind a good Torpid stroke would set this right.' The crew lost their race versus Worcester, but former pupil and founder of Blackwell's bookshop, Basil Blackwell (the main 1st IV coach during the

Magdalen College School Football 1st XI, 1915.
Standing, left to right: J.D. Elliot, J.W.L. Mason, T.A. Allan, E.F. Davies, A.E. Claeyssens, O.R. Slater, J.E. Searby.
Seated, left to right: J.L. Barratt, H.S.H. Read (Hon. Sec.), H.R. Dodds (captain), G.R. Bradley, Ahamed.

war years), put the loss down to not having had the same coach throughout their training and as a result not being able to row 'a sound forty' for the first two minutes of the race. In 1916, during Leslie Barratt's final year at school his younger brother (like Leslie Barratt, also known by his second name, Edmund) also took to the water in the new recruits' boat. The school at the time had a 1st IV, 2nd IV, Reserve IV and a Recruits IV. The following year on 4 October 1917 while at school, Edmund was to receive news that his brother Leslie had been killed in action a few days earlier. Leslie had actually been killed on 27 September 1917, the same day as the MCS community was entertained by old boy 'Piggy' Read doing aerobatic stunts over School Field in his SE5 Fighter plane. Edmund set off to his home in London the following day to be with his family. Edmund himself (born 1 December 1902 and also a Chorister from 1912) was too young to fight and was still at the school when the war ended in 1918.

When rowing did not require Barratt's services he turned his hand to hockey, playing inside right, where he 'works hard, but is not very clever with his stick'. The favoured MCS forward line approaching the 1916 season was Barratt, G.R. Bradley[1] and the Master (Mr Brownrigg) in the centre, but rowing commitments for the two boys and teaching commitments for the Master appear not to have allowed this on every occasion. Interestingly, a plea in *The Lily* at the time asks for the hockey players to 'observe the rules rigidly' as 'during the last two or three years in the playground, the observances of rules has been very lax, and consequently we have been had up for fouls in matches.' The wet conditions on school field during the Hilary term appear to have required matches to be played at the Balliol Sports Ground.

Barratt was a member of the 1916 Cricket XI, but is recorded as having only played one informal game, in which he contributed five runs when beating Abingdon by an innings and 73 runs. In the squad summary at the end of the 1916 season he is titled the 'spare man' and described as 'works hard in the field: as a bat has a shaky defence'. Leslie's greater ability in a boat rather than on the cricket field had not deterred Barratt's father (J.W. Barratt) who still found reason to contribute towards the Cricket Pavilion Fund in 1912.

Leslie Barratt dominated the swimming competitions during his time at MCS. In 1911 he won the U14 competition, swimming very strongly and leading all the way in the final. In 1914 he won the U16 competition, and then in 1915 he won the 'Open' race. It is stated that his strength in swimming would be even better if his strokes were longer and his style less snatchy. These swimming competitions took place in the Cherwell River at Cox's Corner (Parson's Pleasure) on the third Saturday in July each year, with Rev. G.L. Deuchar in charge of and skilfully manipulating the barge from which the boys started the races.

Barratt was a House Prefect from Michaelmas 1915 to Michaelmas 1916. At this time prefects were selected to help with the routine running and order of the school, with five house prefects selected to administer to the boarders and one other prefect to administer to the day boys. Maurice Blagden was a House Prefect at the same time as Barratt.

Earlier, in 1914 (14 March), Leslie Barratt and Maurice Blagdon had been confirmed, along with seven other MCS boys, by the Bishop of Oxford in the Latin Chapel of Christ Church Cathedral.

Barratt was the Sergeant of the 'B' Platoon in the School Cadet Corp in 1916 and for eighteen months was also a member of the Oxford Volunteer Training Corps, along with his prefect partner Blagden (as well as J.C. Callender and the Master and Usher, C.E. Brownrigg and P.D. Pullan respectively). Barratt had a healthy love of the water and boats, and in 1915 even presented the school library with a book by J. Fenimore Cooper entitled *The Pilot, a Tale of the Sea*. However, on leaving school he decided to serve his country in the Army rather than the Navy and joined the Officer Training Corps of the Artists Rifles.

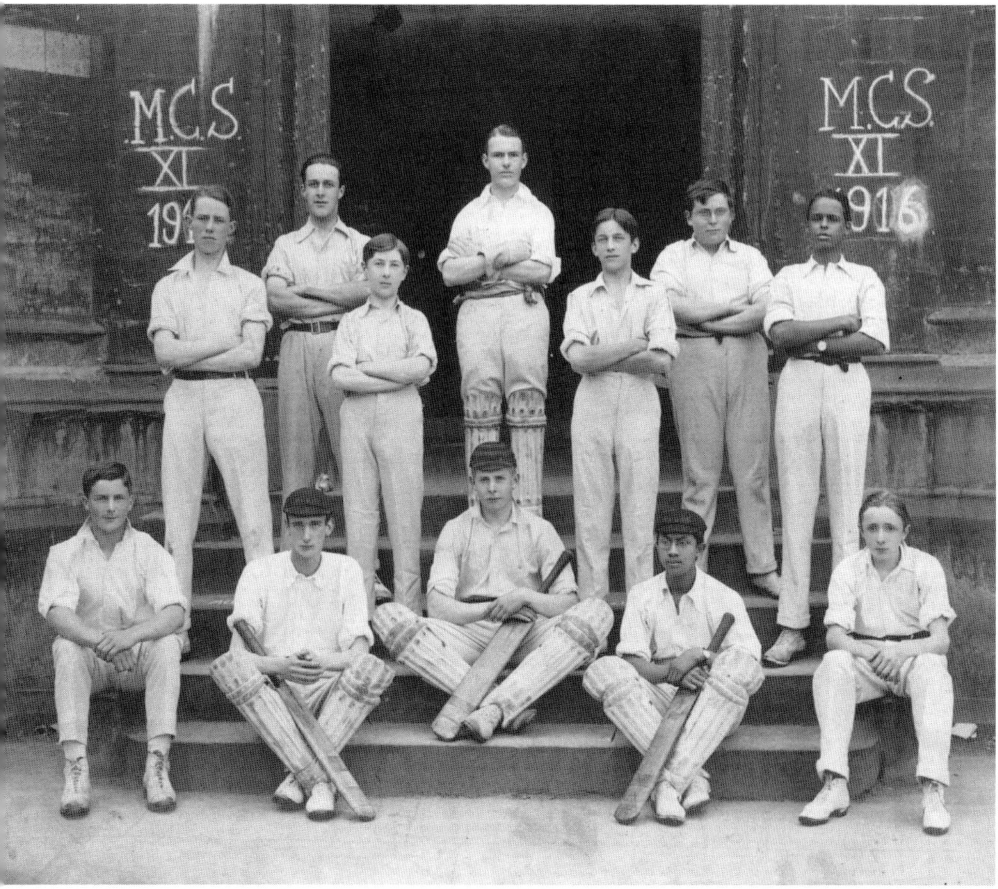

Magdalen College School Cricket 1st XI, 1916.
Standing, left to right: T.A. Allan, J.L. Barratt, J.E. Searby, E.F. Davies (wicket keeper), R.G.T. Fletcher, S.L. Woolmer, A.H.L. Masson.
Seated, left to right: J.Y.E. Myrtle, H.R. Dodds, H.S.H. Read (captain), Ahamed, H.R. Scott.

In 1916 Barratt was accepted by Magdalen College as a commoner, but never matriculated due to joining the OTC of the Artists Rifles.

Barratt's War

Barratt signed his attestation papers on 6 May 1916 in Oxford and joined the army reserve. He was posted to the 28th Battalion (Artists Rifles), The London Regiment on 26 September 1916 and served as a private whilst undergoing officer training in the UK. He completed his training with the 2nd Officer Cadet Battalion in Cambridge before receiving his commission as a Second Lieutenant in the 13th Battalion, The King's (Liverpool Regiment) on 25 April 1917. Following a brief period of further training in the UK, Barratt landed in France on 22 June 1917, eventually joining his regiment in their billets at Fosseux, Arras on the

Somme, five days later. The 13/King's were part of the 9 Brigade, 3rd Division of the army.

By the beginning of July 1917, the battalion had marched to Beugny, where they relieved the 4/OBLI at the front line. The Germans launched an intense attack on the line during 20 and 21 July 1917. Although the battalion was heavily outnumbered in several places they put up a vigorous defence and successfully repelled the attack with heavy casualties sustained by the enemy. On 22 July, following relief by the 4th battalion, Royal Fusiliers, the battalion moved to reserve billets near Vélu. That evening they were entertained with music from the divisional band.

In accordance with the usual rotation of men, the battalion were in the trenches again five days later, but returned to rest at Vélu on 2 August 1917. The following day, Barratt, along with seven other officers, was sent on an entrenching course under the command of the Royal Engineers of the 3rd Division.

By 7 August the battalion was on the move again, this time to relieve the 2/5th Battalion, King's Own Yorkshire Light Infantry in the support trenches at Lagnicourt, before moving on 12 August to spend three days in the front line trenches. The battalion was stationed at Fremicourt Camp in reserve on 16 August where they continued with training and general duties. Thankfully, fine weather favoured the afternoon of 20 August, as regimental sports were being held, with prizes provided by the YMCA Beugny. Such an event must have provided a welcome respite for Barratt after the hardships of the trenches. This light relief did not last long, as the battalion was back in the line the next day.

The battalion moved to Le-Transloy Beaulencourt on 5 September 1917 and remained in camp for the next twelve days before marching through Bapaume, Achiet-Le-Grand and Achiet-Le-Petit to Miraumont, where they took a train to Hopoutre in Belgium. They arrived at Erie Camp near Brandhoek the following day. They remained in camp until 22 September preparing for their next action. By 23 September Barratt had taken up a support position with the rest of his battalion in the front line trenches near Mannebeke Wood on the Ypres Salient. Despite heavy shelling from the enemy, the battalion held their position for the next three days. Then on 26 September the 8 and 76 Brigades attacked the enemy in what was to become known as the Battle of Polygon Wood. Barratt's battalion had remained in divisional reserve, but when word reached the battalion that the front line was falling back due to pressure from the enemy, they moved forward to a support position. At midnight they were ordered further forward, and with much difficulty occupied the position next to the last objective in the day's attack, just opposite Zonnebeke. After heavy shelling, the Germans counter-attacked from Hill 40, but were repulsed. Barratt was killed during this action. He was 19 years of age.

His Commanding Officer wrote to his parents: 'Your boy had just been with the battalion sufficiently long to endear himself to us all, officers and men. On the night that he was killed he was leading his platoon to re-occupy some ground which had been previously captured. He insisted on exposing himself in a most gallant manner, and unfortunately a sniper shot him dead. He had proved himself a popular and gallant officer.'

1. No relation to Gordon Bradley.

John Holland BELLAMY

5 July 1893 – 4 October 1916

Rank and regiment: Lance Corporal (2484), 21st (Service) Battalion (4th Public Schools), Royal Fusiliers (City of London Regiment); Second Lieutenant, 13th Battalion (att. 11th), The Sherwood Foresters (Nottinghamshire and Derbyshire Regiment). **Medals awarded:** Victory, British War, 1914–1915 Star. **Theatre of War:** Western Front. **Memorial:** Dernancourt Communal Cemetery Extension, France.

John Bellamy was born on 5 July 1893 at 10 Tackley Place, Oxford, and baptized seven weeks later at SS Philip and James Church on 24 August. His parents, Edward Holland Bellamy and Zoe Bellamy (*née* Lucas), both local to Oxford, were married the previous summer at St Peter-le-Bailey Church, Oxford, on 7 September 1892. John was their only child. In 1901 the family were living at 123 Iffley Road. John's father, Edward Holland Bellamy (the son of Edward Bellamy, the bookbinder of St Giles' Street) was a clerk to the University Examination Schools. His, and subsequently John's, middle name of Holland was from the maiden name of John's grandmother Caroline Holland (born in Netherbury, Cornwall). His mother, Zoe, was the daughter of the clerk of the Oxford Diocesan Register at 9 New Road (Harry Richardson Lucas).

The Bellamy family later moved to 244 Iffley Road, from where John would walk to school across the bridge.

Life at Magdalen College School (1902–1910) and beyond

John Bellamy was a day boy at MCS for seven years, living only ten minutes' walk from the school. His keenness for all sports and his fine athletic ability during and after his MCS days is clearly documented in *The Lily* magazine. In 1912 he was even able to beat MCS's Olympic sprinter Noel Chavasse in the 150-yard old-boy sprint. Returning to the school to play and race in old boy matches highlights Bellamy's enthusiasm for MCS, the school he had lived so close to for so long.

His early cricketing exploits of 1909 resulted in his batting being described by an old term 'mashie', 'never following through with the body and arms together; in defence he lets the ball play the bat instead of making the bat meet the ball.' Despite this none too flattering description, the following month he did manage to score 'freely' (39) in a seventh-wicket 50 partnership with Frank Wilkinson (22) against an Oxford Police XI. By the season's end he seems to have become a more enthusiastic cricketer, with the season summary stating that he has 'not many strokes and little defence but makes runs when he is at the wickets and can hit the bad ball. Energetic in the field but misjudges a ball in the air.' Definitely a character that would have enjoyed T20 cricket!

In 1912 John Bellamy returned to his old school to play in the old boy game versus the School 1st XI. Captained by Frank Wilkinson and also containing Gilbert Gadney, the Old Boys' XI scored 230, with Wilkinson making 90. The School 1st XI were 207 all out in reply. Playing against the old boys that day were Edward Andrews and Victor Jessel. In 1914 John Bellamy was to return to School Field one last time, along with Thomas Thomas, to play in the annual old boys cricket match. This time, despite Bellamy taking 3 for 20, the School 1st XI featuring Roger Field, Gordon Bradley and Victor Jessel was too strong and won comfortably. Five boys from these two matches, Bellamy, Andrews, Gadney, Bradley and Thomas, were to die in France in the space of three months of each other, during the series of battles between July and November 1916 known as the Battle of the Somme.

John Bellamy's sporting exploits were not limited to cricket, and although he was not the most gifted hockey and football player, he appears to have used his pace to good effect in both sports, eventually winning half colours for football. For these sports he also returned as an old boy to play matches against the school. In 1912 Bellamy made his last appearance for the Old Boys' hockey team alongside Edward Andrews. The school side, losing 5–8, included Roger Field, John Callender and Victor Jessel. Interestingly, the game had to be played on the Lincoln College ground due to flooding on School Field. Some 100 years on, the availability of School Field is still limited in the Hilary term, and indeed in 2013 School Field had been completely flooded three times by February. The installation of a state-of-the-art drainage system at least means the return to suitable conditions is faster than it was 100 years ago.

In 1908 Bellamy's hockey ability was described thus: 'though not very clever has shown fair pace: waits too much for opportunities instead of making them for himself.' Who needed clever play from the boys when in the same team you had the Headmaster Mr Brownrigg, who in the game against the Casuals 2nd XI 'ran through twice in quick succession, bringing the score to 3–1 in the school's favour'.

Bellamy's footballing exploits for the school saw him play mainly in defence, sometimes as a half (a central defender) other times as a back (a full back). In a 1908 2nd XI game versus Clayesmore School mention is made of 'a well-placed shot by Bellamy' which led to a goal and an eventual 3–1 win. In a successful 1909 1st XI season, Bellamy played in, amongst other games, a draw versus MCS's sister school from Brackley and a 'victory over Abingdon for the first time in many years'. The ever-present goalkeeper Bellamy was trying to protect during these games was Frank Wilkinson. Both men returned and played football as old boys versus the School in 1912, this time one at left and the other at right back.

In his last year at the school Bellamy, along with James Roberton, received his full colours for rowing in the school's 2nd IV.

John Bellamy was a gifted runner. In 1909 he won the half mile race, beating Frank Wilkinson into second place in a time of 2 minutes 14.6 seconds (the school record at the time being 2min 10secs). Interestingly, the following year Wilkinson managed to beat Bellamy's time by one third of a second, and then in 1911, after Bellamy had left MCS, he managed to beat Bellamy's time and get to within two fifths of a second of the school record. The question of who was the best half-miler was surely joked about when the two met up for old boys' cricket and football games in 1912. Team mates in cricket and football and friendly rivals on the track, interestingly both men were to volunteer and join the Royal Fusiliers as privates and both men were to sail to France on the same day in 1915 (14 November).

John Bellamy, Football XI, 1908.

In March 1909 a confirmation service was held in the MCS chapel on the Longwall site. John Bellamy (aged 15) was one of eight MCS boys, along with Donovan Leicester (aged 13) and Horace Bradley (Gordon Bradley's elder brother), to be confirmed that day. The choir master, Dr Varley Roberts, after whom the chorister prize is named and still awarded today and known to the choristers as 'Bob', played the organ.

After John had been a day boy at MCS for seven years, he went up to the Queen's College to study under A.C. Clark (a Latinist) in October 1910. Three and a half years later on 25 June 1914, just one month before the outbreak of war and the rush to sign up 'For King and Country', he was awarded his BA degree (Pass) at the degree ceremony in the Sheldonian Theatre.

After graduating John worked for the accountancy firm Wenn & Elsom's on Cornmarket Street, a company he had been articled to throughout his degree. He went back to live with his parents, who had by now moved to 131 Lime Walk (Netherbury), Highfield, Headington. Sadly, within two years a memorial service would be held in tribute to John Bellamy only a quarter of a mile further down Lime Walk from the family home at All Saints' Church. A memorial plaque and stained glass window, still present today, was installed in the church in memory of John.

Bellamy's War

Bellamy enlisted as a private in the newly formed 21st Battalion, Royal Fusiliers on 15 September 1914 and served in the UK for the next year, training at Ashstead in Surrey. He was promoted to Lance Corporal on 4 November 1915 and ten days later as part of No. 4 Company 21/RF, 98 Brigade, 33rd Division landed in France.

On 20 November 1915, the battalion arrived in Béthune and was attached to the 22 Brigade for training. By the end of the month the battalion had moved to join the 'Village Line', 4-Coy taking up billets in Epinette, where they came under German shell fire. The trenches in the area were in a poor state, some being 5 feet deep in water, which meant that the only way to travel between them was to 'go over the top' at night.

The battalion left the Brigade and moved out of the fighting line to GHQ at Saint-Omer on 29 February 1916 in order to provide around 400 men for promotion to commissioned ranks. Brigadier General Strickland commanding the 98th Brigade sent them the following farewell message:

> It is with regret that I am losing your services from the Brigade, but in the interest of the Army generally it is necessary that you should be withdrawn for a time to enable the large number of men who are recommended for commissions to be dealt with. Since you have been in France you have experienced considerable hardships in the trenches and have been under heavy fire. The former you have borne cheerfully and under the latter you have acquitted yourself with credit. The conduct of the battalion has been excellent as was expected of you. The experience thus gained will, I hope, prove of great value to all ranks especially those who may be raised to commissioned rank. Should you not return to this brigade you take with you my very best wishes for your future.

Bellamy was one of these men to take up a commission joining No. 2 Officer Cadet battalion, Pembroke College, Cambridge on 24 March 1916. Bellamy received his commission as Second Lieutenant in the 13th (Reserve) battalion, Sherwood Foresters (Nottinghamshire and Derbyshire Regiment) on 4 August 1916.

He returned to France where he was attached to the 11/Sher.For. (70 Brigade, 23rd Division), joining his battalion in Papot, where they were in reserve in late August 1916.

On 2 September 1916 the 23rd Division began a four-day march via Rouge Croix, Staple and Arques to the Second Army training area near Setques. They began training on 6 September. However, the time in training was only short as they were on the move again on 10 September, this time travelling by train from St Omer to Longueau, and from there marching to Contal Maison where they

John Holland Bellamy.

were again back in the line on 18 September. The battalion spent the next day salvaging rifles, ammunition, bombs and equipment which were lying about in great quantities. On 20 September the battalion marched to bivouacs at Lozenge Wood. The next few days were spent either in the line or identifying the bodies of men who had been killed more than two months earlier in action on 1 July, and burying them by Authvile (Authuille) Wood, half a mile from Thiepval.

On 26 September the battalion relieved the 13th battalion, Durham Light Infantry in the line, occupying the trenches between 'Push Alley' and 'Prue Trench'. The following day, the battalion successfully took an enemy trench (later to be known as 26th Avenue), capturing one prisoner. Perhaps it was in this action that Bellamy acquired the German eagle helmet badge that was later listed in his possessions to be returned to his mother. That night a patrol found that Destremont Farm was occupied by the enemy, and in the ensuring engagement one of the enemy was killed. The following evening, an attempt to take the farm by 13/DLI was unsuccessful. The battalion moved into the support lines where they continued the gruesome task of identifying bodies of men killed more than two months before, and prepared for the coming large offensive planned for 1 October.

The objective of the offensive was to capture the Flers-Le-Sars line, in a front stretching over a mile, with the 23rd Division on the left and the 50th Division on the right. At 09.15 the 11/Sher.For. moved into the assembly trenches, A-Coy on the left and D-Coy on the right in the forward trench (Destremont trench), and C-Coy on the left and B-Coy on the right in a trench dug 50 yards to the rear. The battalion's objectives in the coming battle were two lines of hostile trenches between the divisional boundary on the right and the Albert–Bapaume road on the left. The orders given were that the leading companies were to pass the first hostile line and take the second hostile line, with the supporting companies taking and consolidating the first hostile line.

At 15.10 a barrage of mortars began, and the signal to 'go over the top' was given at 15.15. A- and D-Coy advanced in two waves, with C-Coy advancing in support in one wave, B-Coy remaining in reserve. The battalion achieved its objectives in the fierce fighting and kept in touch with the division on the right. Unfortunately, the battalion on the left failed to hold their objectives and lost touch with the line. It was during this fighting that John Bellamy was wounded in the chest. Bellamy died of his wounds on 4 October 1916, aged 23, at 1/1 South Midland Casualty Clearing Station and may never have heard the message from the GOC 23rd Division congratulating the battalion on their 'complete success which was due to their gallantry and fine spirit they showed'.

Maurice Bernard BLAGDEN

7 April 1899 – 21 September 1918

Rank and regiment: Second Lieutenant, 1st Battalion, The Queen's (Royal West Surrey Regiment). **Medals awarded:** Victory, British War. **Theatre of War:** Western Front. **Memorial:** Epehy Wood Farm Cemetery, France.

Maurice Bernard Blagden, the eldest son of Bernard Henry Blagden and Ada Blagden (*née* Hasluck), was born on 7 April 1899 at 35 Colville Gardens, Kensington, London. His father Bernard was a banker's clerk and by the time Maurice was admitted to Sandhurst Military College had joined the Royal Defence Corps in order to play his part in the war effort. Sadly he was to die on 27 January 1918, eight months before Maurice's own death. Maurice's mother

Ada was born in Gibraltar and died in Canada in 1929 whilst visiting her surviving son Herbert.

Maurice had three sisters Margaret Elinor (1900–1902), Lois Mary (1901–1901) and Ruth Isobel (b. 1902). His two younger brothers, the twins Vincent Henry (1905–1925) and Herbert Charles (b. 1905) also attended MCS.

Life at Magdalen College School (1908–1916)

Prior to attending MCS, Maurice Blagden was privately educated by a Miss Harding at Hook Heath, Woking, near to where the Blagden family was living. When Maurice came to board at MCS in the Hilary term of 1908, at almost 8 years of age, he was the youngest boy in the school. In December 1908 Maurice was assessed for a place as a chorister, but after initially being placed on the reserve list he was turned down and remained at the school as an ordinary boarder. He won the Form III and Form IV prizes for English in 1910 and 1911 respectively and at the early age of 13 was actively participating in the Debating Society meetings. Many of the debates then would still be of topical interest today. In December 1912 Blagden spoke and voted in favour of the motion that 'Military Conscription for Great Britain is desirable', then in November 1913 he supported the motion of 'Home rule for Ireland' by seconding the proposer. On 17 March 1914, Maurice Blagden, along with Leslie Barratt and seven other MCS pupils, was confirmed by the Bishop of Oxford in the Latin Chapel of Christ Church Cathedral. Later that year, war was declared on Germany and yearly routines were knocked out of kilter. Although the school had not yet lost any of its old boys the seriousness of the war started to hit home and the normal school prize day scheduled for 26 October was cancelled. Maurice Blagden did collect the junior certificate he had achieved the previous summer, but four days later MCS was to lose the first of its old boys to the Great War (Hugh Cannon in Ypres, a town that was to become central to the British struggle on the Western Front and a place that MCS boys return to every year on the school's annual pilgrimage). Again in 1915 it was decided not to hold a prize day, but once again Blagden recorded his academic progress by collecting a senior certificate in scripture.

Blagden had always shown an interest in the military and he joined the School Cadet Corps and the Oxford Volunteer Training Corps in 1915, along with his peer John Barratt (as well as John Callender and the Master and Usher, C.E. Brownrigg and P.D. Pullan respectively). In 1915 he was appointed a House Prefect and ultimately given the honour of being Senior Prefect, taking over from John Callender in September 1915. Predictably he became a Commander of the A-Platoon in the School Cadet Corps in 1916. Described as a 'most painstaking senior prefect – a little overburdened at times by the sense of his responsibilities, and at times, therefore, older than his years, but always considerate, helpful and courteous.'

Although Blagden was not known as a sportsman he was certainly gifted academically and was rightfully given a school exhibition for his academic abilities. It was not until his fifth year at the school that he passed his short-pass swimming test. He did however play in goal for the School 2nd XI football team, playing in the same team as Donovan Leicester in 1913. That year the 2nd XI played Abingdon twice, winning at home on a ground in very bad condition and in heavy rain (6–4) and losing away (1–5). In the second game it is reported in *The Lily* that 'Blagden in goal made some brilliant saves'. From 1912 to 1916 he is seen competing in various running events, from sprints to long distance 'paper chases', where boys would take part as either a hare or a hound and the course would take over three hours to complete. In the 1915 paper chase, which started on Boars Hill and returned to school via Bagley Wood and Iffley, Maurice and his friend Basil Donne were leading but arrived back at St Clements before the hares. They therefore had to retrace their steps to try to track their quarry. They eventually finished outside the top twelve, in a time of over four hours.

Blagden always seemed to compete well and achieve a place in some events but would never win, until the 1915 Sports Day. Blagden, having already come third in his heat of the senior 150 yard sprint, was due to race in the senior half-mile handicap race. The previous year he was beaten into second place by his paper chase compatriot Donne, and pushed close for second place by the current favourite, Bell. For a 'never winning but always placed' Blagden this race seems to have been a matter of pride in his penultimate year at the school. It is reported that he 'made the most of his long start, and sticking grimly to his lead succeeded in keeping away from (the favourite) Bell.' Blagden the academic had won on the sports field. This must have been a proud moment for Maurice's two younger twin brothers (Vincent and Herbert both joined the school in September 1914), who were witnessing their first school sports day from the side lines. Their brother, six years their elder, was a school hero.

Blagden's War

After leaving school in July 1916 Maurice naturally progressed from the School Cadet Corps and continued to serve as a Lance Sergeant in the 1st Oxfordshire Volunteer Regiment. At this stage, Maurice's father was also doing his bit for the war effort serving as Lieutenant in the Royal Defence Corps (set up from Garrison [Home Service] battalions for UK defence duties). In October 1916 Maurice applied for admission to officer training at the Royal Military College, Sandhurst, but failed his medical examination (taken in November) as his chest measurement was less than the required 34 inches. Eventually on 23 January 1917 he was accepted into Sandhurst. On 20 December 1917 Maurice passed out from Sandhurst and displayed the loyalty he had for his county of Surrey (where his family home had been for sixteen years) by giving his preference of future regiment as The Queen's (Royal West Surrey Regiment). His wish was granted and on 21 December 1917 he was gazetted as Second Lieutenant in the 1st Battalion, The Queen's. At the beginning of 1918 Maurice received news that his father had died on 18 January. His mother, left with the twin boys (13) and their elder sister (16) to provide for, now faced widowed life knowing that her eldest would soon be off to the killing fields of France.

Blagden did not join the rest of the battalion in France until 7 May 1918, when he and one other officer reached the battalion while they were in a period of 'Reserve and General Routine'. On the 6 August 1918 Blagden was one of two officers in command of 100 other ranks from 1/Queen's who were chosen to form a party that was to proceed to La Lovie Chateau, near Poperinge and line the Avenue to cheer His Majesty King George V as he passed along. The party got very wet in heavy rain.

On 19 September 1918 the battalion (part of the 19 Brigade, 33rd Division) moved across country from Manancourt in battle formation. Unknowingly, they were preparing to join the second great offensive of 1918, to retake the villages of the Somme and drive forward to the heavily fortified Hindenburg Line. On reaching the front they proceeded to relieve the 6th battalion, Leicestershire Regiment (of the 110 Brigade, 21st Division), taking no casualties during a relatively quiet night. On the 20 September the whole brigade was given warning that they would be going 'over the top' the next day. That day and night saw only slight shelling, allowing the ground in front of the trenches to be reconnoitred in preparation for the attack. The night did have one casualty: the officer in charge of conveying supplies to the front was wounded by a shell and later died of his wounds. The following morning, B-Coy, of which Blagden was one of four officers (commanded by Captain E.W. Bethel), together with A-Coy, was in the front line of the attack which began at 05.40. B-Coy was on the left and A-Coy was on the right flank advancing behind a creeping artillery barrage. In the mayhem of battle, and being held up by machine gun fire, A-Coy, whose commanding officer had been wounded at 06.00, sheared off too far to the right and suffered heavy casualties. The front line also had to contend with machine-gun fire coming across its advance from the east. The entire front of the attack was held up, causing the advanced troops to have to halt. Immediately on reaching the line on which his company had been held up, and trying to organize his men for digging in to produce shelter from the very active snipers, Captain E.W. Bethel was killed at about 08.00. During the advance Maurice Blagden had been wounded in the arm but continued with his platoon and was directing his men to dig in when he was shot and killed by a sniper. He was 19 years of age.

In late September 1918, with signs that the war might be in its final stages, Maurice's mother received a devastating rumour that her eldest son had been killed in action on 21 September. Ada Blagden therefore sent a telegram to the Casualty Officer at the War Office politely enquiring if this was correct. The Casualty Officer replied via letter on 30 September to say that they had 'no report of any casualty'. The same day, Ada received a telegram from the War Office delivering the news of Maurice's death. Despite the many miles that separated the war on the Western Front and family back in the UK it was not unusual for rumours to arrive with families before official notification of deaths had been received. Maurice Blagden's death was announced at school on 1 October. In their first year at MCS, Maurice's younger twin brothers Vincent and Herbert had witnessed the finest hour of his school career. In their fourth year at MCS, the twins had now lost their hero.

Lieutenant Colonel P.C. Esdaile, in command of the battalion, wrote to Blagden's mother: 'Your boy had won all our hearts, and his men loved him to, which is I think the greatest testimony I can pay him. He was a splendid young leader of men, and without doubt had a great future before him. What a wonderfully cheery and happy temperament he had.' Brigadier General C.R.C. Mayne, in command of the 19 Brigade, wrote: 'A young officer of exceptional promise; he was keen, energetic, strong, and knew his work well.'

Blagden was originally buried in Deelish Valley British Cemetry, Epehy, north-east of Peronne, but all bodies in this cemetery were exhumed and re-interred at Epehy Wood Farm Cemetery shortly after the armistice.

Gordon BRADLEY

9 March 1897 – 24 August 1916

Rank and regiment: Private (2823), 4th Battalion; Temporary Second Lieutenant, 9th Battalion; Second Lieutenant, 5th Battalion, Oxfordshire and Buckinghamshire Light Infantry. **Medals awarded:** Victory, British War. **Theatre of War:** Western Front. **Memorial:** Thiepval, France.

Gordon Bradley was born on 9 March 1897 at 38 Hertford St, Oxford, on the corner of Percy Street and opposite St Mary and St John Church of England Primary School. The house is now a hairdresser's shop. He was the middle son of Horace Joseph Bradley and Alice Bradley (*née* Gurden). Horace was a well-known Oxford businessman. His main occupation was as a purveyor of milk, owning his own milk firm in Oxford, but his other business interests included a partnership in the electrical engineers, J.E. Elliott and Co., of Broad Street, Oxford, until 1911.

Gordon had two brothers, Horace Frederick (b. 1894) and Norman Douglas (b. 1906), both of whom attended MCS. By 1911 the family were living at Ilford House, 290 Iffley Road, Oxford.

Life at Magdalen College School (1908–1914)

Gordon Bradley joined MCS as a day boy in Michaelmas 1908, with his older brother, Horace Frederick joining a term later in January 1909. Gordon settled quickly into school life, and after only three terms at the school won the repetition and elocution prize for Form I; at the same time Charles Maltby and Donovan Leicester won the repetition and elocution prize for Form Va/VI and Form IV, respectively. In his third year at MCS, Gordon was confirmed in the school chapel on 3 March 1911, along with Andrew Herbertson.

Although Gordon was three years younger than his brother Horace, both boys completed the short-pass swim together on 22 July 1909 at Cox's corner, the site of the MCS swimming sports events. This allowed him to take part in the form fours rowing competition, and he is recorded in *The Lily* as competing in this popular event in 1911 and 1913. The site of Cox's Corner on the River Cherwell is now better known as Parson's Pleasure, a boating station where young men of the University traditionally swam and sunbathed naked right up until 1991. The name 'Cox's' comes from Charles Cox, the proprietor of the bathing place for more than seventy-five years until his death in 1917.

When in Form Vb, Gordon Bradley was to go on and win the main event of the 1914 swimming sports day, the Senior Header race on 18 July, the last swimming event of the summer term and the last event before he left school. Leaving the school at the same time in July 1914 were Donovan Leicester and Roger Field. When the school resumed in September the country was at war. Gordon Bradley's 'valete' in *The Lily* reads that by the time he left school he had 'shown considerable proficiency in English subjects'.

Bradley's War

After leaving school in July 1914 Gordon Bradley joined the offices of Messrs Andrew Walsh and Gray Solicitors as an articled clerk to Mr Frank Gray, but signed up as a private in the 4th Battalion, Oxfordshire and Buckinghamshire Light Infantry on 5 September 1914, one month into the war. He stated his age was 19 years and 2 months, using a birthdate of 9 July 1895. He initially joined H-Coy of the 4/OBLI and was based at the Writtle Camp in Chelmsford, Essex. To enlist in the army you had to have turned 18 and to be posted abroad you had to be 19 or over. Gordon Bradley's real age at this point was 17 years and 5 months. He wanted to fight for his country and was scared he might miss out if the war was over by Christmas, as many people speculated. He need not have worried.

On the 26 January 1915 Bradley obtained a temporary commission as a Second Lieutenant with the 7/OBLI, once again giving a false date of birth. Upon discovering his correct age before the 7/OBLI embarked for France, the Regiment transferred Bradley to the 9/OBLI, a reserve battalion (i.e. based in England for Home Service). After turning 19 in March 1916 Bradley transferred to the 5/OBLI and went out to France as a temporary Second Lieutenant. Upon joining the 5/OBLI he immediately applied for a permanent commission. To provide evidence that he had reached a fair standard of education, Bradley asked Charles Brownrigg to write a letter to support his officer application. In May 1916 the letter arrived with the battalion.

Gordon Bradley's younger brother Norman had joined MCS in January 1916. One can only imagine the pride that the 10-year-old felt for his brother when Gordon's permanent commission as Second Lieutenant in the 5/OBLI was gazetted on 28 July 1916 (effective from 4 July).

Bradley joined the 5/OBLI in the Arras area of France during the snowy March of 1916. Over the next four months the battalion was rotated in and around the Ronville and Bernville support and front line trenches, training at Simoncourt

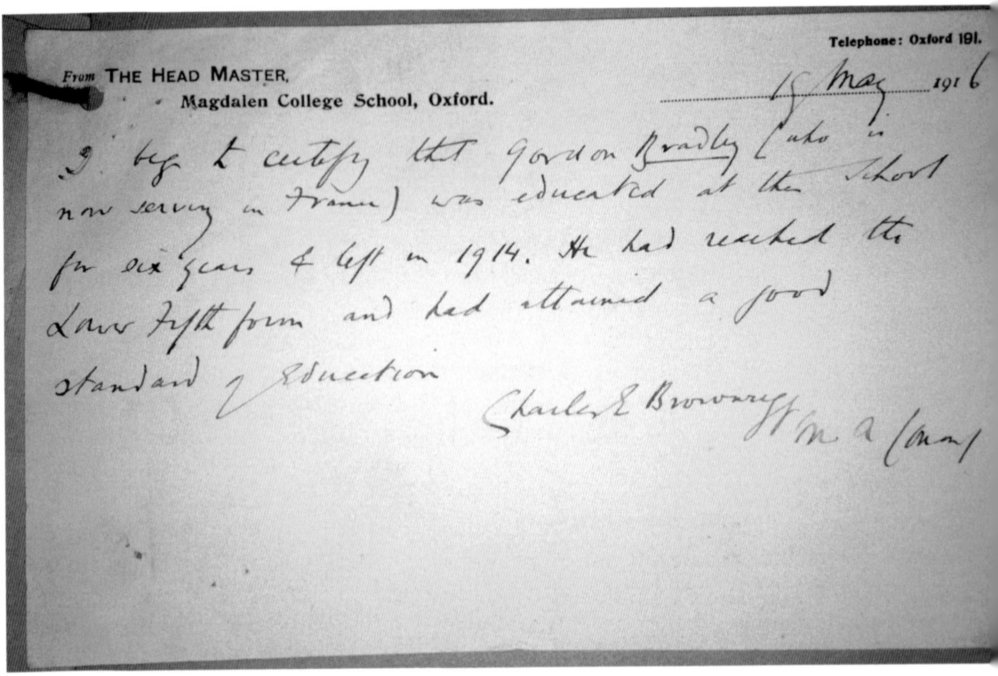

Telephone: Oxford 191.

From THE HEAD MASTER,
Magdalen College School, Oxford.

15 May 1916

I beg to certify that Gordon Bradley (who is now serving in France) was educated at the School for six years & left in 1914. He had reached the Lower Fifth form and had attained a good standard of education

Charles E Brownrigg M A (Oxon)

Charles Brownrigg's letter of support for Gordon Bradley's officer application.

(west of Arras) and in billets in Arras during a relatively quiet period at the front. Thus, despite the occasional heavy bombardment and a gas attack only seven casualties were recorded for the battalion in March, eleven in April, five in May and sixteen in June. On 1 July 1916 the 5/OBLI relieved the 9th Battalion, Kings Royal Rifle Corps in trenches around Arras during a more intense bombardment, when a Maltese cart mule (a lightweight two-wheeled cart usually for transporting medical supplies for the medical officer) and two stretcher bearers of the battalion were 'knocked out'. Seven other men were wounded during the relief. The battalion remained in the front line for eleven days until being relieved themselves by the 5th Battalion, the King's Shropshire Light Infantry on 12 July. The battalion rested in billets in Arras for two days before returning to the trenches at Ronville. When they were relieved on 22 July they had seen the last of the front line trenches for some time. The next month was spent in rest, training at Agnez-lès-Duisans (north-west of Arras, 22–31 July) and Berneuil (31 July–7 August) before heading south by train via Flixecourt and Amien to Buire-sur-l'Ancre (south-west of Albert, 7–12 August) and finally Fricourt (east of Albert, 12–19 August). During the very hot summer weather many men fell out of line on the exhausting training marches during this rest month. The route march from Agnez-lès-Duisans to Sus-Saint-Léger (13 miles) and back on 27 July saw fifty-seven men drop out. Two days later, the march to Mézerolles (25 miles) was so punishing that sixty-nine men failed to complete the route.

Gordon Bradley.

On 19 August the battalion moved forward from Fricourt to Moutauban and occupied the north and north-west defences of the village. After four days enduring slight shelling the battalion advanced on 23 July to trenches in Delville Wood vacated by the 5/KSLI. The following day, the 5/OBLI assaulted and took German trenches in Delville Wood that had been assigned as their objective. One German machine gun was captured, 150–200 German soldiers were killed or wounded, 200 German prisoners including five officers were taken; 172 British soldiers were killed, wounded or missing, including nine officers. One of the officers killed on 24 August 1916 was Second Lieutenant Gordon Bradley, aged 19. His body was never found. Although the 5/OBLI War Diary on this day does not describe the action, when the casualty figures quoted above are digested it is clear that on the 24 August Delville Wood saw fighting of ferocity to match any at the wood since the first Allied attempt to take it on 14 July. Eventually

Delville Wood was secured on 3 September, allowing Allied formations to the north to advance and capture the further high ground of High Wood and Thiepval Ridge, the only tactical gains to cling to after the first few weeks of the stalemate of the Battle of the Somme.

Gordon Bradley's older brother Horace was wounded in action but survived the war, initially serving as a Second Lieutenant in the 11th Battalion, South Staffordshire Regiment but later joining the Royal Flying Corps as a Flying Officer and eventually being promoted to Captain. He was wounded himself while in air combat for the RFC at about the same time as Gordon's death.

Herbert BRERETON

3 October 1894 – 21 December 1916

Rank and regiment: Lance Corporal (1618), The Surrey Yeomanry (Queen Mary's Regiment); Second Lieutenant, 11th Battalion (Pioneers), The King's (Liverpool Regiment); Lieutenant, 15 Squadron, Royal Flying Corps. **Medals awarded:** Victory, British War, 1914–1915 Star. **Theatre of War:** Western Front. **Memorial:** Varennes Military Cemetery, France.

Herbert Brereton was born on 3 October 1894 in Hampstead, London. He was the youngest son of William Henry Brereton and Sarah Brereton (*née* Ambler). He had two sisters, Dulcibella (1886–1964) and Edith Mary Hill (1889–1962), and one brother John Francis (1890–1891). Herbert's parents were musicians and both were members of the Royal Society of Musicians. His father, a bass vocalist, was a teacher of singing who also played the pianoforte and organ. His mother was a soprano vocalist and was engaged in teaching music at the Foundling Hospital in London. In addition to their music teaching, Herbert's parents ran a boarding house in London. It is perhaps no surprise that Herbert inherited his parents' love of music, joining MCS as a chorister in 1904.

Life at Magdalen College School (1904–1909) and beyond

Brereton was a boarder at MCS from 1904 until 1909 and was a chorister during the first four years of this. In 1908 in the MCS Form Fours rowing competition he rowed at stroke for Form I and II. Soon after Brereton's voice broke in 1909 he left MCS to become a day boy at St Paul's, where he remained until 1912. While at St Paul's he represented their OTC in the Shooting XIII. Although he collected the Classics and English prize for Forms I and II while at MCS in 1908, his obituary in *The Pauline*, St Paul's magazine, describes traits in his learning that suggest he was dyslexic. Despite this difficulty, after leaving school he was employed by the Peninsular and Oriental Steam Navigation Company (P&O) in January 1913.

Brereton's War

At the same time as starting at P&O, continuing the military training he had received in the Cadet Corps at St Paul's, Brereton (5ft 6in) joined the Surrey

Herbert Brereton, MCS chorister, 1907.

Yeomanry – a Territorial Force Regiment. At the outbreak of war in August 1914, he went into training with the Surrey Yeomanry and on 17 October 1914 was granted a commission as Second Lieutenant in the 11th Battalion (Pioneers), The King's (Liverpool Regiment).

After six months training in England the men of the battalion arrived in France in the early hours of 20 May 1915. Forming up with the battalion's transport at

Pont de Briques they travelled by train 40 miles inland to billets at Rubrouk. On 26 May, travelling in forty-five motor buses, the battalion relocated 25 miles further east to bivouac at Vlamertinghe, Ypres. At 11.00 the same day they marched to support trenches and began work strengthening existing defence systems and making communication and support trenches. Here they came under enemy shell fire for the first time and four men were wounded. The following day the battalion was advised to work on the least exposed portion of the trenches. They did this in shifts, with two companies working through the day and then the other two companies working through the night. Despite these precautions the battalion suffered its first fatality from shelling on 28 May. Those who thought the Pioneers were going to be a safer option suddenly realized their vulnerability. They continued their work on the support trenches in the area of the Ypres Canal until 11 June, when they moved to billets at Ypres. The same day they marched, proceeding through the famous old Lille Gate, to begin digging assembly trenches to the east of Wieltje. Work in the area became impossible on 14 June due to the severity of the enemy shelling. The battalion therefore returned to its original billets at Vlamertinghe, during which time a new draft of 119 other ranks reinforced the battalion. On 20 June they returned to their Ypres billets and the battalion set up its first workshop for construction and production of items such as trench boards and rifle racks for the trenches. Within days the battalion had plans for three workshops, based upon ideas gained from visits to the Second Army workshops, utilizing the skills of carpenters, blacksmiths and other tradesmen in the battalion to fashion any item that was required for the front line. Thirty men were sent to the workshops of the Second Army for training. Throughout the rest of June, the trench systems were continually improved, despite the heavy rain making earth work difficult. The workshops had a massive boost when Lieutenant Colonel Wickham was appointed the Town Mayor of Ypres, along with a Lieutenant Zonmak as the Belgian representative. These appointments facilitated permission for the Pioneers to remove from the houses of Ypres material that was required in the workshops for 'the making of trench requirements'. A list of everything taken from the houses was catalogued and handed to the Belgian representative each day.

The battalion remained billeted at Ypres throughout all of July, August, September and most of October. During this time they worked on erecting huts, trench digging, widening and strengthening, and employed their machine gun sections for defensive duties. Occasionally the machine gun section of the battalion was also used to relieve other battalions' machine gun sections. During much of this time there were heavy shell bombardments in and around the Ypres area, and casualties, both wounded and killed, were taken daily. The forge built by the battalion at their workshop in Ypres was damaged by shelling on 5 July. At Ypres on 11 July 1915 at 20.30 the machine gun section at the front line was relieved by the reserve section under the command of Second Lieutenant Herbert Brereton and Sergeant Rawson. On 14 July one machine gun was put out of action by a shell and two men were wounded. The next day, work on the trenches was continued by the Pioneers but was hindered by the heavy rain. Sergeant Rawson became sick and was replaced by Sergeant Thompson, who was himself wounded on the same day. After seven days at the front Brereton's machine gun section and the rest of the Pioneers were relieved and they returned to billets near Poperinge, where the baths were put at their disposal. During these seven days of work in the firing line trenches, under constant shelling and machine gun fire, twenty-one men had been wounded or taken ill. It is not known if Brereton was in command of the machine gun section for his entire time or just some of the time while with the 11/King's. In August the heavy fighting continued and the battalion was present in Ypres as St Martin's Cathedral was slowly destroyed by shelling. Casualties in the battalion gradually mounted and on 26 July the senior Major of the battalion was killed by a shell whilst inspecting the Pioneers. The battalion was asked to 'stand to' on 29 July, in case of a German breakthrough. In August the Pioneers' work continued in the area of Sanctuary Wood and Zouve Wood: repairing blown-in trenches, performing carrying duties and setting up a divisional armouries shop to mend rifles. In August they found themselves in the rubble of the cathedral as they dug out bodies of the 6/DCLI from the destroyed cloisters. At this time (16 August) Noel Chavasse's youngest brother, Lieutenant Aidan Chavasse, joined Herbert Brereton and the 11/King's at Ypres. Aidan was to serve with the 11/King's until transferring to the 17/King's in April 1917. He was killed three months later at Observatory Ridge, only a mile from Hooge, on 4 July when patrolling German trenches in no-man's land. At the start of September, thirty-six hours of continual rain hampered the Pioneers' work in the trenches. Once again on 24 September they found themselves 'standing to' during a British attack and two days later they were burying the dead that resulted from the assault. The steady losses within the battalion continued into October as they worked on the defensive systems of Ypres during periods of heavy shelling. Finally, on 22 October, after five months doing front line pioneer work, the battalion was sent for rest. Travelling by train from Vlamertinghe to Poperinge, they then had to march 5 miles to billets at Watou. Here, baths were allocated, route marches were undertaken and football and other games were played. As the weather worsened towards the end of October and into December the roads reached a 'shocking state' and even Sunday Church parade was cancelled on 31 October due to the weather. Training while at 'rest' continued, though, and even the Pioneers received musketry instruction, bomb training and machine gun instruction. After nearly a month away from the front line, the Pioneers moved back to their billets in Ypres on 19 November, but not before they had had another bath! They returned to a similar routine of trench work plus work on the trench tramway system at St Jean in Ypres. To the Pioneers' relief they were not to spend Christmas at Ypres, but on 15 December they returned to their rest billets at Watou, where they stayed until New Year's Eve. On 19 December they were 'stood to' when a German attack at Ypres was launched. At midday they were to hold themselves in readiness and proceed back to Poperinge as it was feared the Germans had broken through the line. Thankfully, they were 'stood down' at 14.00 when it was realized that the attack had been repelled. The battalion concluded the year by travelling to the Elverdinghe vicinity on 31 December 1915, where it billeted, in preparation to work on the Canal Bank trenches.

The battalion moved to rest at Ledringhem on 13 February 1916, 20 miles west of Ypres. Brereton had seen Ypres for the last time. After six days the battalion marched to Cassel and entrained for Longueau near Amien, 70 miles south. They then moved to Villers-Bocage on 20 February, 7 miles north of Amien centre. Then, during a snowstorm on 25 February the battalion moved to Warluzel, 15 miles west of Arras, and three days later moved 5 miles to Fosseux. Finally they moved into a snowy Arras on 3 March. Here they stayed for the next five months, working on the Arras communication trenches and defences at Ronville, Achicourt and Saint Sauveur, supplying miners to build dugouts and helping with the Signals Company. The period was a relatively quiet one compared to their previous time in Ypres, only taking occasional casualties. At last, on 26 July the battalion was relieved from front-line pioneering work by the 14 Northumberland Fusiliers and moved 8 miles west to billet at Wanquetin. They proceeded further west on 27 July, billeting at Ivergny for two days before moving south to billets, split between Outrebois and Frohen-le-Grand. On 1 August the battalion moved 6 miles north to Beaumetz. They stayed here for a week before entraining at Candas to travel the 25 miles to Méricourt-sur-Somme, south of Albert. From here they worked on trenches at Delville Wood and Trones Wood and, on 17 and 24 August, were the reserve in the attacks on the German lines in the area of Delville Wood.

On 26 August 1916 Brereton transferred to the Royal Flying Corps and became an Observer, where he was appointed Lieutenant.[1] When Brereton joined 15 Squadron they were based at Marieux, between Amien and Arras in Northern France, where they had been since late March.[2] It was at Marieux where His Majesty the King inspected the squadron and where they received many visits from the Prince of Wales. After Brereton had been with the squadron for seven weeks they relocated a short distance away to an airfield at Léalvillers. In the latter part of 1916, 15 Squadron was mainly involved with bombing and artillery observation missions. As such they played a prominent part in the taking of Beaumont Hamel in November 1916. Although air-to-air combat for 15 Squadron was relatively rare at this time, due to their non-fighter role, Brereton and his pilot at that time, Lieutenant S.V. Thompson, were involved in a recorded combat on 20 October. Flying in their BE2c plane on this day they were attacked by four German planes while carrying out artillery observations over Beaumont Hamel. The enemy machines spiralled down behind them, so Thompson turned and attacked one machine from above. This machine dived away after Thompson fired 'half [a] drum from [his] front gun on [the enemy plane's] port side at 150 yards'. As Thompson turned they 'attacked two others behind us with [the] front gun, about two more drums [were] fired at them from 100 to 30 yds. All the four of them went off towards Achiet-le-Grand.'

On 21 December 1916, Brereton and his pilot Second Lieutenant Markham were returning to base after a two hour observation flight over the front lines when their aircraft's engine failed. The plane lost speed while they were trying to land, and crashed into the ground. Markham was injured, but Brereton was killed instantly, aged 22. Herbert Brereton was due to return to England in January to retrain as a pilot. He is buried less than a mile away from where he crashed, at Varennes Military Cemetery on the Léalvillers to Varennes road.

In a letter to his parents found after his death Brereton had written: 'I have had the honour to fall for England. Do not on any account grieve for me, but be proud you were able to have a son to offer'. His effects returned to his family included a small prayer book, a Bible, two pipes with a tobacco pouch and a gold ring.

1. The requirement that men possessed a pilot's licence before joining the RFC was dropped in July 1916, as the RFC casualties mounted and the supply of replacement officer's with aviation experience started to dry up. From mid-1916 and throughout 1917 the RFC made periodic appeals to infantry, cavalry and artillery units for men to transfer to the RFC. Many soldiers responded to these recruitment campaigns, others were actively encouraged if their faces didn't fit their current unit, joining what was seen by some as the more glamorous service or by others 'the suicide mob'.
2. Brereton appears in records to have initially transferred to 6 Squadron on 16 July 1916, before joining 15 Squadron, but no further reports of his brief time with them were found.

Archibald Stanley BUTLER

25 May 1890 – 16 August 1916

Rank and regiment: Corporal, Warwickshire Imperial Yeomanry (1908–1915); Second Lieutenant, 2/4th (South Midland) Howitzer Brigade, Royal Field Artillery; Second Lieutenant, 25 Squadron, Royal Flying Corps. **Medals awarded:** Victory, British War. **Theatre of War:** Western Front. **Memorial:** Lapugnoy Military Cemetery, France.

Archibald Stanley Butler was the third son of Charles Dawson Butler and Emily Butler (*née* Brewer). His father was born in Scotland, but as an insurance manager lived in many different locations. Archibald, his two older brothers, Alfred Dawson (b. 1886) and Charles Dawson (b. 1888), and his sister Annie Gertrude (b. 1892), were all born in Dublin, Ireland. The family moved to England sometime between 1892 and 1896, living for a while in Worcestershire, where Archibald's younger brother Albert Cecil was born in 1896. The family was complete with the birth of Archibald's youngest brother, Wallace (born 1900), and at the time of the 1901 census the family were living at 23 Rotton Park Road, Edgbaston, Birmingham.

Life at Magdalen College School (1901–1904) and beyond

Archibald Butler was a boarder and chorister at MCS for three years, joining MCS in 1901 on the same day as Basil Blackwell and Charles Maltby. In total, ten new boys started that September, a typical intake into the school for that era. The total number in the school that year was approximately ninety, making it a very close-knit community. In 1902, in his first year at the school, Butler won the junior gymnastics competition which was held annually in March at the University Gymnasium. In the same year Butler won the Form I prize for his academic studies. The following year Butler was again too 'neat and strong' in the gymnastics competition for the rest of the Lower school and so again won easily. However, fairness being a key ethos of the day at MCS, the prize was awarded to the second-placed W.H. de Souza as Butler had won it the year before. The compassionate and fair Mrs Brownrigg promised Archibald, still only 12 years of age, that he would also receive a prize later on similar to that awarded to de Souza. At the Michaelmas 1903 prize giving ceremony Butler was one of three boys in the Lower school to receive a Master's extra prize for work done out of school.

In 1903 and 1904 Butler appears in the Form Fours rowing competition rowing at stroke for Form I and II. In 1904 he was also the coxswain for the school 1st IV boat, being only 5st 10lbs at the time. The boat, with Gilbert Gadney's younger brother, A.S. Gadney at stroke, beat Bath College for the third year running, this year on home water. The race was an annual event held in March and alternated between racing on the River Avon in Bath and on the Isis in Oxford.

Butler's only other sporting exploits while at MCS appear to have been with the choristers' football team. In 1903 he played alongside Harold Dawes and Charles Maltby in both the home and away games versus Christ Church choristers, both played on Merton Field. The first game ended in a draw (1–1) and the second game played at the end of November on heavy ground ended in a victory for MCS (5–2). Although Butler played as a forward in both games his name did not appear on either score sheet.

It is likely that Butler left school in 1904, aged 14, to start work after his voice broke and he was no longer able to continue as a chorister. It appears that his father, an insurance manager, was able to get Archibald and his elder brother Charles employed in the insurance business, and in the 1911 census the two are reported as being insurance officials. Sadly their father died in 1908. When Archibald joined the Territorial Force in 1908 he was an insurance clerk for the Royal Exchange Insurance Co., Birmingham. In 1915 when he left the Territorial Force for the Army he was a Life Inspector for the Royal Exchange Assurance Co., Pall Mall, London.

Butler's War

On 27 May 1908 Archibald Butler signed up as a Private in the Territorial Force of the Warwickshire Imperial Yeomanry (WIY).[1] For seven consecutive summers he went away for two weeks' training with the Territorial Force (Salisbury Plain 1909 and 1910; Warwick Park 1911 and 1914; Combe Park, Coventry 1912; and Bulford 1913). After five years in the TF, on 1 May 1913 he was appointed Lance Corporal.

After the outbreak of war in August 1914, Butler was promoted to Corporal in the WIY. In May 1915 he was discharged from the Territorial Force to take a commission as a Second Lieutenant in the 4th (South Midland) Howitzer Brigade, Royal Field Artillery. On his commission papers his good moral character was vouched for by the then Bishop of Truro, the Rt. Rev. Winfrid Oldfield Burrows, who had known Butler from the years 1903 to 1912, when Butler had lived in his Parish (St Augustine, Edgbaston). In April 1915 the 4/HB RFA, with the rest of the 61st (2/South Midland) Division, located to Great Baddow in Essex. On 6 August the whole division was inspected by Field Marshal Earl Kitchener. The division was eventually to sail to France in May 1916, after training on Salisbury Plain, but Butler left the Howitzer Brigade some time before this and is recorded in Air Ministry records for the Royal Flying Corp in 1916. He was stationed at Reading (School of Military Aeronautics) in January 1916, then part of the Reserve Squadron in March, 41 Squadron in April and 28 Squadron in May. On becoming a flying officer on 28 June 1916 he was attached to 25 Squadron stationed at Auchel, 9 miles west of Béthune, where the Bristol Scout C, the D.H.2 and the F.E.2(b) were some of the aircraft flown by the RFC at this time.

Everyday life in the RFC was considerably more comfortable than the life experienced in the trenches. At Auchel flying officers had billeted rooms near to the airfield and on the base itself had recreation rooms, bath houses and tennis courts. Even a small stage was erected where members of the squadron performed several revues. One of the pilots with 25 Squadron when Butler joined was Arthur Tedder[2] who became a Flight Commander in August 1916.

In late June 1916, the RFC began an aerial offensive which involved attacks on German observatory kite-balloons and bombing missions on German aerodromes, together with railway junctions, billets and munitions dumps. On 19 July, 25 Squadron supported XI Corps as it began its offensive action on the first day of the Battle of Fromelles (intended to divert attention from the Battle of the Somme, 50 miles to the south), preventing enemy aircraft from observing the British artillery positions. These tasks gave relatively little opportunity for aerial combat, and during his two months with the squadron Butler does not appear in a single combat report. Butler was killed in a flying accident on 16 August 1916, aged 26. He had survived seven weeks as a flyer in France. His observer, Air Mechanic Eric Burslem Brotherton, was injured in the same accident but survived the war. On the same day MCS old boy Flying Officer James Roberton arrived at Auchel to join 25 Squadron. He was to survive only three weeks.

1. The WIY was part of the new Territorial Force (TF). The TF, a volunteer reserve, was formed on 1 April 1908 by the Secretary of State for War, Richard Burdon Haldane, following the enactment of the Territorial and Reserve Forces Act 1907 combining re-organizing the old Volunteer Army with the Yeomanry. In 1920 the TF became known as the Territorial Army (TA).
2. During the Second World War Arthur William Tedder became Marshal of the Royal Air Force, the highest rank in the RAF.

John Clement CALLENDER

24 March 1896 – 21 August 1917

Rank and regiment: Lieutenant, 2/4th Battalion, Oxfordshire and Buckinghamshire Light Infantry. **Medals awarded:** Victory, British War. **Theatre of War:** Western Front. **Memorial:** Tyne Cot Memorial, Belgium.

John Clement Callender was the second son of Clement Boucher Callender and Lucy Agnes Callender (*née* Swabey). He had an older brother, George Herbert (b. 1891). His father was a cement merchant and, with his partner S.H. Blackett, ran Callender and Co., of 32 Saint Mary Axe, London until 1899 when the partnership was dissolved. His father later became an accountant.

John was born at the family home, The Hut, Adelaide Road, Surbiton, Surrey and was christened at St Mark's in Surbiton on 5 May 1896. It appears that John's mother and father separated at some point, as at the time of the 1901 census John, his mother and brother are living with his maternal grandmother at 5 Claremont Gardens, Surbiton, Surrey. By 1911 the family had moved to live with their grandmother at Surrey Lodge, Thames Ditton, Surrey.

John's elder brother George served in the Seaforth Highlanders during the war, attaining the rank of Major and receiving an MC. He survived the war.

Life at Magdalen College School (1906–1915)

John Callender attended Shrewsbury House Preparatory School in Surbiton before joining MCS as a chorister in September 1906, aged 10.[1] He remained a chorister until 1910, when his voice broke. He was a Greene Exhibitioner (a Corpus Christi bequest Prize awarded to the Chorister who was 'best in music, learning and manners'). In 1911 Callender was due to be confirmed in the school chapel on 3 March, just before his fifteenth birthday; however, due to being unwell he had to miss the ceremony, but was confirmed on 23 March in the more salubrious surroundings of Oxford's Christ Church Cathedral. Busy in all walks of school life, John was very able academically and was a good all-round sportsman. Between 1911 and 1915 he won no fewer than five school academic prizes (the Set 1 Science prize; Form Vb Academic prize; English History and Literature prize; Upper V English prize; and a Repetition and Recitation prize). He achieved Lower Certificates (1912 and 1913) and Senior Certificates (1914 and 1915) in the Oxford and Cambridge Examinations. It is not surprising that he was selected to be first a House Prefect (as well as the Librarian) and then in his final year (1914/15) Head Prefect. His scholastic ability also brought him the editorship of *The Lily* in 1915.

Callender played hockey at half-back for the 1st XI for an unprecedented seven years from 1908 when only 12, gaining full colours in 1914. He also captained the U15 side. Playing alongside the likes of Sells, Wilkinson, Jessel, Andrews and Brownrigg, the degree of muddiness of the ground was usually the deciding factor for the outcome of the game, with the school defence sometimes incapable of clearing the ball when the mud was too thick. By 1914, owing to his rowing

John Callender, MCS chorister, 1907.

commitments during the Hilary Term, Callender was making only occasional appearances for the hockey team.

A regular competitor in numerous events on sports days, on 16 June 1910 John Callender came second to Victor Jessel in the Junior 100-yard final, and won the Junior Long Jump with a leap of 14 feet 8½ inches. By the time he was competing in the sun-drenched Sports Day of 20 June 1914 he had progressed his long jump (that year called the Broad Jump) to 17 feet 11 inches, but this was not enough to beat Searby, who jumped over 18 feet to win the senior event. In his final sports day of 1915 Callender won the cricket ball throwing competition with a distance of 85 yards 7 inches; and was part of the winning 400-yard relay team, albeit with help from a stronger team dropping their flag. Callender could definitely compete on the athletics track, but when it came to gymnastics he was always found at the bottom of the competition table each year; the rings, bars, horse and rope were not his thing.

In rowing Callender was pushing for a place in the 1st IV boat as early as 1912, but had to wait until 1914 to gain his place amongst a very competitive crew. The reward for being in the 1st boat was to row in the prestigious head-to-head race against the King's School, Worcester in the Hilary Term. Held annually and alternating each year between the Severn and the Isis, in 1914 the race was on MCS home water. MCS won the toss and chose the Berkshire bank of the Isis with the advantage of a prevailing wind. John Callender (10st 9lb) was at no. 2 and Victor Jessel (11st 11lb) was at no. 3. The start took some time as the boats took a while to settle, then Worcester drifted out of position. When the gun sounded MCS got the faster start and gained advantage from the first bend, taking a quarter of a length lead approaching 'The Gut'. Worcester, taking the bend accidently sharply, actually closed the gap between the boats, leaving MCS with the narrowest lead as the boats straightened out. Along the length of 'Green Bank' Worcester gradually gained on MCS, until just before the 'New Cut' the Worcester boat had a marginal lead. The MCS crew then appeared to go to pieces and lose their rhythm. The stroke of the MCS boat, W.M. Millard, did not try to up the rate at this point, but tried to get the crew back working together. As a result the Worcester boat went further ahead. At 'Talboys' Millard made his move and upped the rate, the crew responded and the MCS boat started to close the gap. The boats were now side by side with Worcester a canvas in front after each of their strokes. The finish line was approaching fast and MCS spectators were preparing themselves for a gallant loss. Millard summoned up one last spurt and his crew again followed, until with 20 yards to go the crews were level. The excitement on the bank was immense, as both crews strained and willed their boats across the line. MCS crossed the line first, winning by just 6 feet. All those involved agreed it was the best race they had seen and that Worcester had been unfortunate to lose. Victor Jessel and John Callender congratulated each other; they had been together at the school for the past eight years, and this was their finest moment. It was also Victor's last year at MCS. The previous October, at the meeting of the Games Committee, Victor had been elected Captain of Rowing and John had been elected the Deputy Captain. Victor would soon be going out into the world, leaving Callender to take on the rowing captaincy for 1915.

Callender played 1st XI Football at half-back in both the 1913 and 1914 season, gaining full colours in 1913. As early as 1911 *The Lily* had reported that Callender 'shows some promise in tackling, but his kicking is not to be depended upon'. By 1913 Callender had 'improved a great deal, putting on weight and [he

Magdalen College School Rowing 1st IV, 1914.
Back, left to right: J.C. Callender (2) 10st 9lb, B.H. Blackwell Esq (coach), B.R. Beasley (bow) 10st 1lb.
Front, left to right: W.M. Millard (str) 9st 12lb, J.D. Elliot (cox) 5st 9lb, V.A.V.Z. Jessel (3, Capt) 11st 11lb.

is] much faster than last year', although on the football pitch he was reported to be 'naturally rather slow' and sometimes relied 'too much on tricking his man by turning inside him, instead of clearing at once'. Playing in that same 1st XI side as Callender were Victor Jessel and Roger Field, and in the 1913 Old Boys game Callender found himself playing against an old boy who had been at MCS four years previously, Frank Wilkinson.

The Lily records Callender's first exploration into the game of cricket in chorister fixtures against Christ Church Choristers from 1909 onwards and against Magdalen College Choir up until 1913; games against the College Choir required the school's ex-choristers to play or else the age difference made the game a little one-sided. Callender was not a gifted cricketer but to his credit in

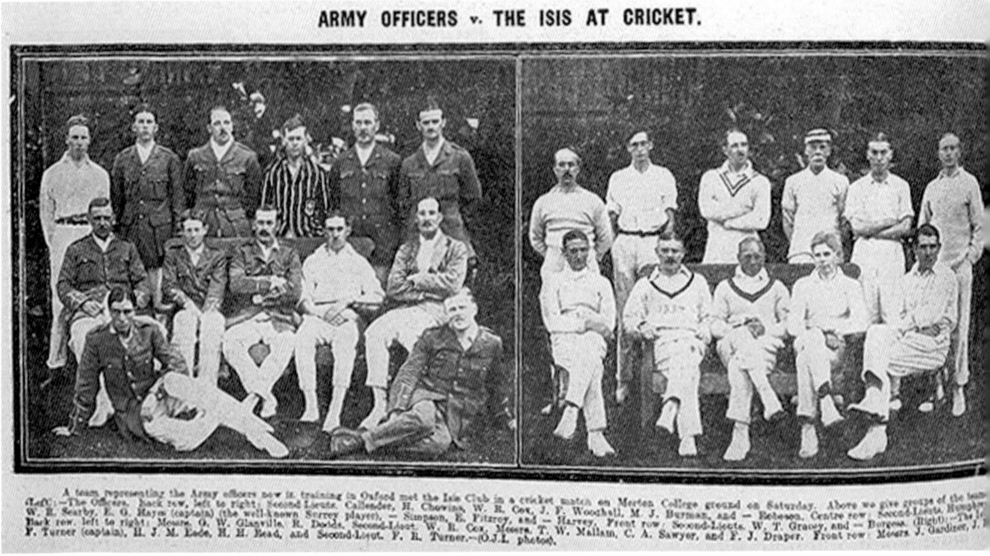

Army Officers (J.C. Callender, back row, far left) versus the Isis Club, Saturday, 4 September 1915.

1915 he played for the 1st XI, gaining half colours, and in *The Lily* was described thus: 'Has learned by steady effort both defence and a forward stroke, and has been rewarded by getting some runs when they are wanted. A very hard worker in the field.' He did not bowl, but came third in the batting averages of 1915, his highest score proudly being 29 not out in the win against Abingdon on 29 May 1915. Interestingly, the fixture list of 1915 pitted MCS against a team from the 3/4 Oxfordshire and Buckinghamshire Light Infantry on 3 July, whom John Callender joined only three weeks later. On Saturday, 4 September Callender found himself playing cricket for the Army Officers team, captained by the well-known Surrey and England player E.G. Hayes, versus the Isis Club.

Callender's fondness for outdoor pursuits is evident from his commitment to sports and to the school cadet corps. One can only imagine the interest he would have shown when on 20 October 1913 he, together with the whole school, attended a lecture at the Town Hall given by Lieutenant Edward R.G.R. Evans (Royal Navy), the leader of the last supporting party to leave Captain Scott on his journey to the South Pole during the ill-fated Terra Nova British Antarctic Expedition.

In 1915 John Callender was a member of the Oxford Volunteer Regiment, along with sixteen other members of the school including Maurice Blagden, Gordon Bradley, John Barrett and four masters, Mr Pullan, Mr Wood, Mr Freeman and Mr Brownrigg. To enable the members of the school who were in the OVR to attend Military Operations, pupils were given half-day holidays on Friday 5 and Monday 15 February.

On 20 February 1915 Callender was one of two hares in the Senior Paper Chase, run over a 9-mile course from school, via Horspath and Shotover, and back again. It took Callender and the other hare, 'Piggy' Read, 1 hour and 35 minutes to complete, with no hounds catching their quarry. For their efforts, Mrs Brownrigg provided a magnificent tea when all had returned. Having previously been a hare on these cross country runs and recognizing the fact that MCS boys required a better appreciation of the school's location and surroundings, Callender took it upon himself to purchase and put up an Ordnance Survey Map of Oxford and the District in the Hall.

After John left MCS, the Callender family was evidently set on keeping a close connection with the school. John immediately paid up his subscription to continue to receive *The Lily* and his mother attended the Sports Days of 1916 and 1917 to present the trophies. In 1916 the Senior Platoon of the School Cadet Corps purchased a set of dummy rifles in order to practise musketry drill. A large part of the cost of the rifles was paid for by a donation from Mrs Callender. The Corps was therefore practising tirelessly so that both A and B Platoons would be able to 'slope' and 'present' accurately when the Lieutenant John Callender next visited on leave. After John's death, his mother presented the school with the handsome silver 'Challenge Cup' that is still awarded annually when the whole school takes part in the cross country running event, the cup being presented to the winning House. The only condition that Mrs Callender attached to the cup was that it should never leave the School.

Callender's War

Callender left school in the summer of 1915 and on 23 July he was commissioned Second Lieutenant in the 3/4th Battalion, Oxfordshire and Buckinghamshire Light Infantry, being appointed machine-gun officer. After a long period of training in England he went out to France in August 1916, where, on 20 August, he joined A-Coy of the 2/4 OBLI (184 Brigade, 61st Division) when it was in reserve at Laventie (14 miles west of Lille). On 22 August at 16.30, A-Coy went into the reserve trenches (at Fauquissart in Laventie) for Callender's first taste of the front, wiring and firing a large number of rifle grenades on enemy trenches. The following day he experienced the German reply for the first time, with trench mortars and artillery doing damage to parapets and communication trenches. After five days in the trenches the battalion was relieved and marched to billets at Laventie (eleven men had been wounded but none killed during Callender's baptism in the trenches), but A-Coy immediately went to man the flanking post positions, remaining on duty to 29 August. From 30 August to 3 September the battalion formed part of the working parties, mainly wiring the Rhonda Sap trench. The brigade went into reserve on 3 September for eight days, marching 7 miles west to billet at Robermetz near Merville. Here they underwent training (with classes in bombing, Lewis gun and signalling), refitting and equipping, as well as parades and a church service. At the end of the first week of September 1916 the brigade held sports competitions, then during 11 September the 2/4 OBLI relieved the 2/6 Gloucester Regiment in the firing line trenches called Moated Grange, and remained in the front line for eight days, carrying out extensive wiring work and patrol duty during the nights. Despite the British pestering the German lines with rifle grenades and trench mortar fire, the Germans remained relatively quiet, but this didn't stop Callender experiencing the first loss from his battalion, on 12 September. A week later, as the weather began to worsen, the battalion was relieved and returned to reserve for eight days at billets in Riez Bailleul. Here they practised trench assaults and also supplied working parties. They returned to the Moated Grange trenches and posts on 28 September for five days. In October the 2/4 OBLI continued to be rotated between the reserve billets at Riez Bailleul (cleaning equipment, route marching, bayonet fighting, and even obtaining demonstration in cooperation between infantry and aeroplanes by the Brigade Signals Corp) and the Moated Grange trenches (Callender receiving his first gas alert while A-Coy was manning flank posts). During this time much offensive work was carried out by the brigade, without significant retaliation.

At the end of October 1916 the battalion began a relocation march, 50 miles south to the Somme. The first day of the march, 30 October, they tracked west from Riez Bailleul to billet at Robecq. Then heading south they marched via Auchel (2 Nov), Magnicourt-en-Comte (3 Nov), Tinques (4 Nov), Estrée-Wamin (5 Nov), Neuvillette (6–15 Nov, pausing for eight days training on wave attacks, working through woods and communications), Bonneville (16 Nov), Contay (17 Nov) and finally to Albert (19 Nov). The battalion went into the front line trenches on the Somme on 21 November, A-Coy initially going to Mouquet Farm trench. They spent one day, 25 November, back in hutments at Ovillers, before returning to the front line trenches for a further four days, A-Coy this time to Hessien Trench. The main work now was clearing up trenches and burying dead (the clear-up operation after the Battle of the Somme), while heavy shelling was in progress from both sides. The first day of December the battalion was back in support hutments then, the next day, they progressed to billets at Hédauville where they spent the following nine days undergoing further training and contributing to working parties. During 12–19 December time was spent in support hutments at Martinsart, overlooked by Thiepval ridge 2 miles to the east. From 20 to 23 December the battalion was back in the front line, with A-Coy remaining in the Wellington hutments and contributing to working parties. On Christmas Eve they moved into Mouchet Farm trenches on the front line and on Christmas Day the British periodically directed concentrated fire on the German trenches. Meanwhile, a German soldier who wandered into the British line was taken prisoner. The battalion took two more prisoners before the end of December when German patrols were challenged, and then on 30 December the battalion returned to support hutments at Martinsart. New Year's Eve 1916 they marched 4 miles west to the relative safety of reserve hutments at Hédauville, where they stayed until 8 January 1917. From 9 to 15 January they were once again moved up to support hutments at Martinsart, then on 16 and 17 January progressed to billets 9 miles further west at Puchevillers. The battalion moved a further 19 miles west on 18 and 19 January, via Longvillette, to billet at Domqueue. Eventually they marched 8 miles further north and on 20 January they reached rest billets at Maison-Ponthieu, where they stayed until 4 February, undergoing platoon and company training, having medical inspections and afternoon recreational training.

The battalion moved south again to rest billets at Brucamps on 4 February and for the next nine days proceeded to carry out practice attacks. After a 15-mile route march on 13 February to Longpré they entrained for Marcelcave, 14 miles east of Amien. From here they marched 2 miles to billets at Wiencourt, staying for two days before moving on to reserve billets 5 miles east at Rainecourt. Six days later the battalion moved a short distance east to Herleville. From here on 23 February the battalion went into the front line trenches of the Ablaincourt sector on the Somme. Occupying trenches deep in water, the troops endured artillery bombardments of exceptional severity on 27 and 28 February 1917, followed by trench raids by the Germans that penetrated the middle section of the British line. Counter-attacks drove the enemy back again. Forty five men of the 2/4 OBLI were killed, wounded or missing during this time. On 1 March the damage done to the trenches was made good and on 2 March the battalion was relieved and returned for a seven-day stretch in the support trenches. By 10 March they were back in the front line trenches for another six days, patrolling and wiring. On 11 March two men from the battalion suffered effects from a gas attack. Returning to reserve billets at Framerville, Rainecourt, Chaulnes and Marchélepot from 16 until 25 March, the battalion supplied working parties for improving roads, old German trenches and ruined houses that resulted from the German tactical withdrawal to the *Siegfriedstellung* (Hindenburg Line). For the remainder of March the battalion were in support billets at Athies and Tertry, holding outpost lines and patrolling roads. On 1 April the battalion moved to Sailors Wood near Caulaincourt, and then on 4 April they took over at the front line trenches at Soyécourt, with the enemy shelling all morning and snow falling all day. At midnight on 6 April, John Callender's A-Coy led a whole brigade attack on the German trenches only to find the enemy wire uncut by previous British bombardments. A second attempt at the attack was made but no breakthrough was achieved and the attacking companies had to withdraw. Twenty-five 2/4 OBLI men were killed, wounded or missing. The battalion was relieved in the front line and returned to support billets on 7 April, then marched to reserve billets on 11 April 1917 and eventually on 13 April to rest billets at Hombleux. From 20 April the battalion was in support trenches at Holnon, near Saint Quentin, receiving heavy morning shelling each day, before moving into the front line at Fayet on 27 April. D-Coy plus two sections of C-Coy raided the German front lines at 04.20 on 28 April, capturing two machine guns and one man but receiving fifty-nine casualties of their own, either killed, wounded or missing. The battalion was relieved on 30 April and went to reserve billets at Attilly to clean up and refit. Two days later they went to billets at Vaux (A-Coy) and Étreillers (B, C, D-Coy) as divisional reserve, undergoing training and shooting practice and were allowed a day's rest. They marched 12 miles on 13 May to new billets at Mesnil-Saint-Nicaise, then on 15 May entrained at Nesle and travelled 30 miles north to Rivery, near Amien. After nearly six months, on 17 May the battalion left the Somme behind and marched north to La Vicogne, then on to Neuvillette (22 May), Barly (24 May), and finally to Duisans (25 May), near Arras, a total distance of 38 miles. The final day of May they marched south-east of Arras to Tilloy(-lès-Mofflaines) and bivouacked, then on 2 June continued 4 miles south-east to take over the reserve trenches at Monchy(-le-Preux), where they received steady casualties over the next five days. On 6 June the 2/4 OBLI took over the front line trenches at Monchy. A-Coy, with Second Lieutenant John Callender commanding, pushed forward their front line by about 100 feet on 7 June and occupied a line of shell holes under the cover of darkness. Here they commenced to consolidate the new positions and dig communication trenches. This they did successfully without observation by the Germans. The work on the advanced line was continuing on 8 June when a patrol of five Germans, surprised at finding the advanced position, were captured by A-Coy and taken prisoner. The battalion was relieved on 9 June and went into reserve line trenches at Monchy, then on 10 June they marched to bivouac at Tilloy. Two days later the battalion moved to billets at Berneville, 5 miles west of Arras. Here they stayed at rest and in training until 23 June, when they marched 4 miles to entrain at Gouy-en-Artois. From here they travelled further west to Auxi-le-Château, detrained and marched 4 miles to rest billets at Nœux(-lès-Auxi). The battalion remained in Nœux at rest from 24 June to 26 July 1917, undergoing training and on the Sundays attending church parade. It is believed that John Callender was given short leave during this time which allowed him to visit England and pay his last visit to MCS. The whole battalion marched back to the train station at Auxi-le-Château on 26 July, from where they travelled 40 miles north to Saint Omer, then marched 8 miles north-west to rest billets at Broxelle. Here they stayed at rest camp until 15 August, when they then marched 5 miles to entrain at Arneke and journeyed east to Abeele, near Poperinge, Belgium. From here the battalion marched to Watau, where they camped for the next three nights, before, on 18 August they marched to Ypres and camped in reserve. The afternoon of 20 August the 2/4 OBLI moved up to relieve the 2/6 Gloucestershire Regiment in the Support Line at Ypres, then later that night they progressed further to the front to relieve the 2/10 GR in the firing line trenches. The following day, the 2/4 OBLI was busy preparing to attack the German positions the next day. During a period of considerable artillery activity, John Callender was out on patrol making observations in preparation for the next day's attack when he was killed by a sniper, aged 21.

His Colonel wrote: 'He is extremely gallant and cool under the heaviest fire, and his men always looked up to him and would follow him anywhere.' His Company Commander wrote: 'I think he was one of the bravest and coolest men I have ever seen, and purely by his own personal example had a tremendous influence over the men.' His Adjutant (when Callender was in England) wrote: 'He was the soul of duty, and that is the simple truth. Always so cheery, so hard working, so liked and trusted by everyone ... I shall always feel proud to have known your dear and splendid son.' Before his death, John Callender had returned home in the summer of 1917 but never got the opportunity to inspect his old Platoon with their dummy rifles.

1. John Callender was first summoned for assessment as a choral scholar at MCS in March 1906. His name was initially placed on the reserve list, and then erased. However, in June 1906 he was called back again for assessment and duly elected to a choral scholarship, starting in September 1906.

Leonard Dobbie CANE

13 May 1883 – 24 January 1916

Rank and regiment: Captain and Adjutant: 20th (3rd Public Schools) Battalion, Royal Fusiliers (City of London Regiment). **Medals awarded:** Victory, British War, 1914–1915 Star. **Theatre of War:** Western Front. **Memorial:** Cambrin Churchyard Extension, France.

Cane's father, Henry Drake Cane, was originally from Lincolnshire but emigrated to Australia in the mid-nineteenth century. Leonard Dobbie Cane, born in Ballaratt, Australia was the only child from his father's second marriage to Margaret Agatha Jessopp (married 1880, Derbyshire), although he had three half-brothers and three half-sisters from his father's first marriage. Cane's father grew wealthy enough to send Leonard to be educated in England. In 1893 Leonard and his mother travelled from Melbourne to Plymouth on the *Matiana* in order for Leonard to begin his education at MCS. His parents ultimately retired to England in about 1904. Leonard Dobbie Cane himself married Kathleen Frances Haslam (daughter of Samuel Haslam, for thirty-seven years Assistant Master at Uppingham School) on 31 March 1910 at the Parish Church of Lymington, Hampshire. They had two children, Sidney Henry Kingsley (born 23 March 1911) and Kathleen Margaret (born 11 September 1915).

Life at Magdalen College School (1894–1900) and beyond

Cane was a boarder at MCS, and for three years a chorister (1894–1897). In November 1897 he received an Ellerton Exhibition (a Prize awarded for the best performance by a chorister in school examinations) and obtained his junior school certificate.[1] After an impressive performance two years later in his senior school certificate he gained a classical scholarship at Sidney Sussex College, Cambridge for 1901. While at Cambridge, Cane was a corporal in the University OTC. In 1904 Cane gained a First Class in the Classical Tripos (along with another MCS old boy, H.L. Clarke, who was at St John's), then following a seven-month stay at the University of Rennes in France he was appointed to a sixth form mastership at Durham School, where he stayed until 1908. A lover of the countryside, while in France he was able to take in a cycle and walking tour

Leonard Cane.

of the Auvergnes, little knowing that he would return to France seven years later with the British Expeditionary Force.

Cane was 5 feet 11 inches tall and the records mention he had a small patch of alopecia above his left ear. He was a keen sportsman, successfully competing in the MCS half-mile race at the university running ground in June 1897 (second place) and in June 1898 (first place). In 1896 and 1897 Cane played football for the choristers and MCS U15 respectively as an outfield player, but by the time 1899 had arrived he had reverted to being the 'fair understudy' goalkeeper for the MCS team in a very successful season (played 17, won 12, lost 4, drawn 1).

On 16 November 1899 Cane showed his acting and comedy skills by playing the part of Blackberry Thistletop in the Amalgamated Comedy Company's 'Tweedleton's Tailcoat'.

Records exist for three cricket matches that Cane played in (two in 1897 for MCS choristers versus Christ Church choristers and one for MCS 2nd XI versus Oxford High School). He did not bowl in these matches, nor did he take a catch, but he managed to score a total of three runs in his three innings! He did, however, have more success with his rowing, gaining 2nd IV colours while at MCS[2] and rowing for Sidney Sussex 1st VIII while at Cambridge.

In 1904, still very much in touch with his old school and its news, and an active member of what was then referred to as the 'Old MCS Club', Cane contributed 5/- (1 crown or 5 shillings) in 1904 to the memorial for his old school friend Frank Twiss, who died in South Africa in 1900 after volunteering to fight in the Boer War. In both 1909 (Thursday, 14 January) and 1910 (Tuesday, 13 December) he attended the Old MCS Club annual dinner at the Trocadero Restaurant, Oxford, where nearly forty old boys had gathered (including William H. Williams) on both occasions. The speeches were interspersed with songs from several of the old boys, including Cane. Both years the evenings were brought to a close with an 'uproarious' rendition of 'Auld Lang Syne'.

In 1908 Cane moved on to teach at Highgate School in London for one year,[3] and then in 1909 became a Junior Inspector of schools for the Board of Education in Bradford. In January 1913 he became a full HM Inspector for the district of Weston-super-Mare and subsequently at Manchester.

On the outbreak of war in 1914 he obtained leave from the Board of Education to join the army. He had until 1909 held a Subaltern's commission in the Middlesex Territorials. On 5 September 1914 he enlisted in Manchester as a private in the 20th (3rd Public Schools) Battalion, Royal Fusiliers.

Cane's War

Cane had joined the 20/RF, the newly formed 3rd Public School's Battalion which, like the other public school battalions was raised at Epsom (Woodcote Park Camp) in September of 1914. In October 1914 Cane was gazetted Lieutenant then appointed Battalion Adjutant on 21 May 1915. On 6 July 1915 he was gazetted Captain. Prior to these two appointments he was offered a captaincy in the East Lancashire Territorials on 7 October 1914, but he had preferred to stay in the regiment he had chosen to join and wait for promotion within the Royal Fusiliers. The battalion was initially based at Leatherhead (October 1914–March 1915) then moved to Clipstone Camp, Nottingham and finally to Tidworth, before sailing and landing in Calais, France as part of the 98 Brigade 33rd Division on 14 November 1915.

Cane being the Adjutant had the job of writing the battalion war diary once they entered the theatre of war. During his two months at the front line the battalion, after transferring to the 19 Brigade on 27 November 1915, was in and out of the trenches around the Béthune area. Cane recorded the daily trench routine, numbers wounded and killed during the day, which company was relieving which company and where, training, location of billets, sniper activity etc., initially signing each entry with a characteristic 'LDC'. He made every entry in

Leonard Cane.

the war diary from 24 November 1915 until he was detailed to take charge of a company in the firing line, replacing an officer who was on leave. His last entry in the war diary is 19 January 1916. Lieutenant Modera, who had taken over duties of Adjutant during Cane's brief command in the trenches, reported in the war diary that Captain Cane was shot and killed by a sniper at 09.30 on 24 January 1916, aged 32. He was buried that evening at Cambrin Church.

Cane was evidently a popular and gallant officer. His commanding officer, Colonel C.H. Bennett, wrote to Cane's mother, even describing his moment of death: 'We had taken over this part of the line after dark the previous evening and so did not know our trenches well. In the one your son was walking along the parapet is low, and one has to stoop to avoid being seen. Poor Cane stopped a minute to speak to a sergeant who was following him, and in doing so must have raised his head, as he was shot through the head by a sniper. Death must have been instantaneous, as he fell and never moved. I had sent your son to command the company temporarily, as I knew I could trust him to keep things right. We buried him in our cemetery behind part of the line [at Cambrin], and have put up a cross to mark the grave. 'Colonel Bennett also wrote to Cane's widow, saying 'We shall all miss your husband greatly, I especially ... [he] has worked hard and not spared himself from the start of the Battalion.'

Interestingly, the Major (Hickley) and also the Major-General (Landon) both took time and wrote letters to the family sending their condolences, as did Lieutenant Modera who had temporarily taken over his Adjutant duties during Cane's command in the front line. Cane was evidently a popular officer who had made a lasting impression on his peers and seniors alike.

Upon hearing the news of Cane's death, his old colleagues at HM Inspector of Schools started to gather a fund to contribute to the education of his two children (Sidney aged nearly 5 years and Kathleen aged 6 months). The Board of Education's Chief Inspector of Schools wrote to Cane's family expressing his 'respect' and 'pride' for Cane, who had the sad fate of becoming the first inspector to die during the war.

College friends also wrote to his family, with supportive words about this 'clean living Englishman, to whom literature and athletics and religion were all intensely real'. Australian by birth, Cane had certainly become a devoted Englishman who, as a college friend wrote, was 'not dazzled by any desire for glory. But he quietly and calmly accepted the dangerous course, and made his sacrifice'.

Cane had no opportunity to win a gallantry award, like several of his relatives in previous wars,[4] but in search of a memento of her only son, Cane's mother wrote to the War Office enquiring if, 'As a mother of an only son killed in the War ... I venture to write and ask if I am not eligible for a copy of "The Scroll of Honour" which I understand is now being presented to the nearest relatives of officers fallen?' The War Office replied, regretting that 'owing to the large number of these memorials to be issued only one can be sent to each individual case', Cane's memorial going to his widow. The War Office kindly advised her to take a photograph of her son's memorial instead!

1. Oxford and Cambridge Public Schools Examination Certificate.
2. Interestingly, in the Scratch IV races of 1899 Cane (bow) was in a boat with the Master (Brownrigg) at stroke.
3. The Roll of Honour of the Empire's Heroes, written soon after Cane's death, records that after graduating from Cambridge he also spent time as a Master at Marlborough, Uppingham and Cheltenham.
4. Cane's great-grandfather, Captain W.H. Dobbie R.N., J.P., Deputy Lieutenant for Essex, was mentioned in Sir Edward Pellew's dispatches in 1806 for his gallant conduct and success in an expedition against pirates. Cane's uncle, Rev. A. Grainger, Chaplain to the Southern Afghanistan Field Forces in 1880, was mentioned in dispatches for his gallantry at the battles of Maiwand and Kandahar and received the associated Campaign medal with two clasps. Other gallant relations of

Cane's were his cousin, Captain L. Cane, 1 Battalion, East Lancashire Regiment, killed in action near Ploegsteerton 7 November 1914; General Sir E.H. Allenby KCB, commanding the 3rd Army Corps, a South African Veteran, who won mention in Sir Douglas Haig's dispatches; and William H. Dobbie CB, MC, who was mentioned in Sir Harry Prendergast's dispatches for his gallant conduct in an expedition against Dacoits (Bandits) in Burma and who was invalided home from the Persian Gulf during the First World War.

Hugh Stanley CANNON

15 October 1888 – 30 October 1914

Rank and regiment: Corporal (28754), 6th Signal Troop, Royal Engineers. **Medals awarded:** Victory, British War, 1914–1915 Star. **Theatre of War:** Western Front. **Memorial:** Ypres Town Cemetery Extension, Belgium.

Hugh Stanley Cannon was born at Sandford-on-Thames near Oxford in 1888, the fourth child of Alfred Cannon and Eliza Cannon (*née* Mewburn).

In 1911 Hugh Cannon was living at Egham, Surrey with his mother, two older sisters (Constance Mary, 1886–1941 and Eva Gertrude, 1887–1974) and a younger brother (Gordon Mewburn, 1890–1943). He had two other brothers, one younger (Herbert Cooper, 1893–1944) and one older (Alfred Edward, 1883–1953). His father (Alfred) died in 1905. In the previous census of 1901 the family were living at Mill House in Sandford-on-Thames. His father was a paper maker and ran the Paper Mill at Sandford-on-Thames.

Life at Magdalen College School (1902–1903) and beyond

In September 1900 Hugh Stanley Cannon joined his older brother 'Freddy' as a boarder at Roysse's School in Abingdon (later to become Abingdon School). After two years, due to his father's illness, Stanley moved to become a day boy at MCS in 1902. In his only year at the school Cannon appears in the Form Fours rowing competition rowing at bow for the Form IV 1st boat in the March of 1903. At bow for the Form IV 2nd boat was Charles Maltby. Hugh's brother Gordon also attended MCS for the same brief period. On leaving MCS in July 1903, aged 14, Hugh joined the Grammar School in Newbury (St Bartholomew School). By 1911 he was employed as a brewer in Surrey, and then moved on to Lamberhurst in Kent.

Cannon's War

At the outbreak of war in 1914 Cannon enlisted in the Royal Engineers and was soon promoted to Corporal, attached to the 6th Signal Troop, 6 Cavalry Brigade, 3rd Cavalry Division as a despatch rider. The 6 Cavalry Brigade formed up on 19 September at Ludgershall, Wiltshire (when the Royal Dragoons with its twenty officers, 558 other ranks and 471 horses arrived from Southampton), joining the 3rd Cavalry Division, which had itself only started its formation days earlier at Windmill Hill Camp, near Salisbury. The Royal Dragoons received orders on 26 September to form the 6 Signal Troop within 6 Cavalry Brigade. Within eight days the 6 Signal Troop was complete with ten Officers, seventy-

Roysse's schoolboys on the steps leading to School House (now Abingdon School)
Hugh Stanley Cannon is one of the boys in the photograph.

three other ranks and sixty-one horses. Cannon left for the Western Front with the 6 Signal Troop on 6 October aboard SS *Algerian*, a Hall Line steamer, from Southampton. Initially steaming to Dover, the ship then waited at the Downs on 7 October until dark and then in convoy with ten other transport ships was

Hugh Cannon.

escorted by twelve destroyers to Ostend. The following day they disembarked and encamped at the race course in Ostend.

The brigade began to march towards Bruges in fine weather on 9 October 1914. They covered a distance of approximately 15 miles on mostly flat paved roads and finally billeted at villages south-west of Bruges. The following day, they concentrated at Lophem and then marched 9 miles to Thourout and settled into billets. Again the weather was fine and the roads good but crowded with disorganized Belgium soldiers. The command of the 3rd Division at this time was taken over by Sir John French. The 6 Brigade halted their march for the day on 11 October, while two armoured motor cars from the brigade travelled and reconnoitred south beyond Ypres, where they surprised a German cavalry patrol and took two prisoners. The following day, the brigade continued its march south towards Ypres, progressing 9 miles to Roulers. In fine weather on the 13 October the brigade continued their march, starting at 07.15 and arrived in Ypres at 11.25. Although Ypres had been occupied by the Germans for the previous ten days, they left in a hurry on 13 October as the British approached from the north and the south. After resting for a short while they progressed on a further 6 miles south-east of Ypres to Gheluvelt. Meanwhile, an officer's patrol scouting ahead ran into a German post 5 miles ahead at Comines and had a man captured. As the afternoon turned rainy the brigade took to billets around Ledeghem. At 05.00 the following morning the Brigade marched 11 miles back to Ypres. Approximately 1½ miles south of Ypres the brigade fired at a German Taube flying at 1,800 feet and brought it down about 2 miles north of Ypres. Both the pilot and the observer were captured in a nearby wood. In the afternoon the brigade marched south-west to Kemmel, on to Neuve Eglise and back north to billets at Wytschaete, an almost circular march of 14 miles. The following day the brigade halted but sent out patrols. On 16 October they marched through Ypres, then on to billets at Zonnebeke by the end of the day. The following day patrols encountered German troops and three men were wounded. Once again on 18 October, after advance patrols, the brigade moved forwards, this time billeting in the villages of Passchendaele and Moorslade. Reconnaissance patrols venturing 4 miles south-east to Rolleghem-cappelle encountered strong opposition on 19 October, so the brigade retreated to Poelcappelle and took to billets for the night. At 04.30 on 20 October the brigade withdrew a further 2 miles and took up defensive positions, entrenching on the Westroosebeke to Passchendaele Road. At 08.00 the Germans attacked.

The brigade held the position until 14.30, then withdrew initially to a mile south of Poelcappelle, then to Langemark. By 15.30 the Germans had caught up with the British and attacked again. After dark the Germans launched another attack on the British positions at Langemark, but their attack was easily repulsed and the British 'stood to arms' for the rest of the night. At 05.00 on 21 October the brigade marched 4 miles south to Ypres, where they were resupplied at the railway station. Continuing on, the brigade marched a further 3 miles south east to Hooge, then laid siege to the canal bridges north of Hollebeke, before taking over trenches at Zandvoorde. The following morning, the enemy commenced shelling at 07.00, necessitating the brigade to move the horses to the woods and the outskirts of the town. An intercepted German message ordering an attack on Zandvoorde prompted the British to reinforce the area, and the eventual attack was easily repulsed. The Germans accurately bombarded Zandvoorde on 23 October so the brigade moved 5 miles to bivouack at Kleinzillebeke, south east of Ypres. After a day away from enemy contact the 6 Brigade returned to Zandvoorde on 25 October to take over the trenches from the 7 Cavalry Brigade at 17.30. At 20.00 over 500 German soldiers attacked the brigade, then after one hour ceased their attack and resorted to heavy shelling the next day. On 27 October the brigade was again relieved in the line and bivouacked back at Kleinzillebeke. After one day's respite the brigade was asked to support an attack towards Zandvoorde, but soon encountered opposition so withdrew back to Kleinzillebeke. A bombardment by the Germans on 30 October forced the 7 Cavalry to retreat still further, requiring the 6 Brigade to cover their rear. The shelling continued when a strong infantry attack developed over the entire front line. The brigade held their positions until relief was finally received and completed in the early hours of 31 October. During the attack three officers had been killed and nine wounded. Twelve other ranks had been killed and thirty-seven wounded. Seven other men were missing, one was Hugh Cannon who had been killed whilst on his motorbike carrying dispatches, aged 26. Hugh Cannon was the first MCS old boy to die during the war. His Commanding Officer wrote, 'He was one of the nicest men to work with I have ever met, and all the officers and the staff think the same. He was always cheerful and keen to do his best'. The final day of October 1914 the brigade marched away from Zillebeke village while a heavy bombardment was underway. As the retreat grew in pace the brigade was asked to support the 2 Infantry Brigade in the woods south east of Hooge. As the gap in the lines was closed the Germans temporarily retired, but as the First Battle of Ypres raged on, the salient that had formed around the city slowly shrank. The British held on and when French reinforcements arrived the static trench warfare of the Ypres salient began.

On 20 November 1914, the *Kent and Sussex Courier* reported that Hugh Cannon 'was very popular in Lamberhurst, and when he volunteered for the Front he placed his house at the disposal of Belgian refugees'.

Herbert Westrup CANTON

6 March 1892 – 13 May 1915

Rank and regiment: Captain, 1st Battalion, East Lancashire Regiment. **Medals awarded:** Victory, British War, 1914 Star. **Theatre of War:** Western Front. **Memorial:** Ypres (Menin Gate) Memorial, Belgium.

Herbert Westrup Canton was born on 6 March 1892 in Walton-on-Thames, Surrey and baptized on 3 April 1892 in the Parish church of Feltham. He was the eldest child of Frank Canton, a wine merchant, and Florence Canton (*née* Smith). Herbert had two sisters, Elizabeth Kate (1894–1984) and Frances Gertrude (1898–1944). Rather than follow his father in the merchant business, Herbert chose to join the Royal Military College, Sandhurst once he had completed his education in 1911, and subsequently gained a commission as a Second Lieutenant in the East Lancashire Regiment on 13 March 1912.

Life at Magdalen College School (1903–1909) and beyond

Herbert Canton joined MCS at the age of 11 in September 1903 and stayed at the school for the next six years. Primarily known as one of the best MCS rowers of his time, he was very active in all aspects of school life and did not restrict himself to the sport of rowing. He was academically very capable and in November 1907 he won the Form IV prize for his academic work. At the prize giving he was applauded to the front to collect his prize at the same time as Charles Maltby and Donovan Leicester, who were collecting the Form V and Form II prizes respectively. In 1907 and 1908 Canton was a member of the Debating Society and in his final academic year of 1908–09 became a School Prefect.

Canton was seen playing football as a forward for the School U15 side in 1905, then progressed to playing as a half back for the 2nd XI in 1906 and 1907. Finally, in 1908 Canton broke through into the 1st XI for his last winter season at MCS and was described as a centre half who 'works hard ... and hustles the opposing forwards, but is slow and clumsy and misjudges a ball in the air'. The team that year played eighteen games in all, winning seven and drawing two. Playing alongside Herbert Canton at right half was Sydney Disney at centre half. Disney was wounded but survived the war, becoming a Major in the 5th Battalion, Lincolnshire Regiment, and returning to take his place at Magdalen College in 1919.

Canton, who had been rowing at the school since 1904 in the Form Fours rowing event and the School 2nd IV boat, eventually won a place in the 1st IV in 1908. He was described in the rowing prospects of 1908 as having 'experience and weight, and if he can get over the tendency of rushing forward when tired, and using his arms at the finish of the stroke, ought to prove of great use to us, and become a really good oar'. The School rowing at the time was very strong and it produced some very exciting commentaries in *The Lily*. Indeed, the 1st IV even competed for the prestigious Wyfolds Challenge Cup at Henley in the July of

1909. The reproduction of extracts of the 1909 Henley race, because of Canton's involvement, is very poignant:

> After only three days serious practice at Henley, the boat was unlucky enough to have be[en] drawn against Kingston on the opening day of the Regatta. This had two disadvantages: the crew were coming on so fast that one more practice would have made them many seconds faster, and stroke would have been able to steer a straight course without continually using his rudder.
>
> In the race itself, Kingston went off at a faster stroke and took a lead of a few feet, but the School, rowing a longer stroke in better style, started to gain after a minute, but just as they were drawing up, they came across the river and nearly fouled Kingston, and in avoiding them nearly ran into the piles. Owing to this mishap, Kingston were still leading at half way. Then the School made a good spurt, and keeping straight took the lead, but immediately after doing so, started wandering over the course again. The two boats then were running side by side till near the finish when Kingston spurted. [W.P.] Roberton [the School Stroke and J.L. Roberton's older brother] held his reply till exactly the right moment and seemed to have the race in his hands, when the boat started to run crooked again, the fatal rudder had to be applied once again and Kingston scraped home by about six feet.

The report added that '[Canton] rowed very well and should turn out very useful'.

Earlier in 1909 Canton had carried out the rowing captain's duties when William Roberton was absent through illness. Roberton, disappointed because it was the second year in a row he had missed the Bath College race, was not let down by his crew. On 13 March the MCS boat beat Bath by sixteen lengths. Previously, on 7 February, the same crew had beaten Abingdon by about twenty lengths. Both races were on the School's home course of the Isis. It was reported that the 1st IV of 1909 were the best IV the School had had for a long time. The crew had even become good enough to be coached on sliding seats, something unusual for the time.

With Canton rowing so much in the Hilary term of 1908, he missed much of the hockey season. The hockey team would dearly have loved to have him (and Broadbent and Francis) included for more games, but as it was they suffered a poor season and it was stated that 'The hockey team suffered more from rowing than influenza' that year. The same rowing commitments in 1909 had again limited his appearances on the hockey field, but in one appearance versus Worcester College it will interest any Astroturf-hockey-playing reader to know that 'Most of the School defence, handicapped of course by the mud, seemed generally incapable of clearing the ball'. Canton played as one of the backs. The school held on to win 2–1, probably because the Worcester forwards also could not shift the ball through the 'unusual muddiness of the ground'.

In 1909 Canton played cricket for the School 2nd XI, finishing second in the batting averages (average 16.3, highest score 36 not out). In the drawn match against Oxford High School on Saturday, 17 July, played at the High School ground, stumps were drawn early before time due to 'the riotous behaviour of some of the [High School] fielders'. In the OHS side was T.E. Lawrence's brother, F.H. Lawrence (who was to be killed in action on the Western Front in 1915). MCS had scored 73 all out in the first innings then bowled the High School out for 48. MCS were 134 for 7 in their second innings when play was drawn to a close with an hour of play still left. The pitch was reported to have been unplayable when MCS were bowling and even 48 to the High School 'was somewhat flattering'. One would imagine that by employing more adventurous tactics, with an early declaration, MCS would have won the game and avoided the High School team losing focus in the field. A week earlier on 10 July, the 2nd XI had entertained Abingdon on School Field. MCS batted first and made 96 all out, with Canton scoring 9. In reply, Abingdon needed only 12 more runs to win with 3 wickets remaining when R.H. Clapperton and W. Moulding came back on to bowl and finished Abingdon off. MCS had won by 3 runs and Clapperton had taken 5 wickets for 33 runs in 11 overs.

Canton did find time to enjoy tennis and in his final summer of 1909 partnered Mrs Brownrigg to second place in the term's doubles competition, a satisfying result seeing that he had come ninth (last place) the previous year, when partnered by his classmate W. Sherard Vines. Interestingly, Sherard Vines, after being wounded and invalided out of the war in 1917, went on to become a successful writer and academic who wrote poetry and novels. Poignantly, his poetry included many war poems, several of which were included in his book *The Two Worlds* published in 1916, while he was still serving in the army, by B.H. Blackwell.

After leaving MCS in July 1909 Canton went to Switzerland, where he was privately tutored from September 1909 to July 1910. On returning to Richmond, England he continued to have a private tutor. Canton donated a book of short stories, *Sailor's Knots* by W.W. Jacobs, to the school library after he left MCS.

Canton's War

On 7 October 1910 Hugh Canton applied for officer training at the Royal Military College, Sandhurst, and was admitted in 1911. After completing his officer training he passed out of Sandhurst on 13 March 1912 and was gazetted Second Lieutenant in the 1st Battalion, East Lancashire Regiment.

At the outbreak of war Canton was amongst the first British troops to go across to confront the Germans in August 1914 as part of the British Expeditionary Force. Initially concentrating with the whole 4th Division (10, 11, and 12 Brigades) on the playing fields at Harrow on 18 August, the 1/E. Lancs sailed from Southampton on 22 August and disembarked at Le Havre on 23 August, Canton's platoon first coming under fire and suffering heavy casualties at Ligny (Le Cateau) three days later on 26 August. As darkness fell on the village, the

1st Battalion, East Lancashire Regiment at Harrow in August 1914.
Lieutenant H.W. Canton is back row, second from right.

British, who had suffered 7,800 casualties in the one day, continued their withdrawal south-west, in what was to become known as the Retreat from Mons. The 1/E. Lancs marched 29 miles to Ham on 27 August 1914, then the following day marched 15 miles and bivouacked at a chateau at Sempigny. They moved 3 miles further south and prepared bridges for demolition on 29 August, before marching 17 miles to Pierrefonds on 30 August, and a further 12 miles through the Compiegne Forrest to Saint-Sauveur on 31 August. The hot weather at the start of September hampered the retreat and the Germans were progressively getting closer, attacking the rear guard of the retreat more frequently. On 5 September the battalion received its first reinforcements since arriving at the front, ninety-eight other ranks. Finally on 6 September the order was announced that it was the end of the retreat, and to stand and fight and stop the German breakthrough to Paris.

Canton's 1/E. Lancs and the rest of the BEF had retreated approximately 164 miles in ten days to the south of the river Marne. The German army, abandoning the Schlieffen Plan, had followed the Anglo-French army all the way to within 30 miles east of Paris, pushing over the Marne, and now lay stretched out along the line of the river. The Germans were now at their most vulnerable, overstretched and a long way from supply lines. As the 1/E. Lancs billeted at a large farm in Les Corbiers on 8 September, the Anglo-French armies prepared to counter-attack. The following day, the 1/E. Lancs, with the help of local guides, reconnoitred the approaches to the river at Conditz (Le Ferté-sous-Jouarre), coming under constant machine gun and sniper fire. They found the eastern bridge over the Marne at Conditz was destroyed. The enemy positions on the far bank were silenced with artillery fire and when the 1/E. Lancs re-occupied their forward position the Germans abandoned their approaches to the bridge locations, and the crossing points easily fell into the hands of the 1/E. Lancs.

At 18.00 on 9 September, A-, B- and C-Coys of the 1/E. Lancs and the 1st Battalion Hampshire Regiment began to cross the River Marne in boats. By 24.00 the crossings were complete, with only D-Coy 1/E. Lancs and machine guns remaining on the south side of the river at Conditz. During the night, Lieutenant Canton led a patrol with two other officers to reconnoitre the high ground that lay ahead and the three objectives they had been ordered to take the following day (Morintru, Le Limon and Bergette, approximately 2 to 3 miles away). The next morning, 10 September, they advanced up the hill in three columns, the left and right columns containing two companies each and the centre column four companies. Despite the centre and right columns being challenged by fire from German patrols the three objectives were reached by dawn. Through several titanic clashes, later to become known as the Battle of the Marne, involving roughly a million Allied troops over the period 5–10 September, the German army had been forced to withdraw to a new line at the River Aisne. From near defeat Paris and France had for the time being been saved.

During the next five days the 1/E. Lancs marched 50 miles north, with both sides bombarding and attacking each other sporadically. Trying to outflank each other, 'The Race for the Sea' and the important channel ports had begun. Eventually in mid-September the 1/E. Lancs entrenched at Bucy-le-Long and for them, from 20 September, the remainder of the month was quiet. On 5 October the Brigade was relieved by the French and started to march west, reaching Compiegne on 10 October, a distance of 48 miles. From here they travelled by train north 120 miles to Blendecques (40 miles west of Ypres, the key market town in Belgium that the German's had captured on 3 October), where they were billeted in a paper mill. Along with the rest of the 11 Brigade, on 13 October the 1/E. Lancs marched east 19 miles and billeted in Flêtre church whilst, a few miles further on, the 10 and 12 Brigades attacked the village of Meteren. The same day, 13 miles north-east from Meteren, the German army was pushed out of Ypres and their ten-day occupation of the symbolic town was ended.

On 14 October, Herbert Canton's A-Coy 1/E. Lancs formed the advanced guard to the 4th Division as they advanced towards Bailleul, encountering only minimal shell fire from light guns. Billeting in a farm for the night, they then marched a further 5 miles east to Neuve Église, where Canton's A-Coy took up an outpost line covering the village, whilst the rest of the battalion found billets. Over the next three days the 4th Division swung south and advanced to Armentieres, via Romarin, Nieppe and Le Bizet. Orders to attack L'Epinette were received then cancelled and orders to billet came and went as the 1/E. Lancs were finally ordered to proceed to La Chapelle-d'Armentières as support to the 17 Brigade. The 1/E. Lancs received orders on 18 October to dig in around the area of Armentières. What followed was a month-long intense period of fighting (the First Battle of Ypres), with attacks and counter-attacks, followed by further digging-in and holding a line. The battalion dug in along a road facing east, but were there only two nights before they were needed a few miles further east at Wez Macquart where, on 20 October, the Germans had broken through the line. Canton's A-Coy rapidly dug a new line east and south-east of the village. After the situation at Wez Maquart had been stabilized with the addition of the 3rd Battalion, the Rifle Brigade, the 1/E. Lancs were ordered to march overnight to Armentieres, then on to Ploegsteert, a distance of approximately 8 miles. Here the Germans had attacked and captured the small village of Le Gheer. Canton's A-Coy along with D-Coy were ordered to counter-attack. Managing to take the eastern edge of the wood outside the village, they were then joined by the Somerset Light Infantry who advanced from the north edge of the wood. Having taken the wood without opposition, the force then encountered the Germans lining a natural ditch in open country. The British took the ditch 'in flank killing and wounding a large number of the enemy', and retook the village after 16-Platoon charged the remaining trenches. Without rest A- and D-Coy pushed on south to support the Essex Regiment and B-Coy in their attack on Le Touquet. From 20 October to 4 November the 1/E. Lancs were rotated between front line trench duty on the Le Gheer to Le Touquet line and rear supporting duties. This two-week period saw intense fighting during which repeated German attacks supported by machine guns were repulsed and long periods of heavy shelling were endured. The weather was particularly wet and at one point the rifles became badly choked with clay. The lines of trenches were continuously added to, with additional support trenches constructed to improve routes for reinforcement. Twice the battalion headquarters had to be abandoned and re-positioned further behind the front line due to being targeted by heavy shelling, and on several occasions companies in support had to be rushed to the front line because large scale attacks were expected. The din of the heavy howitzer shelling, including shrapnel shelling, was described as 'deafening', and on 2 November Herbert Canton's company commander, Captain G. Clayhills DSO, aged 36, was killed during one German infantry attack. The following day a particularly heavy *Minenwerfer* bombardment destroyed part of the 1/E. Lancs forward trench, burying fifteen men, with only two being dug out alive. Finally, on 4 November, the 1/E. Lancs were relieved by the Hampshire Regiment and went into reserve in three farms behind Ploegsteert Wood. There was no rest, though, and the battalion spent the next two days digging trenches on Hill 63. Then at 05.00 on 7 November the battalion was ordered to 'stand to arms', due to a large German attack on the Worcester Regiment on the eastern part of the front near Ploegsteert Wood. At 15.00 the battalion received orders to attack. Canton's A-Coy along with D-Coy attacked and recaptured Le Gheer crossroads and the Worcester main trench. B- and C-Coy then took on the attack of the German positions in the kink of the wood, but the attack was repulsed. The battalion dug in as dawn approached; sixteen of the 1/E. Lancs had been killed and thirty one wounded. During the next eight days another attempt to remove the Germans from the wood was made, but the situation returned to that of soaking up both light and heavy field gun shelling with the loss of a further twenty-one men killed and sixty-seven wounded. The battalion was relieved on 17 November and went to rest for two days at billets firstly in Nieppe and then Armentières, before marching back to Le Gheer and taking over their original trenches from the Essex Regiment on 20 November. The situation had now changed to 'All quiet with occasional shelling', the First Battle of Ypres had come to an end. The 1/E. Lancs, to the south of Ypres, had been right in the thick of the battle for Ypres, during which the Allies received 75,000 casualties and the Germans lost 135,000 men. The Allies had been pushed back in the north and in the south of the town, forming a salient around the town. The town itself stayed in Allied hands, despite being overlooked by the Germans on higher ground and the continual shrinking of the salient. As the end of November approached, both armies had succumbed to exhaustion and the worsening weather, the period of static trench warfare had begun and the German route to the Channel ports was thwarted.

Officers' leave began and replacement officers and other ranks were received. For the remainder of 1914 the 'normal routine' of front line trench warfare was only interrupted by an inspection of B-Coy by His Majesty the King at Pont de Nieppe on 2 December and by one last attack on the Ploegsteert Wood on 19 December, during which the 1/E. Lancs' role was to keep up heavy fire on the enemy trenches while the Somerset Regiment and the Rifle Brigade attacked the wood, supported by artillery and machine gun fire. On Christmas Day the 1/E. Lancs War Diary recorded: 'All [was] quiet [with] no shots being fired at all', an informal truce being held. The tranquillity was maintained until 31 December, when sniping recommenced. The 'normality' of front line routine with its occasional sniping and shelling continued throughout January and February, with regular but fewer casualties. In March defensive operations intensified, reinforcing trenches, building new trenches and fortifying nearby 'Burnt out Farm'. After several cancelled arrangements to be relieved from the front line, the whole brigade was eventually moved to reserve in Nieppe on 19 March and took up defensive duties and training. The battalion did a 9-mile route march on 23 March, during which 'only one man fell out – which was good after five months trench warfare'. The respite was short-lived and on 24 March they returned to the front line at Le Gheer for a period of six days, then swapped into the reserve again at Ploegsteert carrying out fatigue work on the brigade defences. This rotation with the 1st Battalion, Hampshire Regiment of approximately six days in the front line followed by six days in reserve continued in the Ploegsteert / Le Gheer trenches until mid-April.

In March 1915 Herbert Canton had bumped into Sydney Disney, his old football team mate from MCS, in the trenches at Ploegsteert, or 'Plug Street' as it was called by the British troops. Disney was wounded on 19 June and ended up in a hospital in Boulogne. While recovering he wrote a letter to the School and *The Lily* telling them of his meeting with Canton (see Chapter 1, The School, for the letter reproduced in *The Lily* of November 1915). As Disney put it, 'One of the best oars who ever rowed for the school ... a splendid soldier ... absolutely fearless'.

The 1/E. Lancs left the Nieppe area on 15 April and moved 15 miles east to Le Touquet, north of Lille, to take up the trenches occupied by the King's Own Regiment, temporarily joining the 12 Brigade. Here they swapped between the front line and the reserve/support every four days until on 28 April, when they moved 15 miles north-west to Bailleul. The following day they left Bailleul and travelled 10 miles by motor buses to Vlamertinghe (3 miles west of Ypres). They then marched 7 miles to Verlorenhoek (the 11 Brigade Headquarters) along the Menin Road and through the town of Ypres. Amazingly, the march resulted in no casualties despite the road being shelled from both sides continuously during the entire march, due to the acute salient in front of Ypres. For a second time the 1/E. Lancs found themselves in the thick of a battle for Ypres town (the Second Battle of Ypres), this time to the north of the town. The Germans were desperate to take all the high ground around Ypres and dominate the area, so desperate in fact that during the month-long struggle they deployed gas on a large scale for the first time.

On 1 May 1915 the 1/E. Lancs were in the Elverdinge area, north of Ypres, along with the rest of the 11 Brigade 4th Division (1/SLI, 1/Hants, 1/RB), rotating between reserve and front line trenches of the Ypres salient. Unremitting artillery bombardments meant that communication lines were constantly being broken so orderlies/runners had to be used to communicate between the lines. At 08.00 on 3 May A-Coy commanded by Lieutenant Canton, plus HQ and B-Coy, moved up to the front to fill a gap in the line between the 1/RB and the 1/Hants. Orders had been received for a withdrawal, so at 22.30 initially all but one platoon from each company withdrew via Wieltje over the Yser Canal to Elverdinge, where they arrived by 04.30 on 4 May and took up positions in their new trenches. The remaining platoons then withdrew at midnight and joined the battalion at Elverdinge. Between 4 and 8 May the battalion moved with the rest of the brigade to bivouack first at a chateau then at a wood one mile east of Oosthoex, then at Vlamertinge. During the night of 8 May, while marching to new positions to relieve the Monmouthshire Regiment at La Brique to the north of Ypres, the battalion was redirected to intercept a German infiltration around the flank of the salient at Wieltje. The 1/E. Lancs retook the trenches without opposition but the following day were subjected to continual heavy bombardment, though without any further infantry attacks. The situation remained the same over 9 to 11 May, with the battalion digging in an attempt to withstand the unrelenting bombardment. During 12 May Canton's A-Coy in particular suffered severely from the heavy artillery 'Jack Johnson' shells. Finally, on 13 May the German infantry attacked. They were initially repelled on the right by C-Coy, but managed to take Shell Trap Farm, overcoming the Rifle Brigade. This exposed both the rear and sides of A-Coy, allowing murderous enfilade sniping. The devastation of the trench breastwork over the previous four days of heavy bombardment had reduced the cover available to the 1/E. Lancs, and

A-Coy took heavy casualties. Eventually, resilient rifle fire from the surviving members of A-Coy and assistance from C-Coy of the Essex Regiment drove the Germans from the farm. Herbert Canton was killed in this action aged 23, defending Ypres, on 13 May 1915, Ascension Day, the same day as his Company Major and Platoon Captain lost their lives. He had endured over eight months of continual fighting, including the retreat from Mons, the battles of the Marne and the Aisne, and the First and Second battles of Ypres.

The Second Battle for Ypres was to continue until late May. After a month of fighting, the Ypres salient had been reduced in size by two-thirds, Ypres town was in ruins and the British and French had incurred 70,000 casualties. It was to be the Germans' only major offensive during 1915. Canton himself had been promoted to Captain (Temporary) on 31 March 1915, but the promotion was only gazetted after his death. His parents received a telegram informing them of the death of their only son on 16 May 1915. As with all telegrams bearing this sad news during this period it was also communicated that 'Lord Kitchener expressed his sympathy'.

In September 1915 Canton's father received a letter from the War Office reporting the exact burial site of his son. Sadly, over the course of the remaining three years of the war the initial burial site, as with many burial sites on the Western Front, was destroyed and lost by the process of war. Canton is now only commemorated on the Menin Gate at Ypres and has no known grave.

Bernard Robert Hadow CARTER

31 October 1898 – 7 November 1917

Rank and regiment: Second Lieutenant, 19 (Training) Squadron, Royal Flying Corps. **Theatre of War:** Home. **Memorial:** War Memorial, Slimbridge (St John the Baptist) Churchyard, Gloucestershire.

Bernard Robert Hadow Carter was born on 31 October 1898 in Oxford, the youngest son of Rev. James Octavius Holderness Carter and Beatrice Helena Carter (*née* Stone). He had two older brothers: Brian Arundell (b. 1895) and George Christian (b. 1897).

His father studied at Magdalen College, Oxford (matriculating 1883), where he was a Choral Clerk, singing in the college choir with the choristers of Magdalen College School. After obtaining his BA and MA in 1890 he became an Assistant Master at St Edward's School, Oxford (1891–1902), as well as a Chaplain at Magdalen College, Oxford (1893–1902) and Chaplain of New College, Oxford (1892–1902). During his time in Oxford, his father was also associated with other churches, namely Holywell, or St Cross, (1893–1897), St Margaret's (1897–1901) and Iffley (1901–1902) and was an Oxford University Local Examiner from 1899 to 1903.

In 1901 the family were living at 44 Chalfont Road, St Giles, Oxford, but the following year moved to Slimbridge Rectory in Gloucestershire for the Rev.

Bernard Carter, 1916.

Carter to become the Rector of St John the Evangelist church.[1] Ironically, this was the probable birthplace and church of William Tyndale, translator of the Bible, who was resident at Magdalen Hall and attended Magdalen College School in the early 1500s. While living at Slimbridge, Bernard Carter would have witnessed the installation of the carved wooden screen that was erected and dedicated to Tyndale in 1914. James Carter was to remain Rector of Slimbridge until 1925.

With the association his father had with Magdalen College and St Edward's, Oxford, it is not surprising that all three brothers joined Magdalen College School as choristers. In fact, it is something of a record that all three brothers sang in the Magdalen College choir together. All three brothers also later attended St Edward's.

Life at Magdalen College School (1908–1912) and beyond

Bernard Carter joined MCS as a Chorister in 1908 and followed the path of his two elder brothers, leaving MCS after his chorister years and when he was the

St Edward's School Rugby XV, 1916. B.R.H. Carter is third from the left, middle row.

right age to join the rival Oxford Public School, St Edward's.[2] While at MCS he was described as 'a very bright, gentle and lovable boy'. After his first year at MCS, in 1909, he won the Form I/II Prize for French and in his final year, 1912, the Set 1 Music Prize.

In the summer of 1911 he succeeded in swimming the Long Pass in the Cherwell River, a necessity if he was going to be allowed to learn to row the following year. On the sports track in the following summer, despite winning his heat in the 300 yard handicap race, Carter was not placed in the final. *The Lily* also records Carter playing in the annual MCS Choristers versus Christ Church Choristers cricket match of Saturday, 15 June 1912. Batting first, the MCS side lost early wickets before Carter, coming in at no. 4, steadied the ship and put on a stand of 37 runs in the eventual all-out total of 54. A seemingly undefendable total was easily adequate as the Christ Church side was bowled out for 39.

Carter joined St Edward's in the Michaelmas term of 1912. While there he became a sergeant in the OTC, was Captain of the Boats, and was eventually a School Prefect. In the sporting arena he played for the 1st XV Rugby team in 1915 and 1916 and was also secretary of the School Football team. He remained at St Edward's until enlisting in an Officer Training Corps in the Easter of 1917.

Carter's War

Bernard Carter, aged 18, joined the 'The Inns of Court' OTC in Berkhamsted in 1917. In May of that year he progressed to the 1st School of Aeronautics in

Reading and was subsequently commissioned to 25 (Training) Squadron, RFC in Thetford as Second Lieutenant on 15 June 1917, when he 'gained his wings' and qualified as a pilot. After a short spell with 12 (Training) Squadron (also based at Thetford) he joined 19 (Training) Squadron in September 1917, based at Curragh Camp in Ireland. In November he was one of six pilots of 19/TS selected for a 'special duty'. Taking off in bad weather on 7 November 1917, five of the planes were soon forced to land due to worsening conditions. Carter and his observer, Corporal Harold Smith, however, stuck to the task they had been given and tried to fly through the weather front. When over Anglesey their plane was buffeted by a violent wind and was forced to descend near Llangefni. Carter stopped the engine and was circling over the aerodrome when the plane overturned in the wind and crashed. His observer survived, but Carter, aged only 19, was thrown against a wall and killed. His name appears on the War Memorial in St John the Baptist Churchyard, Slimbridge.

The Captain of his squadron wrote to his mother, 'I had a very high opinion of your son, so much so that I had asked for him to be posted to my squadron as an assistant instructor, and he had just been posted in that capacity.'

1. James Carter's predecessor as Rector of St John's, Dr Charles Henry Ridding, had also been a Fellow at Magdalen College. Indeed, five rectors of Slimbridge are acknowledged to have been Magdalen College men which, together with Bernard Carter and William Tyndale, makes a permanent and interesting connection between the two places.
2. Prior to joining MCS, Bernard Carter had been educated at a preparatory school in Great Malvern.

Noel Godfrey CHAVASSE

9 November 1884 – 4 August 1917

Rank and regiment: Captain, Royal Army Medical Corps, attached 10th (Scottish) Battalion, The King's (Liverpool Regiment).
Medals awarded: Victory, British War, 1914–1915 Star, Military Cross, Victoria Cross and bar. **Theatre of War:** Western Front.
Memorial: Brandhoek New Military Cemetery, Belgium.

Noel's father, Francis 'Frank' James Chavasse (1846–1928) became rector of St Peter-le-Bailey in Oxford in 1878. In 1880 he met Edith Jane Maude (1851–1927) when she journeyed to Oxford to seek his advice about the education of a daughter of a missionary from her father's old Parish of Chirk, Denbighshire. Frank and Edith married in 1881. Noel was born in 1884 and lived at 36 New Inn Hall Street, Oxford, for the first five years of his life until moving to Wycliffe Hall (52 and 54 Banbury Road) when his father became Principal of the Evangelical Theological College in 1889. In all, Frank and Edith had seven children, the eldest Dorothea (1883–1937), Noel and his 'older' identical twin brother Christopher Maude (1884–1962), two non-identical twin sisters Edith Majorie and Mary Laeta (1886–1987 and –1989 respectively), and finally Noel's two younger brothers, Francis Bernard (1889–1941) and Aidan (1891–1917). All the children were educated by a governess and a tutor at home until, when the twin boys turned 12, Noel and Christopher became day boys at MCS in 1896. The other children remained at home.

With the home environment of the Church and theology, and the history of surgeons in the family – their great-grandfather (Nicholas Willett Chavasse, 1763–1818) and grandfather (Thomas Chavasse, 1800–1884) both having been surgeons and their uncle ('Uncle Tom', Thomas Frederick Chavasse) a Senior Surgeon at Birmingham General Hospital – it was predictable that the twins would find their career in either the Church or medicine. Noel became the surgeon, Christopher entered the Church.

Noel's Chavasse's life has been thoroughly and accurately recorded in the highly acclaimed biography *Chavasse Double VC* by Anne Clayton. I would strongly advise anyone interested in his story, the RAMC or the First World War to read it. What follows in a small way supplements this biography by giving a detailed insight into Chavasse's experiences at his beloved MCS and summarizes his war years punctuated by the response from the school to the news of his exploits and the ordeals of their decorated 'Old Boys' on the Western Front.

Life at Magdalen College School (1896–1900) and beyond

Noel and Christopher were day boys at MCS and travelled to school each day on bicycles, a ride that took just ten minutes from their Wycliffe Lodge residence on Banbury Road.

Two of Noel's school reports, one in his first and one in his second year in the school,[1] use the word 'mischief' and suggest Noel was not always the first to settle down to his academic studies. The reports also show that he missed school frequently due to illness. However, what is evident is that Noel and Christopher both loved life at the school and participated in as much of the physical activities they could, both excelling at running.

Unsurprisingly, given their father's profession and the Chavasse family environment, Noel and Christopher shared the Form III prize for Scripture in 1898, the prizes being presented in a packed School Hall full of relatives and eminent members of Magdalen College and the University. Chavasse's father, the Principal of Wycliffe Hall, was also a special guest on the platform, along with the President, Vice President and Dean of Divinity of Magdalen College. Interestingly, Noel also collected the science prize, a first inkling of his interest in science and a hint that he would eventually go on to study Natural Sciences at Oxford.

In 1897 at the end of his first year at MCS, Noel witnessed his brother make an impact on the school sports scene, despite his tender age, when Christopher ran well in the 100 and 300 yard events, came second in the long jump and won the sack race at Sports Day. Noel himself only achieved second place in the consolation 200 yard race, designed for the younger runners. Neither of the boys was expected to challenge in event finals because they were still very junior in the school; however, the following year Noel did manage to win the consolation

Noel (left) and Christopher (right) in 1897.

200 yard race and take third place in the coveted sack race, an event taken very seriously at the time. Then in 1899, despite being three to four years younger than some of the boys in the school, Noel won the half mile race in a time of 2 minutes 31.4 seconds, with his brother taking second place. Not to be outdone, Christopher won the long jump and the sack race and came second in the 100-yard final. The first glimpse of the twin's athletic ability had been seen.

During school holidays Noel and his siblings had extended visits to his grandmother's (Mary Fawler Maude) house Pen Dyffryn in Overton-on-Dee near Wrexham, where his mother had grown up; and to Uncle Tom's in Bromsgrove to see his four cousins.

In March 1900 Noel and his twin Christopher, then both 15, were devastated to be told by their father that they were moving from Oxford as he had accepted the offer from the Prime Minister (Lord Salisbury) to become Bishop of Liverpool. A request by the twins to stay on and complete their education at MCS as boarders was refused by their father, who believed the family must be kept together during the most impressionable time in a boy's life. The boys went out and bought a large number of picture postcards of Oxford, pasted them into an

A doodled drawing by Noel Chavasse of his school days at MCS.[2]

album and used them as a constant reminder of the place they loved more than anywhere else. Four years later they would return.

Both the twins rowed in the Form Fours competition each year while at MCS,[3] but neither represented MCS at any team games (cricket, hockey or football). Noel did report to his grandmother, however, in one of his many letters to her while at MCS, that he was the treasurer of both the school hockey and football teams, but admitted they were 'rather in debt'. He refers to the school team by its adopted name of 'Aldebaran', after the giant star that can be found in the constellation Taurus 'which changes from white to red', the team's colours of the time. Both boys did play in Old Boy teams that returned to play the School. Noel returned to MCS in July 1909 to play in the Old Boys' cricket match versus the School the day before the Commemoration service. The School side, which included Frank Wilkinson, Charles Maltby and John Bellamy, dismissed the Old Boys for 103; Chavasse being the last man in was bowled without scoring. The School eventually won by 2 wickets, with Charles Maltby remaining not out on 23. Later that year, Noel returned to MCS to play an Old Boys' Hockey match versus the School, whose team included James Roberton. Noel playing in goal, and helped by a defence that included Basil Blackwell, produced some good saves to keep the scoreline to a respectable 3–1 in favour of the School. Christopher also fostered the twins' close links with the school by returning to

A photograph showing Noel diving during the MCS Swimming Sports at Cox's Corner in 1898.

play against his old school in football and cricket matches; famously in one game he witnessed Harold Dawes score a century.[4]

Noel and Christopher returned to the School on Sports Day and for Commemoration for many years after they had left MCS. Competing in the Old Boys' 150 yards handicap race at these 'reunions' seems to have been a highlight, and predictably Noel won the race in 1907 and 1908. In the 1909 race it seems that a concerted effort was made by the other old boys to stop Noel from winning. Despite some of the entrants being 'very' old boys, they were still fun-loving schoolboys at heart and Noel was blocked off when trying to pass. His winning streak had come to an end. However, it was still a Chavasse win as the blocking tactics had allowed Christopher a clear run, holding off Basil Blackwell to take first place. Not to be outdone by his competitive peers, Noel entered the race again in 1912. Twenty-seven years old at the time and running from scratch (i.e. the full 150 yards), he won the race, but second place, Canon Edwards, over 60 at the time, 'lived with youth till the last strides'.

Both Noel and Christopher subscribed to the Old Boys' Club and by receiving a copy of *The Lily* magazine each term stayed in touch with the happenings and news of the School and exploits of old boys. Likewise the School was kept informed of their progress and careers, reporting in *The Lily* their exploits on the athletics track at University.[5] Midway through the war, in late 1916, Noel wrote a letter to the School which was published in *The Lily* in November 1916.

After their sad farewell to MCS at the Easter of 1900 and a few weeks settling into their new home at the 'Palace' (19 Abercromby Square, Liverpool, then the Bishop of Liverpool's official residence), the twins resumed their education at Liverpool College. In time all four brothers attended Liverpool College, where each of them continued to develop the athletic ability and talent for sport that Noel and Christopher had first shown at MCS.

In 1904 both Noel and Christopher applied to Trinity College, Oxford. Noel was accepted to read Natural Sciences (with the aim of eventually qualifying in medicine) and Christopher was accepted to read a 'Humanities' degree with the core topic being history. Among other achievements while at Trinity, both received Blues for running against Cambridge in 1907. In 1907 Noel was awarded a First in Physiology, but Christopher had failed his degree. Christopher galvanized himself to do a further year and retake his Finals in 1908. Noel, rather than return to Liverpool to continue his Medical Studies, stayed on and continued them at Oxford. The brothers were determined to stay together. Noel again obtained a First in the next stage of his Physiology course, and this time Christopher passed his degree.

During the long vacations and even after his Finals in 1907 Noel would gain extra experience of all things medical by attending on ward rounds, by working and by attending classes at Liverpool's Royal Southern Hospital and Liverpool University Medical School. In addition, he would devote time to the boys of Grafton Street School (a school, industrial training centre and home for destitute children in Liverpool) on their annual summer camps to Hightown.

In 1908 both Noel and Christopher competed in the Olympic Games held in London, taking part in but not qualifying from the heats of the 400 metres event. At this point the boys started to go their own ways. Christopher started to study for eventual ordination back in Liverpool, while Noel stayed at Oxford to further his experiences in anatomy. For this, Noel worked at the University Museum and attended lectures at the Radcliffe Hospital.

In 1908 his younger brother Bernard joined Noel in Oxford when he started his Natural Science degree at Balliol College. In January 1909 both Noel and Bernard joined the Officer Training Corps, with Noel in the Medical Unit. On 5 June 1908 the Oxford University OTC, then more than 700 strong, marched from St Aldate's, passing Chavasse's old school on the High Street and at the Plain, up to Headington Hill Park to be reviewed. At the same time, back in Liverpool, Aidan joined Liverpool College's Cadet Corps.

In July 1909, after acting as a steward alongside Charles Maltby at the MCS Sports Day, Noel finally left Oxford to complete his medical training at Liverpool University. In October 1909 he sat but failed the examination for membership of the Royal College of Surgeons. Continuing with more specialized courses in 1910, in May he retook the RCS exam and, with great relief, this time passed. In 1911 he did his first hospital placement in Dublin, then in January 1912 took and passed his final Medical Exam. In March of that year he was awarded the Derby Exhibition by the University and finally in July he was officially registered as a Doctor with the General Medical Council.

In October 1912 Noel gained his first medical appointment, at the Royal Southern Hospital in Liverpool. This led to him practising at Liverpool for the next twenty-two months. Meanwhile, in 1913 Noel had time to renew his connection with the army and was accepted to the post of Junior Medical Officer of the RAMC, attached to the 10th (Scottish) Battalion, the King's (Liverpool) Regiment, a Territorial Force. To enable him to attend the battalion's summer camp in 1914 he booked two weeks leave, starting on 2 August. On 3 August the battalion was ordered to return to Liverpool and then on 7 August they were recalled to their headquarters of Fraser Street. Britain had declared war on Germany on 4 August. Noel, after being sent away to Chester Castle, was then relieved to be able to re-join his battalion, now based in Edinburgh, when the Senior Medical Officer at that time did not volunteer for foreign service. On 1 November, after three weeks of practice and kitting out at Tunbridge Wells, the battalion were transported by train to Southampton where they left for France aboard the *Maidean* at 7.30pm. They arrived at Le Havre the following morning and finally disembarked on 3 November as part of the 9 Brigade 3th Division.

Chavasse's War

Noel spent his first night on French soil under canvas at No. 1 Rest Camp outside Le Havre. The following day the battalion entrained for the front, a slow journey which took twenty-seven hours. The train passed through Rouen, where May Cannan, the Oxford poet who set up the temporary hospital at MCS, would eventually work as a nurse, and Abbeville to allow the men time to stretch and have a hot drink. The battalion detrained at Saint Omer on 5 November 1914 and marched 3 miles to billets at Blendecques. Here, 25 miles behind the front line, but within earshot of the big guns at the front, the battalion spent the next two weeks training. On 20 November, leaving all ceremonial kit behind, the battalion marched in cold and wet conditions 20 miles east to Bailleul, arriving on 22 November. They were now only 5 miles from the front line. The following day they marched towards the front so that the men could experience the noise and sight of shrapnel shells. The battalion was inspected by General Sir Horace Smith-Dorrien and by the Prince of Wales on 25 November, before moving 5 miles north to billets at Westoutre, Belgium (4 miles south of Poperinge). Removing cap badges and shoulder plates on 27 November, the battalion marched 5 miles to the Firing Line beyond Kemmel (6 miles south of Ypres). Here they spent the next three days experiencing the noise, dirt and horror of the trenches for the first time. During the first night the battalion received its first casualty and Noel lost a good friend, Captain A. Twentyman. It was Noel, with his stretcher bearers, who had to do the duty of retrieving the body while under enemy fire – a duty he would repeat many times during the next two and a half years, retrieving and tending to casualties and often appearing to sprint faster

Noel Chavasse.

than he had on the running track. Returning to billets in support, where the battalion were sited on a hill looking towards the spired town of Ypres, Noel described the scene as 'for all the world like Oxford from the Hinksey Hill'. Noel's everyday concern was keeping the men healthy, free from nutrient deficiencies resulting from the poor diet (he would see to it they drank lime juice) and fighting the effects of the wet and muddy trenches which resulted in a condition eventually known as Trench Foot (he would continually write home requesting hundreds of pairs of socks to be sent by his family, so the men could have several pairs in order to always have a dry pair).

Noel was taught to ride a horse in the early days of the war by a sergeant, and this would become an invaluable mode of transport for him to move around on difficult terrain, especially when in reserve, organizing his medical equipment and dressing stations. Noel's first horse, called Tit, had been a milk-float horse in Everton, Liverpool and by all accounts caused Noel much frustration by enjoying rolling in mud. Bugler Sam Moulton, who from 21 December wangled his way to become a stretcher bearer for Noel, ended up becoming groom for Tit. By the end of December 1914 he was in charge of Noel's medical cart (previously used in Liverpool for delivering the *Liverpool Echo* newspaper to shops). Later in the summer of 1915 Noel had a new horse called Doreen.

At the Christmas of 1914 the battalion was fortunate enough to be away from the front line trenches, and on New Year's Eve 1914 the battalion had moved to reserve trenches at Kemmel, carrying out fatigue work. Noel was affected deeply by the loss of another close friend, Lieutenant Fred 'Tanky' Turner, a contemporary of Noel's from Trinity College, on 10 January. Turner, who was a Rugby International capped fifteen times by Scotland, was organizing the arrangement of a barbed wire entanglement when he was shot. It was Noel who recovered his body.

In early February 1915 Noel was given leave and travelled back to England to visit friends and family. By luck, his twin brother's leave coincided and they managed to catch up with each other's experiences. Christopher had been in France for a longer time than Noel, initially working as Chaplain at the No. 10 General Hospital at Saint Nazaire, comforting the wounded and dying who had retreated from Mons in August and September; then from November he had been at No. 6 Casualty Clearing Station at Merville, between Ypres and Béthune. After the short leave Noel returned to his battalion, the 10/King's, in the Kemmel area, but before long they moved from this familiar front line sector south of Ypres and relocated 6 miles further north to Ypres itself on 10 March. Much of Ypres at this time was still standing but very damaged, and amazingly, despite the civilian population having left, many shops were still operating, much to the benefit of the troops. Part of the sector manned by the 10/King's front overlooked Hill 60, where the battalion improved the front line trenches and built a dug-out that became invaluable to Noel for treating men in relative safety at the firing line during this period.

The 10/King's relocated on 2 April 1915, 3 miles south of Ypres to the southern part of the salient around the Voormezeele area, to a front line sector called 'St Eloi'. The dug-outs that were constructed so that the 10/King's, when in support, could get to the front line quickly were built in a wood, christened 'Scottish Wood' as Noel's own records indicate. Around this time, Christopher Chavasse had been relocated to the Ypres area and had managed to meet up with Noel, even giving a short service to the 10/King's. On 23 May (Whit Sunday) Noel attended his brother's Holy Communion service. In June 1915 Noel received the sad news that his cousin, Captain Francis Chavasse Squires had been killed on 7 June in Aden, aged 30, while serving with the 1st Battalion 23 Sikh Pioneers.

Throughout the day of 11 June the battalion made preparations to move briefly to Busseboom for special training. The men were put through their paces attacking dummy trenches and bomb throwing; a British attack was imminent. On 15 June 1915 the battalion marched 8 miles to the 'jump-up' trenches, ready for their attack on Hooge, the operation during which Noel was to win his Military Cross. Although told to stay half a mile behind the trenches, Noel went up to the front to see the lie of the land. He knew he would be needed there in a short time. The 10/King's were to be in the second wave, going beyond the German front line to take their second line of trenches. At 02.00 on 16 June 1915 the British bombardment began, and after two hours of shelling the troops went over the top. Despite a steady flow of walking wounded and communication trenches being blocked with the worst cases, the 10/King's made good progress, taking not only their original objectives but going further beyond to a fourth line of German trenches. The cost of this progress soon became evident. Many men had been killed or wounded and were lying in the open, being shelled by German mortars. The Germans had also counter-attacked on the left and had come around to cut off the advanced British troops. The British artillery, supposedly shelling the German retreat, were also killing and injuring the advanced and now cut-off British troops. Noel Chavasse worked tirelessly dressing the wounds of injured men and repeatedly searched the battlefield in the most advanced points and collected men, with the aid of his stretcher bearers, and returned them to British lines. The battalion was relieved during the night of 16 June; Noel, however, remained and worked throughout the next two days, not retiring until he was sure that all the wounded had been found and brought in. On 18 June, Sam Moulton and Doreen were out searching for Noel when they found him and his stretcher bearers returning to the asylum on the outskirts of Ypres. Sam put Noel on the horse and took him back to his battalion, arriving at the camp at 05.00 on 19 June. Noel slept for twelve hours. Of the 23 officers and 519 men of the 10/King's that went into battle at Hooge, only 2 officers and 140 men came through unscathed. For his dedication to duty in the face of enemy fire at Hooge, Noel Chavasse received the Military Cross (gazetted on 14 January 1916). No official citation exists for his award, as the recommendation list written by the Commanding Officer of the 10/King's was lost; any honours for 10/King's men from Hooge exist because of recommendations from other Commanding Officers. Noel's award had also been recommended by the RAMC.

At the start of July, Noel was given leave to return to England for a few days. He returned to Busseboom on 9 July and the 10/King's were soon back at the firing line, even with the severely depleted battalion. In August Noel was promoted to Captain, but was reflective enough to point out in a letter that he was the only person left in his Brigade who had been out with a battalion since November 1914. All others in his battalion that he had originally left England with had either been killed or were wounded and not sufficiently recovered for active service. In October 1915 Noel was thrilled to be able to meet up with his younger brother Aidan in France. Aidan had been at the front since 16 August and was then serving with the 11th (Pioneers) Battalion, the King's (Liverpool) Regiment in Ypres, along with Herbert Brereton.

By September the battalion was sufficiently up to number to be involved in the attack on Sanctuary Wood, albeit in reserve. Although not in a charge against the enemy, the job of the reserve battalion following up behind was nevertheless arduous and often under dreadful conditions of battlefield squalor. Noel found himself initially doing a combatant's job, bringing forward ammunition and bombs to keep the front line supplied. His role however soon returned to the familiar one of medical officer, in the 'dreadful wood' he summed up as 'the valley of the shadow of death'. For his 'gallant and distinguished service in the field' during the action at Sanctuary Wood in September 1915 he was mentioned in dispatches by Sir John French, and this was published in the *London Gazette* on 1 January 1916, before notification of his MC won in June 1915.

The new year of 1916 saw the 10/King's transfer to the 166 Brigade 55th Division and in January the battalion moved away from the Ypres area. They initially moved to a training location well behind the front Line at Abbeville, and in February Noel managed to obtain a few days' leave in England. Noel's award of the Military Cross had at last appeared in the *London Gazette* on 14 January and news quickly got back to school about this honour and his mention in dispatches. *The Lily* of March 1916 proudly listed both his awards.

In the spring of the previous year, 1915, Noel had declared his love for his cousin Gladys. Noel had spent much of his youth growing up with Gladys and their relationship had become very strong. Via their exchange of letters while Noel was at the front, and during his short periods of leave in England, both of them became aware that they wanted to spend the rest of their lives together. By March 1916 Noel had written to Gladys and proposed. He received a positive answer. Although apprehensive about disclosing their love for each other to their family, when they eventually did they received full support and blessings. In the same month tragedy again struck the family when Gladys' brother, Captain Arthur R. Chavasse RAMC, died of pneumonia at Le Havre on 12 March. Gladys' mother and sister Esme managed to travel to France in time to be at his bedside.

In May 1916 Noel was granted a short leave, which luckily coincided with Christopher's brief return to England. Both boys met up with family and Noel was able to spend time with Gladys. Only a month later, on 7 June, Noel again returned to England, fortunate to be chosen as one of those to be presented with his Military Cross by King George V at Buckingham Palace. He again managed to see both Gladys and Christopher. Noel soon returned to his battalion in France who for the rest of 1916 spent their days in the rota of firing line, support and reserve duties in the Rivière sector of the line south-west of Arras.

Noel and the rest of the 10/King's were not involved in the 1 July 1916 offensive on the Somme, being kept in reserve at Rivière, but tragically the family was to lose another of Noel's generation that day, Noel's cousin Louis (Second Lieutenant Louis E.J. Maude of the 11th Battalion, The King's Own Yorkshire

Light Infantry). By the end of July the battalion had moved 20 miles south to Ville-sur-Ancre then to Méaulte (just south of Albert), and on 30 July they were moved closer to the front, east of Albert. A week later, on 7 August, an attack was made on Guillemont, with the 166 Brigade and the 10/King's in reserve. By the afternoon of 8 August, despite the attack on the right flank being successful, part of the attack was floundering on the left flank, so the 166 Brigade was sent in to help out. A disastrous night ensued, with enemy shelling zeroing in on the 10/King's march to the jumping-off trenches and in no-man's land, not helped by initially a lack of guides then guides who struggled to find their route to the start point. At 04.20 on 9 August the 10/King's went over the top, only to find progress almost impossible due to the enemy wire being uncut and no preliminary bombardment having taken place. Machine-gun fire made sure the attack on Guillemont past Trones Wood was to fail, despite the battalion regrouping and making a total of four charges on their objective. Of the twenty 10/King's officers at the start of the attack, seventeen were killed, wounded or missing. Over 260 of the 600 other ranks also became casualties. Noel and his stretcher bearers had their jobs cut out for the rest of the day and night, and Chavasse, 'ignoring the snipers' bullets ... carried on with his work ... throughout the hours of darkness', amazingly even using his electric torch as he searched the trenches and mortar holes. At times working within yards of the enemy trenches, and being bombed for their efforts, they effectively cleared no-man's land of the battalion's dead and wounded. When Noel finally retired to sleep, he found he had been wounded by shell fragments in the back of his thigh. Even at this stage his exploits were being followed and his wound made news in the *British Medical Journal* and the *Daily Sketch* newspaper (22 September 1916). A few months later four of Chavasse's stretcher bearers were awarded gallantry medals (two DCMs and two MMs) for their actions during the attack on Guillemont. On 26 October the *London Gazette* announced that Noel had been awarded a Victoria Cross for his 'most conspicuous bravery and devotion to duty' at Guillemont. Chavasse himself had known of his recommendation for a few weeks but had not told anyone in his battalion.

The *London Gazette* of 26 October 1916 said of Chavasse:

> During an attack he tended the wounded in the open all day, under heavy fire, frequently in view of the enemy. During the ensuing night he searched for wounded on the ground in front of the enemy's lines for four hours. Next day he took one stretcher-bearer to the advanced trenches, and, under heavy fire, carried an urgent case for 500 yards into safety, being wounded in the side by a shell splinter during the journey. The same night he took up a party of trusty volunteers, rescued three wounded men from a shell-hole 25 yards from the enemy's trench, buried the bodies of two officers, and collected many identity discs, although fired upon by enemy bombs and machine guns. Altogether he saved the lives of some twenty badly wounded men, besides the ordinary cases which passed through his hands. His courage and self-sacrifice were beyond praise.

To recuperate, the battalion was moved back to billets at Méaulte, near Albert, before in mid-August travelling by train 80 miles to a rest camp at Valines, west of Abbeville. Noel was granted sick leave and journeyed back to England, desperate to see his whole family because of the expectation that the big push would continue. By the end of August Noel was back at the front, again in the Somme area, on the new front line just a mile north of Guillemont at Delville Wood. From here the 10/King's moved back to the Ypres area and Poperinge, 60 miles north of the Somme. The battalion entered the rota of approximately a week in the front line or in support in the Ypres area, and a similar time at camp in Brandhoek. It was while at Ypres that the battalion heard the news of Chavasse's VC and accordingly the officers arranged a dinner to celebrate the award in the chateau at Elverdinghe, where they were billeted.

On Wednesday, 1 November 1916 Noel was featured in the local Oxford newspaper, the *Oxford Journal Illustrated*, as one of the 'Varsity men who have gained distinction'.[6]

As soon as Brownrigg and the school received the news of Noel's VC the Master wrote to his old pupil to offer his congratulations. Noel wrote back:[7]

> Your very kind letter reached me today. Need I say how I appreciate it? I suppose one longs to please one's old Headmaster more than anybody, and when the old school is pleased, it makes me very pleased. My brother and myself were very much touched by the kindness shown us by you and the old school when we came back to Oxford (and before we got our blues), and I know we shall never forget it, and we shall always try to be worthy of the old school we love so well. Thank you very much for your kind letter,
>
> Your old pupil,
>
> Noel Chavasse

The following year, on Monday, 11 June 1917 a whole day holiday was granted by the School to commemorate the winning of the VC by Chavasse. In glorious weather the majority of the school occupied themselves by having fun on and in the Cherwell.

At the end of 1916 Noel was sent away from his battalion for two months, probably because of his criticism of the Field Ambulance organization and a controversial report on minor ailments and morality. During this time he was made to work with the Field Ambulance units. At Christmas 1916 Noel returned to the battalion at 'C' Camp at Brandhoek. In the New Year he returned to England for the Victoria Cross presentation ceremony, held on 5 February 1917 at Buckingham Palace, and spent most of his two weeks' leave with his family in Liverpool. On returning to France he rejoined the battalion at Brandhoek. In late June the battalion moved 30 miles west, away from the front line for training. While there Noel took part in a cross-country race, and true to his previous experience he came first. Meanwhile, at about the same time, but unknown to Noel, Gladys had arranged for a special marriage licence to be prepared and was planning a trip to Paris under the supervision of a chaperone. She was planning

OXFORD JOURNAL ILLUSTRATED, WEDNESDAY, NOVEMBER 1, 1916. 9

'VARSITY MEN WHO HAVE GAINED DISTINCTION.

Many 'Varsity men figure in the latest list of awards for acts of gallantry and devotion to duty. Above are a few to whom awards have been made by the King. (Left top), Lieut. (Temporary Captain) Alan M. Wilkinson, Hampshire Regiment and R.F.C., awarded the D.S.O. for conspicuous gallantry and skill. Captain Wilkinson was an old football Blue, being educated at Repton and Oriel. (Left, lower), Second-Lieutenant J. N. Richardson, of Oriel, Royal Berks, awarded the M.C. for conspicuous gallantry in action. (Centre), Captain Noel Godfrey Chavasse, M.C., M.B., R.A.M.C. (son of the Bishop of Liverpool, formerly Rector of St. Peter-le-Bailey), awarded the Victoria Cross for most conspicuous bravery and devotion to duty. He tended the wounded under heavy fire, and went out at night in front of the enemy's lines, when he was instrumental in saving twenty lives, although fired on by bombs and machine-guns. His courage and self-sacrifice were beyond praise. (Right, top), Captain Hugh K. Ward, M.B., R.A.M.C., awarded the M.C. for gallantry and devotion to duty. Captain Ward is an old Oxford rowing Blue. He entered New College in 1911, and rowed for Oxford in 1913 and 1914. (Lower), Second-Lieutenant Malcolm MacKinnen, Highland Light Infantry, awarded the M.C. for gallantry in action. Second-Lieutenant MacKinnen was an old New College man, and often turned out for the Oxford City Football Club.—(Photos, Gillman, Oxford).

Noel Chavasse (centre).

to marry Noel before the expected next 'big push', and before Noel's plan of marriage at Christmas that year.

On 30 June 1917 the battalion moved approximately 4 miles south to Esquerdes, where training trenches mimicking their planned attack point were dug and training for the attack was undertaken. A repeat of the confusion at Guillemont was to be avoided. While at Esquerdes, Noel received devastating news that his youngest brother Aidan (now serving in the 17/King's) was missing presumed killed on 4 July, only a mile from Hooge.

Noel and the 10/King's marched 5 miles to Saint Omer on 20 July, and then travelled by train to Poperinge. After resting, the battalion marched up to the trenches near Wieltje, Ypres, under heavy enemy shelling. By the time the battalion was relieved in the front line on 24 July they had lost 4 officers and 141 other ranks to the shelling and gas attacks. They were relieved to be able to spend the next six days re-equipping at 'Derby Camp' between Ypres and Poperinge.

At 15.30 on 30 July as the rain began to pour and again under heavy shelling the 55 Division including the 10/King's moved up to their 'jumping off' trenches. At 03.50 the following morning, zero hour, the infantry attack phase of 'The Third Battle of Ypres' began. The 10/King's, already in open ground, rose and moved forward across wet and muddy land, pockmarked by water-filled shell holes. The British attacked and moved beyond the German front line trenches down the gentle slope to reach their initial objective line with limited casualties. They then moved on, crossing the Steenbeke stream, and advanced up the gentle slopes of Passchendaele ridge and moved towards the next objective line, the 10/King's being supported by two tanks and aeroplane reconnaissance. One of the tanks was able to destroy intact German wire that had temporarily halted the battalion's progress and by 07.45 the 10/King's had taken its furthest objective line. The battalion HQ was moved up to stay in contact with its most advanced troops, eventually siting itself on the east side of the Steenbeke stream to escape the concentration of enemy shells. Noel set his Regimental Aid Post up in a captured German dug-out close to Setques Farm, north of the road that runs from Wieltje to the Passchendaele Ridge and at the centre of the German concentrated shelling. The dug-out could hold a maximum of six men and had its entrance facing the German artillery. Once treated, the men left the dug-out to wait in whatever shelter they found nearby, trench or shell holes, until an escort or stretcher team could take them back to the field ambulance stations. Soon after he had established the Aid Post, Noel was hit by a shell splinter while signalling to wounded soldiers the location they could retreat to wait for help. It is possible that his skull may have been fractured by the impact, but importantly, Noel now needed medical help himself. He therefore walked approximately a mile back to the dressing station at the Wieltje dug-out complex, the original location of the battalion HQ before the advance. His wound was dressed and he was advised to stay at Wieltje to wait for transport to the Casualty Clearing Station for further treatment. Noel, however, went back to his Aid Post, knowing that his help was needed with the advancing troops. Before departing for the front in 1914, Noel had drilled with the ranks during their training in Edinburgh, believing that he would better see 'their point of view' and enable him to look after them better during battle. He believed he had a responsibility and duty, and he was staying true to his word.

After making it back to his dug-out, for the rest of the day Noel cleaned and dressed the wounds of his men. When night time came he took his torch and with his orderlies began to search the battle field for the wounded in the incessant rain. As 1 August dawned, Noel continued his work in the most appalling conditions, giving aid to men with horrendous injuries. By this time he had employed the help of a German Medical Officer plus some other captured German soldiers to carry and fetch men to him for help. On the morning of 1 August while at the entrance to the dug-out calling the queue of men forward for treatment a German shell flew past him and entered the dug-out, killing his previous patient. The effect, or wounds suffered by Noel by this close encounter with a shell, are not certain (concussion from a close encounter like this was often fatal), but he did not seek aid and carried on treating men in the 'rearranged' dug-out. This or a later incident that day did produce a further wound which was reported to require his removal from the battlefield, but Noel refused to leave his post and told his stretcher bearers to take another wounded man instead. Amazingly, it is suspected that he received three separate wounds on 1 August, but remained with his men on the battlefield. That evening and into the night he continued to treat and tend the wounded, who were lying out in the open or who were brought back to the Aid Post. It was while he was back at the Aid Post at 03.00 on 2 August that another shell entered through the doorway of the dug-out and killed or seriously wounded all those inside. Noel himself received four or five wounds, the most severe a gaping hole in his abdomen. Without any assistance available he dragged himself out of the dug-out and found the muddy road. Despite losing much blood he orientated himself and headed, stumbling and falling in the dark and wet, in the direction of Wieltje. He eventually came across help and the temporary sanctuary of a dug-out occupied by a North Lancashire Regiment officer. Noel sent the medical personnel from the dug-out to assist any casualties remaining in his dug-out, while he inspected his own wounds. He was eventually moved to the 46 Field Ambulance, which was under the command of Lieutenant Colonel Martin-Leake,[8] and from there ended up at Casualty Clearing Station No. 32, Brandhoek, between Ypres and Poperinge. At 11.00 on 2 August he was operated on. The splinters were removed from his abdomen, and his ileum, which had been punctured in several places, was repaired. X-ray photographs showed no splinters remained inside. Noel was tended to by a nurse, Sister Ida Leedam, who had been on the staff at the Royal Southern Hospital in Liverpool while Noel was a registrar there. Resting, drifting in and out of sleep, the next day he talked with Ida. After an initial relatively comfortable day on 3 August, showing concern for his men, Noel became restless during the evening and that night. He asked Ida if he could dictate a letter to Gladys. This he did, including his words, 'Duty called and called me to obey'. When he realized a chaplain was amongst the beds, he requested communion. At 05.00, Noel took his last communion. By 10.00, with the help of morphine he became quiet and restful. At 13.00 on 4 August 1917, three years after the start of the war, Noel Chavasse passed away, aged 32.

Noel was laid to rest at Brandhoek New Military Cemetery. It is reported that his men, who had been relieved from the trenches on 3 August, were present at his funeral, with many hospital staff and his horse. Noel's servant at the time, Private C.A. Rudd, died six days later from his wounds received in the same incident. He is buried a few yards away from Noel.[9] Noel's brother Bernard had been wounded in the knee in an earlier stage of the same battle just a mile or two south of where Noel and the 10/King's were advancing. When he heard of Noel's wound, he endeavoured to visit him, but arrived on 6 August. He was, however, able to garner the full story of Noel's last few days from the hospital and relay it to the family. Noel's twin brother Christopher had been stationed at Bullecourt on the Somme at the time of Noel's death, but during a short period of leave at the end of August he managed to visit Noel's grave. For Gladys, going to Paris in a Church Army post now seemed even more important, to fill the hole in her life and at the same time bring her closer to Noel's resting place.

On 14 September for his gallantry at the Third Battle of Ypres the Bar to Noel's Victoria Cross was announced in the *London Gazette*:

> Though severely wounded early in the action whilst carrying a wounded soldier to the dressing station, he refused to leave his post, and for two days, not only continued to perform his duties, but in addition, went out repeatedly under heavy fire to search for and attend to the wounded who were lying out. During these searches, although practically without food during this period, worn with fatigue and faint with his wound, he assisted to carry in a number of badly wounded men over heavy and difficult ground. By his extraordinary energy and inspiring example was instrumental in rescuing many wounded who would have otherwise undoubtedly succumbed under the bad weather conditions. This devoted and gallant officer subsequently died of his wounds.

In the first *Lily* edition of the new academic year, November 1917, it was announced that Noel had been killed in action. The report ends, '*Sic itur ad astra*' (this is the way to the stars).

1. The two surviving reports of Noel's are his Hilary (Spring) Term Report 1897 and Michaelmas (Autumn) Term Report 1897.
2. From a letter written to his grandmother, Mary Fawler Maude, in 1898.
3. In 1899 they rowed in the same boat, Noel at no. 2 and Christopher at stroke.
4. Christopher Chavasse returned to play against his old school on several occasions. On 30 November 1904 he organized a football team of 'Trinity Freshmen', including himself, to play against MCS; the school won 7–1. On 2 June 1906 he played cricket for the 'MCS Past' versus the 'Present'; the 'Present' scored 219, which included a 'lucky' 117 by Harold H. Dawes. In reply 'MCS Past' could only reach 86 before being bowled out, Christopher making 4 runs. On 19 June 1908 he returned to play cricket against the School; Old Boys 67 all out and 87 for 8, MCS 75 all out and 64 for 9. The game ended in a draw, with Christopher making 2 and 4 in the Old Boys' innings. Frank Wilkinson and Charles Maltby played for the School.
5. December 1905, 'Chavasse has been running for the OUAC'; December 1906, 'C.M. and N.G. Chavasse ... have been playing Lacrosse for the University Club'; March 1907, C.M. and N.G. Chavasse (Trinity) have both obtained their blues for running, the one in the 100 yards, and the other in the quarter mile'; November 1907, 'On the running path the twin brothers Chavasse have added lustre to our and their records, N.G. running a dead heat in the hundred against Cambridge, while C.M. won the quarter, with his brother a few inches behind. Those who know them will suspect a dead heat, for with them to beat a brother was, though they may deny it, food for tears. Mr Sherwood will perhaps remember years ago sending one of them with a bad headache over to the School House, and then finding him weeping in the playground – and remember answer to his rebuke, 'Please, Sir, it's not me that has a headache, it's my brother'; November 1908, 'The Chavasse twins represented us in the Inter Varsity athletic sports and the Olympic games.' It is interesting that the Olympic Games (the Fourth Olympiad, held in London) and the Chavasse brother's involvement only commanded this one small comment in *The Lily* of 1908.
6. The other four men pictured are Lieutenant Alan M. Wilkinson (top left), Hampshire Regiment and RFC, DSO, Oriel College. Captain Hugh K. Ward (top right), RAMC, MC, New College.

Second Lieutenant J.N. Richardson (lower left), Royal Berkshire Regiment, MC, Oriel College. Second Lieutenant Malcolm Mackinnon, Highland Light Infantry, MC, New College.

7. Published in *The Lily*, November 1916.
8. Lieutenant Colonel Martin-Leake was the first man ever to receive a double VC (VC and bar).
9. A servant or batman was an officer's uniformed orderly, performing voluntary extra duties, for which the officer paid. In addition to his normal duties, he was responsible for the officer's clothing and kit and also for preparing and serving meals. He would carry the officer's personal kit and often acted as a bodyguard.

Richard Colin CHRISTIE

19 October 1893 –15 December 1915

Rank and regiment: Lieutenant, 80th Field Company, Royal Engineers. **Medals awarded:** Victory, British War, 1914–1915 Star. **Theatre of War:** Western Front. **Memorial:** Corbie Communal Cemetery, France.

Richard Christie's father, George Robert Christie, was himself an old boy of MCS (joining in January 1870) and a contemporary of Richard Garnons Williams.[1] George married Lilian Emma (*née* Row) in January 1893, and Richard and his twin brother Robert Gilmer were born later that year, on 19 October. They had a younger brother Dennis Halsted, who was born on 16 April 1896. In 1911 Richard and Robert were living together in Petersfield, Hampshire. At this time their parents and younger brother were living in Brighton, Sussex. Richard's twin brother Robert (Major, Royal Engineers) survived the war, but Dennis (Second Lieutenant, 16th Battalion, The Royal Sussex Regiment) was killed in action in France on 21 September 1918.

Life at Magdalen College School (1911) and beyond

Richard Christie was initially educated at a day school in Brighton for one term (September 1903), then spent two and a half years at Bedales School (Petersfield) before attending Clayesmore School (then at Pangbourne, Berkshire) for a single term in the summer of 1906. In 1906, at the age of 13 he moved on to the Royal Naval College, Osborne,[2] and then progressed to the Royal Naval College at Dartmouth before being appointed to HMS *Cornwall* in 1910.[3] However, owing to defective vision he was forced to retire from the Navy only three months into his appointment. He therefore decided to apply and complete his education by doing a single year boarding at his father's old school, MCS.

Christie seems to have thrown himself into MCS life. The Form Fours rowing competition in the Hilary term of 1911 saw 'the most wonderful boat of the lot, and considering that two of its members had never touched an oar in their lives before, they have come on splendidly. With three days practice they practically gave up "deep sea fishing" altogether … and drive the boat along at quite a fast pace'. The four were Webb (Bow), Christie (2), Wilkinson (3) and Amon (Stroke). Three of the four were to die during the war. In the summer of 1911 Christie partnered R.H. Clapperton in the Doubles tennis tournament for that term. During the Swimming Day he excelled: in two races held at Cox's he came second (Senior Headers) and first (swimming on the back); then at the events held at Merton Baths he once again claimed a second (long distance dive; managing over two lengths underwater before surfacing) and first place (diving for plates; managing to collect nineteen out of twenty plates from the bottom of the pool). On the Sports Day of July 1911 in the mile race Christie finished in third place, 5 yards behind second-placed Wilkinson (the winner's time was 5 minutes and 5.25 seconds). In the team race (4 × 100 yard relay) he was part of the winning team. In November he was involved with the Debating Society, along with two other boys who were to lose their lives in the war, Dennis Webb and Victor Jessel.

That winter saw the fourth and last ever football fixture between MCS and Christie's former school, Clayesmore. The Football Prospects in *The Lily* that year read that Christie was 'the right build [for centre half], though [he] is not used to the association game'. However, the selectors saw fit to include him in the fixture versus his old school. The team, which included Victor Jessel and Leslie Roberton, journeyed to Pangbourne on Saturday, 4 November. Always a thrill for any boy to beat his old school, MCS and Christie beat Clayesmore 5–0; however, the description of Christie's play is amusing: 'runs straight and tries but has no knowledge of the game and tackles his own side, apparently, for choice.' Maybe he had split loyalties or was confused as which side he was playing for!

After leaving MCS at Christmas 1911 he joined the Royal Military Academy, Woolwich on 31 January 1912. While at Woolwich, he distinguished himself by winning three prizes in the Swimming Sports, for plate diving and lifesaving. He attended the RMA for two years, passing out on 18 December 1913 and taking a commission with the Royal Engineers. Christie was third in the order of merit (out of forty-eight) on leaving Woolwich, winning the prestigious Armstrong Memorial Prize for obtaining the highest mark in Advanced Electricity.

Christie's War

After gaining his commission with the Royal Engineers at the end of 1913, Christie spent some time at the Royal School of Military Engineering in Chatham. At the start of the war in August 1914, the Royal Engineer battalions already based at Chatham were deployed to defend the local area. Later, Christie was posted to the newly formed 80th Field Company, one of the initial two field companies assigned to the new 18th (Eastern) Division, part of Kitchener's Second New Army. In May 1915 the 18th Division moved to Salisbury Plain, and at the end of July sailed across to France. The Division initially concentrated near Flesselles, just north of Amien.

In December 1915 Christie was working with the 99th Trench Mortar Battery, Royal Field Artillery (99 Brigade, 33rd Division) and a battery of four trench mortars, commanded by Lieutenant Martin Kirke Smith.[4] On 14 December 1915, while at work in his trench near Fricourt on the Somme, Christie had seen a fellow officer who was outside his trench fall after being hit by sniper fire. Christie, rushing to his side, was himself shot by a sniper. Lieutenant Kirke Smith gallantly attempted to rescue the wounded Christie and bring him back to shelter; however,

Kirke Smith was killed whilst in the open. The battery then apparently went mad at the loss of their officers and 'swarmed over, and the snipers, no doubt scared, ceased fire, and then all the dead or alive were got in'. Christie was taken back 12 miles behind the front line to a Casualty Clearing Station, at La Neuville in Corbie, but died of his wounds on 15 December 1915, aged 22.

One of his section wrote, 'A more cheerful gentleman I never knew, and as brave as a lion, and a man I would have gone anywhere with, and he was loved by everybody in the Company.' Another letter sent to his parents and signed by all thirty-three men of his section is testimony to Christie's character:

> From the men of Lieutenant Christie's Section, 80th Field Company Royal Engineers, on active service:- He was more like a brother to us than an officer. A soldier every inch of him, he knew no fear. In fact, his bravery cost

Part of the memorial window in the Clayesmore School Chapel.

> him his life. He never asked us to do a job he would not do himself; and there is none among us but would willingly have laid down his life rather than anything should have happened to him. We cannot realize that he has passed away – to us he is not dead, nor ever will be. We shall always treasure the memory of as true, gallant, and noble a soldier as ever donned His Majesty's uniform. We hope you accept these few lines of condolence from 'Christie's boys' who are carrying on the work from which he was so untimely taken. We know it is poor solace for so great a loss, but we feel the loss, and our sympathy is with you.

Although Christie had only attended MCS for one year, his father sent £5.5s to the school to contribute to the War Memorial, the equivalent of several hundred pounds in 2014. His parents were obviously determined for their son's life not to have been in vain and forgotten, for their donation to Clayesmore was a stained glass window marking their son's sacrifice. In a letter to Clayesmore School his mother wrote, 'Every day of that dear son's was lived finely, and his record is one that I, as his sorrowing mother, can lift up her heart, and be proud of, but the loss is bitter and overwhelming. He always remembered Clayesmore and its chief affectionately and gratefully.' The window carries the simple motto 'Carry On'.

Richard Colin Christie was also one of the thirty-seven Old Clayesmorians to die in the First World War.

1. George Christie and Richard Garnons Williams were both active members of the MCS Debating Society in 1872.
2. Osborne House is a former royal residence on the Isle of Wight, where in January 1901 Queen Victoria died. From 1903 to 1921 it was used as a Junior Officer Training College for the Royal Navy.
3. HMS *Cornwall* was a relatively new ship, a Monmouth-class armoured cruiser commissioned in 1904. She was to later see action during the Battle of the Falkland Islands in 1914 and the Dardanelles Campaign in 1915/16.
4. Trench mortar organization was still in its infancy in 1915 and it was still common for infantry, artillery and engineers to be involved in the mortar weapon deployment.

Arthur Dukinfield DARBISHIRE

14 February 1879 – 26 December 1915

Rank and regiment: Private (S12370), 15th Battalion, Argyll and Sutherland Highlanders; Second Lieutenant, Royal Garrison Artillery. **Theatre of War:** Home front.[1] **Memorial:** Brookwood (United Kingdom 1914–1918) Memorial, Surrey.

Arthur was born in London on 14 February 1879, the eldest child of Samuel Dukinfield Darbishire (1846–1892) and Florence Darbishire (*née* Eckersley, 1854–1917). Arthur had two younger sisters; Helen (1881–1961) and Rachel (1883–1911). Helen, like her brother, was academically minded and became a lecturer in English and later the Principal of Somerville College, Oxford.

Arthur Darbishire.

Arthur's father Samuel was a medical doctor and famous Oxford rower in the late nineteenth century. Samuel was in the Balliol VIII that was Head of the River in 1873. In 1868, 1869 and 1870 he was stroke for Oxford in the Boat Race. In 1868 and 1869 the Oxford boat beat Cambridge and stretched their winning run to nine consecutive wins. In 1870 his inclusion in the Oxford boat caused some controversy as he was not resident in Oxford at the time, but still had sufficient association with Oxford to qualify. Cambridge protested, but Darbishire was allowed to row. Cambridge won by one and a half lengths and ended Oxford's nine-year winning streak. In 1869 he rowed in front of 500,000 spectators in the first transatlantic amateur boat race (a coxed four race) between Oxford and Harvard on the Thames. Oxford won. Due to the news coverage that the race achieved in the US it generated such interest in rowing that it was directly responsible for the formation of hundreds of rowing clubs in America.

Arthur's father came from a large family which originated in Bolton, Lancashire. Samuel's father and Arthur's grandfather (also Samuel Dukinfield Darbishire) was a slate quarry owner in Penmaenmawr, Wales, and a personal friend of William Gladstone, the Liberal Prime Minister, who was a frequent visitor to Penmaenmawr. One of Arthur's cousins, Godfrey Darbishire (son of his uncle Robert Dukinfield Darbishire, a naturalist), was to play for Wales alongside the MCS old boy Richard Davies Garnons Williams in the first ever International Rugby Union match between Wales and England in 1881 (see section on Garnons Williams).

Life at Magdalen College School (1890–1896) and beyond

Soon after Arthur was born, the Darbishire family moved to Oxford and were living at 15 New Inn Hall Street in 1881. In 1882 the family moved into the Magdalen Gate House,[2] opposite Magdalen College and on the corner of Rose Lane and the High Street, overlooking the Botanic Gardens. It was here where Arthur's two sisters were born. The family remained at the Gate House until Samuel Darbishire's retirement in 1887, then moved to Caernarvonshire, Wales, when Arthur was 8 years old. As a young child Arthur had rheumatic fever, which left him with heart trouble. It has been reported that due to his medical condition he was not sent to a boarding school. However, after attending Merton House School in Penmaenmawr, MCS record him as a boarder from 1890.[3] Along with Arthur Steward, Darbishire was one of two boys of 'the fifty' to be present at the school prior to and after the transfer of boarding location to the new school house building by the Plain in 1894. After his father's long illness and death in 1892, Arthur's family moved back to Oxford in 1894, initially to 20 Polstead Road, later to 22 Winchester Road, then eventually to Grey House, Boars Hill. Whether Arthur remained boarding or became a day boy after his family returned to Oxford is not known.

An indication of his ultimate career in biology was given when in 1893 he won Mr Manley's prize for practical work in science. Two years later he won Mr Brownrigg's prize for science.

Predictably, his heart condition stopped him playing any sport while at school; however, after leaving MCS he did return to play in a few old boys' games. In 1897 he played football in the same side as Charles Brownrigg (who was in goal) and in 1900 he played cricket for the old boys, this time with Mr Brownrigg in opposition opening the batting for the school.

In 1896 Arthur left MCS, and in October 1897 took his place at Balliol College to read Natural Sciences. He achieved a Second in Zoology (BA degree) in 1901. While at Balliol he was very involved with rowing but did not compete himself, because of his weak heart. However, he was so well thought of that he was awarded an 'honorary' eights blazer and cap.

In 1901 Arthur worked as a demonstrator in Comparative Anatomy in Oxford, then in 1902 he moved to Manchester University for three years and eventually to Imperial College[4] in 1905 until 1911 as a lecturer in Heredity. In 1904 he found time to take a BSc in Zoology. In his final year at Imperial College he published a book on Breeding and the Mendelian Discovery (see bibliography).[5] Later in 1911 Arthur took up his final university post as a Lecturer in Genetics at Edinburgh University. Sadly, his youngest sister Rachel died (aged 28) in the same year.

Arthur was noted for his 'Untiring diligence in research, minute accuracy in recording, dispassionate criticism of premature theories or interpretations ... a love of the practical ... side of his work, and a growing consciousness of the philosophic basis of his subject'. It was predicted at the time that he would have gone far as a biologist. As it was, he was already a published academic who was a 'successful teacher; he lectured without notes, was admirable in diagrams and illustrations, and got into touch with an audience at once'. So much so that in July 1914, while on a lecture tour in America, he was offered a research professorship at the University of Missouri, Columbia. On 4 August 1914 Britain declared war on Germany and Darbishire responded to the offer by saying he would not leave England while they were at war.

Darbishire's War

Due to his previous poor health Darbishire was told that he would never be fit enough to serve in the army. He therefore trained himself for munitions work at Heriot Watt Engineering College, but found it difficult ultimately to obtain a suitable job with the munitions industry. However, he was determined to serve his country and on 22 July 1915 he enlisted at Edinburgh as a private in the 14th Battalion, Argyll and Sutherland Highlanders. His initial training was in England at the Witley Camp, Godalming, Surrey, then when he joined B-Company of the 15th Battalion Argyll and Sutherland Highlanders he was stationed at Gailes Camp, Ayrshire.

In September 1915 Darbishire applied for a commission and on 17 December he received a letter from Major H.F. Dawson to tell him that his application had been accepted and that he was to be gazetted to officer status.[6] He replied on 20 December acknowledging receipt of the notification and that he understood he would be serving with the Royal Garrison Artillery, stationed at Plymouth. He signed the letter 'your obedient servant A.D. Darbishire'. Six days later, Arthur Darbishire died of cerebral spinal meningitis in Kirklandside Fever Hospital, Kilmarnock on 26 December 1915, aged 36.[7] On 29 December a letter was received at the Gailes Camp officially confirming that he had been appointed to Second Lieutenant in the Royal Garrison Artillery, Special Reserve at Plymouth.

Arthur's surviving sister, Helen, took care of the administrative duties after Arthur's death because their mother Florence became seriously ill. His mother eventually died in 1917 two years after her son, aged 63.

1. Arthur Darbishire was not eligible for any campaign medals.
2. Magdalen Gate House was later to become the home of the Cannan family, and the author May Wedderburn Cannan, from 1895 to 1920. See section on The School, The War Years.

3. It has been indicated (http://www.headington.org.uk/oxon/sunningwell/17_darbishire.html) that Arthur was taught at home by a Governess with his two sisters, prior to attending MCS. In the entry in the School Register at the time of joining MCS it is claimed that he previously attended Merton House School. The MCS School Examination Lists then establish his presence at MCS from July 1890 until the summer of 1896.
4. The Royal College of Science.
5. When Arthur Darbishire died in 1915 he left unfinished a second book, with the proposed title *An Introduction to Biology*. His sister Helen completed the publication of this book for her brother (see bibliography). In addition to his two books he also published various papers on heredity.
6. Sir Arthur Shipley (the eminent Zoologist, Master of Christ's College Cambridge, and later Vice-Chancellor of the University of Cambridge) completed Darbishire's officer application forms to certify his moral character. James Leigh Strachan Davidson (Master of Balliol College) signed to certify that Darbishire had a good standard of education.
7. He had been taken to the hospital from Gailes Camp in an unconscious condition and died shortly after admission.

Harold Henry DAWES

8 May 1888 – 30 October 1917

Rank and regiment: Private (8352, 762365), 28th Battalion (Artists' Rifles), The London Regiment. **Medals awarded:** Victory, British War. **Theatre of War:** Western Front. **Memorial:** Tyne Cot Memorial, Belgium.

Harold Henry Dawes was born on 8 May 1888 in Chiswick, London, the only child of Ralph Jones Dawes and Sarah Annie Dawes (*née* Chappell). Both his parents were musicians, describing themselves in census records as professors of singing, so it not surprising that Harold was to join Magdalen College School as a chorister.

Life at Magdalen College School (1897–1906) and beyond

Harold Dawes joined MCS in September 1897 as a 9-year-old chorister. He was to be at the school for nine years, was an outstanding sportsman and left as a Prefect at the Christmas of 1906. Like his parents, Harold was a 'first-rate musician, and one of the mainstays of the [school] choir'. He won the Form II Maths Prize in 1898 and Music Prize in 1899, the Form IV Prize in 1902 and the School's Music Prize in 1903. In 1901 he sat on the Games Committee as the chorister representative. Very able with his school work, in 1903 and 1904 he gained Junior Certificates and in 1906 a Senior Certificate for his academic studies. In his final year at MCS he presented the library with a copy of Arthur Conan Doyle's novel *Sir Nigel*.

Representing MCS at football, Dawes eventually got his full colours in 1906 after rising through the ranks of the chorister team, the 2nd XI (in 1904) and eventually the 1st XI in 1905 and 1906. *The Lily* of December 1906 records that 'Dawes [at the back] is the most persistent trier' and his character is reported thus: 'As left-back has shown good form: is not fast but gets back more quickly than used to be the case: is a strong kick.' Ever-present in this team were forwards Leslie Hoyne-Fox and Francis Pitts. Dawes played for the MCS chorister team against Christ Church choristers on five occasions between 1897 and 1903, appearing in goal on the first three occasions.

Harold Dawes.

Dawes also played hockey for the school in 1904 and 1905. Described in *The Lily* as 'The strongest hitter in the team and can clear well from full back: has improved in pace but is still rather slow when pressed. Was very useful', he obtained colours in his final season.

It is probably correct to rate Dawes as one of the best cricketers the school has ever produced, both as a batsman and as a fast bowler. *The Lily* records that 'as a youngster he was the terror of the junior sides which came against him, and he was for four years in the School [1st] XI.' In 1898 he played for the MCS Choristers versus Christ Church Choristers. In 1901 he was playing for the MCS U15 side and also the MCS 2nd XI, taking 4–10 against Oxford High School 1st XI. In 1902 for the U15 side he took 6 wickets in one game against Summerfields. In 1903 he broke into the 1st XI, taking 3–20 in the win over Abingdon. He received his half colours in 1903 aged 15 and his character profile in *The Lily* read: 'Will be very useful in years to come. A straight bowler who has, though only occasionally serviceable to the eleven, done great things for the "under fifteens" and other teams. Has a good idea of batting but at present retreats from a fast bowler and thereby loses his wicket. Must learn to field and if possible run.' In May 1904 in the 106-run win over Abingdon, coming in at no. 2, Dawes made 60 with the bat and took 4–28 with the ball. On the last day of the 1904 season, in July, he took 5–16 in the win over St Mark's School. Playing in the same side was Wilfrid Pearson. Harold's cricketing character profile in *The Lily* of 1904 reads: 'Has the makings of an excellent bat with crisp off strokes. Has a really good cut but too fond of trying to bring it off from a straight ball. Has improved in pace as a bowler, gets quickly off the pitch and seldom becomes loose. Not quick in the field but can throw.' In the 1905 season Dawes captained the 1st XI side and obtained full colours. The 1905 team was to lose only one game 'mainly to the all-round ability of Dawes'. In May a 13-run win over Abingdon saw Dawes take 4–25 with the ball. Then, in the emphatic victory over Leighton Park School in June he made 103 not out with the bat and took 5–4 with the ball. The only loss came in the return game against Abingdon in the last match of the season on 15 July, when Dawes made 81 and took 3–54. His cricket profile in *The Lily* read: 'One of the best cricketers we have had for some time. A fast scoring bat with a good off drive and a nice wrist cut, but sometimes loses his wicket through impatience. A hard working bowler who bowls very well when he is getting wickets; best on a fast ground as his balls come very quickly off the pitch.' [This sounds amusing or even painful, but all cricketing buffs will know what the writer of the time was trying to say]. In the same year, Dawes also won the 'Throwing the Cricket Ball' event at Sports Day, with a throw of 75 yards, despite the rain making the ball rather slippery. Disappointingly, in 1906 all school-versus-school cricket matches had to be scratched due to continuous outbreaks of mumps throughout the summer term. The only games that took place were those against adult college and touring sides. In the game versus the 'MCS Past' team, which included Christopher Chavasse, Dawes made 117 with the bat. Against St Catherine's he took 5–55 with the ball. Finally, against Oxford City 2nd XI in June, Dawes played his last match for the school, scoring an unbeaten 144 in the MCS total of 227 for 2. In reply, Oxford City were bowled out for 114, with Dawes taking 3–31. A fitting way to end his school cricketing career, but a shame he did not have the chance to add to his 1st XI statistics versus other schools. No school averages are given for 1906 because no inter-school matches were played; however, studying Dawes' previous three seasons' averages does make one wonder what he would have been capable of in his final year had it not been for the mumps scare.

Harold H. Dawes: 1st XI Averages

Bowling

Year	Overs	Maidens	Runs	Wickets	Average
1903	14.1	1	35	4	8.7
1904	175.2	30	472	40	11.8
1905	205.5	46	608	45	13.2
1906	no inter-school matches were played in 1906 due to a mumps scare				

Batting

Year	Innings	Not Outs	Highest Score	Total Runs	Average
1903	5	3	11	13	6.5
1904	15	1	60	172	12.3
1905	16	2	103	466	33.2
1906	no inter-school matches were played in 1906 due to a mumps scare				

Dawes' cricketing exploits limited his rowing experience to that of competing in the Form Fours in 1900 and 1901.

After leaving MCS, Harold Dawes joined the Bank of England at its headquarters in London. In 1908 Dawes and another MCS old boy, R.V.N. Wiggins, who he had previously played cricket with and against, were Secretary and Captain respectively, of the Bank of England Cricket team.[1] In 1909 Dawes was still subscribing to *The Lily* and in 1911 he and his Bank of England colleague R.V.N. Wiggins returned to Oxford to play hockey for the Old Boys against the school team that included Frank Wilkinson, Edward Andrews, Victor Jessel and Charles Brownrigg. The game ended in a 4–4 draw.

Dawes' War

Dawes attested (or enlisted) for the army on 10 December 1915, and joined the ranks of the 2/28th Battalion (Artists' Rifles), London Regiment. However, the Bank would not release Dawes for service, his occupation being 'starred' or deemed vital to the war economy; therefore Dawes entered the Reserves. He was finally released from the Bank and posted for Home Service (training for two months) on 6 September 1916.

Ironically, while at MCS Dawes had been an active member of the Debating Society and in the open debate of 1902, where the proposed motion was 'The abolition of war is desirable', Harold 'who spoke from the practical point of view ... denounced war as expensive and ineffective'. In this debate the House decided war was desirable by a majority of ten. Fourteen years on, the war was real and Dawes was journeying to the front.

On 4 November 1916 Dawes sailed from Southampton and landed in France two days later. He was probably one of the 150-strong draft of men to join his battalion at Hesdin, 14 miles to the east of Montreuil (home of British GHQ on the Western Front from March 1916), on 9 November 1916. The London Regiment amalgamated the 1/28th and the 2/28th Battalions at this time, with the newly formed 1/28th Battalion becoming an officer training battalion and part of the GHQ troops. Dawes would have spent his time training according to the Brigade syllabus as well as carrying out guard duties at the GHQ facilities in Montreuil, a pleasant, picturesque town surrounded by beautiful countryside. The non-commissioned officers were also given free time to undertake pastime activities and play sports. Behind tranquil scenes at Montreuil, the commanding officers of the British army, headed at this time by Field Marshal Sir John French, coordinated the British efforts and planned the strategies for the battlefield.

On 25 June 1917 half the battalion moved with GHQ troops by motorbus to Bajus, 18 miles east of Hesdin, the other half remaining in Hesdin. On 27 June they did a four-hour route march to Cambligneul. The next day saw a two-and-half-hour route march to reach Ecoivres, where they joined the 190 Brigade, 63rd (Royal Naval) Division. The two halves of the battalion were reunited at Aubrey Camp by 5 July 1917. Two days later saw Dawes and the rest of C-Company fitted with box respirators and undergoing tests in preparation for the coming deployment in the trenches. The box respirators were the best designed gas masks used in the war. They were designed in two pieces: a mouthpiece which was connected via a hose to a box filter which contained chemicals to neutralize the gas. Two designs of box respirators were used, but by 1917 the small box respirator was favoured, and it is probable this version was issued to Dawes. The advantages of the SBR was that it included a close-fitting rubberized mask with eye pieces, and the box filter was more compact and could be worn around the neck.

The battalion spent a few days in the trenches before marching to Bailleul on 22 July 1917 where they relieved the 2nd (Hawke) Battalion, 63rd Royal Naval Division entrenched in a railway cutting, remaining there until 7 August. They returned to Aubrey Camp and spent a few days in training before going back into trenches on 16 August, this time relieving 5th (Nelson) Battalion, before returning to the railway cutting on 25 August. Casualties were suffered almost every day during this time in the trenches and Dawes will have witnessed the true horrors of daily warfare. The battalion was relieved during the night of 2 September and marched back to Aubrey Camp, arriving at 02.40. The next few days were spent in training, including night marches wearing box respirators.

By 10 September, the battalion were back in the trenches near Oppy Wood, and for four days did not suffer any casualties. They were relieved by the 22nd Battalion, London Regiment (47th Division) on 24 September and marched back to the railway cutting from where they travelled 40 miles south-west by train to Écoivres and then by motorbus a further 14 miles north-east to La Comté, near Béthune, where they were allowed a day of rest before training began again on 26 September.

On 2 October the battalion marched 7 miles south to Ligny-Saint-Floche, where they entrained for a 35-mile journey north to Cassel, west of Poperinge. From here they marched 5 miles to Rietveld. Here they trained until moving on to Houtkerque on 7 October to continue their training. On 25 and 26 October they moved forward to the Dombre camp and Reigersberg camp respectively, before reporting to Nelson Battalion at Irish Farm and going into the line at Albatross Farm on 28 October 1917.

On 30 October 1917 the battalion launched an attack on German positions as part of the second stage of the Second Battle of Passchendaele. The 1/28/London were caught by German artillery fire at their jumping-off line and made only slight progress in deep mud against heavy machine-gun fire and were unable to reach their objectives. Harold Dawes, aged 29, was last seen wounded in action, and at the end of the day was reported missing. It was feared that while being taken by stretcher to the dressing station he and the stretcher party were hit by a shell. Harold Dawes' body was never found; he is commemorated at the Tyne Cot Memorial. He was one of 324 men from the battalion that were either killed, wounded or reported missing in action during 28–31 October 1917.

1. Ironically, four years earlier Dawes had been an expert witness for the defence when Wiggins' brother had pleaded 'not guilty' in a mock trial set up by the Headmaster Mr Brownrigg and the Usher Mr Pullan, in which Mr Brownrigg even provided wigs and gowns for the occasion.

Cecil MacMillan DYER

17 January 1894 – 9 April 1915

Rank and regiment: Second Lieutenant, 6th Battalion (att. 4th), Rifle Brigade. **Medals awarded:** Victory, British War, 1914–1915 Star. **Theatre of War:** Western Front. **Memorial:** Ypres (Menin Gate) Memorial, Belgium.

Cecil MacMillan Dyer was the second son of Louis Dyer and Margaret Anne Dyer (*neé* MacMillan). He had an older brother, Charles Volney Dyer (b. 1890) and a younger sister, Rachel Margaret Dyer (b. 1897).

Cecil's father Louis was born in Chicago, USA and after studying at Harvard moved to the UK in order to study at Balliol College, Oxford (matriculating in 1874). He became an assistant professor of Greek at Harvard (1881–87), a lecturer at Lowell Institute (1889) before returning to Balliol College in 1893 for a further three years. He was acting professor of Greek at Cornell University (1895–96), lectured before the Royal Institution in 1896 and in 1900 he gave a series of lectures at the University of California and at many colleges and universities across the USA.

In the 1901 census the family is recorded as living at 68 Banbury Road (Sunbury Lodge), Oxford, where they remained until Louis' death in 1908.

Cecil's maternal grandfather, Alexander MacMillan, founded MacMillan Publishers with his brother Daniel. Cecil was a second cousin to Maurice Harold MacMillan, 'Super Mac', who was later to become the British Prime Minister.

Life at Magdalen College School (1906–1908) and beyond

Cecil Dyer joined MCS at the age of 12 and was only to stay at the school for two years before having to move. In his second and final year he rowed in the Form Four rowing competition and was in the same boat as Graham Matheson. After Dyer's father died in 1908 his family moved from Oxford to London and Cecil left MCS to board at Clifton College for the final four years (Form IVβ to VI) of his school education. Clifton College was the *alma mater* of the man who was to become the overall commander of the British army on the Western Front during the First World War, Field Marshal Douglas Haig. In 1912 Dyer left Clifton and went up to Christ's College, Cambridge.

In 1914 he was elected a member of the British Ornithologists' Union, after having shown a great interest in ornithology at school. While at Cambridge he was recognized as 'one of the two leading spirits in ornithology . . . and did a great deal of work in the neighbourhood, chiefly in estimating the number of each species of bird in the various districts and finding out in which spots they breed. He kept careful lists of the results, and his work was most accurate . . . he added a good deal to our knowledge of the birds of remote villages to the west of Cambridge'.

His education at Cambridge was then rudely interrupted after his second year when war broke out in the August of 1914. Having already been a private in the OTC at Clifton and continuing this at Cambridge, it is not surprising that Dyer immediately volunteered for the Army's Special Reserve.

His nickname at Clifton appears to have been 'Bill', as it is by this name that he is referred to in a letter from one of his contemporaries just before the Battle of Loos in 1915.[1]

Dyer's War

In August 1914 Dyer obtained a commission in the 6th Battalion, Rifle Brigade at Sheerness. As he was under 21 years of age, he needed permission to join the Army, and his uncle, G.A. MacMillan, duly sent a telegraph to the War Office

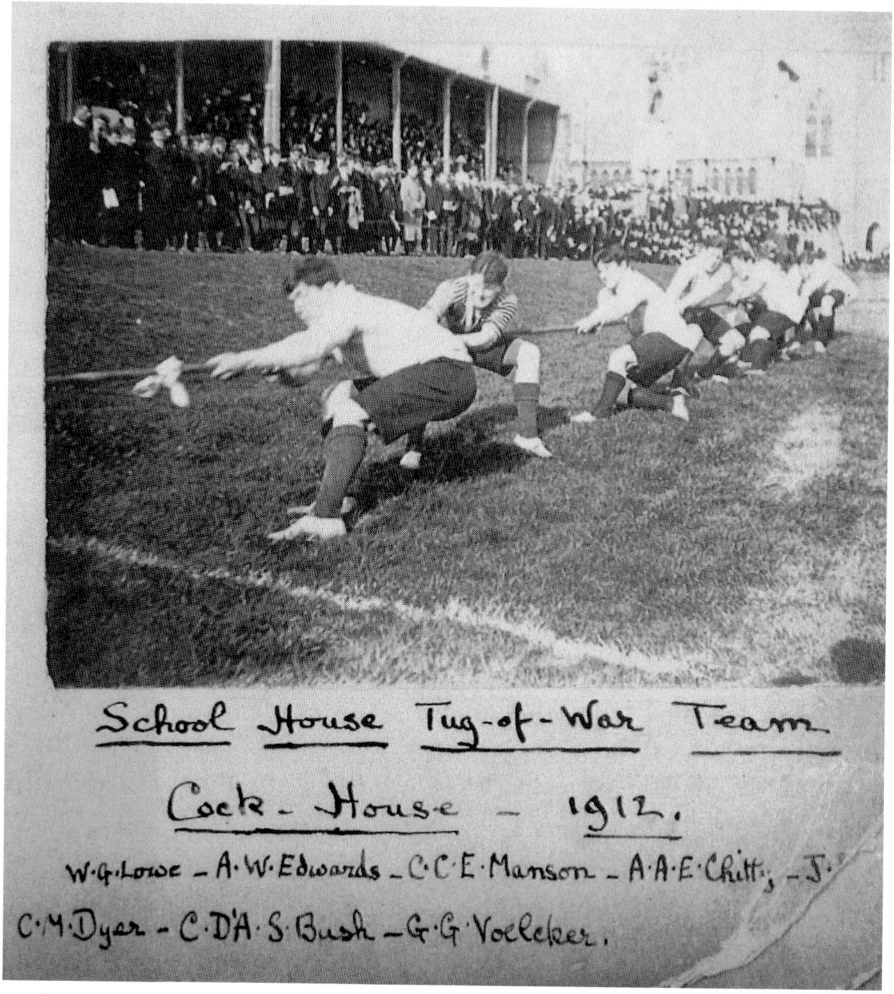

School House Tug-of-War Team
Cock-House - 1912.
W·G·Lowe - A·W·Edwards - C·C·E·Manson - A·A·E·Chitty - J·
C·M·Dyer - C·D'A·S·Bush - G·G·Voelcker.

Cecil Dyer (position six, mostly hidden) competing in the Clifton College Tug-of-War competition in 1912.

giving permission in October 1914. Dyer transferred to the 4th Battalion, which was attached to the 57th Division, and went out to the front in December 1914.

Dyer, along with 27 officers and 921 other ranks sailed on board *Austerlind* from Southampton and landed at Le Havre on 22 December. They marched overnight on 23 December to their billets at Blaringhem. The battalion spent the next two weeks digging trenches, before embarking on a 13-mile march to Meteren and then on to the front line trenches at Voormezeele near St Eloi. After spending four days in the trenches in dreadful conditions the battalion was relieved by the Argyll and Sutherland Highlanders. The battalion's war diary records that the march of about 8 miles to the reserve location of Boeschepe on

11 January 1915 was a considerable tax on the men's endurance, their feet having suffered in the trenches and through the want of boots. The following day saw 100 men in hospital unable to march further.

The respite in reserve did not last long as they were back in the trenches four days later. The hard winter was taking its toll on the battalion, and by 20 January 1915, 313 men were either sick or unfit for duty. On 4 February, Dyer was taken to the 2nd British Red Cross Hospital at Rouen with frostbitten feet. Five days later he was discharged to a convalescent home in Nice. The weather across Europe at the time was particularly bad, with biting winds, and even the Kaiser returned home from the Eastern front with a chill.

Dyer rejoined his battalion at Reninghelst on 13 March 1915 and was straight back into action, with his battalion moving overnight to St Eloi, where at 03.00 on 15 March they launched an unsuccessful counter-attack against the Germans. The next respite came only on 24 March when the battalion moved back into reserve and were billeted just south of Poperinge for the rest of the month.

On 5 April the battalion moved to Ypres and two days later took over trenches in Polygon Wood from the French. It was in these trenches that Dyer was killed in action, aged 21. Initially, there was some confusion whether his date of death was 8 or 9 April. Although the war diary reports his death on 8 April, for certificate purposes the date of 9 April 1915 was agreed. Second Lieutenant Cecil Dyer was buried in a field on the west side of Polygon Wood, by the side of Charles Aubrey Vintcent (Pembroke College, Rugby Blue) with whom he was at Cambridge, but due to the processes of war over the coming years their graves were lost. They are both commemorated on the Menin Gate at Ypres.

Cecil Dyer is also commemorated on the Clifton College Memorial Arch (designed by Charles Holden), 'a mini Menin Gate', along with a further 577 Clifton boys and staff lost during the First World War. A bronze statue of Douglas Haig lies just beyond. Fittingly, both are within a stone's throw of where Dyer boarded in Clifton's School House and where he pulled in the Tug-of-War competition of 1912.

1. The letter (24 September 1915) is written by George Whitehead (53rd Squadron, RAF and RFA), reminiscing about his Clifton days and seemingly unaware that 'Bill Dyer' had been killed in April. George was killed in action on 17 October 1918.

Roger Gwynne FIELD

14 October 1896 – 20 December 1916

Rank and regiment: Private (9352), 20th (Service) Battalion (3rd Public Schools), Royal Fusiliers (City of London Regiment). **Medals awarded:** Victory, British War. **Theatre of War:** Western Front. **Memorial:** Assevillers New British Cemetery, France.

Roger Gwynne Field was born at 19 Abbey Road in the parish of St Thomas, Oxford, the youngest child of Walter William Field and Catherine Rhoda Field (*née* Williams). He had an older sister, Catherine Myfanwy Field (b. 1892) and a brother, Francis William Field (b. 1894). His father originally studied law but by the time Roger was born had become a brewer of ales.

In 1901 the family were living at 23 Park End Street in the parish of St Thomas, Oxford. The family moved to 41 Park End Street some time before 1903. At the time of the 1911 census they were living at Abbey House, 4 Botley Road, Oxford.

His brother Francis also attended Magdalen College School and served with the Queen's Own Oxfordshire Hussars during the First World War.

Life at Magdalen College School (1907–1914) and beyond

Roger Field joined his older brother as a day boy at MCS in January 1907, starting in Form I. Evidently a good orator, in 1911, while in Form IV, he won the Master's Prize for repetition and elocution. In 1913 he won the Form Vb prize for repetition and recitation, repeating this win again in 1914, at the same time as Donovan Leicester won the R&R Prize for Form VI. In 1913 Roger Field was an active member of the Debating Society, on one occasion contributing a good argument against Home Rule for Ireland. Interestingly, this debate was presided over by Charles Brownrigg, who was an Irishman himself. Amongst Field's peers taking part in the discussion were John Callender, Gordon Bradley and Victor Jessel. Masters were regular participants in these debates, with the Usher, Mr Pullan, and an assistant master Mr Etty, joining this particular debate.

The boys would train and practise gymnastics throughout the year, then in June each year those good enough to enter the school competition would compete at the University Gymnasium. Field competed in the junior competition in 1911 and 1912 and the senior competition in 1913 and 1914, winning the Cup in 1913. From the results of each discipline during these years (rings, horizontal bars, parallel bars, rope, horse, exercise) Field was evidently a talented gymnast and justifiably Captain of Gymnastics in his final two years at school.

Playing football for the U15 side in 1911, Field was described as 'rather clumsy, but hard working'. Initially in defence for the U15 team, at half back, when he matured to play with the 1st XI in 1913 he swopped to playing as a forward, at inside-right, in the side captained by Victor Jessel. He received half colours in 1913 and was described as being 'on the slow side, and not to be relied on to alarm a goal-keeper; has improved lately, and has fed Searby quite well.' As if to confirm this observation, in the game against Abingdon in December 1913, with Abingdon leading 2–0, Field found himself in front of an open goal, only to place the ball wide! Abingdon went on to win 3–0 against the MCS side weakened without Victor Jessel. Fittingly, in his last match for the school, Field played against a very strong Old Boys' XI that was captained by the talented Frank Wilkinson; alongside him, playing in defence and thwarting Roger in his efforts to get on the score sheet, was his brother Francis. The old boys won 9–2 in a game that did not become one-sided until the last quarter of an hour.

For hockey Roger Field played in the 1st XI in four consecutive seasons 1911–1914, deservedly receiving his full colours in 1914, with *The Lily* recording,

'Much improved as a back player, though he occasionally misses the ball altogether. A little lacking in pace, but watches the game well.' Once again, his last game for the school was against an old boy side that included his brother. Played on the Lincoln College ground due to the unfit state of School Field, the old boys again beat the School (5–8).

In 1911 Field started playing for the U15 cricket team, alongside Edward Andrews and John Callender. His one direct mention in *The Lily* of 1911 was a comment on his 'excellent fielding and catching'. By 1913 he had progressed to playing in the 1st XI, but despite making no significant contribution during the season he actually ended up top of the batting averages (9 innings; 41 runs; 13* highest score; 6 not outs; 13.7 average), indicating a relatively weaker 1st XI side than normal. *The Lily* of July that year reports that he 'has some idea of batting, and watches the ball, but doesn't always play straight. As a bowler gets very short and wouldn't frighten a good batsman.'

The 1914 cricket season at MCS will always be significant for the reason that it was the first season using the new cricket pavilion (built in 1913). Since then, its understated shape has been as much a part of the beautiful scenery and view on School Field as the Botanical Gardens and Magdalen Tower. If any old boy, or Old Waynflete as they are now referred to, pictures School Field it is undoubtedly this building that is in the centre of their memory. The first match to be played from the new pavilion did not disappoint. Bloxham School were the visiting team. Batting first, MCS scored only 88, with Roger Field being caught without scoring. In reply, Bloxham edged their way to the MCS total, reaching 79 for 7, then 87 for 9. A single was then snatched and the scores were level. With the next ball, Field's bowling partner K.L. Dams took the final wicket; a 'remarkable' tied match, wrote *The Lily*. Roger Field had played his part, finishing with 6–24 off 17 overs; there was one run out and Dams took the other 2 wickets. Only two home games later, on 26 May, the pavilion was properly 'christened' in a game versus the Master's XI. While chasing down the School's score of 142, H.P. Hansell, on his way to 25 not out, 'had the honour of being the first to break a window in the new pavilion'.

Field had a good summer with the ball and top of his performances were 5–61 against Abingdon; 5–74 against Magdalen College 'A' XI; and 6–32 against Ruskin College. Thankfully, the 1914 season had been a more successful season than the 1913 season and this time with a batting average of 6.9 Field did not even feature in the top five of the batting averages. His bowling efforts did, however, put him at the top of the bowling averages (120 overs; 21 maidens; 356 runs; 33 wickets; 10.8 average) for 1914. *The Lily* records that Roger Field was 'the steadiest bowler on the side as he keeps a good length and can go on for a long time. Rather disappointing as a bat and deserved to do better: slow in the field.' Roger Field was awarded half colours.

Roger Field did not go on to University but opted to leave MCS when in Form Vb, in July 1914, to take a position in a local bank. Living in Oxford and still in touch with his old school, Field returned to School Field to play cricket on 20 May 1915 for the C.B. Shepperd Esq XI versus the School. Despite making a brief last wicket partnership with his old headmaster Charles Brownrigg, the school won by 41 runs. At about this time, when a Royal Fusilier Battalion was stationed in Oxford, Field felt compelled to join up.

Field's War

After joining the 20th Battalion, Royal Fusiliers (98 Brigade, 33rd Division), Field and the entire infantry of the 33rd Division assembled at Clipstone Camp, Nottinghamshire in July 1915. After progressively moving south, both the infantry and the artillery of the 33rd Division concentrated on Salisbury Plain in August 1915. On 8 November Her Majesty the Queen inspected the division at Figheldean Down, then four days later entrainment began, and between 16 and 21 November the infantry of the 33 Division and Artillery Division of the 54th East Anglian Regiment arrived at the Morbecque area. The 33 Division had arrived in France and was to stay on the Western Front for the remainder of the war. After being attached to the 19 Brigade on 21 November, the 20 RF were transferred to 19 Infantry Brigade (33 Division) on 27 November. On 21 and 22 November the 20/RF occupied front line trenches for the first time, east of Cambrai, taking its first casualty on 22 November. At the end of November the battalion moved to rear quarters at a tobacco factory in Béthune. For the remainder of 1915 the 20/RF were rotated in and out of front line sections in the area in and around Béthune (using billets at Annequin and Beuvry and in reserve at Le Quesnoy amongst others).

As was usual for front line divisions, its three brigades were rotated from the front line, to reserve line, to the rear. Of the four battalions in each brigade two were at the front and two were in reserve at any one time. Finally, the four companies of each battalion rotated between front line and support trenches. The time spent in each line or reserve depended on many factors, but over the course of the next three years the 20/RF endured this rotation system, only to be interrupted by offensives.

As well as the hazards of patrols, bombardments and the constant threat from snipers, the 20/RF were involved in three offensive actions during 1916. On 10 July at 03.00 the battalion left by train for Longueau (Amien), relocating further south to participate in the Battle of the Somme. Specifically, the 20/RF had a major part in the Battle of Bazentin Ridge and the attacks on High Wood between 14 and 21 July. The 19 Brigade was relieved by the 100 Brigade on 20 July; sixteen officers and 375 other ranks had been killed, wounded or were missing. The 33 Brigade withdrew to reorganize and reinforce. Fast forwarding to the heavy rain period of late October and early November, the 20/RF was involved in several actions to take German trenches (the capture of Dewdrop and Boritska trenches) in the Albert area; nine officers and 174 other ranks had been killed, wounded or were missing.

At the start of December 1916 the 20/RF had been sent to the rear at Merelessart to rest. Then on 8 December they started the long, convoluted journey back to the front. By 14 December they were back in support trenches at Priez Farm, then on 18 December they moved in to relieve the 1st Battalion, the Cameronians (Scottish Rifles) at Rancourt, opposite St Pierre Vaast wood. During the relief two officers were wounded by shrapnel even before they had reached the reserve trench. Between 18 and 22 December the front line companies were relieved each night from the support and reserve companies. Over this period a hard frost was succeeded by a thaw, and trenches and tracks became impassable in places. As a consequence, movement was very slow and relief of the companies in the front line, always carried out under cover of dark, occupied most of each night. During this time it is reported in the Battalion War Diary that as well as the two officers that were wounded, one other rank was killed, fourteen were wounded and two were missing. The one other rank killed was Roger Field on 20 December. He had just turned 20 years of age.

Arthur Edward FOSTER

17 June 1893 – 10 April 1917

Rank and regiment: Private (1487), 18th (Service) Battalion (1st Public School's), Royal Fusiliers; Second Lieutenant, 3rd Battalion (att. 7th), The King's Own Yorkshire Light Infantry. **Medals awarded:** Victory, British War, 1914–1915 Star. **Theatre of War:** Western Front. **Memorial:** Neuville-Bourjonval British Cemetery, France.

Arthur Edward Foster was the youngest of six children born to Myles Birket Foster and Christine Foster (*née* Lorimer). He was born on 17 June 1893 at 6 Dean Road, Willesden Green, London. He had two sisters, Dorothy Margaret (b. 1885) and Mabel Christine (b. 1888), and three brothers, Myles Birket (b. 1884), John Lorimer (b. 1886)[1] and Robert Spence (b. 1891).

Sadly, their mother was to die in 1901, leaving their father, who was a composer and music examiner, a widower. The eldest son, Myles Birket, died on 19 November 1918.

Life at Magdalen College School (1906–1908) and beyond

Arthur Foster joined MCS in 1906, at the same time as Cecil Dyer. Dyer and Foster were at the school for the same six terms, and in the same form as each other in their second year. Arthur's brother Robert was already at the school (MCS 1902–1910) and had been a chorister from 1902 to 1905. While at MCS Arthur was a member of the Debating Society. In 1908 after obtaining his Junior Certificate in the Lower Fifth Form he left school to work in London and ultimately became an engineer, while his class mate Dyer went on to Clifton College. When war broke out in August 1914 Arthur was an engineering apprentice for the North Eastern Marine Engineering Company and was studying at Chelsea Polytechnic.

His brother Robert matriculated to Magdalen College, Oxford in 1911. During the war, while serving with the Shropshire Light Infantry he was wounded twice but went on to join the King's African Rifles in East Africa and survived the war.

Foster's War

Arthur Foster enlisted in the 18th Battalion (1st Public Schools), Royal Fusiliers on 3 September 1914, aged 21. At the same time, his brother Robert joined the King's (Shropshire) Light Infantry. Also in the 18/RF at this time were ex-MCS boys and fellow 21-year-olds Horace Amon and Frank Wilkinson. Foster's time at MCS coincided with Wilkinson and remarkably they shared the same birth date, both being born on 17 June 1893. The 18/RF were initially based and trained in England, going out to France on 14 November 1915. It is while Arthur was still training in England that he received the news that Cecil Dyer, his old MCS class mate, had been killed in action at Ypres on 9 April 1915. Foster and the 18/RF were part of the 19 Brigade, 33rd Division and stationed at La Bassée near Béthune during the winter of 1915/16. The battalion was transferred to GHQ Troops on 26 February 1916 and then disbanded on 24 April 1916.

In March 1916, while a Private in the Machine Gun Section of the 18/RF, Arthur was wounded and transferred back to England to convalesce. Later in March 1916 he was admitted to No. 4 Officer Cadet Corps in Oxford (9 Alfred Street), along with Frank Wilkinson and Horace Amon, and then in August 1916 they were all gazetted as officers in different regiments. Arthur Foster was commissioned as a Second Lieutenant in the 3rd (Reserve) Battalion KOYLI, based at Withernsea, near Hull.[2]

Foster was attached to the 7/KOYLI and went back out to France in November 1916, joining his new battalion (part of the 61 Brigade, 20th Division) on 14 November at Métigny on the Somme. On 15 November the 7/KOYLI paraded and had practice of open warfare tactics. At 22.00 a fire broke out in the barn allotted as D-Coy billet. Great excitement followed at the very fierce fire, which continued to burn for three days. No one was hurt and luckily there was little wind or else the whole village might have burnt. The cost of repairing the damage was estimated to be £250, although no good property was lost.

On 18 November the battalion moved a short distance north to billets at Airaines. Here they stayed for five days, parading and training, before relocating 7 miles east across the river Somme to billets at Bourdon. The battalion travelled by train on 28 November from Hangest to Corbie (10 miles east of Amien), the transport section of the Brigade having left by road the day before. At Corbie they billeted and resumed training until 11 December, when they moved on to Ville, and then the following day proceeded to Carnoy Camp No. 18 via Méaulte, Fricourt Cemetery and Mametz. Camp No. 18 was situated on the west side of the road from Carnoy to Montauban(-de-Picardie). Along almost the entire 2 miles of this road and on both sides were erected many camps, each containing about fifty huts described as 'elephant huts'. The weather at the time made movement around the camp very difficult due to the muddy conditions. At 10.00 on 14 December the battalion left the camp to proceed to the front line trenches. They stopped for a hot meal at Guillemont, and then proceeded towards Ginchy at 16.30 carrying two days of reserve rations. Beyond Ginchy a walkway, two duckboards wide, was followed to within 1,000 yards of Morval. The remaining 2,500 yards to the front line had to be reached over the top on single-width duck boards. Men had to be continually helped along as in the dark one false step resulted in a man getting engulfed in the surrounding mud. The extraction of a man could take hours of work by his comrades. Even when the front line trench was reached some men got stuck so badly that they had to be dug out. One man who got stuck took twelve hours to dig out. During this first night a man who was wounded in the front line required sixteen men and fourteen hours to bring him out by stretcher. The battalion relief of the front line was completed by 05.00 on 15 December; it had taken nineteen hours to perform an operation that usually took a few hours. When each company reached the front line, the men were so exhausted that they could do no work for several hours. The battalion was relieved in the front line on the night of 16/17 December. After reaching Carnoy camp they had a hot meal and spent the next few days cleaning their kit and resting. Thankfully, on 20 December the weather was very frosty and the ground became much better to travel across. That night the 7/KOYLI again relieved the 7th Battalion Somerset Light Infantry in the front line at Morval, doing another three days' tour in the firing line before returning to Camp No. 18 at Carnoy. The battalion then proceeded on the morning of 23 December to Plateau and entrained for Méaulte, near Albert. They were relieved to be going further west where they spent the next six days training and doing fatigue work; on Christmas Day they were given Christmas presents in their billets. At the end of 1916 the 7/KOYLI was congratulated for being the battalion with fewest cases of trench foot in the division (only eight out of the thousand-plus men in the Division who had been treated for trench foot were from the 7/KOYLI).

At the start of January 1917 the 7/KOYLI left their billets at Méaulte and proceeded to Maltzhorn (2 January), Combles (3 January), Sailly-Saillisel (4 January) and into the front line trenches. Here they remained for only two days before being relieved and returning to Combles in support. They were back in the front line trenches on 9 January, but were relieved the following night. The men marched back to Combles after saying they preferred to walk rather than wait for the delayed and painfully slow train. The battalion had two stints in the front line during January, eventually going to a rest camp at Cardonnette on 25 January. They stayed at this camp for thirteen days, training in the hard and frosty weather and being visited on more than one occasion by enemy aeroplane bombers. On 8 February they travelled by motor bus via Albert to Carnoy, where they were billeted in Nissen huts. Two days later in extremely cold weather they moved up to rest huts at Guillemont, where they were only supplied with a very small issue of fuel. From here they moved up to the front line at Morval on 11 February. The battalion found this section of the line not complete or joined up, so had to cover the gaps with machine guns. This stay at the front in 1917 was during a very quiet period, and while it was impossible to work on the maintenance of the trenches due to the hard ground, the poor wiring on the front of the line was repaired. A shortage of water at the front during this time led to fewer hot drinks being prepared and the men suffering from the cold even more than normal. After leaving the trenches on 14 February the battalion was greeted by the 'Cookers', who supplied the men with a hot meal. Within three days they were back at the front and under heavier artillery fire. Intense artillery fire from the Germans on 19 February halted the relief by the 6/OBLI, which had started at 18.35. Following the barrage, German infantry attacked the left of the line but were repulsed. The relief was finally completed at midnight. Trains had been arranged for the men leaving the line to take them to Carnoy camp. However, due to heavy shelling the troops were unable to take advantage of this transport, and the last train left at 00.45, with most men still sheltering from a renewed bombardment. Only thirty-five men from the Division managed to leave on trains. The others had to walk the 7 miles back to camp, so did not arrive until about 05.00.

On 22 February 1917 the whole battalion moved by train to camp at Guillemont, but were recalled to the front line again the following day and occupied the firing line until 27 February. During this time the silence of the German trench line meant that patrols were sent out at night to ascertain if the Germans were still occupying their front line trenches. They were, and the patrols made a hasty retreat to the safety of their own trenches. The battalion returned to camp at Carnoy on 28 February, before moving forward again to Guillemont on 4 March. The next day the battalion went into the front line near Morval, where it snowed in the early hours of 6 March but quickly thawed. On 8 March the men in the post trench of the right withdrew to allow the artillery to shell the enemy front lines, although a few British shells still fell on the 7/KOYLI front line trenches. The following day the Germans retaliated heavily, shelling the British lines. It was snowing again, and two more cases of trench foot were reported. The 7/KOYLI were relieved on 10 March and returned to Camp No. 3 at Guillemont. Twenty cases of trench foot were reported but were given the 'French method' of washing feet then sent away. Having moved to Camp No. 3 at Carnoy on 12 March the battalion witnessed an explosion in the neighbouring Camp No.4 (thought to be an old German mine) on 15 March which caused heavy casualties. On 16 March the 7/KOYLI relocated 5 miles to Maurepas Ravine to form working parties on roads during the following week. They then moved on to Camp No. 3 at Guillemont on 24 March and the following day to Le Transloy, where heavy rain on ground already badly cut up by shell fire meant the camp was in a very bad state. At the end of the month the battalion moved 3 miles to Barastre (27 March), where their HQ was located in old German dug-outs. During the night of 28 March an officer patrol went out and stumbled upon a German outpost on the Ruyaulcourt Road, threw its bombs and withdrew rapidly. At least the recent sharp frosts made it easier to run on open ground. Between 29 and 31 March the battalion took part in the attack on the village of Ruyaulcourt, which was found to be deserted. The battalion was relieved on the first day of April and went back 4 miles to billets at Barastre, where it stayed for four days. The 7/KOYLI then took over front line position at Havrincourt Wood on 5 April, ready to commence the building of the planned line of resistance from Metz (Metz-en-Couture) to Bertincourt the following day. Digging and wire-laying for this enterprise began on 6 April, but in places this work was incredibly hard due to the thick undergrowth and deadly resistance from a series of enemy snipers. The battalion therefore worked to drive the snipers away. At 04.00 on 9 April the 7/KOYLI line was in position again and the men recommenced their digging, wiring parties were sent out and a screen put up to hide the labour from the enemy's eyes. It was during this operation that Arthur Foster, aged 23, and another officer were killed on 9 April 1917, two years to the day after his school friend Cecil Dyer had died.[3] Arthur Foster's personal effects, a wrist watch and a signet ring, were shipped back to his next of kin.

1. In July 1917 John Lorimer Foster, aged 31, was working for the Western Telegraph Company in Montevideo, Uruguay. He died aged 88, in 1974.
2. In August 1916: Frank Wilkinson was commissioned as a Second Lieutenant in the 3rd (Reserve) Battalion, The Buffs (East Kent Regiment) at Dover (for the rest of Wilkinson's story see his biographical section in this chapter). Horace Amon was commissioned as a Second Lieutenant in the Royal Sussex Regiment and was eventually to be promoted to Captain and win an MC (gazetted 18 October 1917) and bar (gazetted 16 September 1918). Amon became acting Major and second in command of his battalion for April and May 1918 and ended up fighting as part of the Northern Russian Expeditionary Force in the second part of 1918. He survived the war.
3. Some confusion over Arthur Foster's date of death is seen in the war records where it is recorded as 10 April 1917; however, the war diary records no casualties on 10 April but records two officers as casualties on 9 April.

John FOX RUSSELL

27 January 1893 – 6 November 1917

Rank and regiment: Captain: RAMC (TF), attached 1/6th Battalion, Royal Welsh Fusiliers. **Medals awarded:** Victory, British War, Military Cross, Victoria Cross. **Theatre of War:** Egypt and Palestine. **Memorial:** Beersheba War Cemetery, Israel.

John Fox Russell was born at Tanalltran in Holyhead, Anglesey, on 27 January 1893. He was the eldest son of Dr William Fox Russell and Mrs Ethel Maria Fox Russell (*née* Thornbury). His father was a physician and surgeon. Both his father and mother were born in Ireland, and according to his obituary in *The Lily* magazine John appears to have inherited some of his Irish nature from his parents. He had six brothers: William (b. 1894), Henry Thornbury (b. 1897), Thomas (b. 1899), twins Kenneth and Charles Barrington (b. 1903) and Dacre Philip (b. 1906), and one sister, Ethel Elizabeth (b. 1895). In 1909 with the call to scouting in Holyhead, John and his brothers William, Henry and Thomas all joined the 1st Wolf Patrol, Holyhead Boy Scouts, of which John became Patrol

John Fox Russell.

Leader. As with any new adventure, the novelty for many of the Patrols formed at that time waned until the only surviving Patrol was the one led by John.

Three of John's brothers were too young to serve during the war, but his other brothers all saw service. Captain Henry Thornbury Fox Russell MC served with the Royal Welsh Fusiliers and the RFC and died in an air accident on 18 November 1918; Lieutenant William Fox Russell served with the Royal Army Service Corps; and Thomas Fox Russell served as a midshipman in the Royal Naval Reserve, surviving the sinking of his ship during the battle of Jutland.

Life at Magdalen College School (1904–1907) and beyond

John Fox Russell had his primary schooling at the National School and his initial grammar schooling at the County School, in his home town of Holyhead.

1st XI Wolf Pack, 1st Uniformed Scouts, 1909.
Back row: William Fox Russell, Henry Fox Russell, John Fox Russell, Robin Jones.
Front row: Allan Williams, John Tanner, Thomas Fox Russell, William Tanner.

After much help and preparation from Miss W. Thomas of the local vicarage, John then gained a place, after the usual interview and examination, at MCS as a chorister. He started in September 1904, the same year as fellow choristers Herbert Brereton and Dennis Webb. In his first year at MCS Fox Russell won the Form I Prize for 'General Work' and also successfully swam the 'Short Pass' in the Cherwell. Unlike Brereton, however, who did his entire schooling at MCS, Fox Russell left MCS after only three years when his time as a chorister came to an end, in July 1907.

After leaving Oxford John donated a book to the Library entitled *The Challoners* by E.F. Benson. He then moved to St Bees School in Cumbria, where his father knew the Headmaster and where three of John's cousins were educated.

While at St Bees, John was a member of the OTC of the Border Regiment. After passing the entrance exam for the Royal College of Surgeons at the tender age of 16, John decided to attend Medical School at the Middlesex Hospital in London, having turned down the opportunity to go to Medical School in Dublin. Beginning his medical studies in October 1909, he is recognized as one of the

John Fox Russell in MCS chorister uniform, 1907.

youngest students ever to have joined the school. After gaining Certificates in Practical Pharmacy (1911) and Practical Anatomy (1913) he returned to Holyhead in 1913, working in his father's practice in order to gain experience.

While in London Fox Russell continued his connection with the army, joining the Senior Division of the University of London OTC (Medical Unit) and becoming a Cadet Sergeant.

In November 1910 he achieved his 'A' OTC Certificate and in March 1913 he achieved his 'B' OTC Certificate. On returning to Anglesey, Fox Russell applied for a commission in the army and was gazetted on 13 January 1914 as a Second

The Fox Russell family (John Fox Russell standing, dark suit), c.1908.

The Fox Russell family (John Fox Russell fourth from right), c.1913.

Medical Cadet John Fox Russell (standing far right).

Lieutenant in the 6th (Anglesey and Caernarvonshire) Battalion, Royal Welsh Fusiliers (dated 5 December 1913). The following August he was with the battalion when war was declared.

Fox Russell's War

Embodied with his Battalion at the start of the war, the 6 feet 2 inches tall Fox Russell was gazetted to the rank of Lieutenant on 2 September 1914, and on 27 January 1915 he was further promoted to Captain (temporary, gazetted 27 March 1915). On 31 March he is recorded as having received 1st Class instruction in bayonet fighting at Aberystwyth. Fox Russell then returned to his studies, qualifying as LMSSA MRCS in 1916, and gained a commission as a Lieutenant within the RAMC (TF) on 24 April 1916 (gazetted 22 May 1916), thus having to relinquish his commission of Captain with the 6/RWF.

He was initially attached to serve with the Royal Field Artillery, but after a specific request he was attached to his old battalion, the 6/RWF, as the medical officer. Before he departed for Egypt, where the 6/RWF had been since December 1915, Fox Russell married Alma Grace Isabelle Taylor at St Mark's Church, Tunbridge Wells in September 1916. He sailed from Devonport a few weeks later on 10 October 1916 and eventually caught up with the 6/RWF (158 Brigade, 53rd [Welsh] Division) on 7 November at El-Ferdan (North Camp), Egypt on the banks of the Suez Canal (today this is the site of the El-Ferdan Swing Bridge or Al-Ferdan Railway Bridge, the longest rotating metal bridge in the world, spanning the Suez Canal in north-eastern Egypt, from the lower Nile River valley near Ismailia to the Sinai Peninsula). The battalion was in Egypt as part of the strengthened defence of the Suez Canal after the Turkish attempt to seize the canal in 1915. On 24 October Fox Russell was promoted to Captain RAMC (TF) (gazetted 1 November 1916). Throughout November the battalion worked on defensive positions and dug-outs around the El-Ferdan area of the Suez Canal,

Lieutenant John Fox Russell in 1916.

but as December approached this work was replaced by exercises in preparation for a move into Sinai and an advance on Palestine and the West Bank. The brigade trained doing full scale exercises with camels as their first line transport.

On 3 January 1917 the battalion received instructions to join the rest of the 53rd Division at Romani. The following day they marched 15 miles north to Kantara (Al Qantarah) via Ballah (Al Ballah) during bad weather. A few days later they marched on 12 miles to Bir El Gilban, via Hill 70. After progressing to Pelusium, they marched on to Maham Diya on 8 January. Here they stopped for twelve days, rested and received special training. In addition, all the time they were wire track laying, creating a wire mesh track surface which was better to march on than sand. From 21 to 23 January they progressed on to Bir El Abd, via Rabah and Khirba. During the three days of 29 to 31 January they marched on to Salmana, Tilul and finally Mazar. At the start of February they marched to Maadan (1 Feb), Bardawil (2 Feb) and then on to El Arish (3 Feb). From then until 23 February they spent time in the outpost lines and doing fatigue work laying wire. They moved away from the coast to El Burs on 23 February, and then pressed on to Sheikh Zowaiid (Sheikh Zuweid) on 25 February, spending their first week here digging wells. The battalion moved on 8 March to the Long View position, taking over the outpost line and constructing trenches on the three positions of Bedouin Hill, Middle Knoll and Monte Carlo. On 19 March the battalion took part in a Divisional Exercise in the neighbourhood of Karm Ibn Musleh and Shokh El Sufi; two days later they were moved into reserve to a position north-east of Rafa (Rafah). Marching north through the town of Kahn Yunus (Khan Yunes) on 24 March, the battalion next bivouacked in a garden about 1½ miles east of the town. The next day the battalion progressed on to Deiral Belah (Deir al Balah), where they had a hot meal and water bottles were replenished. In the early hours of 26 March the battalion crossed the Wadi Ghuzze and marched upon Mansurah. However, owing to the fact that the guide supplied to them by the 53 Brigade got lost as soon as they left Deiral Belah, causing a delay, as well as the very thick fog of the early morning, the circuitous, rocky and often steep route, the march was a very arduous one. What was more crucial was that their advance now taking place in daylight hours had been discovered by the Turks. At 11.20 the attack on Mansurah (and the Ali Muntar ridge) began with the 6/RWF supporting the 5/RWF, but as they got within 5,000 yards they came under heavy artillery fire. The advance was continued to within 600 yards of the Turkish trenches, when under intense rifle and machine gun fire from the mosque and surrounding houses the Fusiliers became pinned down. When the 161 Brigade of the 54th Division attacked from the west the 6/RWF were asked to then push their attack home at 18.00. Within ten minutes they had captured Green Hill on the Ali El Muntar position and collected and formed up the battalion to repel any counter-attack. The battalion bivouacked behind the Mansura Bluff for the night but at 07.45 the next day shelling began and did much damage to the camels and the bivouac houses. The battalion moved to the north-east and dug themselves in. From this position the 5/RWF watched as the 161 Brigade retired from Green Hill and the 6 Battalion, Essex Regiment retired from El Sire, both followed and pursued by the Turks. Due to a staff error the infantry had retired when only the cavalry, whose horses were suffering from lack of water, had been recalled. The good British progress and positions had been lost, the Turks quickly counter-attacked and the British were forced to break off from battle on 28 March. For his part in this action John Fox Russell was awarded an MC on 17 May 1917 for 'the greatest courage and skill in collecting men of all regiments, and in dressing them under continuous shell and rifle fire' (*London Gazette*, 14 August 1917).

The Battalion rested, training and route marching (deceiving the Turks into thinking they were advancing) from their bivouacs at Deiral Belah during the first two weeks of March 1917. On 17 April the Second Battle of Gaza took place, with the 6/RWF staying in reserve and digging defensive positions while only one division attacked the now improved positions of the Turks along a 2-mile front of the Gaza to Beersheba road (Samson's Ridge). Needless to say, the attack was a big failure and the Commander of the EEF, Lieutenant General Sir Archibald Murray, was relieved of his position in June. He was replaced by General Sir Edmund Allenby, who insisted on substantial reinforcements to do the Palestine job professionally.

Over the months of May to October 1917 the British forces (XX Corps) trained, refitted and reinforced. The 6/RWF spent time in the defensive line

Captain John Fox Russell (standing far left), in Gaza 1917.

trenches and in reserve, occasionally subjected to artillery fire but mostly suffering from the heat and disease. On 17 June, John Fox Russell was admitted to Hospital and spent twelve days there. Details of his ailment are not reported.

The battalion moved out under urgent orders at 11.15 on 27 October to take up a position in support of the 1/1 Battalion, Herefordshire Regiment. The following day, cable burying operations were undertaken from El Buggar towards Towail. The last day of October saw the battalion move out via El Buggar to dig in. On 31 October the battalion moved out onto the Wadi at 20.30 in support of the 230 Brigade, who led the attack on the high ridge north of Beersheeba. From 1 to 5 November the battalion advanced, consolidating the outpost positions taken by the vanguard of the attack and by 3 November they had reached the Beersheba to Khuweil-Feh road. At 04.00 on 6 October an artillery barrage began whilst the 7/RWF were still not in position for their next advance. The 6/RWF immediately moved forward to the right of the 7/RWF and in so doing had to cross the brigade front, and the two battalions became mixed as the advance began. The battalion advanced under a heavy barrage but met only light opposition apart from in two isolated places. By 04.55 the objectives were reached and flares were let off to signal their success. At 05.15 the British artillery opened fire on the positions occupied by the 6/RWF and the Herefords and compelled the troops to withdraw about 200 yards back. During this time the enemy machine guns worked around the flank, taking advantage of the mist which had descended, and immediately the shelling had ceased the Turks advanced against the new positions both from the front and from the right flank. They were immediately attacked with three successive bayonet charges allowing the British to regain the ground they had originally occupied. Owing, however, to enemy machine guns, which were now in position on both flanks and the rear, the British found it necessary to withdraw to their second position. This position was consolidated under heavy machine gun fire and held for the remainder of the day in spite of very heavy casualties. Over 50 per cent of the officers and 30 per cent of the men from the battalion were killed or wounded. John Fox Russell was one of the officers killed near Khuweil-Feh during the action on 6 November 1917, aged 24. The battalion was relieved at about 21.00 and moved back into reserve. Later that day and the next, Beersheba was successfully taken by the

Collectors card of John Fox Russell.

British. For his devotion to duty during the action on 6 November John Fox Russell was posthumously awarded the VC, 'for most conspicuous bravery displayed in action until he was killed. Captain Fox Russell continually went out to attend to the wounded under murderous fire from snipers and machine guns, and in many cases where no other means were at hand, carried them himself, although almost exhausted. He showed the highest possible valour.' In mid-November Gaza was bombarded from the sea and occupied by the British on 16 November. The Third Battle of Gaza had been won by the British and signalled the beginning of the end of the Turkish army in the Great War.

John Fox Russell was originally buried at Khaweilfeh Military Cemetery, Palestine. Sometime later it was found necessary to exhume all the bodies buried in the area and to re-inter them. His body is now at rest at Beersheba War Cemetery.

Gilbert Sims GADNEY

8 May 1886 – 3 July 1916

Rank and regiment: Second Lieutenant, 8th Battalion, Gloucester Regiment.
Medals awarded: Victory, British War, 1914–1915 Star.
Theatre of War: Western Front. **Memorial:** Thiepval, France.

Gilbert Sims Gadney was born on 8 May 1886 in Oxford, the youngest son of Frank John Gadney and Elizabeth Ann Gadney (*née* Sims). Gilbert's father was a partner in the tailors and robe makers firm Hookham, Gadney & Embling Bros of 3 Cornmarket, Oxford. This was a relatively successful business, employing over fifty workers in 1881. The family were living over the shop at the time of Gilbert's birth. They had moved to 163 Woodstock Road, Oxford, by the time of the 1901 Census, and to 199 Woodstock Road in 1908.

Gilbert had one sister Ethel Mary (b. 1873) and two brothers, Herbert George (b. 1874) and Cyril Frank (b. 1885). All the children were born in Oxford and baptized at SS Philip and James' Church. Cyril also attended MCS and was a Day Boy Prefect in his final two years.

Gilbert's father was not only a well-known businessman in Oxford, but also the Vice-President of the Oxford Gleeman Male Voice Choir in 1889. The President of the choir was the ex-Magdalen College Organist and famous composer John Stainer, and the Librarian was Basil Blackwell (OW). The Oxford Gleemen went on to take third place in a National Choir Competition in 1902. In the same year, Gilbert's father donated to the School's photography scheme, whereby boys at the school were encouraged to take photographs with the school camera and learn to develop the pictures themselves in the newly set up darkroom. Sadly, Gilbert's father died in 1914.

Life at Magdalen College School (1898–1901) and beyond

Gilbert Gadney started at MCS in January 1898, joining his brother Cyril, who had been a day boy at the school from the previous January.

Hookham, Gadney & Embling Bros (tailors and robe makers), 3 Cornmarket, Oxford.

In the Form Fours Rowing Races of 1899 Gilbert Gadney rowed at no. 2 for the Form II boat. His older brother rowed at no. 3 in Form IV's 1st boat. The following year, Gilbert had progressed to stroking the Form III 2nd boat. Cyril had progressed to rowing at no. 2 for the Form Vb 1st boat. In his final year Gilbert stroked the form III 1st boat, progressing four places and finishing above three boats that were from older forms.

In 1901 Gilbert was playing in the forward line for the School's 2nd XI Football team, whose wins that year included games against Bloxham and Abingdon. That year also saw the school hold a 'Scratch Sixes' Football Tournament. Eight teams from the school competed against each other over four days at the end of November and the start of December. Interestingly, Gilbert's team were knocked out in the early rounds by his brother's 'Gadney's Side'. Gilbert Gadney evidently participated well despite not being the most gifted boy at games: his character profile in *The Lily* reads, 'inside right ... is a promising forward who has a good idea of the game and has made some good shots. In dribbling, he must learn to go forwards and not backwards. Should be useful next year when he is stronger and heavier.' Alas, Gilbert Gadney was to leave MCS at the end of that year, December 1901. His brother Cyril stayed on at MCS until July 1904, progressing on to Lincoln College, but tragically died a year later, aged 20. In 1911 Gilbert was working as an Auctioneer's Clerk.

Although never representing the school at cricket, Gilbert Gadney did return and play in the Old Boy XI versus MCS 1st XI match of 13 June 1913. Batting at no. 3, he came to the crease and had a small partnership with the talented Frank Wilkinson, who had opened, before Gadney himself was clean bowled. Eventfully, the game ended in a tie, both sides scoring 142 all out.

The Lily of July 1916 recalled, 'unlike his older brother, who was Rowing Captain for four years and also Football and Cricket Captain, he [Gilbert] did not make a mark in games while at School, but he "came out" afterwards. He was a most loyal "Old Boy".' Indeed, he definitely did make his mark afterwards, playing cricket for Oxford City Cricket Club, hockey for Isis Hockey Club and ultimately for Oxfordshire in 1910.

Gadney's War

Soon after the outbreak of war Gilbert Gadney joined the Public Schools' Battalion and went to Epsom for Training. He received a commission in the Gloucestershire Regiment and went out to France with the 8/Gloucs in July 1915 as part of the 57 Brigade 19th Division. Gadney and the 8/Gloucs arrived in Boulogne at 22.30 on 18 July 1915 and stayed in K rest camp on their first night on French soil. The next day they entrained at Pont de Briques railway station (rejoining their transport section who had left the day before and crossed to Le Havre) and travelled 40 miles to Watten, north of Saint-Omer, then marched 7 miles to camp at Nort-Leulinghem. After three days physical training they marched south 14 miles to billets in the vicinity of Renescure, then the next day marched a further 10 miles to Isbergues. After six days of physical training

Gilbert Gadney.

they marched east to Haverskerque (5 miles), then on to Caudescure (5 miles), near Merville the next day on 31 July.

After three days in billets at Caudescure the battalion marched on 6 miles to billets at Estairs. From here they attended training with grenades and trench mortars and washed at baths in La Gorgue. From 9 to 11 August each of the four companies of the battalion went into trenches at Laventie, experiencing the firing line for the first time. On 12 August 1915 the battalion lost its first man killed in action. The battalion returned to their former billets at Caudescure on 16 August, where they were based until 28 August receiving instruction in trench warfare. They then moved 10 miles south to occupy trenches at Richebourg-l'Avoué, 2 miles from Neuve Chapelle, rotating the four companies between the firing and reserve line until mid-September. Tit-for-tat firing between front lines, as well as artillery and aeroplane activity during attempts by both sides to work on their trenches and parapets, brought about several casualties on both sides. Frustration was shown in the front line when on 12 September a shout from the German lines was heard saying, 'Come over and finish it'. Under cover of dark on 13 September the 8/Gloucs were relieved in the front line and returned to billets near Locon. After two continuous weeks in the trenches the men visited the baths at Lestrem (a 4-mile march) over the following two days, cleaning up and receiving new clothes. The battalion remained at rest for eleven days, supplying working parties, parading and route marching. Marching from Locon on 25 September, the battalion moved towards Givenchy, before their advance was cancelled and the battalion remained in the Le Hamel area for the next four days. In the pouring rain on 29 September, they took over very muddy front line trenches from the 9th Battalion, Cheshire Regiment near Festubert. Over the next two days the men had the gory duty of burying the dead of the 9th Battalion, Welsh Regiment killed in action on 25 September at the Battle of Loos. The 8/Gloucs were relieved by the 2nd Gurkhars on 2 October, when they moved initially to Le Hamel, then to support trenches near La Couture (north-east of Béthune). On 7 October the battalion went into reserve in billets in Vieille-Chapelle, again paying a welcome visit to the baths at La Gorgue on 8 October. Within three days they were back in the front line trenches just north of Givenchy(-lès-la-Bassée) for a nine-day spell, during which time the activity of machine guns, snipers and artillery was constant. The eight days in reserve at Le Hamel that followed, with time spent at the baths in Locon, was very welcome. Their return to the trenches on 28 October 1915 saw them exposed to some of the worst trench conditions imaginable. During a time of constant action much rain fell, making movement down the communication trenches eventually impossible. Ration supply was becoming increasingly difficult and food had to be carried over the top to keep the men fed. Men killed during the day were buried near the front line at night, as carrying bodies back to the rear lines was impossible. After seven days in the front line, with the trenches in a dreadful condition, the battalion was relieved on 5 November. The misty conditions that were prayed for, to cover their 'over the top' return to the rear, did not prevail, but fortunately only two men from the battalion were wounded during this risky relief.

During November several men were sent on leave while the remainder of the battalion supported working parties in the area of Festubert. The battalion returned to the muddy trenches on 17 November 1915. Their relief on 21 November was done in relay style with the help of the light from the full moon. Two platoons from each of the three companies in the front line came out in waders, handing them over to the platoons of the 8th Battalion, North Staffordshire Regiment, who waded up to the front line and handed the waders over to the remaining platoons for them to wade out, and so on. The battalion went into Army Reserve on 25 November and marched to billets in Robecq. Again leave was opened and several men were chosen to go on leave. The leave restrictions at this time were that only four men of any rank could go on leave *per diem*, but officers' leave was extended to ten days. Gilbert Gadney is known to have returned home on leave twice during his time in France. The exact dates are unknown, but the final time was only a few weeks before he was eventually killed in action in July 1916. The battalion moved 8 miles south-east on 4 December to billets in Le Touret. The battalion went back into the front line on 11 December for four days, during which time the trench conditions were described as 'deplorable' by the battalion adjutant. A further period in reserve followed by four days in the trenches then saw them go into reserve between Locon and Les Lobes on Christmas Eve until 3 January. Christmas Day was not recognized except for an easy day and Divine Service in company billets.

Throughout the first four months of 1916 the 8/Gloucs rotated between the trenches (including Neuve Chapelle, Riez Bailleul) and reserve billets (including La Gorgue, Régnier Leclercq) in and around the Estaires area. During this time much intense fighting was seen. On 19 March the 8/Gloucs had a German soldier of the 13th Bavarian Regiment walk across no-man's land and give himself up at their trench. The intense fighting was not only from artillery, rifle and machine gun fire, but mine explosions were also common, with a small mine exploded by the British at 17.00 on 20 March causing a German mine gallery to collapse near the 8/Gloucs' trenches. At 22.00 on the same day a further five mines were exploded by the British in 8/Gloucs' sector and rapid fire was kept up for three minutes and then at intervals of five minutes for one minute until 23.00. During the intense retaliatory bombardment by the Germans on the front line at Neuve Chapelle on 21 March, many shells that were lachrymatory and painful to the eyes exploded. Conditions in the trenches were often wet and muddy, and extremely cold. It is recorded in the Battalion diary that it was snowing heavily in the Estaires area as late as 24 March. The soldiers billeted in civilian areas when not in the trenches or camps. For civilians whose home towns and villages were cut across by the Western Front it was a dangerous place to survive if one chose to stay and not become a refugee. The 8/Gloucs held a Court of Enquiry on 14 April over the death of a civilian from a rifle grenade when the battalion had been staying at Hamet-Billet.

On 7 May the battalion, after being located between Hazebrouck and Béthune for nine months, entrained at Aire(-sur-la-Lys) at 04.37 for the Somme area, 60 miles south-west. Arriving at Longueau, south-east of Amien, they then marched 14 miles north to billets at Vignacourt. Here they rested and trained until 30 May, when they then marched 15 miles further north to the training area of Saint-Riquier. The battalion sensed they were being prepared for an imminent attack on a grander scale than they had seen before. On 10 June they marched back south, towards the Somme area, to Vignacourt, then progressed 9 miles closer to the front lines during 16 June, billeting at Rainneville. Here they underwent ten more days of tactical exercises. The battalion moved forward a further 8 miles to Franvillers Wood on 27 June, where for three days they paraded and route marched to avoid boredom. The battalion moved up to the Corps reserve line on 30 June, then the following morning, 1 July, at 07.00 the 8/Gloucs moved forward to the intermediate line at Millencourt, north-west of Albert. At 17.00 they advanced to the valley near the Albert-Pozieres road, then at 22.00 moved forward to trenches on the Tara-Usna line (Tara and Usna are two hills in the area) and remained there for the night. The next day they were ordered to remain in these trenches, then on 3 July at 01.30 they moved forward to attack the German lines at La Boisselle via St Andrew's Trench. At 03.15 they attacked La Boisselle and consolidated the position, remaining there all that day and night. During the attack Second Lieutenant Gilbert Gadney was one of six officers from the battalion to be killed, aged 20. Fourteen other officers were wounded, 282 other ranks were killed, wounded or missing. Gilbert Gadney's body was never recovered, but his name is commemorated on the Thiepval Memorial just a mile and a half from where he was killed. Gilbert's mother contributed towards the Magdalen College School War Memorial.

Richard Davies GARNONS WILLIAMS

15 June 1856 – 25 September 1915

Rank and regiment: Lieutenant Colonel, 12th Battalion, Royal Fusiliers (City of London Regiment). **Medals awarded:** Victory, British War, 1914–1915 Star. **Theatre of War:** Western Front. **Memorial:** Loos Memorial, France.

Richard Davies Garnons Williams was born at Llowes, Radnorshire, Wales, the second son of Garnons Williams and Catherine Frances Williams (*née* Hort). He had five brothers, Arthur (b. 1854), Aylmer Herbert (b. 1857), Gerald (b. 1859), Mark Penry Fenton (b. 1867) and Penry (b. 1873). He also had three sisters, Katherine Frances Helena (b. 1860), Annabella Mary (b. 1862) and Mary Elizabeth (b. 1871).

His father was the Vicar of Betws Penpont, a JP and a landowner at Abercamlais, Breconshire. Abercamlais is the ancestral home of the Williams family, with many of the owners, like Garnons Williams, being in Holy Orders.

Richard married Alice Jessie (*née* Bircham) on 8 January in 1885. They had two daughters, Frances Mary Barbara (b. 1889) and Alice Katherine (b. 1894) and one son, Roger Fenton (b. 1891). At the time of his father's death Roger was serving in India with the Brecknock Battalion, South Wales Borderers.

Life at Magdalen College School (1870–1872) and beyond

For the three years prior to attending Magdalen College School Garnons Williams was educated by Reverend George Woods near Cardiff, from September 1866 to December 1869. Recorded on his entry register for MCS is the fact that he had already had whooping cough and chickenpox some years earlier, but was now quite well and healthy.

Garnons Williams joined MCS in January 1870, aged 14. Unquestionably a gifted athlete and sportsman, as his time at MCS was to show, he eventually went on to play international rugby. He competed in numerous events each year in all of his three Sports Days while at school. These took place in April or May during this era and were held at the University Running Ground at Marston. In the

Richard Garnons Williams.

Sports Day of May 1870, competing in the junior events, he came second in the High Jump, fifth in the Long Jump, fourth in the Half Mile, fourth in the 110 yard Hurdles; but won the Cricket Ball Throwing event with a throw of 67 yards 2 feet 10 inches (his throw beat R.H. Murphy's throw by only 2 feet, but Murphy was forced to leave the competition as he had fractured his arm with his first throw). In the Sports Day of May 1871, again competing in the junior events, with fine weather and plenty of spectators, Garnons Williams came second in the 100 yard Sprint final, won the High Jump with a clearance of 4 feet 6 inches, won the Long Jump with a distance of 14 feet 3 inches, won the 120-yard Hurdle race, 'going over his hurdles in a very good style' in a time of 20 seconds, and won easily the Cricket Ball Throwing competition, with a throw of 77 yards 2 feet. In his final Sports Day in March 1872, competing in the senior events, he came second in the High Jump (clearing 4 feet 11 inches; the winning clearance was 5 feet), won the Long Jump with a leap of 16 feet 3 inches, won the 120 yards Hurdle race (having led all the way and winning by 2 yards), and was second in the Cricket Ball

Throwing event with a throw of 81 yards 1 foot (the winning throw was 91 yards 1 foot).

During his three summers in Oxford Garnons Williams played many cricket games. He was a batsman (highest score 18), seemingly never bowling, in games whose totals rarely went past 100. Many of the fixtures that he appeared in were unconventional by today's school fixture standards and included: Clergy v Laity (essentially boys of Clergy fathers versus the rest); North v South (based on boy's family locality); 1st IX (nine) v Next XVII (seventeen); Lower School XI v XXII (twenty-two); and many 'scratch' matches. Conventional XI-a-side fixtures versus other schools and Oxford colleges were also played. In 1872 Garnons Williams was on the same 'clergy cricket team' as fellow South Walian T.W. Edgeworth David, who had joined MCS in 1870 at the same time as Garnons Williams. Edgeworth David was to become famous for leading the first expedition to reach the South Magnetic Pole in 1909 and for being the geological mining brain behind the tunnelling on the Messines Ridge in which seventeen mines were exploded at 03.10 on 7 June 1917, signifying the start of the Battle of Messines Ridge and a significant victory for the allies.

The *Magdalen College School Magazine* (the school magazine from 1870 to 1880) records Garnons Williams as a member of and playing for what was called the School Football team in 1870 and 1871 (his only two Michaelmas terms at the school). Playing with fifteen a side, with drops, touch downs (tries) and conversions and clever dodging being reported, this is definitely Rugby Football and not Association. Amongst other active pursuits Garnons Williams competed in the Junior Pair rowing event in June 1870 and in the Fives Competition in December 1871.

In 1872, Garnons Williams was heavily involved with the Debating Society, taking his turn in the Chair, as well as speaking For and speaking Against motions.[1] The topics of debate give an interesting insight into the era, and included the motion 'That the study of Medicine on the part of women ought to be encouraged'. The motion was voted against, seven to one.

After leaving Magdalen College School, Garnons Williams was privately tutored and prepared for University for two years by Mr J.M. Brackenbury in Wimbledon. He was successful and in 1874 he went up to Trinity College Cambridge, matriculating in October 1874. His tutor at Trinity was Coutts Trotter, then Lecturer in Natural Sciences and later Vice-Master of the College. Garnons Williams went on to Sandhurst and obtained a commission in the Royal Fusiliers in 1876. He initially served as a Second Lieutenant in the Staffordshire Regiment in 1876, then as a Lieutenant in the Royal Fusiliers in 1877, becoming Captain in 1884. He served in Gibraltar and Egypt.

Garnons Williams played club rugby for Brecon Rugby Football Club and Newport Rugby Football Club and in 1881 was selected to represent Wales in the first ever rugby international versus England. Played at Blackheath on Saturday 19 February 1881, the Welsh lost a very one-sided game by seven goals, a dropped goal and six tries to nil (considered to be equivalent to 82–0 by modern

Wales Rugby Team, 1881.
Standing at the back, furthest right, is R.D. Garnons Williams (interestingly, third from right at the back is G. Darbishire of Bangor, cousin of Arthur Dukinfield Darbishire).

scoring standards). The Welsh team selection was not only based on a set of trials but also on the geographic location of clubs the players represented and their affiliation to particular universities, rather than just rugby ability. It was to be Garnons Williams' only Welsh rugby cap.[2] He is one of eleven Welsh rugby internationals killed in the First World War. The photograph above was taken just prior to the match, most likely in the back of the Princess of Wales Public House in Blackheath, where the team changed.

From 1886 to 1892 Garnons Williams was Adjutant to the 4th (Militia) Battalion Royal Fusiliers (The City of London Regiment). During this time he read for and was called to the Bar (admitted at the Inner Temple, 26 April 1887) and also became an active member of the Charity Organization Society. Retiring from the full time army in 1892 (aged 36) he joined the 1st Volunteer Battalion of the South Wales Borderers as Major in 1894, in his native county of Breconshire. In 1895 he was appointed Brigade Major, and then in 1899 he was granted the honorary rank of Lieutenant Colonel. He resigned his Volunteer Commission in 1906, retaining his rank and with permission to continue wearing his uniform.

He was also a member of the Breconshire County Council Territorial Force Association and was on many diocesan committees.

Garnons Williams' War

In 1909 Garnons Williams became organizing secretary for the National Service League for the counties of Brecon, Radnor, and Montgomery and worked unceasingly for the cause of national service. At the outbreak of war in 1914 he immediately formed a strong volunteer body in his neighbourhood.

On 26 September 1914 Garnons Williams, aged 58, joined the 12th Battalion of his old regiment (Royal Fusiliers) as second in command, Lieutenant Colonel. The 12/RF had been newly formed in September 1914 and from November until April 1915 was billeted at the neighbouring seaside towns of Shoreham and Brighton. In June 1915 they moved to Pirbright, Surrey and at the end of August their training was nearing completion. The battalion practised entrenching and bivouacked for the night on Chobham Common in the fine weather of 23 August. The following day they practised assaulting the trenches and on 25 August three companies of the battalion returned to the Common to fill in the trenches during very hot weather. The same day the battalion was brought up to strength by a draft of eighty men. The Adjutant for the battalion noted in the diary, 'Amongst the number were one or two of the undesirables or weaklings which had previously been transferred from the battalion to the 5/RF, but such is the system military!' The men were allowed 'Embarkation Leave' on 26 August, but when Embarkation Leave expired the next day, over 100 men were still absent. The slackers slowly returned over the following two days, until on 31 August the battalion transport and machine gun section (72 horses and 108 men) marched to Woking station for eventual embarkation to Le Havre, while the remainder of the battalion marched to Brookwood Station, where they entrained in two trains for Folkestone en route for Boulogne. Lieutenant Colonel Garnons Williams commanded the second train with Nos 3 and 4 Companies. The whole battalion had embarked on the fast Channel boat *Queen* by 21.00 and was then escorted across to France by destroyer. One officer and nineteen men were attached as details for lookout duty.

The 12/RF (part of the 73 Brigade 24th Division) disembarked at Boulogne at 00.30 on 2 September; whilst the Colonel and the Quartermaster motored up to their rest camp the rest of the battalion assembled and marched the 2 miles through the sleeping streets of Boulogne 'with drums a-beating to remind the inhabitants that a war was on'. Their first night on French soil was spent in tents on a beautifully warm night, with the men allowed to sleep in until 06.00. That day they stayed resting and confined to camp. At 03.00 on 3 September the whole battalion paraded and once again marched with 'much banging of drums' to Gare Centrale where they entrained into one long train and received orders to proceed (24 miles) south to Montreuil. On arriving at their destination a private soldier 'thrust his head into the Headquarter carriage and asked for the Order of Movement ... He took it, and vanished up the platform, only to return a minute later bringing it back with the destination Montreuil changed to Maresquel'. After progressing another 8 miles by rail they detrained at Maresquel(-Ecquemicourt) to find that the transport section had initially been at Montreuil to meet them and had now covered the extra miles to catch up with them at their new destination. The horses were now very tired and could not move for at least three hours. So after they had knocked open a few ration boxes and issued some 'bully' to the men the battalion marched in the torrential rain east to their billeting area at Embry, which required them to retrace their steps for some way along the route they had travelled from Montreuil. Fifty men dropped out as a result of the conditions, carrying full pack and rations, and twenty-three men went sick. The battalion spent the day of 6 September 'pulling ourselves together', with a Divine Service and a bath. They spent the next two weeks at Embry training and 'practising the attack', rehearsing Divisional concentration, advancing in the dark and receiving special instruction in bombs and machine guns. On the afternoon of 7 September, after parading, the battalion had a campfire concert. The Adjutant wrote that it was 'quite a success! – much talent [for concert not for parades]'. During 9 September, 3-Coy had musketry practice 'and nearly shot a dozen Sherwood Foresters by accident – Sherwoods quite annoyed about it'. The following day 4-Coy was having musketry practice when one man changing his magazine nearly shot the Quartermaster. Also on this day Garnons Williams, the Colonel and four other officers went 3 miles to Divisional Headquarters at Royon to be lectured about gas, where they wore their gas helmets and walked through a trench filled with gas. A full-scale battle practice, between 72 and 73 Brigades, took place on 11 September. The inevitability of action was sinking in with the men and on 21 September three men were tried by Field General Court Martial, one for insubordinate language to a NCO and two for refusing to obey an order. The same day, the battalion also received their marching orders eastwards, and in weather that was fine but cold marched 16 miles via Créquy, Fruges and Lugy to a billeting area around Beaumetz-lès-Aire. The next day the battalion marched on a further 17 miles via Saint-Hilaire(-Cottes) and Lillers to billets at Busnes. The second half of the march was on 'pavé', which made the march more wearing on the men. Halts were taken every hour for ten minutes to allow men to take off their packs, but heavy motor lorries constantly passing the column smothered the men with dust. The battalion reached the billets at 01.30 in the early hours of 23 September, and for the first time since arriving in France they heard through the night the booming sound of heavy guns in the distance. The battle noises persisted throughout the day as the men bathed in the nearby La Busnes River. That night, as sand bags were drawn, men were starting to get jittery and one man, after getting drunk and refusing to go on parade, was court-martialled.

On 24 September the Colonel attended a meeting at Lillers where the General explained the situation and the plan for carrying out the forthcoming attack. At 21.00 the battalion paraded and marched 10 miles to Beuvry, near Béthune, where they arrived at midnight; then at 08.50 on 25 September the Colonel reported to the Divisional Report Centre to accompany it in the forthcoming advance. The battalion, now under the command of Lieutenant Colonel Garnons Williams, paraded at 11.00 and marched southwards into action via Vermelles (5 miles) heading towards Loos(-en-Gohelle). Soon after Vermelles they occupied some trenches, but the evening was so dark that they did not know which trenches they were in. Orders were then received to proceed forward to Fossé Numéro 8 de Béthune (a colliery with giant slag heaps), following the 9th Battalion, Royal Sussex Regiment in 2, 1, 3, 4-Company order. After going 300 to 400 yards the second platoon of No. 1 Coy lost touch with the leading platoon of that company. No. 2-Coy and the leading platoon of No. 1 Coy proceeded under Lieutenant Colonel Garnons Williams towards Fossé Numéro 8 de Béthune following the 9/RSR who were being led by a guide. When they came within about 400 yards of a heap of clinkers in the farming part of the colliery they came under heavy shell and machine gun fire and became detached from the rest of the battalion. They had come across an incredibly well fortified German position, part of the Hohenzollern Redoubt. When the Fusiliers reached the bank of clinkers they were reformed and led by the Brigade Major (73 Infantry Brigade) through the colliery and placed in trenches occupied by the Black Watch. As soon as the Fusiliers were in control of the trench position the Black Watch withdrew. These trenches were then continuously shelled from this point until the 12/RF were relieved from the position on 28 September. The Germans attacked these trenches in the morning and the evening of 26 and 27 September but their attacks were beaten off by the 12/RF. On the morning of 28 September, after a horrendous bombardment of the battalion's position, the Germans attacked in force and gained a foothold in the trenches on the left flank (7th Battalion, Northampton Regiment) and the right flank (7/RSR). The Germans then proceeded to bomb the Fusiliers out of their trenches from both flanks, so that they had to retire. This they did under heavy shell and machine gun fire. It was during this retirement that most of the battalion's losses occurred. During the whole time they occupied the trenches the troops were without rations and water, and owing to the continuous shell fire sleep was impossible. The Fusiliers went into action without any bombs so were unable to meet the final attack of the Germans. All ranks behaved with great gallantry and coolness under their first experience of shell fire and after their retirement they joined various units and took part in three or four bayonet charges driving the Germans back on each occasion. Lieutenant Colonel Garnons Williams had been severely wounded before these charges and there is some confusion over the date of his death. It was some time between 25 and 28 September. He was aged 59.

The Battle of Loos, was the original 'Big Push' over a 20-mile front from Arras to La Basseé. It is famous for the first use of chlorine gas by the British Army and for the tactical mistakes that resulted in Sir Douglas Haig replacing Sir John French as Commander in Chief of the BEF. Almost 8,000 British men died in the battle, many of those from New Army units like the 12/RF who had been rushed into battle without any previous experience of any conflict and after only being in France for three weeks.

1. Also actively involved with the MCS Debating Society in 1872 was George Christie, the father of Richard Colin Christie.
2. A report by *The Times* (13 October 1915) indicates that the multitalented Garnons Williams also represented Wales at Association Football, but the author was unable to find confirmation of this.

Edward Wrey HANBY

27 July 1896 – 30 April 1917

Rank and regiment: Second Lieutenant, 6th Battalion (att. 23rd), The Duke of Cambridge's Own (Middlesex Regiment). **Medals awarded:** Victory, British War, Silver War Badge. **Theatre of War:** Western Front. **Memorial:** Hastings Cemetery, Sussex.

Edward Wrey Hanby was born in Saidpur, India on 27 July 1896. His father Wrey Albert Edward Hanby (1862–1947) was also born in India and was a Deputy Charge Engineer for the East Bengal State Railways. Edward's mother, Maud Margaret Hanby (*née* Warton) and father were married in Calcutta in 1891.

Edward had one brother, Dennis Wrey (b. 1894), with whom he was to share his school days both at MCS and later at Felsted. He also had two sisters, Barbara Wrey (1893–1898) and Agnes Wrey (b. 1901). All of the siblings were born in India.

At the tender age of 4, Edward was already at boarding school with his older brother Dennis in Willesden Green, London. Their parents remained living in India for their entire educational life.

Life at Magdalen College School (1904–1908) and beyond

Edward and his brother Dennis both joined MCS in the September of 1904, when Edward was only eight years old. Despite being two years younger than his brother he was always in a class higher throughout his time at MCS, and their school friends referred to them by the nicknames of 'Hen' and 'Egg' (probably a reference to 'which one came first?'). *The Lily* records Edward as 'never very strong', and in 1908 he had to have an emergency appendectomy. His army records also state he had diphtheria as a child. Earlier in 1908 and in keeping with his youth, despite being in Form IV, Edward was borrowed by the Form I/II boat to row at no. 2 for them in the Form Four races, while his brother Dennis rowed at stroke for the Form III boat. In 1907 Edward received a Form III prize for repetition and a prize for French.

Edward and Dennis left MCS at the Christmas in 1908, when Edward was twelve, and started at Felsted School, Essex in January 1909. Their application to join Felsted was only received in August 1908 but the change from a classical schooling in Oxford to that of Felsted was likely to benefit Dennis, who was suited to a less academic training.

On joining Felsted Edward started in Class III (referred to as 'the Classical Third') and Dennis joined the less academic 'Army and Engineering Second Form'. Edward is recorded in the *Felstedian* magazine playing for the 2nd XI cricket team in 1914. In 1915 he also gained 2nd XI hockey colours and is reported playing and scoring in house hockey matches. Dennis stayed at Felsted three years, leaving in 1912. Edward left Felsted two years later in April 1915.

Despite leaving MCS some years earlier the brothers stayed in touch with the school and Dennis even wrote to Mr Brownrigg in June 1914 saying that he was hoping to get a job on the Indian Railways, in the footsteps of his father. Indeed, although originally in the Honourable Artillery Company, by 1917 he had been transferred to Railway Transport.

Hanby's War

While at Felsted Edward had been a Quartermaster Sergeant in the school's Officer Training Corps and obtained Certificate A. In his final year he had an episode of haemoptysis (coughing up of blood, a potential sign of lung disease and the much feared tuberculosis) but a few months later when he applied for a temporary commission in the 6th Battalion, Duke of Cambridge's Own (Middlesex Regiment) he was found, by three RAMC doctors, to be healthy, have no evidence of tuberculosis and was passed fit for general service in April 1915. After his initial training and a year's home service, on 29 May 1916 Second Lieutenant Hanby went out to France and was attached to the 23rd Battalion Middlesex Regiment (123 Brigade, 41st Division).

Hanby joined the 23/Middx in the Le Touquet trenches on 17 June 1916. On 24 June 1916, the battalion was relieved from the line and went into billets in Armentières, where they remained until 3 July 1916. The following day the battalion were back in the trenches, where they remained for the next ten days.

After less than two months in France, on 12 July Edward reported sick with haemoptysis and was invalided home having been diagnosed with tuberculosis. He sailed back to Southampton on 19 July 1916 and was admitted to the Pinewood Sanatorium, near Wokingham. This was a special hospital for the treatment and containment of tuberculosis, situated in a pine forest which was believed to be beneficial for sufferers of TB. In early 1917 and after much argument between the army and himself he received news that the War Office considered his illness was not caused by military service and as such was not prepared to take responsibility and pay the cost of sanatorium treatment. Hanby had wanted to serve his country so this disappointing outcome would have been a psychological setback during his convalescence. Suffering from worse health, but wanting to be recognized for his short service and willingness to fight, Hanby wrote to the War Office on 2 February 1917 asking if he was entitled to be issued with a Silver War Badge, since he had to relinquish his commission on account of ill health. Hanby died of 'phthisis'[1] just twelve weeks later on 30 April 1917, aged 20, at St Leonards-on-Sea, and is buried in Hastings cemetery.

1. The word 'phthisis' was commonly used for tuberculosis (TB), a disease that typically attacks the lungs.

Charles Eric HEMMERDE

30 August 1896 – 27 September 1918

Rank and regiment: Bombardier (74769), III Brigade, Royal Horse Artillery; Officer Cadet, 28th Battalion (Artists Rifles), The London Regiment; Lieutenant (acting Captain), 6th then 1st Battalion, The Queen's Own (Royal West Kent Regiment). **Medals awarded:** Victory, British War, 1914 Star, Military Cross. **Theatre of War:** Western Front. **Memorial:** Gouzeaucourt New British Cemetery, France.

Charles Eric Hemmerde, born at Lee, Kent, was the only son of Charles Louis Hemmerde (1867–1945) and Maud Hersee Hemmerde (*née* Howell, 1877–1951). His father, after attending Winchester College and Magdalen College became a 'stock dealer', eventually becoming a member of the Stock Exchange. Charles had one sister, Audrey Pauline (1906–1990). Charles' uncle, Edward George Hemmerde KC (1871–1948) was a barrister, politician and playwright who had been a Liberal MP (East Denbighshire 1906–1910, North-West 1912–1918) before defecting to the Labour Party in 1920 to become the first MP for Crewe (1922–1924). Charles married Emilie Maurtizen in January 1918 in Baltimore, USA.

Life at Magdalen College School (1907–1909) and beyond

Charles Hemmerde joined MCS as a chorister in January 1907 at the age of 10 and stayed until his voice broke in 1909.[1] He then went on to Ongar Grammar School,[2] but stayed an active member of the MCS Old Boys Club. In the summer of 1909 he was in the choristers' cricket team that played the Christ Church choristers twice, in June on School Field then in July on the Christ Church Sports Ground. On both occasions MCS choristers were victorious, with Hemmerde taking two catches in the first game, but only making 6 runs in his two innings. He did not bowl. His only other sporting exploit during his time at MCS was in the summer of 1908 when he swam and won 'by a couple of yards' the Short Pass race at Cox's.

Hemmerde's War

On 29 January 1914 Hemmerde, aged 17, enlisted at Glasgow in the Royal Horse Artillery, giving his age as 23 years and 152 days and his occupation as Actor. The reference from his previous employer (Walter Maxwell, Theatrical Manager) stated that Hemmerde left his employment as an actor due to his 'inability'! He is classed as 'an exceptionally fine recruit. Strongly recommend his acceptance' on his army application form. However, upon discovering his true age to be below 18 (and hence requiring parental consent) the army dismissed him from service on 16 March 1914 for having made an incorrect statement on attestation. His parents responded to this by writing a letter of consent for Hemmerde to enlist in the Army below the age of 18. This time (17 March 1914) he enlisted at Woolwich for the Royal Horse Artillery using his correct age of 17 years and 200 days, along with his parents' letter of consent. His assessment at Woolwich in

Charles Hemmerde, MCS chorister, 1907.

May 1914 concluded that Hemmerde was 'AVG [A Very Good] recruit. Well educated. Has done some work as Battery Officer. Likely to make NCO later'; he was posted as a Gunner to 'O' Battery, RHA. His army adventure was to become very real sooner than he thought, when war broke only two months later, on 4 August. Hemmerde sailed to France on 15 August 1914 with the III Brigade, Royal Horse Artillery (part of the 1st Cavalry Division), some of the first British Expeditionary Force troops to enter France and respond to Germany's encroachment into Belgium. By the beginning of September the German Army had advanced so far south that they had crossed the River Aisne and some sections had progressed beyond the River Marne. Over the period 5 to 10 September the

Battle of the Marne raged, during which time the over-stretched German army had been forced to withdraw, as the British and French Armies finally decided to retreat no more, but to stand and fight. The Germans withdrew to a new line at the River Aisne. At the end of the first week of September 1914 Hemmerde was posted to E-Battery, who were at this time 40 miles east of the centre of Paris, near Les Pottées and in the middle of a mobile battle against the German rearguard. During the next days both sides bombarded and attacked each other; the Germans had the advantage of initially retreating on to higher ground, but the British exploited the exposed position of the stragglers and the outnumbered German rearguard. E-Battery advanced in very wet and heavy conditions to Mouroy (5 miles, 8 September), Rougeville (5 miles, 9 September) and crossed the Marne at Nanteuil-sur-Marne (3 miles, 10 September), where they captured a German convoy and rear guards. The wet and resultant heavy going was recorded as being 'very hard on the horses'. The battery advanced 24 miles to near (Parcy-et-)Tigny on 11 September, then on the following day their progress north was hampered after 15 miles by a surprise German rearguard attack near Chassemy. Here they stayed on 13 September as the infantry attack at the Aisne was developing. When the battery went to support the attack and cross the Aisne at Vailly the next day, they were repelled by heavy shell fire from the Germans and had to fall back 11 miles to Limé. The following day they had advanced 4 miles to about a mile south of Chassemy, then went into action, responding to artillery fire from behind Fort de Condé, just north of the river. At this point, on 17 September E-Battery transferred to be part of the 5 Brigade, 2nd Cavalry Division. The following day the battery went to rest at billets at Cerseuil, their first relief since arriving in France. To this point twenty-seven of their horses had become casualties (nine from wounds, or destroyed on account of them; the remainder had either become lame or sick).

On the last day of September 1914 the battery began to relocate, initially south-west, via Hartennes(-et-Taux) (11 miles), Saint-Rémy(-Blanzy) (3 miles, 1 October) and Précy à Mont (12 miles, 2 October); then they tracked north via Villeneuve(-Saint-Germain) (25 miles, 3 October), crossing the River Oise (4 October), Le Neuville (15 miles, 5 October), Longpré-Lès-Amien (48 miles, 7 October), Noyelles(-sur-Mer) (33 miles, 9 October), Roquetoire and across the canal at Aire (50 miles, 10 October), Wallon-Cappel (8 miles, 11 October) and Eecke (8 miles, 12 October). Here, when billeting at a farm one mile east of Eecke, the battery found the bodies of Prince Maximillian of Hesse (the nephew of Kaiser Wilhelm II of Germany) and twelve others in a nearby wood which they had earlier shelled.[3]

Marching on to Boeschepe (5 miles, 13 October) then to Kemmel (8 miles, 14 October) they had now entered Belgium. Although the battery were a mobile force with the motive power of over 200 horses and able to relocate more quickly than marching infantry, much of their race north had been done on congested roads against the flow of the French Army or across water-sodden countryside. The miles covered in the relatively short time are therefore very impressive. Now for the first time the battery entered a more static phase of the war near the town of Ypres. The Allied armies had avoided being outflanked in the 'Race to the Sea' and stopped the Germans getting to the important Channel ports. For the remainder of October the battery billeted near Wytschaete, south of Ypres, and made significant contributions with its guns in the surrounding area in the period of fighting known as the Battles of Messines and of Gheluvelt. In November they had billets in Lindenhoek, Saint-Jans-Cappel, La Crèche, Dranoutre and Steenwerck and continued their actions from positions nearby before they retired on 25 November to billets at a 'very good farm', 1¼ miles south-west of Bailleul. Here, on 2 December, the 5 Brigade was treated to a visited by HM The King and the battery played sports. They stayed in reserve at Bailieul, 8 miles behind the now fairly static front line, until 15 January 1915.

In the cold of mid-January 1915 E-Battery relocated, marching via Saint-Venant (15 miles, 15 January), Maisnil (18 miles, 16 January) and Aire(-sur-la-Lys) (23 miles, 31 January), with the last leg marched during heavy snow. They were now 1¼ miles north-east of Merville, billeted in a series of small farms. At the end of February they moved back to Maisnil, billeting there for a week before marching 23 miles to Caudescure (north of Merville) on 9 March and 9 miles to Pont du Hem on 10 March to be in close support of the First Army in their attack on Neuve Chapelle. After the capture of Neuve Chapelle, E-Battery moved to billets at Caudescure (2 miles south of Merville) on 13 March, moving to new billets near Vieux-Berquin (at La Rue du Bois) four days later. Here they stayed for five weeks until they marched 10 miles to Boeschepe on 23 April, then on to a mile north of Vlamertinghe (9 miles) the following day in extremely cold weather. They went into action a mile north of Brielen (3 miles north-west of Ypres) on 25 April, in support of the French Infantry at the Battle of St Julien, and registered on the ridge to the east of the canal and south of Pilkem. Their artillery support for the French continued until 1 May when they were relieved by French artillery. During this final day of the battery's involvement in the offensive, 'two men [of E-Battery were] wounded during [the] morning as [the] Battery came under a good deal of heavy shell fire'. One of these men was Charles Hemmerde. He received a 'GSW Right arm', gunshot wound to his right arm, and was taken to No. 2 Canadian Field Ambulance for treatment. During the rest of May he was slowly evacuated along the medical line via No. 18 General Hospital and No. 12 Stationary Hospital until reaching a Convalescent Camp at Rouen. After convalescing for three weeks he was sent to No. 2 General Base Depot before being re-posted back to E-Battery on 17 June 1915, when they were in reserve near Le Nieppe, Ebblinghem and east of Saint-Omer. They stayed in reserve until 4 September, moving to billets near Noordpeene, Morbecque and Blaringhem. The battery went back into the line on 5 September and stayed rotating in and out of firing duty and resting in billets in the areas around Le Quesnoy, (Beuvry), Blaringhem, Cauchy and Nédon. No major battles took place during this time, but on 29 September 1915 Charles Hemmerde was promoted to Bombardier (equivalent to Corporal). Hemmerde's final billet location with the RHA was at Ergny, during very heavy snow, for on 18 November 1915 Hemmerde was posted to the 28th Battalion, London Regiment, the Artists Rifles (an Officer Cadet Battalion) at Saint Omer to attend Cadet School. Due to his service in the field it was not long (16 January 1916) before he was commissioned Second Lieutenant to the 6th Battalion, The Queen's Own (Royal West Kent Regiment), 37 Brigade, 12th Division. He joined his new battalion on 21 January 1916 at Gonnehem near Béthune, where they were in reserve. Hemmerde was posted to C-Coy and for the majority of the next two months they were in training and route marching, with the 6/QORWK moving to Manqueville on 5 February and to Fouquereuil on 15 February before moving into the Brigade support trenches near Vermelles on 21 February. During the next two months the battalion went through the cycle of spending short periods in support trenches, in the front line trenches and linked craters near Vermelles, and in reserve at billets in Annequin and Béthune (at École Michelete, the tobacco factory and the orphanage). In March in particular they saw much action, but even when in support they were employed in exposed positions carrying supplies to the front line troops. On 5 April the battalion detonated a tunnelled mine in front of their trenches, destroying a German observation and sniping post. At the same time three other mines were detonated to the right of the 6/QORWK lines but assaulting parties from the neighbouring 6th Battalion, The Queen's (Royal West Surrey Regiment), trying to occupy the rear lip of the new craters, were driven back. Eventually the wet weather of the spring turned to hot Easter weather and on 25 April the whole 12th Division was relieved from front line duty and went into reserve and rest. The 6/QORWK went into billets at Allouagne, 7 miles west of Béthune. The 37 Brigade moved 15 miles west to Bomy on 8 May 1916, where they underwent training in open warfare for most of the rest of May. During the 27 May the 6/QORWK moved back towards Béthune, to Allouagne, where they were 'stood to' ready to respond and support the front line in the event of an expected attack.

The beginning of June brought yet more training, until on 16 June the battalion marched the short distance to Lillers and entrained for Longueau, Amien, 54 miles to the south. Hemmerde and the 6/QORWK were now on the Somme. On 17 June 1916 they marched 11 miles to Flesselles, where they arrived at billets, whilst a party of the battalion's officers visited the trenches near Albert. The battalion's training stepped up again and assault practices took place repetitively over the next ten days. Even to the normal rank and file soldier, it was obvious that a big offensive was imminent. The battalion marched 8 miles east to Saint Gratien, via Villers-Bocage and Rainneville on 27 June, then three days later they moved a further 8 miles to billets at Bresle. As the opening charges of the Battle of the Somme got under way on 1 July 1916, the 6/QORWK moved up via Millencourt to the reserve trenches at Bouzincourt, and then in the early hours of 2 July they stepped forward to take their places in the firing line trenches. The day was spent removing the wounded and dead from the trenches, which had resulted from the previous days shelling. They then readied themselves for an attack on the German positions early the following day. At 03.15 on 3 July the battalion, just 617 men strong, rushed the German trenches south of Ovillers-la-Boisselle, with A-Coy and Hemmerde's C-Coy leading the attack. The German first line was taken without significant losses, but when B- and D-Coys charged past them towards the second German line, only a few elements made it. The Germans counter-attacked and drove the battalion back to their original trenches. After being heavily shelled the 6/QORWK was relieved before the end of the day by the 7th Battalion, East Surrey Regiment. The 6/QORWK had suffered almost 400 casualties (19 officers and 375 other ranks). Hemmerde and the remnants of the battalion marched back to Bouzincourt reserve trenches to rest and reorganize. They were relieved on 9 July and over the next few days marched via Albert and Warloy-Baillon to Vauchelles-lès-Authie, 11 miles behind the front line. Here they stayed in training until 20 July before moving to Bertrancourt and receiving a draft of 475 men. The newly populated battalion then made its way back to the front, and on 27 July took over old German trenches at Ovillers-la-Boisselle, making new fire steps and deepening the trench.

After less than a week, on 4 August 1916, the 6/QORWK were back in the thick of the action again when they were in support of the 6th Battalion, the Buffs during their attack on a German strong point east of Ovillers, taking over to consolidate the captured position during an intense bombardment that continued throughout the next day. A week later the 6/QORWK attacked the same line at 22.30, and got within 15 yards of the German positions before being forced to return to the relative safety of their trenches.

The remainder of August and all of September was spent in the trenches at Ovillers and Wailly, east of Albert and in billets at Bouzincourt, Riviere, Monchiet and Lucheux. On 7 October, in trenches to the east of Albert, the 6/QORWK were subjected to intense shelling from the Germans and lost eighteen men when one shell landed directly in their trench. At 13.45 the battalion rose from their trenches and attacked the German front line. Despite being confronted by fierce machine gun fire the battalion advanced 150 yards to the cover of a bank and Hemmerde's C-Coy to the cover of the sunken road. When night came the battalion had to withdraw, carrying their wounded with them. They had suffered 197 casualties. The following day they were withdrawn to a rest camp at Bernafay Wood. After almost two weeks regrouping, the battalion returned to alternate between billets at Ribemont, Beaumetz, Riviere and Sombrin and the wet and collapsing trenches at Wailly for the remainder of the year.

In January 1917 the 6/QORWK switched back and forward between the billets and trenches near to Arras. In mid-February the battalion moved to billets 10 miles west of Arras at Lattre-Saint-Quentin and a week later moved to Beaufor (-Blavincourt), 4 miles further west, where they spent significant time until the middle of March, practising attacks over dummy trenches near Givenchy (-le-Noble). When one sees film of troops 'going over the top' during the First World War it is more often a clip of practice attacks rather than a real attack, as a cameraman exposing himself to record real action on film would have been almost impossible and definitely suicidal. The 6/QORWK returned to the trenches at Arras on 26 March, and three days later Hemmerde's C-Coy conducted a night-time raid on the German trench in front of their line, attempting to gain information ready for the upcoming offensive, only to find the German trench in this section unoccupied. After a night in billets at Arras the battalion spent 31 March practising moving in and out of the St Sauveur caves of Arras. This network of caves underneath the Ronville and Saint-Saveur districts of Arras was constructed during the previous twelve months by the New Zealand Tunnelling Companies. They dug new tunnels and rooms and joined them up with the existing extensive ancient tunnels and quarries already under the city. The tunnels were fitted with running water and electricity supplies and provided accommodation in an 'underground city' for soldiers to live and sleep in. There was even a large hospital with 700 beds and operating theatres. Today the caves are known as the Wellington Quarry, after the capital city of New Zealand, and are open as a museum. Up to 20,000 soldiers were billeted in the tunnels in the days prior to the start of the Arras offensive on 9 April 1917.

On 3 April, referred to as 'U-Day' in the 6/QORWK war diary, the battalion moved from cellars in the city of Arras in to the caves; C- and D-Coy were in the 'Manchester' and A- and B-Coys in the 'London' section of the cave system. At 04.30 on 9 April the 6/QORWK moved out of the caves and formed up on the reserve line ready to advance at zero hour. At zero hour, 05.30, exits from the caves were blown to enable troops in the caves to storm into no-man's land and take the German trenches. The 6/QORWK following the lead troops helped to take all three objective points, taking many prisoners and much 'booty'. The following day was spent consolidating the newly gained positions.

The 6/QORWK suffered 138 casualties during the attack, and it is likely that it was for his actions during this battle that Hemmerde was mentioned in dispatches during the following month. Although the Germans had been taken by surprise and were pushed back 7 miles, the offensive soon became bogged down and it was eventually called off after three days. After initially moving back into the caves on 12 April, the battalion then went into a period of training during the rest of April, billeting at Montenescourt, Coullemont, Habarcq, Duisans and Arras.

The 6/QORWK moved up into position on 3 May 1917, in the trenches north of Monchy(-le-Preux) to support the 7/ESR with their attack on the German lines at 02.30. After the initial attack had failed a second attack was launched by the 6/QORWK at 21.45. This attack was also beaten back due to intense machine gun fire from the front and from both flanks. The battalion, having suffered 262 casualties, including twelve officers, held their front line under heavy shelling until relieved at dawn. It is likely that Hemmerde's Military Cross, gazetted in July 1917, was awarded in recognition of his actions on this day, 'For conspicuous gallantry and devotion to duty in personally reconnoitring an obscure situation under heavy shell and machine gun fire in order to ascertain the whereabouts of our advanced troops. The valuable information which this gallant action afforded enabled our artillery to give closer support to the infantry, whose attack had been held up.'

Four days later, on 7 May, they were back in the line for a further ten-day tour in the trenches south of Rœux, during a period of much shelling by the 'very nervous' Germans and wet weather, both of which demanded constant reconstructive work on the trenches. The battalion was relieved on 17 May and went into reserve, marching west and away from the front line, through Arras, Duisans and arriving at Montenescourt on 19 May, 14 miles behind the front lines. After a week's rest they were transported by bus a further 12 miles west to Ivergny, near Beaudricourt. Here they rested for three further weeks, training and competing in battalion sports.

The battalion moved back to Arras on 18 June, but continued training until going back into trenches between Feuchy and Wancourt on 1 July. On 17 July the battalion was involved in the successful attack on and capture of the German 'Long Trench', suffering 106 casualties including 8 officers. Their success was rewarded with a week's rest at a camp at Beaurains. On the second day of August they were back in trenches to the east of Monchy when the Germans attacked at 21.00 after a heavy all-day artillery bombardment. The Germans managed to get a foothold in the sapheads and the northern part of 'Hook Trench' and it took the whole of the following day and much stiff fighting to recapture all the front line, the battalion suffering approximately 100 casualties during the two days. For the next two months, the 6/QORWK continued with the constant rotation in and out of the trenches to the south east of Monchy and in billets around Arras.

Hemmerde had now survived three years on the Western Front, quite a feat considering the average survival time for a subaltern in France during the First World War was six weeks. At the start of October he was presented with and accepted an opportunity to be posted away from the relentless dangers and harsh conditions of the front line. On 5 October 1917 he left France to journey to the USA to join the British Military Mission at Camp Meade in Baltimore. Once there, the purpose of his posting was to instruct the US 79th Infantry Division in the art of sniping, in preparation for their entry into the war on the Western Front. Within little over three months, Captain (Temporary) Hemmerde was married, on 17 January 1918, to Emilie (Mitsie) Maurtizen (b. 1897) who was from Copenhagen and staying with her uncle in Baltimore. In July 1918 Hemmerde was ordered to return to Europe. Relinquishing his temporary captaincy status, he joined the 1/QORWK in the trenches in France on 9 August. Meanwhile, Mitsie sailed to England on the SS *Carmania*, arriving in Liverpool on 3 August, and lived with Hemmerde's parents in London.

During his stay in the USA Hemmerde, taking advantage of his new environment and rank and enjoying a relatively lavish lifestyle, had built up debts amounting to greater than $700 (money was owed to Stadler and Stadler 'Uniform Makers', Baltimore Country Club and the Belvedere Hotel) some of which he tried to settle by cheque (account with Cox and Co.) without sufficient funds being available. On his return his debts started to catch up with him and requests for payment reached his Battalion Headquarters. At the end of August 1918 Hemmerde was ordered to see the Lieutenant Colonel commanding the 1/QORWK to answer questions regarding his debts. Hemmerde admitted liability for the debt but stated that he was unable to defray the whole account himself. However, he informed the Lieutenant Colonel that his Uncle Will was able and willing to settle the account for him if necessary and that he had arranged for the account to be defrayed by monthly instalments of $30. He subsequently wrote to his uncle asking for financial assistance.

Hemmerde's begging letter to his Uncle Will reads as follows:

1st September 1918

Dear Uncle Will

Terrible trouble has now arisen, owing to the fact that when I left America I owed a bill for my marriage of $489. I arranged as you will see by the enclosed to pay them $30 per month. Cox's evidently have omitted to send them this money presumably because I had not sufficient funds available. The Belvedere Hotel Company have now reported the matter to the Embassy Washington and from there to the War Office and it has now arrived at these Battalion Headquarters. I went in front of the Colonel last night and he was extremely nice about the whole matter and asked me what I intended to do about it. I told him that all I could do was to write to you. He then told me that he would give me to the end of the month to settle the whole thing up. If it was all settled by then all well and good. If not he would have to put me under arrest and I should of course be court martialled. I can not forward you the papers as there is only one copy and they are of course being kept by the Colonel. If you do fix this up, as I am sure you will, would you send them a cheque through D Dept. Cox and Co. so that the authorities will know that everything is O.K. Will you telegraph to me what you intend to do so that I can report at once to the Colonel and free myself of the terrible shadow that has been cast on the name of the Regiment and my own name as well.

Apart from the actual damage that I shall do the name of the Regiment it will absolutely kill Mitsie. So please do all you can to get me clean.

Believe me

Your loving Nephew

C.E. Hemmerde

To avoid further debt, Hemmerde was forbidden by his Lieutenant Colonel from drawing money from either Cox and Co. or the Field Cashier. The Lieutenant Colonel concludes his notes by saying that this is 'another … [case] … of an officer being suddenly in a position to make use of a banking account which they have no conception of what a banking account is or their responsibilities with regard to it'. He strongly urges that 'some arrangement be made by which officers newly gazetted from the ranks receive their pay and allowance through the Field Cashier in the same way as the soldier by means of a B64 or its equivalent.'

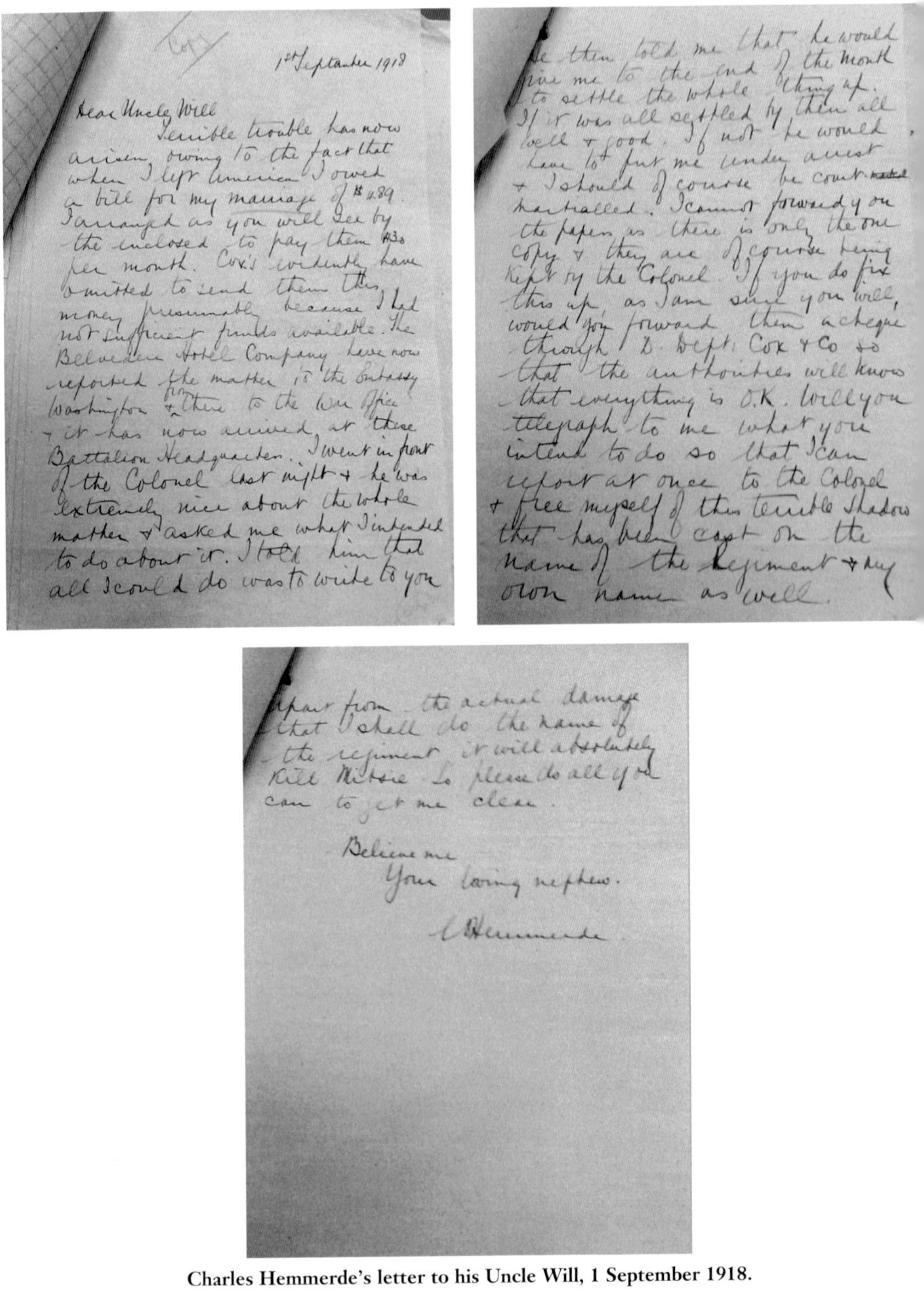

Copy

1st September 1918

Dear Uncle Will

Terrible trouble has now arisen, owing to the fact that when I left America I owed a bill for my marriage of $489. I arranged as you will see by the enclosed to pay them $30 per month. Cox's evidently have omitted to send them this money presumably because I had not sufficient funds available. The Belvedere Hotel Company have now reported the matter to the Embassy Washington & from there to the War Office & it has now arrived at these Battalion Headquarters. I went in front of the Colonel last night & he was extremely nice about the whole matter & asked me what I intended to do about it. I told him that all I could do was to write to you

He then told me that he would give me to the end of the month to settle the whole thing up. If it was all settled by then all well & good. If not he would have to put me under arrest & I should of course be court-martialled. I cannot forward you the papers as there is only the one copy & they are of course being kept by the Colonel. If you do fix this up, as I am sure you will, would you forward them a cheque through D. Dept. Cox & Co so that the authorities will know that everything is O.K. Will you telegraph to me what you intend to do so that I can report at once to the Colonel & free myself of this terrible shadow that has been cast on the name of the Regiment & my own name as well.

Apart from the actual damage that I shall do the name of the regiment it will absolutely kill Mitsie. So please do all you can to get me clear.

Believe me

Your loving nephew.

C Hemmerde.

Charles Hemmerde's letter to his Uncle Will, 1 September 1918.

In September 1918 the 1/QORWK were based near Beugny preparing for the next offensive against the Hindenburg Line and in rotation in the trenches near Neuville. At 05.20 on 27 September the divisions to the north of the 1/QORWK commenced a heavy bombardment of enemy lines, signifying the start of the Battle of the Canal du Nord. The attack by the1/QORWK did not commence until 07.58, however, by which time the Germans had plenty of warning of the attack to come. With the aim of capturing 'African trench', Hemmerde, commanding C-Coy, advanced on the left under a heavy trench mortar barrage. After heavy fighting and suffering many casualties the battalion advance was held up 250 yards short of their objective. Heavy enemy artillery rained down on their advanced position for the remainder of the day. Charles Hemmerde, aged 22, lost his life during this action and was eventually buried at Gouzeaucourt. The following day, after the 1/QORWK had suffered 236 casualties, the objective was finally taken, with the capture of ten enemy machine guns (in working order) and about 300,000 rounds of ammunition, indicating that the enemy had finally retreated in a hurry.

1. Before attending MCS, Charles Hemmerde was educated privately by a Miss Lewis at Belgrave Villas, Lewisham. Hemmerde's parents applied for a choral scholarship for Charles in January 1905 and after three assessments in 1906 (March, June and December) he was finally elected to a choral scholarship.
2. Hemmerde's obituary in *The Lily* of November 1918 incorrectly states that he went to Framlingham School after leaving MCS.
3. Reports indicated that Prince Max had been lying there for three days, stripped of everything but tunic and socks. He supposedly had five wounds made by revolver bullets from behind which indicated that he was a victim of his own Prussian soldiers. The British made a rough coffin for him and he lay in the outbuildings of the farm for three days before being sent to the German lines.

Neil Emslie Nelson HENDERSON

31 October 1897 – 11 April 1918

Rank and regiment: Second Lieutenant, 1st Battalion, The King's Own Scottish Borderers. **Medals awarded:** Victory, British War. **Theatre of War:** Western Front. **Memorial:** Ploegsteert Memorial, Belgium.

Neil Emslie Nelson Henderson was born in Dulwich, London, on 31 October 1897 to Nelson Faviell Henderson and Frances Isobel Emslie Henderson (*née* Smith). He had four sisters, Marjorie Lavinia Nelson (1892–1966), Sheila Frances Nelson (1894–1969), Kathleen Nina Nelson (1896–1939) and Dulcie Patricia Nelson (1903–1978). None of his sisters ever married.

His father attended Dulwich College, London, and studied at Magdalen College, Oxford (Matriculation 1883, BA 1887), before joining his father's publishing and newspaper company, James Henderson and Sons, as a newspaper editor. He took over as publisher some time before 1911. The company, James Henderson and Sons, was started by Neil's grandfather in Scotland in 1823 where it published the *Glasgow Evening Mercury* and the *Glasgow Daily News*. It moved to

London in 1865 where it launched a weekly tabloid magazine, *Our Young Folks Weekly Budget* in 1871. It was in this tabloid that Robert Louis Stevenson's *Treasure Island* was first serialized. Three years later the company launched the first British comic, *Funny Folks*.

Neil's father was a keen rugby player, being an Oxford blue, and in 1892 represented Scotland in the match against Ireland. During the war Neil's father was a special constable.

Life at Magdalen College School (1907–1910) and beyond

Neil Henderson joined MCS in the Michaelmas term of 1907. In his second summer at the school he won the Junior Quarter Mile race (in 76.4 seconds) on Sports Day, plus the all-important sack race. The following year he was second to John Callender in his 100 yard Sprint semi-final race but, a natural in hessian, he won the sack race for the second year running. At the age of 12 he played football for MCS U15s versus Summerfields. On the academic side, in his final year at MCS he received a Form II Prize for Classics.

In September 1910, aged 13, Henderson moved back to his birthplace and on to his father's old school, Dulwich College. While at Dulwich he played 1st XV Rugby (1915 and 1916) and 2nd XI Cricket (1915) and became a School Prefect in his final year. He was also a cadet in the Dulwich College Officer Training Corps. He left Dulwich in April 1916 and progressed on to the Royal Military College at Sandhurst.

Henderson's War

Despite failing the Army entrance exam in February 1916, Henderson (5ft 6ins) was selected for admission to the Royal Military College. He entered Sandhurst in April 1916 and gained a commission as a Second Lieutenant to the King's Own Scottish Borderers in October. Early the following year he was posted to the 1/KOSB and sailed to France on 5 February 1917.

Arriving in France on 5 February, Henderson initially stayed at Étaples on 6 February before continuing his journey to join his battalion (part of the 87 Brigade 29 Division), who were in billets at Méaulte (near Albert) on 13 February. The next four days were taken up with training, practising bayonet fighting, skirmishing, bombing and parading, only being interrupted on 16 February by enemy aeroplanes dropping a large number of bombs on the village. On 18 February the whole battalion marched in company formation, keeping a distance of 200 yards, to Bronfay Camp. Next afternoon the battalion moved into the support line close to Combles (south of Bapaume). Here the whole battalion received treatment for prevention of trench foot at the Main Dressing Station. The following day they went into the firing line for three nights, working hard to clear the trenches of water and mud. The enemy was fairly active with *Minenwerfer* (huge mortars) and rifle grenades during each of these nights. On 22 February they were relieved from the front line and marched back to Hardecourt, a few miles behind the front line. The next day they moved back to Bronfay Camp, but on 24 February they were back in support lines. The following day they marched to Combles, where their feet were again treated, before going into the wet and muddy firing line trenches. When they moved in to take relief of the firing line they did so under heavy shell and mortar fire. Later that night two patrols from the 1/KOSB attempted to get into the enemy trenches, but were unsuccessful due to rifle fire. The following night a patrol was more successful and managed to cut through the German wire and bomb the trenches. Those not on patrols, the majority, stuck to clearing mud and water from the bottom of the trench. After three days in the firing line they were relieved and marched back to Hardecourt, to receive yet another feet inspection. At this time

Neil Henderson.

100 men were sent to help at the front line as stretcher bearers, but the rest of the battalion had seen the last of the firing line for the next six weeks.

The 1/KOSB relocated to La Neuville on 3 March, where they billeted until 18 March. During this time they 'rested', overhauled kit, did drill, trained, practised skirmishing, bayonet fighting, rapid loading and firing, bombing, and got Lewis gun instruction. A church service was also held each Sunday. Company commanders were lectured on fire discipline and control, writing reports, outpost duties and the use of a compass. A half day holiday for the battalion was declared for 10 March, while Neil Henderson went on a course at the Divisional School.

On 19 March the battalion entrained for Hangest then marched to Le Mesge, 40 miles west of Albert. For nine days the battalion was put through its paces learning how to manoeuvre in attack. A special Field Day (26 March) was organized so the movement of the whole division together could be practised. All surplus kit of officers was sent back to England due to forthcoming movement and operations and all leather jerkins had to be returned to stores. Again a half day holiday was given on 24 March, then the following day a Divine Service was held, followed by a 2-mile march to the baths at Riencourt – luxuries before going into battle. Three days later they were given full marching orders. During the next fifteen days they were to march approximately 50 miles en route to the Arras area.

The battalion crossed the River Somme at Picquigny and La Chaussée-Tirancourt on 29 March, hiking a total of 12 miles, via Saint-Vaast, to billets at Flesselles. The next day they marched 7 miles to billets at Bonneville via Havernas, Canaples and Fieffes-Montrelet. Resting the following day they underwent running drill and gas helmet inspection. The first day of April they marched 8 miles to Hem, via Fienvillers and Hardinval, then the following day 6 miles to Lucheux via Doullens. On 3 April they rested and an order was issued for all ranks to get their hair 'cut close' to minimize danger of infectious wounds in the head. A course on erecting wireless apparatus was given the next day before they marched to Lienvillers via Sus-Saint-Léger and Grand Rullecourt on 5 April. A route march back to Grand-Rullecourt on 7 April was used as a practice attack. Arras was now getting close and the sound of enemy guns was in the vicinity. A march of 8 miles to Monchiet via Barly, Fosseux and Gouy-en-Artois on 8 April put them in a location where they were now on six hours' notice to move out in support. They rested until 12 April then marched 8 miles to Arras. At 19.00 the battalion moved up to the support line trenches, arriving at midnight. On13 April the 1/KOSB moved up to the firing line, the whole battalion being in place by 04.45. A large number of gas shells fell close by which necessitated use of their box respirators, with several men slightly gassed. The following day the battalion held the firing line and dug a new advanced line 200 yards east of Sunken Road, in view of the enemy. They worked to improve the new trenches and slowly moved forward to hold this new line. By 18 April they had been at the firing line without blankets or greatcoats for six nights and 'having been wet through on two occasions were looking tired and worn'. Thankfully, they were relieved on 18 April and went into support lines.

During the morning of 19 April 1917 the 1/KOSB rested, then cleaned and repaired the support line trench. After an inspection on 20 April they were relieved and moved back to the reserve in Arras. The whole battalion was treated to a bath at the Deaf and Dumb Institute in Arras on 21 April, but their pleasure was short-lived as they received orders for a big offensive to begin within days. On 22 April, they returned to the firing line at Monchy-le-Preux under heavy shelling, and early the following morning at 04.45, under artillery barrages, the battalion left the trenches to capture and consolidate a new line. It was reported that by 04.46 everybody in the battalion was 'over and doing well'. At 04.57 some British shells were reportedly dropping short of their planned targets. At 05.50 a 'very heavy mess' was reported, with British shells dropping short and German machine guns opening fire. The Division put up white flares to signal to the artillery to raise the barrage. The Worcestershire regiment were even shelled out of their most advanced position by the British Artillery. Any further advance was therefore held up by the friendly barrage. By 08.05 the battalion was dug in to escape the heavy shelling, German and British, that was now surrounding them. The Germans were seen massing in Sack Wood, but heavy artillery fire broke them up, causing many casualties. Many more casualties were caused when the Germans fled into the open and were cut down by rifle and Lewis gun fire. The Germans counter-attacked strongly and the Worcestershire Regiment had to check these to hold their advanced position. During the morning trenches were being dug to consolidate the new advanced line. Very few prisoners were taken as the battalion had to pass over and move beyond the German trenches rather than take them, but several Germans were killed by British as they passed over them. At 14.00 the battalion was relieved by the Lancashire Fusiliers and they retired back to Arras.

Henderson was one of seven officers wounded in this action near Monchy-le-Preux on 23 April 1917. Three officers and sixteen other ranks had been killed and 116 other ranks wounded from the battalion. Henderson had received a gunshot wound to his left forearm that caused a fracture of his ulna. He was evacuated from the battlefield via the well-established casualty line of Field Ambulance, on to a Casualty Clearing Station, then on to the General Hospital at Camiers. On 25 April Henderson was sent back to England to convalesce. In April Henderson was also gazetted to the rank of Lieutenant. He had fragments removed from his arm and the wound healed well, but despite having good movement of his fingers his fourth and fifth fingers remained semi-flexed (assessment done at Caxton Hall, London on 11 May 1917). While recovering at home Henderson visited his old teachers at MCS. He was passed fit for light duty in May and joined the 3 (Reserve)/KOSB in Montrose. In August and October his progress was assessed at Dundee Hospital, until finally he was adjudged well enough to rejoin the 1/KOSB in France in the New Year. Sailing on 26 January, Henderson caught up with his old battalion on 31 January 1918, this time not on the Somme but at Ypres, where they were in reserve working on division defences. The battalion returned to the firing line on 3 February, deepening the trenches, laying duckboards and revetting. Although it was a relatively quiet period for shelling, with 'activity normal', the German machine guns cried out constantly at night in an attempt to reduce the number of British offensive patrols that were going out each night. The battalion war diary records a 'German aviator' being shot down near the battalion line on the 4 February. On 10 February the 1/KOSB were relieved in the firing line at 04.00 and immediately entrained at Wieltze, travelling 10 miles west beyond Poperinge to Abelle. Here they billeted for the next sixteen days, in isolated and widely scattered farmhouses, resting and doing the usual training. They marched to and billeted at Poperinge on 26 February, before, on 4 March Henderson and his 'servant' were transferred to the 87 Trench Mortar Battery. They spent the majority of March on this secondment, but then re-joined the 1/KOSB on 29 March at 'B' Camp in Brandhoek (4 miles from the centre of Ypres). The battalion companies were inspected in 'trench order' on 29 March, before returning to firing line duty the following day for a relatively quiet three-day duty. On being relieved on 2 April they marched back to rest in 'Junction' and 'California' Camps. After resting for three days they returned to the front line on 5 April for another three-day duty, when trench and wiring work was carried out, and the situation was considered 'normal' with 'little or no activity', despite twelve ranks being killed. The battalion returned again to rest, this time by train to Poperinge. However, their rest this time was short-lived and on the night of 9 April they proceeded by bus to Neuf Berquin. Here they billeted during the day of 10 April, during which time a German plane was brought down by D-Coy. The whole battalion then moved off shortly after 17.00 to take up positions between Estaires and Steenwerk, where the Germans had broken through the front line. At 06.00 on 11 April the Germans attacked in overwhelming numbers. B-, C-, and D-Coys met the full force of the attack, with A-Coy in reserve. B-, C-, and D-Coys found themselves surrounded. The remnants of the division were compelled to retire fighting stubbornly throughout the day. During the night A-Coy took and held a number of posts but had to retire the following morning under cover of dark. Fifteen officers and 260 other ranks were killed or missing and 207 other ranks were wounded on this day. Field Marshal Sir Douglas Haig's Army Order of the Day of Thursday 11 April 1918 stated: 'There is no other course open to us but to fight it out. Every position must be held to the last man: there must be no retirement. With our backs to the wall and believing in the justice for our cause each one of us must fight on to the end. The safety of our homes and the freedom of mankind alike depend on the conduct of each one of us at this critical moment.' Lieutenant Neil Henderson was reported wounded and missing at Dieulieu near Estairs on 11 April 1918. He was subsequently declared killed in this action, aged 20. The German offensive across a 50-mile front was soon to run out of momentum and the tide of the war began to swing significantly in favour of the Allies. Henderson, who is remembered at Ploegsteert Memorial, had answered Haig's call.

Andrew Hunter HERBERTSON

1 August 1894 – 16 May 1917

Rank and regiment: Lieutenant (acting Captain), 14th Battalion (att. 9th, 10th, 7th), The King's Royal Rifle Corps. **Medals awarded:** Victory, British War, 1914–1915 Star. **Theatre of War:** Western Front. **Memorial:** Arras Memorial, France.

Andrew Hunter Herbertson was born on 1 August 1894 in Edinburgh, Scotland to Andrew John Herbertson and Fanny Louisa Dorothea Herbertson (*née* Richardson). He had one sister, Margaret Alice Louisa (b. 1899), who was later to become a physician.

The family had moved to Oxford by 1900, when Andrew's father took up a Readership in Geography at the newly formed School of Geography at Oxford University. He had originally obtained his doctorate from the University of Freiburg im Breisgau, Germany. By 1911 his father was an eminent Professor at Oxford University and his mother an author (also on geographical topics). His mother and father both wrote textbooks for secondary schools. Sadly, Andrew and his sister were to lose both their mother and father within two weeks of each other in 1915, their father dying after a long illness on 31 July 1915 and their mother on 15 August 1915.

Life at Magdalen College School (1907–1912) and beyond

From the age of 8 to 13 Herbertson attended the Dragon School in Oxford, as a day boy. It is reported that he was absent for several terms during this time owing partly to illness and partly to travelling with his father. While at the Dragon, he was renowned for his 'gift of commanding a following', as well as his ability 'for getting into and out of scrapes', 'his quick brain' and 'his complete indifference to the chance of punishment'. After completing his Prep Schooling, Herbertson joined MCS in September 1907 and obtained a School Exhibition in 1909. Known at MCS as Hunter Herbertson, he was academically strong and especially gifted at English subjects (Form IV English Prize in 1908; English, History and Arithmetic Prizes in 1909), going on to study History and Classical Greats at Balliol in 1912. Herbertson was involved with the debating society and in 1910 was the 'opposer' of the motion, 'That in the opinion of this house the policy of the Government as regards the Navy places the country in imminent danger of invasion'. The 'mover' of the motion was Leslie Yeo. Herbertson proved the more persuasive and the motion was defeated by twelve votes to nine. In 1910 and 1911 Herbertson donated books to the school library, *Britannia Poems* by H.V. Storey and *Barchester Towers* by Anthony Trollope. On 3 March 1911 Herbertson was one of eight boys, which also included Gordon Bradley, who were confirmed by the Bishop of Oxford in the school chapel. Later in 1911 he obtained a senior certificate as well as winning three school prizes (an English prize, the Form Va prize, and an English History prize that he shared with Donovan Leicester). In his final year at MCS, 1912, he achieved a further senior certificate. After leaving

MCS Herbertson subscribed to the Old MCS Club and *The Lily* magazine, and also made a donation towards the building of the cricket pavilion of 1913.

Herbertson was described as a kindly and unselfish, quiet and reserved person, who after matriculating at Balliol College in October 1912 began reading History and later the Literae Humaniores (a course focused on Classics). After two years at Balliol his education was interrupted by the war and he signed up for the army in October 1914.

Herbertson's War

On 2 December 1914 Herbertson was gazetted to temporary Second Lieutenant in the 14th (Reserve) Battalion, The King's Royal Rifle Corps and based in billets at Westcliff-on-Sea, Southend.

Herbertson was promoted to temporary Lieutenant on 7 September 1915 and attached to the 9th (Service) Battalion, KRRC joining them for duty in France on 11 October 1915. Herbertson went immediately into the firing line of the 'Kaaie Salient and Seminaire' trenches at Ypres, as the battalion had just started a two-week stint in the front and support line when he caught up with them. The previous three days had been a quiet period in this sector but on 12 October a heavy bombardment of neighbouring trenches meant the whole battalion had to 'stand by' in case they were required to fend off an attack. This shelling made the already poor condition of the trenches even worse than the fighting of 25 September had left them. Much work was done during this time on repairing and improving the defences, including the wire in front of the trenches, but at least the weather during this period was fine with light easterly winds and misty mornings. During 13 and 14 October, Ypres town and the Menin Road were heavily shelled, then on 16 October, in the vicinity of Hooge, Herbertson received a gunshot wound to his forehead. He was removed from the battlefield via the usual casualty evacuation chain and ultimately admitted to 20th General Hospital at Étaples on 17 October with a two-and-a-half inch wound in his forehead. Three days later he was at Calais embarking on a ship for Dover to recuperate in England. Arriving back in England he was placed on 'Home Duty' and returned to the 14 (Reserve)/KRRC at Seaford on the south coast.

He was eventually passed fit to return to 'General Service' in February 1916 and rejoined his regiment, attached to the 10th Battalion in France on 17 February 1916. That night, the 10/KRRC slowly relieved the 11/KRRC in the firing line trenches ahead of Canal Bank at Ypres, the relief being made difficult due to the very bright moonlight. For the two days of 18 and 19 February the battalion endured much artillery fire, but with little damage. The battalion's trench was infiltrated on 20 February by a German patrol during a gas alert, but the Germans were driven off without incurring casualties. Another larger German patrol attacked the trenches of the 10/KRRC on 22 February under the cover of a considerable artillery barrage, but were again driven off by rifle fire. In the early hours of the following morning the 10/KRRC were relieved in the front line by 11/KRRC and returned to support trenches at Canal Bank in cold, snowy

Andrew Hunter Herbertson.

conditions. After four days they swapped into the firing line again as the weather turned wet and cold. On the night of 2/3 March the battalion was relieved by the 6/OBLI and marched to the railway station. Those who arrived in time caught a train, arriving at their rest huts to the north-east of Poperinge at 07.40. Those that missed the train had to march the 10 miles, arriving exhausted at 10.30. Here they rested and re-equipped themselves over the next six days, before relieving the 12/KRRC in extremely poor and wet trenches neighbouring their previous location on 9 March. The next five days saw a number of skirmishes as the British attempted to continue their offensive policy and to gain information about the enemy's strength and the accuracy of British artillery fire, using patrols and manned dug-outs close to the German lines. For the remainder of March and the first few weeks of April the 10/KRRC rotated from Canal Bank reserve trenches to front line trenches and back. The only break from the floods and slush was a week's rest at Poperinge in the first week of April 1916. After eight weeks back at the front, in mid-April 1916 Herbertson was sent back to England to read for the entrance examination at the Royal Military Academy in Woolwich, to try for a commission in the Royal Engineers. Upon arriving in England he reported to 10/KRRC HQ at Winchester on 19 April, but was informed that RMA Woolwich had no officer training places available until 27 June 1916. He was therefore sanctioned leave until the end of June. Herbertson took up residence at Balliol College in the Trinity Term of 1916 while preparing for his entrance examination, but in June he reported that he was suffering from nausea, vertigo and headaches. After a medical examination at the 3rd Southern General Hospital in Oxford on 5 July he was declared unfit for general service for one month, but fit for home service. At this time he rejoined his original battalion, the 14/KRRC, and was engaged in training recruits at Seaford, Sussex. Here his condition was re-evaluated every month at the Ravenscroft Military Hospital, where he was eventually prescribed glasses to help his myopic astigmatism. On 1 September the 14/KRRC was absorbed into the Training Reserve Battalions of the 4 Reserve Brigade, and Herbertson was gazetted Lieutenant and acting Captain for the 16 Training Reserve. At the end of 1916, on 29 December, he declared himself fit and able to return to 'General Service'.

Herbertson was eventually attached to the 7/KRRC and posted back to France, joining his new battalion near Arras on 2 May 1917. Along with four other officers and nine other ranks that joined the battalion that day, he went straight into the support line trenches near Wancourt. At 00.30 on the 3 May the 8th Battalion, Rifle Brigade and the 8/KRRC launched an attack on the German lines. The 7/KRRC moved up in support and were subjected to 'tear' shells. The British barrage during the intensely dark morning was described by the battalion adjutant thus: 'The flashes of the guns presented a wonderful sight, one saw nothing but a maze of flashes stretching as far as the eyes could see.' The battalion was subjected to heavy artillery fire themselves the entire day. In the evening of 3 May the 7/KRRC relieved the 8/RB and the 8/KRRC in the front line. The following day they continued to be shelled. On the night of 5 May and early morning of 6 May the battalion was relieved in the front line, having to go over the top to do so during heavy shell fire. Amazingly, only two casualties were suffered. From 6 to 14 May the battalion was employed in digging trenches, during which time there were many casualties from shelling. The battalion, now under the orders of 41 Brigade, relieved the 6/KOYLI in the front line on 14 May. During the night of 16 May, acting Captain Herbertson plus a corporal and one other rank went out on patrol in no-man's land to reconnoitre the German defences, in the area around Fontaine-lès-Croisilles, Riencourt-lès-Cagnicourt and Chérisy. None of them returned. The following night a patrol intercepted four Germans approaching the battalion's trenches carrying two machine guns. One of the Germans was killed and two were wounded and taken prisoner together with the machine guns and a tripod. The war diary tells that the prisoners provided much useful information. A telegram was sent to Herbertson's grandfather in Beechwood, Galashiels on 20 May reporting him missing in action.

A circulation list of missing officers was always sent via the Netherlands Legation to German prisoners of war camps and hospitals to find out the fate of missing men. In reply a statement was received from Rifleman 9389 G.A. Wood of the 7/KRRC, who wrote from Schneidemuhl prisoner of war camp, that 'whilst on patrol Lieutenant Herbertson attempted to return, but was caught in the barbed wire entanglement where he was killed. I was accompanying this officer. I am confident that this officer was killed.' Herbertson's batman, Rifleman 12512 H. Glasspoole (D-Coy, 14 Platoon), tells the story that the night after Herbertson went missing a German patrol was captured by the 7/KRRC and when interrogated told a different story, that Herbertson was taken prisoner and that he 'shot himself through the body'. It is likely that Rifleman Wood's eyewitness version of events is closer to the truth than the version given by the two very scared German soldiers trying to save their own lives.

Herbertson's grandfather, Andrew Hunter Herbertson, was finally sent the news of his grandson's confirmed death on 12 April 1918, aged 22. His Colonel wrote: 'He had only been a short time with the battalion, but we were all impressed by his character both as a man and as a most capable officer.' Herbertson left Balliol College a sum of money with which the Master and Fellows founded a prize, named after him, for History and Science in alternate years.

Frank Magens Caulfield HOUGHTON

11 December 1895 – 6 May 1918

Rank and regiment: Second Lieutenant, Shropshire Light Infantry; Second Lieutenant, Army Cyclist Corps; Lieutenant, 73 Squadron, Royal Flying Corps. **Medals awarded:** Victory, British War, 1914–1915 Star. **Theatre of War:** Western Front. **Memorial:** Dorrington (St Edward the Confessor) Churchyard, Shropshire.

Frank Magens Caulfield Houghton was born in Birmingham on 11 December 1895 to Frank Edwin Caulfield Houghton and Rosa Steele Houghton (*née* Perkins). He had an older sister, Dorothy Rose Felicia (b. 1892) and a younger brother, John Arden Caulfield (b. 1908). All three children were christened at St Thomas' in Dudley, the birth place of their father.

Frank's father was a surgeon and physician, and at the time of Frank's birth the family were living at 259 Stratford Road, Birmingham. The family had moved to Hill View, Headington, some time between 1903 and 1905 when Frank initially joined Milham Ford School[1] in Cowley Place,[2] then swapped to join MCS as a day boy. However their stay in Oxford was not long and by 1908 the family had moved to Dorrington, Shropshire, where Frank is now buried.

His younger brother John followed in Frank's footsteps, becoming a pilot in the RAF (gaining his wings in 1930).

Life at Magdalen College School (1905–1908) and beyond

Houghton joined MCS as a day boy just prior to his tenth birthday in Michaelmas 1905, starting in Form I the same day as Donovan Leicester. In 1906 Houghton applied for a choral scholarship and was summoned three times to be assessed; but after initially being placed on the reserve list he was turned down and remained at the school as a day boy. He was only at the school for three years before he moved to Shropshire with his family, when his father became the local GP in the village of Dorrington. While at MCS, Frank won the Form II English Prize in 1907. After moving to Shropshire he boarded at Denstone College in Staffordshire for the remaining six years of his schooling. At Denstone he was known as a boy with 'unusual ability', writing several 'distinctly clever' articles for the *Denstonian* magazine. In 1914 he was due to go to Cambridge to study Medicine, but at the outbreak of war immediately enlisted in the army and applied for a commission.

Houghton's War

Houghton was gazetted Second Lieutenant in the King's Shropshire Light Infantry on 30 September 1914, but did not go out to France until the following September. During his training year in England he found time to continue his passion for motorcycle racing, having the idea for and organizing the All-Khaki Motor Cycle race at Brooklands in 1915.[3] He went out to France in September 1915 with the KSLI; however, due to his skill as a motorist and the fact that relatively few people had experience of driving motorised vehicles, he was soon transferred to the Army Cyclist Corps. The primary roles of the cyclists were reconnaissance and relaying messages. They were armed as infantry and could provide mobile firepower if required, but most of their time was spent in trench-holding duties and on manual work.

While in France it was common for the men to come across their old school pals, indeed one of Houghton's Denstone College friends (J.N. Knight) wrote back to the College mentioning that he had seen Houghton at the Front. Houghton himself wrote back to his old College, describing life at the Front. On one occasion he described an alert:

> Somewhere in the distance was a voice yelling 'Stand to! Stand to! Stand to!' coming nearer and nearer. And machine guns, the noise was indescribable. Then began an irregular boom, boom, boom – bombs. By this time we were dressed and anxiously waiting for a message on the phone; but all was silent as far as that was concerned. Never knew what it was. By and by we crawled into bed once more, and as the noise abated we fell asleep.

On another occasion he described the scene of a Christmas celebration:

> Our Church was the barn in which my platoon was billeted. It lacked all the beautiful vestments and music which make our Denstone service what it is, but none the less we felt awed as of yore. You can perhaps imagine the scene – the altar, composed of the little oaken table from my 'bedroom', raised on top of some boxes, and some spotless napery, and on each side of the Cross a candle, in sticks brought specially by the padre. Around stood men in khaki – rough men, some, but strangely silent. The only sounds were the dull murmurs of the guns and the rustling of our feet in the straw, and occasionally the squeak of a rat. There was no 'Gloria' at the end – we just crept quietly out.

In May 1916 the Army Cyclist Corps was reorganized, with the 'Divisional' cyclist companies being replaced by 'Corps HQ' cyclist battalions. At this time Houghton transferred to the Royal Flying Corps, 3 Squadron and carried out duties and trained as an Observer.[4] On 27 September he returned to Oxford, to the School of Military Aviation, as an instructor in flight observation and artillery aeronautics. At the same time he received elementary training in flying with 5 (Training) Squadron, receiving his pilot's 'wings' in March 1917. The following month he was gazetted Lieutenant, then on 20 October 1917 he was appointed Flying Officer with 73 Squadron at RFC Lilbourne, near Rugby. The squadron were being readied for combat operations and were preparing for deployment to France on 22 December. In only his second week with the squadron, on 29 October, Houghton was forced to crash-land his plane after a mid-air collision in which his machine had its propeller damaged and the other plane lost part of its lower left wing and aileron. Houghton and the other pilot both survived, but it is reported that, although Houghton did not suffer unconsciousness from the effects of the crash, he had three nights with poor sleep and occasional headaches and was generally suffering from the mental strain of combat training. When he attempted to return to flying he found he was nervous in any machine other than his own. On 23 November 1917 he appeared before the Army Medical Board, suffering from 'Nerve Strain', for assessment of his condition. Interestingly, a note sent to the Medical Board asking for Houghton to be examined pointed out that Houghton was 'urgently required for the EF as a Camel Pilot tomorrow'.[5] He was passed fit for general service, but less than two weeks later he was admitted to hospital on 5 December, cancelling his scheduled transfer to 65 Squadron. He was assigned to 'Home Establishment' and eventually on 18 February he was posted to be a test pilot at the Wireless Experimental Establishment at Biggin Hill, Kent. During his time with the RFC and RAF[6] Houghton had become an experienced pilot,[7] but despite this experience, on 6 May 1918 while flying Sopwith Camel B6303[8] he was killed, aged 22, when his machine spun into the ground from a low altitude. Houghton's body was brought back to Shropshire and was buried in St Edward's Church Yard, Dorrington, Shropshire.

His CO wrote: 'He was one of my best pilots, and it is a very real sorrow to me to lose him like this. He was a very popular officer and all feel his loss.'

Frank's younger brother went on to have a distinguished career with the RAF and when he died in 1997 his ashes were interred in his brother's grave, reuniting the two brothers after almost eighty years.

1. Frank was in Miss Moody's class at Milham Ford School.
2. The site of Milham Ford School on Cowley Place is now occupied by MCS and St Hilda's College.
3. Brooklands (Weybridge, Surrey) was the world's first purpose-built motor racing circuit, opened in 1907. Motor racing stopped at Brooklands in 1914 with the outbreak of the war. However, two motorcycle events were held on the track during the war, both organized by the British Motor Cycle Racing Club for men serving in the Armed Forces. One of these was the 'All Khaki' Meeting held on 7th August 1915 organized by Frank Houghton.
4. Houghton served in 3 Squadron at the same time as the pilot Cecil A. Lewis MC, who went on to co-found the BBC and write, amongst other books, the aviation classic *Sagittarius Rising*, inspiration for the film *Aces High*.
5. EF probably refers to the Egyptian Force, i.e. the EEF.
6. On 1 April 1918 the RFC, amalgamating with the Royal Naval Air Service, become known as the Royal Air Force (RAF).
7. Houghton had experience flying many machines, including the MF.7 Longhorn, Avro, Sopwith Pup, Sopwith Camel, Sopwith two-seater, R.A. Factory BE, Armstrong Whitworth, Airco DH4 and R.A. Factory FE.
8. Camel B6303 had been used as the receiving aircraft for wireless transmissions from Camel C1614 since March.

Leslie Vincent HOYNE-FOX

24 May 1890 – 13 October 1918

Rank and regiment: Captain, 120th Rajputana Infantry. **Medals awarded:** Victory, British War, 1914–1915 Star. **Theatre of War:** Mesopotamia. **Memorial:** Baghdad (North Gate) War Cemetery, Iraq.

Leslie Vincent Hoyne-Fox was one of seven children of Henry Hoyne-Fox and Alice Louise Elizabeth Fox (*née* Hannah). His father, who like Leslie was born in India, was a Civil Engineer for the Public Works Department, Rangoon. Leslie's mother came from London and married Henry Hoyne-Fox in 1877 in the Parish Church, Clapham. Leslie's father, who was responsible for the design of many buildings for the Burmese government, moved to the UK after he retired in 1910, and was the architect for Hove Pier (which sadly was never built).

According to the 1911 census records, three of Leslie's siblings died before 1911, including two sisters who died in India before Leslie was born: Doris died as a baby in 1884, Brenda Alice aged only 1 in 1880. His youngest sister, Alice May died in England aged 16 in 1909. Leslie had two other sisters who married in India when Leslie was still a schoolboy: Elsie Ellen (b. 1878) married Lionel Herapath in 1902, and Marjorie (b. 1888) married Alfred John Reginald Gregory in 1908. He also had an older brother, Bertram (b. 1882), who was a Major in the Royal Engineers.

Life at Magdalen College School (1903–1907) and beyond

Leslie Hoyne-Fox joined Form IV at MCS in the Michaelmas of 1903, at the age of 13. From the following year, 1904, until he left school he is first seen as a key member of the 2nd XI and then, in 1905 and 1906, the 1st XI Football team, playing as a forward alongside Francis Pitts and Edmund Tarbet and in the same team as Harold Dawes and Basil Blackwell.

In *The Lily* of 1905 'Football Prospects' described Hoyne-Fox as able to 'go straight and play a fairly bustling game' and said that he had learnt to use his head. The school team travelled by train to places such as Reading and Windsor, to play Leighton Park School and St Mark's School respectively. Hoyne-Fox was a frequent goal scorer, who was not unknown to try his luck from a long distance. *The Lily* of 1905 describes him as 'A fair inside-right: "traps" the ball better than any of the other forwards, but starts with it slowly and doubles back too much. On his day not a bad shot.' While playing school football he received a horrific

Magdalen College School Football 1st XI, 1906.

The following players represented the 1st XI in the 1906 season: H.H. Annetts (goalkeeper), A.P. Bell (captain), B.H. Blackwell, H.H. Dawes, L. Hoyne-Fox, F.A. Jones, G.H. Mawson, F.B. Pitts, W.P. Roberton, E.A. Tarbet, L.F. Tebbutt, F.R. Turner.

injury to his leg; without the 'providential appearance and instantaneous operation' by Dr A.P. Parker he would probably have lost his 'leg through blood poisoning'. Hoyne-Fox also played Hockey for the school 1st XI in 1907, in a side that included Victor Jessel.

An active member of the Debating Society, interestingly in November 1906 he spoke against the motion, 'That this House favours the extension of Parliamentary Suffrage to women'! *The Lily* of December 1906 reported that, 'To publish the speeches would simply provoke the "suffragette", the opinion of the House, however, is evident in the voting. The motion was lost by 10 votes to 6, one member withholding his vote.'

After leaving MCS in 1907 Hoyne-Fox passed the Army Preliminary Examination in late 1907, and subsequently passed into the Royal Military College, Sandhurst in 1908. In 1907 he presented the school library with the book *The Vultures* by H. Seton Merriman.

Hoyne-Fox's War

At Christmas in 1908 Hoyne-Fox received his first end of term report from Sandhurst, describing his ability as 'good', his conduct as 'very good' and his characteristics were that he 'tries hard at his work'. At Sandhurst, as well as the usual military studies, Hoyne-Fox studied Hindustani.[1] At the end of his Junior Division year he was placed 58th and at the end of his Senior Division year he was placed 23rd out of 100 cadets in the order of merit. After passing out of Sandhurst he received a commission as a Second Lieutenant in the Indian Army on 8 September 1909, and was initially attached to the 1st Battalion, The York and Lancaster Regiment. The 1/Y&L had been based in India since 1902 and were to remain there until the start of the First World War. After serving with the 1/Y&L for a year Hoyne-Fox was transferred to the 120th Rajputana Infantry on 23 December 1910. The following year, on 8 December 1911, he was promoted to the rank of Lieutenant.

During the Great War the 120/Rajputanas were attached to the 6th (Poona) Division and served in the Mesopotamian campaign fighting against the Turks at four major Battles (Basra, Qurna, Es Sinn and Ctesiphon). After securing the Anglo-Persian Oil Company's installations at Abadan in southern Mesopotamia, the British and Indian Army advanced 35 miles northward, up the Shatt-el-Arab River to Basra by 22 November 1914. With new reinforcements the armies advanced further, via two routes, one along the Tigris and one along the Euphrates, with the aim of capturing Baghdad. The 120/Rajputanas managed to reach Ctesiphon via the less heavily defended Tigris route, just 20 miles short of their target Baghdad, by September 1915, after marching over 300 miles through the extreme heat of the Middle Eastern summer. At this point the continued support of the river steamers was not possible because of the drying rivers. The overstretched and poorly supplied Indian troops had to fall back nearly 100 miles to Kut after an unsuccessful attack on the Turks. At Kut, Major General Townsend planned to wait for reinforcements and for the river to return to full flow. After digging a defensive position around the city the British and Indian Armies sat tight and defended their ground strongly, but multiple rescue attempts were too small-scale and unsuccessful, with much loss of life. In the new year of 1916, supplies were so short that the army's horses were slaughtered for meat. It was during this heroic defence of the city of Kut that the now Captain Hoyne-Fox was severely wounded. The RFC had managed to airdrop some supplies, but the amount was insufficient and Townsend was given authority to negotiate surrender in April 1916, after holding out for 147 days. Despite reassurances that his men would be fairly treated, the troops were subjected to an appalling 1,200-mile forced march north via Aleppo in Syria to Anatolia in Turkey, during which over 4,000 men died. Despite his wounds, Leslie Hoyne-Fox survived the journey and the year and a half of captivity before being released in October 1918, only to succumb to pneumonia and die on 13 October, aged 28, three weeks before the defeat of Turkey and the signing of a peace agreement. Hoyne-Fox was initially buried in Anatolia, but later his grave was relocated to the North Gate Cemetery, Baghdad, where many other graves from other burial grounds in Baghdad and northern Iraq and from battlefields and cemeteries in Anatolia were centralized after the war.

1. At the Royal Military College, Sandhurst as well as studying one of three languages (French, German or Hindustani) the Gentleman Cadets studied Administration, Law, History, Geography, Tactics, Engineering, Topography, Riding, Musketry, Gymnastics, Drill, Signalling and Sanitation.

John William JENNER-CLARKE

2 December 1897 – 16 September 1916

Rank and regiment: Second Lieutenant, 6th Battalion, Duke of Cornwall's Light Infantry; Captain, 43rd Trench Mortar Battery. **Medals awarded:** Victory, British War, 1914–1915 Star. **Theatre of War:** Western Front. **Memorial:** Thiepval Memorial, France.

John William Jenner-Clarke was the youngest child of the surgeon William Jenner-Clarke MRCS and Edith Clarke (*née* Waldron). John's mother died in December 1897, shortly after his birth. John had an older sister, Edith Jenner (b. 1893) and an older brother Reginald Jenner (b. 1891, Captain, Essex Regiment). All three had been born in Newbury and in 1901 were living at 66 Oxford Street, Newbury, with their widowed father and their Aunt, Jane Waldron. Their father was to later marry his sister-in-law Jane in 1908. The family moved to Devon (Mansfield, Douglas Ave, Exmouth) by 1915, where John's father continued to practise medicine. His brother Reginald interrupted his medical studies when war broke out, and finally qualified as a doctor in 1919.

Life at Magdalen College School (1908–1909) and beyond

John William Jenner-Clarke attended MCS as a boarder in Form I/II for just two terms, Michaelmas 1908 and Hilary 1909. In 1911 he was attending Wykeham

Hall School in Lee on Solent, then from May 1912, when aged 14, John went to Blundell's School in Devon. He left Blundell's in July 1914 when aged 16. While at Blundell's School he was a member of the School OTC and attended the Corps camp in all three summers he was there.

Jenner-Clarke's War

On 15 August 1914 John William Jenner-Clarke applied for a temporary commission in the infantry of the regular army. Being under 21, John's father had to countersign the application. John's old Headmaster at Blundell's School signed the forms to certify he was of 'good moral character', and that he had attained a 'good standard of education'. Interestingly, his Headmaster crossed out 'good' for his standard of education and replaced it with 'fair'! He was passed fit for service on 17 August and on 22 September he was made Second Lieutenant (temporary) in the 9th (Reserve) Battalion Duke of Cornwall's Light Infantry.

After a year of training in England, Second Lieutenant Jenner-Clarke sailed for France in September 1915, aged 17, arriving in France on 26 September and joining C-Coy of the 6/DCLI (43 Brigade, 14th Division).

Jenner-Clarke joined the 6/DCLI as they returned from the front line at Ypres to bivouacs near Vlamertinge, on 29 September, for five days rest. On 5 October, Jenner-Clarke had his first taste of the firing line trenches at St Eloi (Sint-Elooi, near Voormezele), where C-Coy worked improving the trenches before being relieved and going into reserve trenches on 9 October. The battalion was relieved by the 9th Battalion, Royal Sussex Regiment on 14 October and returned to rest billets at Watou, near Vlamertinge. The whole 14th Division was passed into Corps Reserve on 20 October and the 6/DCLI therefore remained at Watou in billets. After nearly a month at rest and in training the battalion returned to front line duty on 11 November, briefly attached to the 18 Brigade, 6th Division, with C-Coy taking up position at the Kaaie Salient defences near Ypres. After a six-day stint in the line they were relieved and moved back to billets at a large hop warehouse by Poperinge railway station. The next trenches they had to occupy on 22 November, near Wieltse and St Jean (Sint Jin), were in a very poor, wet and collapsing condition. The communication trenches were impassable and the front line was only reached across open ground at night. Work was done on thickening the parapet and improving the revetment whilst fog gave them cover. Precautions against trench foot were taken by men greasing their feet, changing their socks and wearing thigh-length gumboots.

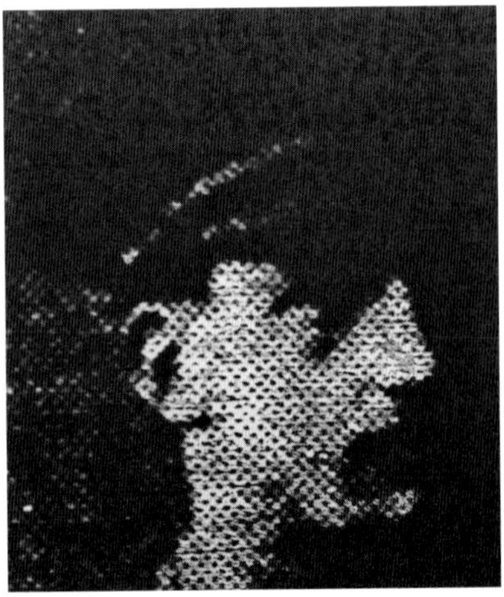

John Jenner-Clarke.

Drying dugouts were prepared in each trench, at the HQ and at the transport camp, and trench boards were laid on piles. As the end of November approached the weather turned cold and very hard frosts froze the ground to a depth of over a foot, making work on the trenches and pumping out of dug-outs very difficult. Finally, on 30 November the battalion returned to billets. At the start of December the battalion was in support, before going into the front line trenches near the village of Wieltje. During this very wet period they were constantly shelled and suffered numerous casualties, before on 12 December the battalion moved back to rest, initially at 'B' Camp, then from 16 to 27 December at 'C' Camp, carrying out fatigue duties and training. On 25 December work continued with the laying of a trench railway, and when operational orders were received in the afternoon for an expected move the camp was readied for clearing. These orders were cancelled, however, and Christmas Day was able to be observed with the troops receiving extra food and puddings, and a concert was provided at night. The men were reported to be extremely cheerful. The 6/DCLI moved up to 'A' Camp in the Vlamertinge area during the daytime of 29 December and then progressed up to the front line later that night. The trenches were in low ground and consequently were very full of water. Thigh boots were provided and helped to reduce the discomfort. Although 30 December was relatively quiet, at about noon four 9-inch shells fell near the support trenches, two falling directly in the trench but doing no damage. Several shells passed near the HQ, but no casualties were received during the day. At night Second Lieutenant Jenner-Clarke led a patrol into no-man's land and found the body of a French soldier. His papers being in good condition, they were taken from him and letters found dated January 1915 led them to believe that he may have been gassed earlier in the year. Wind directions were continuously monitored during this time to give early warning of potential gas attacks and are reported in the war diary. On New Year's Day the troops could hear a band playing behind the German lines.

The battalion stayed in the trenches until 4 January 1916, when they were relieved by the 6th Battalion Somerset Light Infantry, and returned to Rest Camp No. 4 by a combination of marching and motor bus. After four days in camp they moved up to the front line trenches north of Ypres town. The trenches here were in urgent need of maintenance, and communication trenches from the front line back to HQ were non-existent. The only communication with the front line was therefore the telephone, which was very susceptible to being cut off due to shelling, and on 9 January communication with the front line was lost for five hours. During this period, despite the lively shelling and rifle fire, work on the front line was carried out and patrols were conducted at night (finding the German wire was in good condition). At approximately 21.00 on 13 January 1916 the men in the listening post in front of the firing line trenches captured a German who was out in no-man's land on patrol. He showed a good deal of fight and unfortunately had to be brought to submission by a bullet from his own rifle. He was identified as Augustus Hirsch of the 234th Reserve Regiment, called into the army as a labourer in July 1915 and sent to the Western Front in November 1915. The battalion was relieved in the front line on 14 January and returned to camp No. 4 for rest and refitting, returning to the same trenches on 20 January.

During a relatively quiet period a German plane flew two separate sorties on 23 January to bomb Poperinge and Elverdinghe. Patrols into no-man's land took advantage of the cover of mist, and on one occasion a sample of the German wire was collected for analysis. The battalion were relieved on 26 January and returned to rest Camp No. 4, although they formed working parties for the Royal Engineers back in the front line trenches during this time. They again 'moved up' to the front on 1 February, helped by motor bus transport as far as Brielen. At 10.30 the following morning the Germans attacked the 10/DLI line to the left of the 6/DCLI, getting as far as the parapet. The 6/DCLI stood to during the attack. The remaining days until relief on 7 February saw much artillery action. On 10 February the battalion route-marched to a camp consisting of 'A huts' just west of Vlamertinge, on the north side of Poperinge to Ypres road. Jenner-Clarke had seen the last of Ypres. The battalion moved via train to Poperinge on 12 February, then by road via Watou to billets north of Houtkerque. Here they stayed for the next ten days, practising on the rifle range, route-marching and refitting. At 03.00 on 22 February they marched 8 miles to Esquelbecq station, and then journeyed 80 miles south to Longueau, a suburb of Amien. Jenner-Clarke now found himself on the Somme.

From Longueau the battalion travelled by motor bus 13 miles north, in very cold and snowy weather, to billets at Vignacourt, where they stayed for two nights. At 03.40 on 24 February 1916 they marched at short notice in the direction of Arras. They stayed at Beauval that night, after an 11-mile march, then moved on to billets at Coullemont, a further 12-mile march, the next day. The steep and frozen roads caused problems for the troops, as they had been used to the flat countryside of Ypres. Snow fell continuously throughout their march, which was also hampered by blocked roads due to disorganized French and British motor transport. They remained at Coullemont until 27 February, then marched 10 miles to Simencourt as the thaw set in, stayed one night in billets previously occupied by the 9th French Infantry Regiment, then moved 7 miles into reserve positions at Agny (a suburb of Arras), where they billeted throughout the village.

On 1 March 1916 the 43/1 Trench Mortar Battery was formed at the 3rd Army Trench Mortar School, at Valheureux, near Arras. Jenner-Clarke joined as the officer commanding the Battery, still in the 43 Brigade 14th Division, and was gazetted Second Lieutenant (Temporary). The war diary for the 43/1 TMB from March to September 1916 was written and signed by Jenner-Clarke, detailing the number of mortar rounds fired each day and their target. For the first seven days of March the newly formed Battery were trained on the 3.75-inch trench mortar. Equipped with four mortar guns, the battery proceeded by rail from Candas (east of Arras) 15 miles to Saulty, then by road 10 miles to Dainville (Arras) on 8 March. Four days later the 43/1 Battery went into action for the first time around Arras, digging emplacements and dug-outs for the guns and men in the 43 Brigade's front line. The battery fired a mortar for the first time in action on 16 March, when it fired three registration rounds at a German sap trench. Before firing at enemy positions on 22 March, underground mine listening posts had to be evacuated due to their closeness to the target. On 18 June the battery received 3130 rounds of the new Stokes ammunition (a 3-inch mortar that allowed a more rapid rate of fire). The 43/1 and 43/2 Batteries were amalgamated on 20 June and Jenner-Clarke became Commanding Officer of the new 43 Brigade TMB, having been gazetted to Captain (Temporary) on 14 June. Three days later, on 23 June, the battery was fully relieved in the front line for the first time in almost four months. They proceeded to billets in Arras, where they stayed for five days. Half the battery relieved the 95 Brigade TMB in trenches north-west of Arras on 28 June 1916, while the other half proceeded to the 8th Army Trench Mortar School to be re-armed with the Stokes Mortar.

The battery increasingly utilized its new mortars throughout July. Then on 23, 24 and 25 July, in response to a German raid on the front line, the 43/TMB fired 297 rounds in three days. One of the mortar guns and a large quantity of rounds was buried in a bombardment. The Battery was relieved on 28 July and proceeded by motor bus to Warluzel, 13 miles west of Arras. Two days later they marched with the rest of the brigade 12 miles further west to a rest camp at Le Meillard, near Remaisnil. The brigade entrained for Méricourt(-sur-Somme) on 7 August, 33 miles south-east. From here they marched a short distance north to camp under canvas for the next five nights, about a mile north of Dernancourt, near Albert. From here they moved up and took over the front line trenches in Delville Wood and at Longueval on 12 August.[1] Bombardments and raiding parties were conducted with disastrous results over the days leading up to the brigade's attack on the German lines on 18 August, when finally the brigade went over the top. After two days of intense fighting the brigade was relieved and returned to camp. They were back again to relieve the 42 Brigade at Delville Wood on 25 August, and over the next two days the 43 Brigade helped to completely clear the wood of enemy for the first time. This removal of the last Germans from the wood resulted in the enemy incessantly bombarding the wood, resulting in the brigade suffering considerable casualties. The relief by the 72 Brigade took place on the night of 30/31 August, but due to the intensity of shelling and the poor weather, was not complete until 1 September. The brigade proceeded to rest areas, with the 43/TMB travelling by train 44 miles west to the safety of Hornoy(-le-Bourg). The brigade had suffered 1,295 casualties from approximately 4,000 men.

The 6/DCLI had lost fifteen of its officers, either killed, wounded or missing, more than half of its officers, during the Battle of Delville Wood. The battalion was needed in action again soon, and officers to lead the infantry were urgently needed. Jenner-Clarke was therefore relieved of his position as officer commanding the 43/TMB on 7 September 1916 and re-posted to command a company with his old battalion, the 6/DCLI. The 6/DCLI were recouping in billets just 10 miles north of Hornoy(-le-Bourg), at Aumont (Oisemont), west of Flixecourt.

Here they stayed until 11 September when they marched the 8 miles to Laleu. At 04.15 the following morning they marched 2 miles to Airaines and entrained at 06.00 for Méricourt(-l'Abbé) 32 miles east and beyond Arras, then marched 4 miles to camp near Albert. At 07.15 on 15 September the 6/DCLI marched to Pommiers Redoubt and bivouacked there at 09.30. At noon they began to move up through the defensive trench systems of Montauban Defences, York Alley, Trones Wood and Crucifix Alley. As evening came they moved up in single file to consolidate Gap Trench in support of the 10/DLI and the 6/SLI, but found direction difficult due to the very dark night and the ground being cut up by the previous heavy shelling.

At 06.45 on 16 September 1916 the preliminary bombardment began during a fine but misty morning. At 09.45 (zero hour) the 6/DCLI began to advance towards the village of Gueudecourt over open ground and in one wave, supporting the attack led by the 10/DLI (who were on the left) and the 6/SLI (who were on the right). The artillery barrage was weak and erratic and did not appreciably increase in intensity at zero hour. The village having been heavily barraged appeared to be weakly held as only occasional sniping came from it. More worrying was the relentless machine gun fire coming from both flanks of the village that inflicted heavy casualties on the 10/DLI and the 6/SLI, although initially only minor casualties on the 6/DCLI. The message for artillery to knock out the most murderous machine gun fire from the right was never communicated during the battle, and the suffering of the 6/SLI continued. They therefore changed attack formation to advance in waves of half companies in extended order and with 100 yards between waves. Each wave suffered terribly, but the 6/SLI managed to reach advanced positions along with the 10/DLI. Attempts to get two Vickers machine guns to the forward positions were unsuccessful. Two men of the 6/DCLI were sent to mount the crest protecting them from the machine gun fire to determine the situation, but neither returned. At noon, two more men were sent forward; this time one returned to report the status of the attack. Signals were sent to overflying aeroplanes to inform the brigade headquarters why the attack had broken down, but the only message received in reply was to 'Hang on where you are until situation has been cleared up on Divisional right'. No extra artillery help was given.

At 13.40 the Germans counter-attacked in four waves from the west of Gueudecourt. To the relief of the 43 Brigade the artillery responded, the attack was broken up and the Germans disappeared into trenches. The German artillery responded with a heavy barrage on the British lines. Now reinforced by the 42 Brigade, the 43 Brigade were ordered to resume their attack at 18.55, the objective being to capture the Gird Support position and if successful continue on to Gueudecourt village. Dissemination of this order to the companies in the field, due to the loss of many officers and the mixing of battalions, was very difficult at this stage. However, at 18.55 the whole line rose and advanced with the utmost gallantry. After advancing 200 yards the casualties from the intense machine gun fire from both flanks became overwhelming. Every company commander was either killed or wounded and only two very junior officers remained in the firing line. The surviving men crawled back hugging any and every feature of the land to achieve protection from the savage machine gun bullets. At 21.40 the 6/DCLI together with all units from the 43 Brigade formed a defensive line at the Bulls Road trench system, reinforced by four Vickers machine guns. Orders were received from Brigade HQ cancelling the attack on Gueudecourt. Despite supposedly being in support, the 6/DCLI had received heavy casualties. In total, 294 other ranks out of 550, and 15 officers out of 20 were killed, missing or wounded. Jenner-Clarke was one of the officers initially reported as 'wounded' after the attack.

After hearing nothing from his son, Jenner-Clarke's father made several desperate attempts to find out what had happened, asking the War Office to seek out Private J.W. Collier (12190), a close friend of Jenner-Clarke, to see if he had any information, and even employing Petherick & Sons, Solicitors (Exeter) to fight for information on his behalf. A letter sent by the War Office to his family on 21 November 1916 stated that he was now officially 'wounded and missing'. Finally, almost a year later on 16 August 1917 a letter was sent to Jenner-Clarke's father regretfully concluding that 'in view of the lapse of time since anything has been heard of this officer, he is now presumed dead', having died on or since 16 September 1916, aged 18. Jenner-Clarke has no known grave.

1. Delville Wood, 'Devil's Wood', was a heavily defended German vantage point near the village of Longueval. The wood, only approximately 500 yards by 600 yards in dimension, was first attacked on 13 July 1916 by a South African Brigade, who managed to get a small foothold in the southern edge of the wood. For the next month the struggle to take the wood resulted in horrific loss of life and almost every tree in the wood being destroyed and left as a shattered stump.

Kenneth Vivian KING

5 December 1896 – 30 July 1918

Rank and regiment: Private (765274), 28th Battalion (Artists Rifles), The London Regiment; Lieutenant, 52 Squadron, Royal Air Force.
Medals awarded: Victory, British War. **Theatre of War:** Western Front.
Memorial: Varennes Military Cemetery, France.

Kenneth Vivian King was the son of George Edward King (a veterinary surgeon) and Maude Amelia King (*née* Parmeter), of 2 The Vineyard, Abingdon. He had a sister, Marjorie Horne (b. 1890) and a brother, Eric Hume (b. 1892). Eric served with the Royal Navy during the First World War.

Life at Magdalen College School (1909) and beyond

Kenneth King was initially educated at Abingdon School from March 1906 to April 1909. He then attended MCS for two terms (Trinity 1909 and Michaelmas 1909) before going on to Lancing College in January 1910, where he was in Olds House. While at Lancing College he served in the Lancing OTC. He left Lancing in July 1913 to become an assistant in his father's veterinary practice. In

Old Abingdonian swimming event, 1914.
Kenneth King (centre front).

1914 he returned to Abingdon School to compete in an Old Abingdonian versus School swimming match (see photograph).

King's War

Kenneth King completed his attestation forms for the Army in December 1915, joining the Army Reserve list as he turned 19. He returned to Abingdon to continue his apprenticeship in his father's veterinary practice until just over a year later, when, on 3 February 1917, he was mobilized and posted to Hare Hall Camp, Gidea Park in Romford, where he joined D-Company of the 2nd Artists Rifles OTC as a Private.[1]

In March 1917 the very slightly built King, 5 feet 8 inches tall and only 8 stone in weight, applied for a commission with the Royal Flying Corps. On 2 April 1917

Kenneth King.

he was posted to the School of Aeronautics (5 Squadron) at Reading. He was commissioned as a Second Lieutenant on the General List of the RFC on 1 June 1917 and assigned for flight training at the Beatty School in Cricklewood, obtaining his Aero Certificate (No. 4977) on 14 July flying a Beatty-Wright biplane. On 17 July he joined 50 (Training) Squadron at Spitalgate, near Grantham in Lincolnshire, and was appointed Flying Officer on 21 September. Later that month, on 27 September, he was sent for further training at the Wireless and Observers School and on 30 September he was assigned to 82 Squadron. From 5 December 1917 he spent five days with the 2nd Aeroplane Supply Depot, before being posted on 10 December to the 53 Squadron, as part of the Home Establishment. King moved to the 16 (Training) Squadron on 19 February 1918, where he was promoted to Lieutenant on 1 April 1918. Finally, on 22 May 1918 he was posted to France to join 52 Squadron RAF, becoming part of C Flight on 20 June. King joined the squadron at the end of its retreat from the advancing German Army that had begun on 22 March 1918, during its massive Spring offensive.

On 30 July 1918, at 09.35, King and his observer, Second Lieutenant John Kelly, took off from Auxi-le-Château in their RE8 C5056 aeroplane with other aircraft of the squadron for a mission to bomb a German Divisional Headquarters. They became engaged in combat with enemy aircraft and at 11.30 were shot down in flames to the south west of Albert by Vizefeldwebel (Staff Sergeant) Michael Hutterer (Jagdstaffel 23), a famous German flying ace.[2] In total, four aircraft from 52 Squadron were shot down during the mission. King, aged 21, and Kelly, aged 18, are buried in Varennes Military Cemetery, two plots away from each other.[3]

1. 2/28 (County of London Regiment) Battalion (Artists Rifles), No. 15 Officer Cadet Battalion.
2. King and Kelly were Hutterer's third 'victory' of an eventual eight. Hutterer survived the war and died in 1964.
3. Probably because of his short stay at MCS, King's sacrifice remained unknown to the school and his name does not appear on the original MCS memorial that hangs in the School Chapel. In November 2013 acknowledgement of his sacrifice began, his name was read out in Chapel for the first time and plans are in hand to include his name on an additional memorial in Chapel.

Percy Beresford LEES

12 June 1890 – 11 March 1915

Rank and regiment: Second Lieutenant: 3rd (att. 2nd) Battalion, Northamptonshire Regiment. **Medals awarded:** Victory, British War, 1914–1915 Star. **Theatre of War:** Western Front. **Memorial:** Le Touret Memorial, France.

Percy Beresford Lees was born at Newton Hall, Middlewich, Cheshire on 12 June 1890, the eldest son of Charles Percy Lees and Anna Madeleine Lees (*née* Allpress). His father was a justice of the peace (JP) at the time of Percy's birth, but by the time of the 1901 census was listing his occupation as a Major in the 3rd (Militia) Battalion, Northamptonshire Regiment. He was to come out of retirement and serve with the Cheshire Regiment during the First World War.

Percy had a younger brother, Eric Vernon (b. 1895) and a younger sister, Vivien Madeleine (b. 1899). His brother joined the Royal Navy, served with distinction at Jutland, and then came out of retirement during the Second World War to serve as a convoy commodore in the Atlantic. He survived both wars.

Although no photos of Percy have been found, he and his brother Eric inherited a striking appearance from their maternal grandmother, who was Costa Rican, tall, very upright and blessed with a spectacular nose.

Life at Magdalen College School (1900–1903) and beyond

Percy Lees was a boarder at MCS from 1900 to the Christmas of 1903. In 1903, Percy's last summer term at MCS, the Master, Brownrigg, organized and offered prizes for a walking competition during the period that School Field was out of action due to wet weather. Percy Lees was one of the junior winners, walking a 6-mile course. During the wet Trinity term of 1903 the school employed a fire engine to drain off the water as quickly as possible, in a desperate attempt to prepare the field for cricket fixtures.

House Group (Boarders), Summer Term, 1901.
The House Group of 1901 included C.E. Brownrigg (centre), P.B. Lees and H.H. Dawes.

After leaving MCS Percy went on to complete his schooling at Wellington College. As was the ritual after moving on, Percy Lees presented the MCS school library with a book, his was entitled *The Red Army Book* by P. Dandy. Percy progressed on from Wellington in 1908 to become a student at Manchester University, attending the Cambourne School of Mines (Cornwall). While a student he was a private in the Manchester University OTC (October 1912 to September 1913). After obtaining his Geology honours degree in 1912 he was employed as a geologist's assistant (a mining engineer) in the mining industry in Canada. At the outbreak of war he returned to England and applied for a commission in the army.

Lees' War

On 6 October Percy wrote from his parents' home in Oundle, Northamptonshire to apply for a commission, requesting that he be gazetted to the 3rd Battalion, Northamptonshire Regiment (24 Brigade, 8th Division), his father's old regiment. On 13 October 1914 Percy, a slightly built man but almost 6 feet in height, was gazetted as a Second Lieutenant to the regiment of his choice.

He went out to France on 1 March 1915 and joined B-Coy of the 2nd Battalion Northamptonshire Regiment in their billets on 4 March, in the La Bassée region. After 21.00 they left the relative safety of their billets and returned to the front line trenches, which in parts were only 250 yards away from the enemy trenches. Reconstructive work on this section of trenches over the previous nights had seen, on average, eight men killed or wounded per night out of up to 950 men who were in the working parties. During the night of 4 March the German lines were reconnoitred by many parties of officers from the 23 and 25 Brigades. The ranks sensed an attack was imminent. One of the officers was wounded by splinters from a shell while observing the enemy trenches. Work on reclaiming the fire trench (the very front line trench) from collapse was continued by the Royal Engineers. On the day of 5 March the battalion diary records there was 'nothing to report'. The 2/North'n went back to billets at Rouge Croix on 6 March and then on 8 March the battalion returned to the trenches.

On 9 March the battalion was holding the front line trenches called the 'B'-lines, north-west of Neuve Chapelle. At midnight on 9/10 March the order was received to clear away the obstacles from the front and move A-Coy and D-Coy to the right and left into the C-Coy and D-Coy trenches, leaving the central trenches free to be occupied by the 23 and 25 Infantry Brigades. At 06.00 on 10 March 1915 a few shells were fired by the British artillery into the enemy trenches and to the rear; the artillery were getting their range! Then at 07.30 a very large bombardment of the enemy positions started. At 08.05 the 23 Brigade advanced, stormed and seized the German first line and cleared the village of Neuve Chapelle. C-Coy and D-Coy of the 2/North'n advanced to assist the 25 Brigade in digging trenches beyond the village facing Bois de Biez. Later, three companies were ordered back to assemble at Sign Post Lane. At approximately 17.00 the whole 2/North'n was ordered to make an attack in the south-east direction, with A-Coy and Percy Beresford Lees' B-Coy leading. C-Coy and D-Coy were in support. The 7th Division were on the left and 1st Battalion Worcestershire Regiment were on the right. The battalion advanced amidst heavy rifle and machine gun fire, progressing about 1,000 yards before digging in about 440 yards on the further side of the village. The number of casualties was very high.

The following day, 11 March, at 07.00, C-Coy and part of A-Coy attempted to renew the attack several times but were repulsed by heavy fire from enemy machine guns, suffering very heavy casualties. At 12.00 D-Coy then attempted to advance but was repulsed by heavy fire, Lieutenant Coldwell being shot in both legs and Lieutenant Gordon in the throat. While pinned down and having to remain in these advanced trenches, Percy Lees was killed, aged 24. He had been at the front for seven days. The battalion was heavily attacked at dawn the following day (12 March) but managed to repel the enemy. The 2/North'n then launched their own counter-attack, with some four men reaching the enemy trenches to find them vacated. Returning to their own trenches the battalion was relieved on the night of 12/13 March by the Devon and the Middlesex Regiments.

The night before the start of the battle the 2/North'n strength was 22 officers, 594 other ranks. It was now reduced to 2 officers and 158 other ranks. The battalion returned to billets but was ordered to stand ready to return to the trenches in case of attack. The two remaining officers, exhausted and suffering from the effects of being in waist-deep water for the last two days, were sent for medical attention. In the meantime, the Regimental Sergeant Major and twenty-three other men who had become separated during the battle rejoined the battalion. The battalion returned to the trenches the next day, consisting of an officer with 181 other ranks.

Donovan Nicolas LEICESTER

28 March 1895 – 8 May 1917

Rank and regiment: Second Lieutenant, 12th Battalion, Gloucester Regiment. **Medals awarded:** Victory, British War. **Theatre of War:** Western Front. **Memorial:** Arras Memorial, France.

Donovan Nicolas Leicester was born on 28 March 1895 at 8 Richmond Terrace, Clifton, Bristol. He was the eldest son of James Leicester and Constance Mary Leicester (*née* Woods). His father was a Lecturer in Chemistry and Metallurgy in Bristol, but by 1901 had become a HM Inspector for Schools and the family had moved from Clifton to Derby. Donovan's younger brother Peter was born in Derby in 1904. The family moved to Oxford and by 1907 were living at 17 Staverton Road. Donovan's father was later appointed HM inspector for Schools in Gloucestershire, and some time between 1911 and 1914 the family moved to the Vatch House, near Stroud.

Life at Magdalen College School (1905–1914) and beyond

Donovan Leicester joined MCS in May 1905 and was at the school for nine years. He was a day boy for seven years and then became a boarder for his two final years. During this time he regularly appeared at the end of year Prize Giving Ceremony, winning a History Prize five times, an English Prize four times, a Form Prize once, and the Repetition and Elocution Prize four times. Leicester donated three books to the school library, the titles of which indicate his interest and passion in History and writing. The first, presented in 1911, was *A School History of England* by Kipling and Fletcher, the other two, presented after he left in 1914, were *A Modern History of the English People* by R.H. Gretton and *Modern English Literature* by G.H. Mair.

On Wednesday, 17 March 1909 Donovan Leicester was one of eight MCS boys to be confirmed in the School Chapel by Bishop Mitchinson (Master of Pembroke College). Also in the confirmation group was John Bellamy, another MCS boy to be killed in action.

Donovan Leicester is recorded once playing for a school sports team, the 2nd XI Football team against Abingdon in October 1913. In this game Abingdon led twice, before MCS eventually came out 6–2 winners. Leicester played as a back in defence; also in the side was Maurice Blagden (in goal). He also flirted with tennis, appearing in the school tournament in 1913, partnered by H. Amon, but coming bottom of the table. Leicester was more suited to rowing. In the 1911

Sports Day, 20 June 1914, the 150 yard handicap race.
Donovan Leicester, second from left, coming second to Searby on School Field. The new cricket pavilion, used for the first time that year, is seen in the background. John Callender is one of the other boys in the race.

Form Fours Races he rowed in the Form Vb 2nd boat, and although at that time was recorded as being 'late with nearly every stroke' he progressed well over the next two years to row with the school's 2nd IV squad in 1913. In athletics he was a regular Sports Day feature in the 100 and 150 yard sprint races and the high jump competition. In the 1909 Junior High Jump event he tied for first place, clearing 3 feet 11 inches. By the time he won this event again in 1914 he cleared 4 feet 11½ inches in the Senior Section. In the sprint events he seems to have narrowly missed out on winning several years running. His final attempt to capture a sprint win was captured by a photographer for the local newspaper in 1914. The picture shows Searby winning 'by inches' in a time of 16 seconds with Donovan Leicester seemingly flying in second place.

In September 1912 Leicester became a House Prefect (at the same time James Roberton was also made a House Prefect) and in September 1913 he became Head Prefect. Also in his final year he was Editor of *The Lily* magazine.

In December 1913 Leicester was awarded an Exhibition in Modern History at Hertford College, taking up his place and matriculating in the autumn of 1914. After one term in residence at Hertford he took up a commission in the Gloucestershire Regiment.

Leicester's War

After spending one term in Oxford University OTC, on 3 December 1914 Donovan Leicester attested for a temporary commission in the Army for the duration of the war. He was gazetted as Second Lieutenant in the 11th (Reserve) Battalion, Gloucestershire Regiment the same month.

Donovan Leicester.

Leicester was held in the highest esteem by his peers and the masters at the school, although one teacher, Mr J.L. Etty, had identified him as being 'far from robust and I, in common with many others of his friends, thought that he would never be able to stand the strain of Active Service'. Their predictions were partly accurate, for after several months of ill health in the first half of 1915, to Leicester's disappointment he was 'marked' for Home Service. However, after many months of training in the relatively healthy atmosphere of camp on the Sussex Downs he was, 'to his great delight', passed fit for General Service and posted to France in September 1916, after recovering from bouts of neurasthenia as a result of pneumonia contracted during training.

He joined the 12th (Service) Battalion, Gloucestershire Regiment as a Signalling and Intelligence Officer (SIO) on 27 September 1916 just south of Bapaume, before entraining to billets in Sorel. At the beginning of October the battalion moved by train to Béthune and by 5 October were in the line near Givenchy. This time in the trenches was thankfully relatively quiet with no casualties being taken, and the battalion moved back into reserve billets at Le Quesnoy on 14 October. After four days in reserve, the battalion returned to the trenches for another ten days before moving forward into reserve again. This was the pattern of life for the next few months, interspersed with enemy raids on the British trenches as well as periods of trench repair work due to the increasingly wet weather conditions. Whilst in reserve the battalion continued with specialist training such as musketry and anti-gas measures.

Leicester withstood the severities of winter in the trenches well and even returned on leave to Oxford in December 1916 in good spirits. Like many of the other boys he was still subscribing to *The Lily*, enabling him not only to keep up with the goings-on of the school but also to find out the fate of his school friends also serving at the front.

The pattern of life in the trenches continued in much the same way in 1917, with the battalion in the front line at Cuinchy, near Béthune from the beginning of January. On 5 March, A-Company carried out a successful raid on the enemy trenches, capturing two prisoners. The battalion moved to the training area at Burbune, west of Béthune by the middle of March where they were schooled in a new attack formation as well as other general training. April saw the battalion move to Bois Des Alleux, west of Mont St Eloy, where they were billeted in huts. The early part of April was cold and the battalion had to cope with frequent rain and snow storms. On 14 April they moved into the support trenches at Quarries, north-east of Souchez whilst under enemy shell fire. They spent the next few days carrying supplies to the 1st Battalion, Devonshire Regiment and 1st Battalion, Duke of Cornwall's Light Infantry, who were in the front line. On 19 April the battalion moved, under heavy shell fire, into the front line, taking up positions in a line of outposts running south-east from the Souchez River through Cité Des Petits Bois, with C- and D-Coy holding the main line of resistance about 300 yards to the rear. Heavy shell fire continued for the next three days, when the 1/Devons and 1/DCLI moved forward taking up positions in front of the 12/Gloucs. On 23 April the 1/DCLI attacked with the 12/Gloucs being in support. Following yet another period of heavy shell fire, the 12/Gloucs were finally relieved on 24 April by 47th Battalion, Canadian Expeditionary Force and moved back to huts at Niasara Camp near Bois de la Haie. The rest of April was spent in training before the battalion marched to Petit Servins on 30 April to prepare for the next attack.

Unable to perform reconnaissance during the day time the 12/Gloucs proceeded to relieve the 1/CEF on 4 May in trenches captured the previous day (east of Fresnoy) without any knowledge of the terrain or exact location of the Canadians or surviving enemy positions. On 5 May, after heavy shelling during the day, large numbers of the enemy were spotted preparing for a counter-attack on the British lines. An SOS signal was sent up and the artillery successfully prevented the enemy attack developing. The enemy laid down continuous shelling of the lines and on 6 May enemy aircraft were spotted overhead photographing and reconnoitring the lines. This reconnoitring was clearly successful, as the following day the artillery was accurate, with shells falling in all trenches, A-Company's trench being obliterated by the evening and the men reduced to sheltering in shell holes. That evening the battalion was warned that a German attack was expected and the artillery were put on standby.

It started to rain at midnight and at 03.45 on 8 May the enemy started a heavy barrage on all lines as well as the battalion's HQ. Thick mist limited visibility to about 50 yards. An SOS was sent to the artillery for support as the enemy, the 5th Bavarian Division, attacked in force. The British managed to repel the attack and fall back to regroup, ready to mount counter-attacks. Donovan Leicester's role as SIO for the battalion stopped him taking part in the first wave of any attack but, due to a shortage of officers after the initial German attack, he volunteered to help lead the B-Coy counter-attack in the late morning of 8 May. Showing confidence and carelessness, he was able to rally a very tired company and led them into the attack. He was killed, aged 22, by machine gun fire when close to enemy trenches. It was reported by the battalion that Donovan Leicester died with a smile on his face at about 11.00.

In Mr Etty's tribute to Donovan Leicester in *The Lily* of June 1917, only a month after Leicester's death, it is evident that Leicester was held in incredibly high regard by all who knew him. He wrote:

> I have had plenty of cleverer boys to teach, but none for whom it was more worthwhile to take the trouble. He was not only extraordinarily conscientious – almost too much so ... and absurdly grateful, but he made the effort (which few boys can make), to get in touch with his teacher's mind, to understand his point of view, examine it and get whatever he could get out of it. His antiquarian knowledge of architecture, brasses, and local history and customs in Oxfordshire and the Cotswolds, would have put to shame many an older student. But he was no mere antiquarian, and my pleasure in teaching him history was largely due to the fact that I could always feel sure he would realize that the people around about whom we read together were not mere lay-figures of this or that century, but real men and women whom we liked or disliked and (quite often) laughed at.

It is this effect that this book tries to accomplish, showing the fifty boys to have been real characters, not just names, who we may have liked or disliked and in several cases smiled at.

While at the front Donovan Leicester wrote many letters back to the school communicating a spirit of duty, self-sacrifice and inevitability. He read and appreciated Donald Hankey's *A Student in Arms*, a series of dispatches sent by Hankey from France and published as anonymous essays in *The Spectator* in 1915. The essays were eventually compiled and published in two volumes. Hankey's writing became incredibly popular for its insight into the ordeals of the ordinary soldier. Donald Hankey himself was severely wounded near Ypres in 1915 and was eventually killed on the Somme in October 1916.

Mr Etty wrote poetically that Leicester 'was of those who ... tendebantque manus ripae ulterioris amore ['were stretching forth their hands in longing for the further bank'; from the *Aeneid* by Virgil], ... like Donovan Leicester, have died because duty was not to them just duty, but the brightest possible object of desire, [they] have concentrated into their short lives, especially their last months, the value and experience of a long lifetime. It is [therefore] we who, still left in the darkness of the nearer bank, must stretch out our hands in vein to them as they stand smiling at us from the further shore.'

After Donovan Leicester's death the family still subscribed to *The Lily* and his father donated a large amount of money towards the War Memorial.

Charles Robert Crighton MALTBY

9 July 1890 – 27 August 1916

Rank and regiment: Private (5288), 20th Battalion, Royal Fusiliers; Lieutenant, 12th Battalion, Rifle Brigade (The Prince Consort's Own). **Medals awarded:** Victory, British War, 1914–1915 Star. **Theatre of War:** Western Front. **Memorial:** Dive Copse British Cemetery, France.

Charles Robert Crighton Maltby was born on 9 July 1890 at 50 Arboretum Street, Nottingham. He was the eldest son of Charles Langley Maltby and Isaline Philippa Maltby (*née* Bramwell). He had a younger brother, Patrick Brough Maltby (b. 1893). His father was a bank manager in Nottingham so it was perhaps particularly frustrating to his father that, whilst an undergraduate at Oxford, Maltby showed a blatant disregard for the appropriate management of his own finances.

Life at Magdalen College School (1901–1909) and beyond

Charles Maltby came to MCS as an 11-year-old Chorister in 1901. Starting chorister life on the same day was Archibald Butler, also aged 11. Butler only remained at the school for his three chorister years, whereas Maltby stayed at MCS for the remaining seven years of his school life, leaving in July 1908. Born in the same year as each other, the two boys were eventually killed in action within eleven days of each other in 1916.

Maltby's school career brought many academic prizes. He was awarded a Green Exhibition (a Corpus Christi bequest Prize awarded to the chorister who was 'best in music, learning and manners') and won the Ellerton Exhibition in 1906 (a prize awarded for the best performance by a chorister in school examinations). He remained a chorister for six years. Amongst his academic prizes he won a Repetition and Elocution Prize twice, a Form Prize twice, a Maths Prize and a Classics and English Prize. He was awarded Lower Certificates in 1904 and 1905 and Senior Certificates in 1907 and 1908, gaining a Distinction in English. For his studious efforts he was also rewarded with an under fifteen Exhibition at the school and was given a 'chorister pension'. He was a School Prefect from 1907/08, then in his final year 1908/09 he was a Senior Prefect and the Editor of *The Lily*. He was the Librarian from 1907 to 1909. Heavily involved in many aspects of school life, Maltby attended the Debating Society and in November

1906 he seconded the motion, 'That this House favours the extension of parliamentary Suffrage to women'. The following year he was elected on to the committee of the Society. In his later years at MCS, Charles Maltby was also the School Organist (1907–1909) and was fundamental in raising money and support to purchase and install a new organ for the School Chapel, fitted in 1908. One of the money-raising schemes involved putting on a Grand Concert in the New Examination Schools.

Maltby's strengths when it came to games and sports were rowing and cricket, but he did have brief dalliances with the other sporting pursuits. He appeared in two matches for the Chorister football team (which also included Harold Dawes and Archibald Butler) versus the Christ Church Choristers in 1903. In 1908 he played tennis in both the doubles and singles competition. In the doubles, with Roberton (Senior), he came sixth out of nine. In the singles, played in a knockout format, he was runner-up, losing in the final but notably beating the sporty, though four years younger, Frank Wilkinson in the first round. Maltby was also a good sprinter and in the Sports Day of 1908 he won the Senior 150 yard Handicap Final in 16.4 seconds. The following year, in front of a large crowd consisting of parents, old boys and friends, he was just unable to repeat this feat but still finished a creditable second, by just 2 yards. Maltby served on the organizing committee for sports days along with notable old boy Noel Chavasse.

Maltby first appeared in the cricket records in 1905, with *The Lily* saying he 'has sound ideas about batting but has no knowledge of the length of a run'. By 1908 he had progressed to playing in the 1st XI, gaining 'quite a fair idea of the game, but lacks height and strength [to be successful]'. That year he made a total of 82 runs in 16 innings at an average of 5.5, but did not bowl. In 1909 he was made Honorary Secretary to the Cricket Club. That season, not only did Maltby briefly bowl for the side, but in the absence of the regular wicketkeeper he went behind the stumps. *The Lily* politely acknowledged his wicket-keeping skills saying that at least he was 'beginning to stop them in that position and has held some catches, but so far has not been within throwing distance of a stump[ing]'. In the Old Boys' cricket match on the Friday before Commem of that year, three boys whose names were to become House names played in the same match. Noel Chavasse had returned to play for the Old Boys XI and Frank Wilkinson and Charles Maltby were representing the school. Maltby scored 23 not out to help the school defeat the Old Boys XI. He finished the season with a total of 114 runs in 11 innings at an average of 11.4, bowling 4 overs and taking 2 wickets for 27 runs. *The Lily* described Maltby as 'probably the straightest bat on the side, but loses many chances of scoring on the off – and often puts up a catch – by facing too much full front to the bowler. He has played some useful innings. Not quick enough for a wicket-keep[er].'

Boys were encouraged to swim the Long Pass, a specific course in the Cherwell which would indicate they would be able to swim to safety if they capsized while rowing on the river. Maltby, along with Herbert Canton and Edmund Tarbet, took and passed this swimming test in the summer term of 1905.

In 1903, 1904 and 1908 Maltby rowed in the Form Four Races. In 1904, aged 13 and weighing 5st 2lbs, he was the cox for the 2nd IV boat that raced against Bath College on the Isis, on a drizzly Saturday in March, 1904. The 2nd IV race started immediately after the 1st IV race, which MCS had won by a good margin. The MCS 2nd boat had a disastrous start and immediately lost two lengths when a 'slight hitch occurred in the proceedings of the Magdalen boat'. The Bath College boat very sportingly offered to start again, but MCS turned this offer down and just redoubled their efforts. By the time the boats had appeared from the Gut the MCS boat had a three lengths' lead. Before the finishing line was crossed the lead was increased to five lengths. Benefiting from his coxing experiences, Maltby would have rowed in the 1st or 2nd IV crew himself in his later years at the school if he had not remained so light in weight.

Maltby's commitment to the school was evident even before leaving, when he joined the organizing committee for the Old Boys' annual dinner and sports fixture in 1908. After leaving MCS, Charles Maltby (or 'Tim' as he was referred to by his friends at school)[1] made a very kind donation of three books (totalling seven volumes) to the Library, reflecting his interests and his kindness. The books were *The Letters of Queen Victoria, 1837–1861* and *Great Buildings and How to Enjoy Them* and *Greek and Gothic Architectures* by E.A. Brown. He had previously made a donation of four books to the Library while he was still at the school in 1909: *The New Far East* by Arthur Doisy, *The Cruise of the Cachalot* by Bullen, *The Harbours of England* by Ruskin, and *Micah Clarke* by Conan Doyle.

Maltby was elected to a Classical Exhibition at Worcester College, matriculating in October 1909. While a student at Worcester, despite being very light in weight (9st 4lbs), he rowed for the College. In Torpids in February 1910 the Worcester College boat achieved four bumps (Day 1, Bumped Univ II; Day 2, Bumped Queen's; Day 3, Bumped Merton; Day 4, Rowed Over; Day 5, Rowed Over; Day 6, Bumped New College II). It appeared as if the entire College was on the bank to receive them after their final success, and several students jumped in the water to meet them, nearly drowning in their celebrations. After achieving their fourth bump the crew persuaded the Dean to organize a celebratory dinner that evening. They celebrated in style, with a bonfire in the Meadow after the dinner, followed by refreshments in the pavilion with speeches, toasts and the College song. In the Boat Club diary the Captain recorded that Maltby, 'Made a very good seven, had quite a pretty form and kept good time. His only trouble is his weight.' In the Summer Term of 1910 Maltby was swapped to rowing at bow during the preparations for Eights Week. Originally planned for 19–25 May, Eights Week was postponed due to King Edward VII's Funeral on 20 May and moved to start on 23 May (and also reduced to four days' racing). The Worcester boat rowed over on the first day then was bumped (by Keble, Pembroke and Exeter) on each of the next three days. There were no celebrations this time. Once again the Boat Captain's comments on Maltby were, 'too light to help the boat along much'. Despite this, Maltby kept his place in the boat the following year and in the summer of 1911 he rowed again at bow (now weighing 9st 8lbs).

The boat had a disastrous week, rowing over three times but also being bumped three times. The Captain's comments on Maltby in the Boat Club diary read: 'Though he has put on a few pounds in weight, he is still rather ineffective, as he is very slow into the catch, and does not hold at the finish. Has no idea of rowing himself out.'

This was the least of Maltby's worries. For in February 1911 a letter from the College to Maltby's mother revealed that he had been spending his money rather freely and that his battels were higher than anyone else's in the College. At the same time, Maltby had written to his parents saying he was hard up for money. Already struggling financially to send his son to Oxford, Maltby's father wrote back imploring his son to 'pull himself together'. In June 1911 things got worse and the College wrote to Maltby's father to say that his son's 'industry has not been thought satisfactory by the College, which has therefore decided not to re-elect him to his exhibition after this term. It seems doubtful whether he is making so good use of his time here that it is desirable for him to take a four years course. It might be better for him to take his degree at the end of his third year, or some work elsewhere.' Entering his third year at Worcester, Maltby by this stage should have already taken his Classical Mods (a second year exam course to read Greek and Latin fluently) but had not even sat his first year exams. In the Michaelmas Term of 1911 he attempted to further delay these assessments by appealing to the College, writing that he had 'a very good offer to play Polixenes in *The Winter's Tale* at the Court Theatre on October 12 + 13' and 'as the Stage is to be my profession I do not wish to lose such a good opportunity'. Not seeing his precarious situation at Oxford, he went on to request specific improvements he required to his three College rooms. Understandably, the College was not approving of him missing Mods or his request to refurbish his room. In March 1912 the College finally refuses Maltby residence until he has passed 'Final Groups' (exams). The College informed his father this action had been taken due to his son's 'idleness and irregularity'. They also disclosed that Maltby's College expenditure had remained unusually extravagant, that he was in debt to a tradesman (Maltby had taken it upon himself to refurbish his College rooms, but not paid the bill) and as a result his son had been summoned to the Vice Chancellor's Court. On Sunday, 17 March 1912, after a request from the College, Maltby writes (on Oxford University Dramatic Society headed paper!) to the Provost to remove his name from the College books. Rather cheekily, in the same letter Maltby asks if the College can reimburse him for the new chintzes on the sofa, two chairs and three window seats and the new matting on the floor of the third room. Maltby came up to College the following Friday and cleared the last belongings from his College rooms.

Maltby's War

Following the outbreak of war he enlisted in the Public Schools Corps along with Dennis Webb, Arthur Foster, Gilbert Gadney and John Bellamy. In February 1915 he obtained a commission in the 12th Battalion, Rifle Brigade. Maltby's

Charles Maltby.

journey to the Western Front started at the Larkhill Camp on the southern edge of the Salisbury Plain. On 21 July the battalion entrained for Southampton and sailed to Le Havre on the SS *Viper* the following day. The battalion followed the common route for many men, journeying through France to the front, initially marching to No. 1 Rest Camp, then travelling 160 miles by train north to St Omer, billeting at Tatinghem, before marching westwards. During the extreme heat of the final week of July the battalion marched west, reaching Outtersteene on 30 July. As they passed through Hazebrouck on 29 July, they were inspected by Sir John French (Commander-in-Chief of the British Armies in France and Flanders), before they progressed to their overnight bivouac site at Borre. Twenty-four men had fallen out from the march that day due to heat exhaustion, despite many halts and packs being removed temporarily during each stop.

The battalion remained in billets at Outtersteene until the early morning of 10 August 1915 when, under cover of darkness, they marched 10 miles south-west to Fleurbaix. That evening, two platoons from each of the four companies of the battalion went into the front line trenches for the first time. The following day, the remaining platoons of the battalion swapped into the trenches. Their introduction to the front line was very quiet, with no shelling, and only sniper fire on the second day. Despite this, the battalion still received its first killed in action casualty, by sniper fire, on 11 August. The platoons of the battalion rotated in and out of the firing line trenches at Fleurbaix until 16 August, when they were relieved and marched back to billets at Outtersteene. Here they carried out fatigue work until 26 August, when they were ordered to march 5 miles south to an overnight billet at Estaires, then on the next day 7 miles north-west to Ferme de L'Epinette on the outskirts of Armentières. Here they took over the defensive post positions in the rear line. From mid-August heavy rain made it difficult to move up and down the trench system. For the last few days of August and the first few days of September the battalion returned to billets on the outskirts of Armentières and supplied working parties to strengthen the weathered trench work. On 3 September the battalion returned to firing line rotation duty in 6 inches of mud. The conditions resulted in both sides carrying out only limited firing.

The battalion spent 3–9 September 1915 in the firing line trenches, patrolling at night and carrying out parapet and wire repairs when possible. During this time two German prisoners (17th Bavarian Regiment) were taken and warning of a mine explosion was gleaned. The Battalion HQ was therefore withdrawn and the men stood to arms; the mine duly exploded on 8 September but did no damage. The battalion was relieved and returned to billets at Laventie, 7 miles south-west of Armentières, where they recommenced their working party duties.

After another period in the firing line from 16 to 22 September, the battalion had spent three days in reserve when on 25 September the Meerut Division (the 7th Division of the Indian Expeditionary Force) made an assault on German lines. The 12/RB stood to arms in reserve, whilst a large pre-attack bombardment took place followed by a large mine explosion. At 06.00 the assault began and by 06.25 the Meerut Division had advanced as far as the German third line trenches. Starting at 07.30 the 12/RB were ordered to advance and connect up with the left of the Meerut Division. By 09.30 B-, C- and D-Coys had crossed no-man's land, while Maltby's A-Coy was occupied digging a new sap trench. Enfilade rifle and machine gun fire from approximately 600 yards caused heavy casualties throughout all companies of the 12/RB. The sap work was found to be almost impossible under such heavy fire, despite efforts to sap backwards from the captured German line. By 10.15 D-Coy had reached and was consolidating the German third line, while A-Coy was regrouping behind the parapet of the British lines (it had lost almost all the men from its first two sections to attempt the sap work). As soon as A-Coy was relieved from the sap work, two platoons of A-Coy commanded by Second Lieutenant Maltby went over the top, but were held up half way across no-man's land and were unable to advance. They had to lie flat in the open, in any ditch they could find. As the attack slowed, ammunition and bombs for the advanced troops began to run out. Sections of the Meerut Division began to stream back towards the original British lines. Despite reinforcements from the 6th Battalion, The King's (Shropshire Light Infantry) and the 1st Battalion, Black Watch, the Germans began to counter-attack in such force and with such a supply of bombs that the Meerut Division gave way and began to retire in a disorganized manner. British shrapnel shell fire was also doing much damage to the British troops in the German trenches. Soon after 11.15 a decision was made to retire and all battalions were advised to do the same. By 12.30 all the Coys of the 12/RB were back in the original firing line trenches. Here they reorganized and were then led back to the support trenches. The KSLI and King's Royal Rifle Corps were left to hold the front line as heavy rain began to fall, while the 12/RB were ordered to move back to billets at Laventie, leaving the support trenches free for new troops to move up. In all the 12/RB had taken 339 casualties (7 officers and 332 other ranks, of whom 123 were killed) and lost nearly all their equipment. The attack had failed chiefly due to the most advanced troops progressing too far and losing touch with the support lines, the supply of bombs being inadequate and the Meeret Division not being equal to the strain and breaking line, leaving the Black Watch unsupported.

By 29 September the 12/RB, reduced to just 375 men in total, had been refitted and left its billets to relieve the KRRC in the firing line. The rain over the previous three days made the communication trenches almost impassable, so the relief had to be carried out above ground down the railway line. During October the battalion, temporarily amalgamated into two companies (A+C and B+D) due to there only being 350 men, was rotated in and out of the firing line, in increasingly wet conditions that necessitated constant repair of the trenches. Artillery and sniper fire was constant throughout this period, and a large mine exploded behind the German lines on 8 October, but its intensity was considered quiet compared to the end of September. At one point German fire did increase significantly when dummy infantry were put up on the British parapets to attract

German fire in order to assess front line strength. Maltby was gazetted Lieutenant after this period of fighting known as the Battle of Loos.

The battalion spent November and half of December 1915 rotating in and out of the firing line and billets near Fleurbaix, and new recruits were received, increasing the battalion's strength. Initially, November was very wet with the trenches in a terrible state, but as the month progressed the colder weather took hold, fog and frost started to set in and excavation work and filling of sand bags was increasingly difficult due to the hard ground. The Germans stretched their shelling all the way to Fleurbaix on 10 December where the 12/RB were billeted, so the area had to be evacuated for a period. When 12 December arrived it had been raining for three days continuously. Water lay 18 inches deep in the fire trench and the River Lys was 5 feet deep in places instead of 2 feet. No-man's land was flooded. On 14 December the battalion marched back into Divisional Reserve a few miles away at Sailly-sur-la-Lys and Bac Saint-Maur. Here they cleaned up, refitted their equipment and supplied work parties to help the Royal Engineers. They stayed in reserve over Christmas and then on 28 December returned to the rotation in and out of the firing line, holding approximately 1,800 yards of front, during a very quiet period. The British kept up patrols, though, listening in to the Germans front line trench at night and generally harassing the enemy. Despite being relieved and returning to their billets on 8 January 1916 the battalion learned that a British gas attack was imminent. In the early hours of 9 January, the battalion 'stood to' in smoke helmets (gas masks), as a precaution in case the favourable wind direction changed or the Germans retaliated with gas shells, while 1,500 rounds were fired by the British artillery.

Finally, on 12 January 1916, the battalion went into Corps Reserve for the first time since landing in France in July. They marched 9 miles north-west to Strazeele, where they billeted for the night, then marched a further 8 miles with the whole brigade to No. 5 camp near Morebeque. During the previous six months they had spent sixty-five days in front line trenches and suffered 421 killed, wounded or missing. On 22 January the brigade moved north to Stenvoorde (west of Poperinge), an 8-mile march. Training, route-marching and general cleaning duties filled their time; then on 5 February the battalion moved to a 'very comfortable' Camp B, 3 miles from Poperinge. The battalion marched to the railway station on 11 February, and after gumboots were issued, the men entrained for Vlamertinge, where C-Coy was left to form the Battalion Reserve, before the rest of the battalion progressed on to Brielen (north west of Ypres). From here, under enemy shell fire they progressed to take up their new front line trench positions, consisting of isolated pieces of trench varying from 40 to 300 yards in length. The trenches they found were in a very poor state of repair, with parapets very low and weak. The trenches ran either side of the canal and the five bridges of the canal were under constant shell fire. Only one bridge was considered practical for use. No communication trenches existed and it was impossible to get to the trenches in daylight. While the relief of the front line was still taking place on 12 February the Germans attacked two sectors of the trenches to be controlled by the 12/RB, bombarding them with artillery and trench mortar fire. The Germans launched raids and infiltrated trench systems, going on bombing runs through the trench lines. Grenades to repel the Germans were running out and resupply was slow as mud over knee height was making movement difficult, but with eventual help from two bombing sections of the 12/KRRC a counter-attack was launched, recapturing much of the British trench system and infiltrating the German trenches. The German artillery and mortar fire now took the lead and blew many of the already poor trenches away. When dawn broke the artillery fire slackened and the morning was comparatively quiet. At 14.30, however, the enemy artillery increased considerably. The battalion trenches and outposts were reinforced by sections of the 12/KRRC and 6/KSLI as the front line trenches were slowly obliterated by an estimated 300 enemy guns. At 16.30 the enemy artillery fire lifted and formed a moving barrage covering infantry attacks against three sections of British trenches. The British managed to repel the attacks, but at considerable cost. As the evening came and work was hurriedly begun repairing defensive systems, the battalion roll call identified 153 men killed, wounded or missing. The 12/RB had only been in the north Ypres salient sector for twenty-four hours. This action of beating off the sustained German attack when the Battalion was still in the process of taking over the trenches brought much praise from Brigadier General J.W.G. Roy (60 Brigade). In a letter to Major H.L. Riley, the officer commanding the 12/RB, he thanked them for 'the splendid way they played the game on the night of 11/12th and 12th'.

Enemy shelling continued on 13 February 1916, and with telephone lines cut and bridges not crossable, communication across the canal was impossible. As soon as night time came the Royal Engineers set about mending the bridge. At 22.30, with a bridge useable again, relief of the stranded outposts was commenced. Maltby, now a Lieutenant, took parties to relieve two outposts (S32 and F31), but due to the very wet ground and the innumerable shell holes, the party only arrived at S32 just before day light. The relief of F31, from whom no sign of life had been heard, had to be abandoned until the next night. The following night a new patrol, stumbling through the churned up battle field and finding it hard to keep direction, found five men from F31 in an almost unconscious state in the bottom of a crater. Continuing on to find the remains of F31, the patrol eventually had to return unsuccessful and were unable to relocate the five injured men to guide them back to the British lines. It was not until 15 February that a further patrol again found the five men and this time carried them in. The remains of the destroyed F31 outpost were discovered but no bodies were found; it was presumed the garrison had been captured. The 12/RB returned to camp at Elverdinghe on 16 February to reorganize and reequip. On 19 February the Germans captured one trench and the British had to abandon two other trenches in the sector, so when the 12/RB relieved the 12/KRRC on 20 February they were back in a much shortened front line. The battalion was exposed to severe bombardments over the next few days until they were relieved and went to camp near Poperinge on 24 February. In very cold and snowy conditions the battalion slipped and skidded the 3 miles from Poperinge station to the camp, with many men suffering from frozen feet. Here they stayed until on 2 March, at a reduced strength of only 350 men, the battalion went back into trenches just north of Ypres. In places the German lines were only 80 yards away, but at others stretched to 500–1,000 yards away. The parapets were in need of rebuilding and many sections of the trenches needed reclaiming, so care had to be taken to remain out of sight of snipers; but at least protective wiring in front of the trenches was in a good state. During this period the weather was extremely cold, but the snow that fell added to the wet in the bottom of the trenches, so much so that pumps had to be kept going continuously to keep the water level down. The battalion was relieved from the firing line on 6 March only to go into reserve at Canal Bank, from where they made up working parties for the next four days, until they returned to camp at Poperinge on 10 March. After four days in support they returned to the poor trenches they had occupied on the night of 11 February north of Ypres. When they went again into reserve on 18 March they were used as working parties, digging new trenches and carrying equipment to the firing line. On 22 March they were relieved and went to camp to reorganize and re-equip, during which time it continued to snow heavily. Entraining at Brandhoek on 30 March, they travelled back to spend four days in the front line around Ypres, before again moving into reserve. They returned to camp on 7 April for four days' respite before returning to the firing line trenches at Ypres on 11 April. After five days they again rotated briefly back to the support trenches before going to billets in Poperinge on 17 April; then on 19 April they moved to a rear echelon camp for a week, forming working parties for railway maintenance, attending courses and undergoing training. Finally, on 26 April the battalion marched 4 miles to a railway siding and entrained for a rest camp at Calais, where they held parades on the sands and had sports competitions, winning the trench clearing competition and the individual throwing competition.

At 04.00 on 6 May 1916 the whole 60 Brigade marched 13 miles to billets at Zutkerque. The next day, setting off at 03.15, they marched a further 17 miles up several very steep hills to Merckeghem. Only two men of the 12/RB fell out – the best performance of the brigade. They marched a further 11 miles to Wormhouton 8 May and billeted around the town for the next ten days, parading and training. The battalion set out at 04.30 on 19 May and marched the 12 miles back to Poperinge, where they billeted in the town. Two days later the battalion travelled back to Ypres by train and then progressed onwards to the Potijze area to take over the firing line trenches for the next four days. They then billeted in and around Ypres until returning to the firing line trenches on 31 May. The trenches on the right flank of the 12/RB at Sanctuary Wood, held by the Canadian Division, were heavily bombarded and attacked by the Germans on 2 June, causing the Canadians to lose the sector. The 12/RB were therefore ordered to put every available man into holding and strengthening the traverses. During this eight-day tour at the firing line, the battalion withstood heavy shell bombardments, rifle and machine gun fire and even a tunnelled mine explosion underneath the trenches. By the time they were relieved on 9 June they had suffered a further thirty-two casualties. The next seven days were spent in reserve at billets in Poperinge under orders to be ready to move at half an hour's notice. On 16 June the battalion moved to billets in Ypres where, in support, they carried out working party duties under constant shell fire. Maltby, who was for some time the Signalling Officer of the battalion, became Adjutant on 21 June 1916. The battalion moved again into the firing line near Potijze on 23 June and for seven days experienced a mix of quiet periods followed by intense action. The British artillery carried out several wire cutting bombardments during this time, with the Germans responding with heavy shelling and night-long rifle and machine gun fire on the British trenches. On the final day of this tour, 1 July, the British released gas from the 6/KSLI trenches, to the right of the 12/RB. The Germans responded with a severe bombardment of the Shropshire trenches. Sixty-six men of the battalion were either killed or wounded during these seven days at Potijze. The battalion returned to billets and support duties at Ypres on 2 July for six days.

Their next stint in the firing line was only four days long, but of similar intensity due to the British again antagonizing the Germans by releasing gas towards their trenches. On 11 July the battalion marched back to Ypres then went on by train to billets at Poperinge. The action followed them, however, with the Germans shelling Poperinge in the morning, afternoon and into the evening. Orders were given to evacuate the town and occupy Camp B at Brandhoek. The battalion marched out of the town at 21.30 and arrived at the camp at 00.30. Two days later the battalion received news they were to go to a rest area the next day; however, these instructions were soon cancelled and a new order was received stating that the whole brigade was to move 'elsewhere', destination secret. Entraining at Poperinge station the following day, they travelled 12 miles south to Steenwerck, from where they marched to a camp near Erquinghem-Lys. Later that night they took up a position in the front line that the battalion had occupied back in November 1915, now an ANZAC Corps area. They found the trenches to be the best they had encountered, 10 feet deep and clean, with parapets up to 25 feet thick, good dug-outs, and excellent wire in front. On the evening of 15 July, when a gas cloud was seen blowing between the trenches, the gas alarm was sounded and the men put their gas helmets on, but not before five of them were gassed. Firing and shelling began, but within the hour the situation returned to normal. It was discovered that the gas was let off by the 5th Australian Division, but the 12/RB had not been warned. The battalion remained in the front line until 22 July, during which time gas cylinders installed in their trenches were planned to be opened on two occasions and the men were dispersed accordingly; however, wind directions were never favourable and the gas attacks were postponed. This date marked the 12-month anniversary of the 12/RB at the Western Front, something that did not go unnoticed by the battalion. In the War Diary the statistics for their year were totalled up: 116 days in the front line;

43 officers killed, wounded, missing or sick; 1,030 other ranks killed, wounded, missing, gassed or sick.

The battalion bivouacked in a field near Steenwercke on 22 July, the following day marching 6 miles to billets at Bailleul; then on 25 July they marched 9 miles to Hopoutre Siding near Poperinge and entrained for Frevent (50 miles south-west). After the six-hour train journey the battalion immediately set off on a hilly 7-mile march to billets at Le Suich. With most of the men only getting three hours sleep they were again on the march, this time 10 miles in very hot weather to Sarton. At this stage the men of the battalion had only had two proper nights rest in five weeks and three days. Approximately thirty-five new recruits fell out during the march, but all except two completed it. Twenty men were sent to hospital on 27 July 1916 suffering from influenza and thirty-five reported unfit to march further due to bad feet. All these were new recruits with less than two months previous training. The next day the rest of the battalion marched 6 miles to Bus-lès-Artois and camped in a wood near the village, then marched to billets at Courcelles-en-Bois the following morning. The working party for that night was cancelled as the guide did not turn up and a heavy bombardment was taking place in the direction of Thiepval; the battalion was now on the Somme. The battalion gradually went into the trenches at Serre near Hebuterne during 5 and 6 August, where the front line had been severely damaged on 1 July and was until this time held only very lightly by small groups of men. The smell in the front line was very bad and no-man's land was covered with corpses. Practically the whole of the line was under reverse enfilade fire from the left, where German trenches were behind the British trenches. To the front the Germans were very quiet. Every available man in the battalion was put on digging duty to reconnect destroyed trench lines. The working parties were interrupted periodically by mortar bombardments from the Germans and replies from the British artillery. On 13 August the sap trench from the 12/RB front line was blown in by the Germans, causing the roof entrance to the sap to collapse when the blast travelled down the tunnel. Six men on guard in the tunnel were injured. From other locations the Army Listeners had picked up conversation between two German Officers that an attack on the 12/RB trench would take place that night. Preparations were made to repulse the attack. Further signs of intent from the Germans were made, mortars being fired attached to white tape, forming a directional path from the German front line to the British. All remained quiet and no attack came, and the 12/RB was relieved by 12th Battalion, The King's (Liverpool Regiment) on 14 August.

The 12/RB marched back, 6 miles west to the relative safety of the camp at Couin. They then marched 8 miles further west to a camp to Amplier on 16 August, then two days later progressed a further 9 'hilly' miles west to billets at Fienvillers. The battalion entrained at Candas on 20 August, travelled 28 miles south-east to Méricourt-sur-Somme, then marched 3 miles to billets at Ville-sous-Corbie. The next day they progressed to a mile south-east of Méaulte. Here they received orders that they would soon be attacking Guillemont, with the

60 Brigade (including the 12/RB) in reserve. During 22 August the battalion went in to the old British support line trenches of the original Carnoy-Montauban Road front line. The 12/RB stood and watched as the 17th, 18th and 24th Divisions marched down the road after being relieved in the front line. The following day two officers from each company plus the CO of the battalion went up to Montauban, Bernafay Wood and Trones Wood to reconnoitre the approaches up to the front line. For three days, 23 to 25 August, the 12/RB practised their attack and formations over old trenches and sent working parties to dig in Trones Wood, but on 26 August the Germans started shooting at the British Gun Batteries behind the 12/RB lines, so practice attacks ceased. Rain fell at intervals in the afternoon and the Germans continued shelling intermittently. At about 20.30 that evening a shell dropped right into the D-Coy officer's mess in a trench. Second Lieutenants M.L. Taylor and G.W. Parmenter were killed instantly. They were buried close by at Carnoy in plots next to each other. Second Lieutenant Tudor Owen was seriously wounded. Lieutenant C. Forster-Brown (D-Coy CO), aged 22, and Lieutenant and Adjutant C.R.C. Maltby, aged 26, both severely wounded, were evacuated back 9 miles behind the lines to the XIV Corps Main Dressing Station at Dive Copse. Both men died the following day, 27 August 1916, and were buried just one plot apart from each other in the cemetery just south of the Dressing Station.

A letter from Maltby's Commanding Officer, Colonel H.L. Riley (ex-Magdalen College) to his mother read:

> I want to write to tell you how much we all sympathize with you in your great loss. Personally I have lost a most excellent officer, one whom I cannot hope to replace and a very great friend. He has been absolutely invaluable to me as Adjutant, and the men were devoted to him. He had just gone to speak to one of the Company Commanders and a shell fell right among them, killing or wounding all five officers. I saw him just afterwards and he was wonderfully cheerful and collected; he asked me to write to you, and I did so hope that he might pull through, though I don't think he thought so himself. I have never known anyone who was so devoted to his duty and he did his share or more than his share in the great cause.

Charles Maltby (or 'Rob' as he was referred to by close University friends) had a natural gift to entertain and he had become more involved with musical and dramatic performances as the years progressed, eventually gaining a considerable reputation for his acting skills before war broke out. After his death his father wrote to Worcester College indicating that they were correct to have awarded him the Exhibition originally (including three letters indicating Maltby's well-meaning character) but that the attractions of the drama and music had distracted him from his academic studies.

1. Referred to as 'Tim' Maltby by his contemporary Walter N. Sage. See letter from Walter N. Sage (from Canada, MCS 1904–5), *The Lily*, January 1949.

Graham Groves MATHESON

26 July 1891 – 7 June 1917

Rank and regiment: Corporal (14035), 14th Reinforcements NZEF; Private (14035), 1st Battalion, Auckland Regiment. **Medals awarded:** Victory, British War. **Theatre of War:** Western Front. **Memorial:** Messines Ridge (New Zealand) Memorial, Belgium.

Graham Groves Matheson was born in New Zealand on 26 July 1891. He was the eldest son of William Brooklyn Matheson and Annie Elizabeth Matheson (*née* Speedy). His father was born in Nottingham, England, and moved to New Zealand some time after 1881 where he became a sheep and cattle farmer. The family lived at Tiratahi, Eketahuna, Wellington. Graham had two brothers: James Percy (b. *c.*1898) and Leonard David Penn (b. *c.*1902); and four sisters: Elizabeth (b. *c.*1890), Annie Dorothy (b. *c.*1893), Marjorie (b. *c.*1896) and Ruth Mary (b. *c.*1907). On his death Graham left his money to his brothers and sisters, but it was his brother James to whom he left his personal possessions.

Graham's uncle Percy Ewing Matheson was the Secretary of the Oxford Examination Board and lived in Oxford, so it is perhaps not so surprising that Graham was sent to England and MCS to complete his schooling.

Life at Magdalen College School (1903–1909) and beyond

Graham Matheson joined MCS in September 1903. He had brown hair and grey eyes and was not athletic or sporty, only being recorded once as obtaining a place in a Sports Day event (a heat of the Senior 150 yard Handicap), once rowing in the Form Fours in Hilary 1908, in the same boat as Cecil Dyer, and not appearing for any of the Schools teams. He was moderately studious but reserved, winning an English Prize and a Form Prize during his six years at the School. He left MCS at the Easter of 1909 to return to his native New Zealand. His parting present to the school library reflected his interest in Classics, the book *Social life at Rome in the Age of Cicero* by Warde Fowler.

Back in New Zealand, Matheson matriculated at Victoria University College in 1910 and for the following two years is recorded as studying English, Latin and Greek. In 1915 he took and passed examinations in Latin, Greek and French that constituted the first section of his two-part BA degree. During this period he was also going through Teacher Training and at the time of his enlistment was teaching at a school in Pirinoa, a very rural area to the east of the Tararua Ranges and south of Lake Wairarapa.

Despite being thousands of miles away from Oxford he kept in touch by writing to the school informing them of his whereabouts and experiences. He was also subscribing to *The Lily* magazine through to his death. In a letter to the school in 1914 he describes his teaching role in Pirinoa, saying that it is not an easy job as he has to teach both well-to-do farmers' and Maori children. The main advantage of the position he described was that he could at any time decide to declare a few days' holiday and go off on a shooting expedition.

Matheson's War

Graham Matheson tried to enlist in the Army at the outbreak of war in 1914; however, owing to his poor eyesight he was originally rejected. Not to be deterred, the 5 feet 10¾ inches tall and 156lb Matheson kept trying to persuade the Army to take him, and was eventually successful, joining G-Coy, 14th Reinforcements New Zealand Expeditionary Force as a corporal on 10 January 1916. He embarked on the troopship *Tahiti* for the two-month journey to Europe from Wellington on 26 June 1916, waving goodbye to his family for the last time. The ship docked at Devonport on 22 August 1916, at which point Matheson reverted to the rank of Private on joining a training battalion (Wellington Coy) in Sling, England. A month later, on 26 September 1916, Matheson was sent to France, arriving in Étaples the following day where he was attached to the NZEF General base depot for the next eighteen days. The New Zealand Division had earlier in the month made its debut in the war on the Western Front, taking part in the third major offensive on the Somme that year, the Battle of Flers-Courcelette, where tank warfare was seen for the first time. At the end of September the main objective of the Flers-Courcelette offensive, the third German defensive line, was finally captured during the Battle of Morval. Unfortunately, the Germans had been busy digging a fourth defensive line (a fifth and sixth were also under construction) along the Transloy ridge. On 14 October 1916 Matheson was attached to the 1st Battalion Auckland Regiment (New Zealand Division) and within three days he had joined the Light Trench Mortar Battery, in time to enter the final offensive on the Somme of 1916, the Battle of Le Transloy, an attempt to capture the new German line along the Transloy ridge. In an ever increasing struggle against the resilient German defences and the wet and muddy conditions the offensive had its last throes in early November 1916, before the Battle of the Somme eventually petered out.

During the winter months of 1916/17 the New Zealand Division relocated north towards the Ypres area, where in June 1917 they were to play a large part in the storming of the Messines ridge and the capture of the village of Messines. On the night of 6 June the Division moved forward to the assembly trenches in preparation for the following day's attack. Completion of the troop assembly was delayed until about 02.30 on the 7 June due to a German bombardment with gas shells. Then, after the detonation of seventeen huge underground mines (a total of 420 tons of high explosives) at 03.10,[1] the 2 and 3 Brigades of the New Zealand Division went over the top, moving up the cratered slopes of the Messines ridge behind a creeping barrage. The New Zealanders, supported by the Australians, passed through the German front and support lines and beyond towards the heavily fortified village of Messines. Graham Matheson and the 1 Brigade then drove on through, supported by a solitary tank, to attack the village. The New Zealanders were initially held up by artillery and machine gun fire from a farm north of the village, but with the help of the tank driving through the farm this was neutralized. After rushing two more machine gun posts on the outskirts of the village, and penetrating the village under a slow (100 yards in eleven minutes)

Graham Matheson.

creeping barrage, the New Zealanders eventually captured the German commandant and the garrison surrendered.

While digging themselves in to their new positions in the village the New Zealanders were subjected to heavy artillery fire from the Germans and their own artillery which was falling short. Graham Matheson was killed by a shell at Messines on the night of 7 June 1917, aged 25. Between 1 and 14 June the New Zealand Division suffered a total of 4,978 casualties. In spite of the huge losses suffered by the New Zealand, Australian and British troops, the battle was considered a tactical and operational success, with the Germans not only losing a significant strategic vantage point but also suffering a significant dent to their morale.

1. See chapter 'The Theatres of War' for more detail and the contribution of T.W. Edgeworth David (OW) to the mining operation.

Henry Stephen MINTOFT

2 June 1897 – 4 October 1917

Rank and regiment: Second Lieutenant: 3rd Battalion (att. 1st), East Yorkshire Regiment. **Medals awarded:** Victory, British War. **Theatre of War:** Western Front. **Memorial:** Oosttaverne Wood Cemetery, Belgium.

Henry Stephen Mintoft was born in Crieff, Perthshire and was the youngest son of Thomas John Mintoft and Margaret Mintoft (*née* Lesley). His father was a timber merchant from Yorkshire. Henry had two older brothers, Thomas Christian (1886–1976) and John Philip (1889–1909). The family lived at Alne Low Hall, Yorkshire, but temporarily moved away for some time after Henry's father, then a Church Warden at Alne Church, was cited as a co-respondent in a divorce case with the wife of the Vicar of Alne in 1900. Shortly after the divorce suit, which ordered Thomas John Mintoft to pay £4,000 damages, he filed for bankruptcy. To complete the tragedy, Henry's mother died only a few years later in Yorkshire in 1906, and his youngest brother John died in 1909, aged 20, after the two youngest brothers had moved to Oxford with their father. In 1911 Henry and his father (whose occupation was given as 'Private means') were living in Oxford with their housekeeper, Louise Crosby (from Alne in Yorkshire). When Henry entered Sandhurst four years later his father's occupation is recorded as 'Gentleman'. Henry's older brother Thomas joined the Army, served with the Yorkshire Regiment during the war and survived.

Life at Magdalen College School (1908–1912) and beyond

Henry Mintoft started at MCS as a day boy in the Trinity Term of 1908, aged 10. He joined Form III, which at the time included John Callender and Donovan Leicester. In Michaelmas 1910 he progressed up to Form IV, but was absent for the majority of the Trinity Term, reportedly due to a severe illness. He returned to school in the Michaelmas Term of 1911, still in Form IV, but achieving his highest end of term Science exam score of 60 per cent. Mintoft was present at school the following term, but was absent for the Trinity and Michaelmas Terms of 1912 despite being on the register. In his later period at MCS, in Form IV, Mintoft became a boarder. It is uncertain where Mintoft went after leaving MCS in 1912 and until he joined the Royal Military Academy in 1915.

Mintoft's War

From 21 September 1915 to 7 April 1916 Henry attended the officer training course at the Royal Military Academy, Sandhurst; and on 18 July 1917 he was gazetted Second Lieutenant 3rd (Reserve) Battalion, East Yorkshire Regiment. Soon after, he was attached to the 1/E.Yorks and posted to France. Mintoft arrived in France on 25 August 1917 and immediately made his way to join his new battalion in the area of Boisleux-au-Mont, between Arras and Bapaume. When he arrived at the front the 1/E.Yorks had recently been relieved by the 6 Connaught Rangers. Between 26 and 28 August the 1/E.Yorks additionally received a draft of 193 other ranks and the whole battalion moved to hutted billets at Simencourt (8 miles east of Arras town centre) during very high winds and heavy rain. The battalion was reorganized on 29 August, absorbing new drafts of men, and for the next seventeen days they remained at 'rest' billeted at Simencourt. During this time they were kept incredibly active with training (including 'trench to trench attack', 'attacking a strong point', 'assistance to another platoon on a flank', 'consolidating and wiring of captured positions'); with inspections of the ranks, the billets by the Brigadier and gas helmets by the Divisional Gas Officer; with ceremonial drills and parades; Divine Service on Sundays; route marches; and evening lectures from the CO. For recreation brigade sports were organized on 8 September, in which the 1/E.Yorks came second out of the four battalions (1/E.Yorks, 9/KOYLI, 10/KOYLI, 15/DLI) and the 64/MGC and 64/TMB. A marathon and relay races were run and a tug of war was contested (the officers taking part in a separate tug of war competition). On 9 September a revolver shooting competition was held and won by the 1/E.Yorks, the team of eight included Henry Mintoft. In the inter-unit football, the 1/E.Yorks beat 9/KOYLI 2–0 in the first round, but the following day in the semi-final lost 3–1 to the 10/KOYLI. The officers even had a divisional gymkhana on the afternoon of 10 September, and Brigade boxing was fought on 12 September. A Brigade Day was held at Wailly on 13 September, where training attacks on the enemy were carried out, with 10/KOYLI representing the enemy. The following day was the Brigade's final day in billets at Simencourt and a message from the town mayor was read out stating his appreciation for the improvement they had made to their accommodation. The battalion left Simencourt on 15 September and moved 50 miles north by train to billets immediately north of Hazebrouck (east of Ypres).

On 18 September the Brigade underwent a short route march and tactical exercises followed by 'attack practice with contact aeroplanes' the following day. All officers of the brigade were given a lecture on field cypher on 20 September and were made to practise their compass work on 22 September. The brigade was gearing up to go into action and on 23 September the whole brigade marched approximately 6 miles to new 'scattered farm' billets around Thieushouk and over the following four days undertook practice attacks and route marches. The Brigade moved again on 28 September, marching 11 miles to La Clytte, where the 1/E.Yorks stayed at Murrumbidgee Camp. The evening of the next day saw the battalion practising forming up for an attack under a bright moonlit sky, which attracted considerable aerial activity from the Germans. A number of bombs were dropped around their practice area. On Sunday 30 September the battalion held a Church Parade, after which there was considerable air activity again during the evening.

On 1 October the officers of the brigade were shown a 'picture ground' of the sector for the forthcoming operations. The following day at 16.00, with Henry Mintoft as one of four officers in A-Coy, the battalion marched 2 miles to Chippewa Camp near Reninghelst. At 23.00 on 3 October, in very cold and rainy conditions, the 1/E.Yorks left their camp at Scottish Wood and marched to form up by 05.00 on 4 October at Glencorse Wood. Under a heavy enemy barrage 'all ranks displayed great steadiness'. At zero hour the battalion advanced in separate companies, with A-Coy on the right of the 10/KOYLI. At zero plus 1 hour 40 minutes A-Coy assisted in the capture of a second objective point. Their commanding officer, Captain A.R. Case, reorganized them and they dug in at Reutel Ridge. Several times during the afternoon and evening the Germans counter-attacked and the front line troops had to send SOS signals to the British artillery on each occasion to help disperse the attacks. Sadly, but predictably, some of the British artillery shell fire fell short, causing casualties on each occasion. Henry Mintoft was killed, aged 20, during this action on 4 October; he had survived six weeks at the front and one day in battle. He is buried close to where he fell, 4 miles south of the centre of Ypres at Oosttaverne Wood Cemetery. His name also appears on the War Memorial of St Mary's Church, Alne in Yorkshire. The brigade managed to hold the positions they had won until relieved on 6 August by the 7th Battalion, Leicestershire Regiment.

Michael Ambrose MORRIS

6 April 1883 – 6 August 1915

Rank and regiment: Lieutenant, 13th Battalion (att. 2nd), Hampshire Regiment. **Medals awarded:** Victory, British War, 1914–1915 Star. **Theatre of War:** Gallipoli. **Memorial:** Helles Memorial, Turkey.

Michael Ambrose Morris was born in Stoke Fleming, Devon, and was one of seven children of Reverend Charles Morris and Penelope Morris (*née* Dunn). His father was a graduate of Corpus Christi College, Oxford, and at the time of Michael's birth was the vicar of Street, near Dartmouth, Devon. The family moved to Oxford in 1888 when his father became the vicar of Marston. He had three brothers, Charles Edward (b. 1881), Henry Rowland (b. 1884) and George Philip (b. 1892). He also had three sisters, Penelope Mary (b. 1887), Henrietta Dorothy (b. 1889) and Milicent Helen (b. 1890). His father died in 1899, aged 56, whilst Michael was still at school.

Michael's eldest brother, Charles, served with the Indian Army during the First World War, eventually rising to the rank of acting Lieutenant Colonel and winning a DSO in 1919. Henry served with the Royal Engineers, Pioneers Corps; and George served with the 8th Battalion, Oxford and Buckinghamshire Light

Infantry and the Royal Flying Corps in the Egypt Expeditionary Force. All three survived the war.

Life at Magdalen College School (1896–1902) and beyond

Michael and his two eldest brothers, Charles and Henry, all joined MCS in January 1896. Charles appears to have been the sporty one of the MCS brothers, playing cricket and football while at school and indeed returning to play old boy games, whilst neither Michael nor Henry appear for any of the teams while at MCS. Academically and socially, while at MCS, all three boys appear to have been reserved, and it was only Charles who succeeded to the position of School Prefect in 1900. Interestingly, none of the Morris brothers attended science lessons while at MCS. George, the youngest of the brothers by eight-plus years, attended St Edward's School as a boarder.

In 1901 Michael passed the Royal Military College exam for Sandhurst. The same year, despite not winning the school Modern Language Prize, he was cited as being among the *proxime accesserunt*. In 1902 Michael left school and passed into Sandhurst. Poignantly, eight years later, in 1910, Michael donated a book to the school library entitled *The Three Brothers* by Eden Phillpotts (himself the son of an Indian Army Captain).

Morris' War

Michael Morris attended the Royal Military Academy, Sandhurst from July to December 1902 and gained his first commission on 21 April 1903 with the 1st Battalion, Hampshire Regiment. He joined his new battalion at Aden in South Arabia, the strategically important port city at the entrance to the Red Sea. In February 1905 he resigned his commission and took up employment doing consular service work at Cadiz in Spain. In 1914 he was returning to Spain after a short break in England when he heard news of the outbreak of war. He responded by taking the first boat back to England to rejoin the army. He was gazetted Lieutenant to the 13th Battalion, Hampshire Regiment in October and was posted to the Dardanelles in May 1915, attached to the 2nd Battalion, Hampshire Regiment (48 Brigade, 29th Division). Morris, along with a draft of five other officers and 360 other ranks, joined up with the 2/Hants in the early morning of 15 June, disembarking at Cape Helles. The 2/Hants had already been in Gallipoli seven weeks, originally landing at the cape on 25 April. Z-Company (which Morris was to join) had landed in the collier boat *River Clyde*, which drove herself on to 'V' beach and delivered the men down ramps in broad daylight into a mêlée of withering machine gun fire and shrapnel shells. By nightfall the 29th Division was in disarray and its ability to make progress towards its first-day objective, the high ground of Achi Baba and the village of Krithia (5 miles in land), was in ruins. On 26 April the 2/Hants did capture the coastal village and fort of Sedd-el-Bahr, but the battalion continued to suffer many casualties as they struggled to work inland with the rest of the 88 Brigade towards the town of Krithia. The Turks had prepared well for the invasion over the previous month. They continually bombarded, raided and sniped at the Allied troops as they tried to get a foothold on the peninsula, pinning them down and producing a static trench war.[1] The initial objective of Krithia was never taken during the entire campaign, despite three major battles to do so. When Morris arrived, the third of the battles for Krithia had recently ended and a period of consolidation ensued, improving trenches, burying the dead and fending off Turkish raids. The battalion was relieved from the firing line on 19 June and returned to reserve at Y-beach, where the Turks continued to bombard with shrapnel shells, causing ninety casualties. The French attacked and captured two lines of Turkish trenches on 21 June, killing 7,000 Turks and suffering 3,000 casualties themselves. The Turks counter-attacked at 23.00 and the 2/Hants stood to ready to assist. These small scale battles or raids continued throughout June and July and the casualties mounted. Interestingly, on 11 July, the 2/Hants drew about 40,000 rounds of ammunition out of the Turks and located three of their machine guns by cheering and waving their bayonets, but even with this tactic twelve casualties were suffered. After Morris had been at the front for a month the battalion was withdrawn on 17 July and embarked on the *Elkahira* for Lemnos, a small Greek island, for some much needed rest and reorganization. Here they were inoculated against cholera, practised attack formations and route-marched from one side of the island to the other. After ten days, on 28 July they returned aboard the *Newmarket*, leaving Lemnos at 16.00 and arriving at W-beach, Cape Helles, at 23.30. Here they bivouacked on Gully beach, before advancing to previously held trenches. On 1 August they commemorated Minden Day[2] by wearing flannel roses, as real roses were not available. Unfortunately, the commanding officer of the battalion, Lieutenant Colonel Beckwith, was shot through the index finger on this day whilst looking over the parapet during an inspection. His finger was amputated, but whilst recovering in hospital a cliff fell on him. He was eventually brought to using an artificial respirator and removed to a hospital ship.

For the month of August, General Sir Ian Hamilton, commanding the Mediterranean Expeditionary Force (MEF), had planned a decisive battle to break the Gallipoli deadlock. The plan was to make new landings at Suvla Bay in the north part of the peninsula then, together with the Anzac Cove troops, take the objective of the high ground of the Sari Bari ridge in the north. At the same time the troops in the south at Cape Helles (including the 2/Hants), were to be used in a diversionary attack on Achi Baba. On 2 August details of proposed diversionary attack in the south at Achi Baba were given out to the 2/Hants officers. Morris' Z-Coy were to be in the front line, with the 4/Worcs on their right and Y-Coy of 2/Hants on their left, with the 1/Essex Regiment further along. Officers of the battalion reconnoitred the trenches they were to attack on 4 August, concluding that 'details of [the] attack appeared to be suitable ... and it is expected that no opposition will be met with'. In the early hours of 6 August the battalion moved up, under heavy gun-fire, to their starting positions in the fire trenches, relieving the Royal Fusiliers. In the afternoon, after the planned one-and-a-half hour bombardment of the enemy trenches, the 2/Hants launched their attack at 15.50. Morris and the 'first line advanced at proper time' but many machine guns in front and in the flanks had not been knocked out by the bombardment and the attack met murderous fire. It was reported that the 'attack did get home', but the majority of the first line of the 2/Hants were either killed or wounded. The second wave of the attack lost its commanding officer as soon as he left the trench, and the attack failed. Casualties from the 2/Hants for the day totalled 22 officers and 439 other ranks, with Michael Morris initially listed among the missing officers. During the night, patrols were sent out to check whether any men were holding isolated parts of the enemy trenches, but it was found that all had either been killed or returned to their own lines. The following day the 88 Brigade, including the 2/Hants, were relieved by the 86 Brigade and moved back into reserve at Gully beach. During the night of 8 August patrols were sent to the front to search for any wounded still out between the two front lines, but none were found. It was concluded that Michael Morris was killed in the attack on 6 August 1915, aged 32. His body was never recovered and he has no known grave. The attacks in the north and the south of the peninsula both failed with the loss of many thousands of men. Hamilton was replaced as commander of the MEF and the decision was made to plan for the complete evacuation of the peninsula.

1. The Allied forces at Gallipoli included not only the British and the famous ANZACS of Australia and New Zealand, but also the French Oriental Expeditionary Force. Together they constituted the Mediterranean Expeditionary Force (MEF).
2. Commemoration of the Battle of Minden on 1 August 1759.

Joseph Leonard Milthorp MORTON

21 March 1895 – 22 October 1917

Rank and regiment: Captain, 22nd then 23rd Battalion, Manchester Regiment. **Medals awarded:** Victory, British War. **Theatre of War:** Western Front. **Memorial:** Tyne Cot Memorial, Belgium.

Joseph Leonard Milthorp Morton was born in Church Green, Redditch, the third son of Dr Edwin Morton and Anne Emily Morton (*née* Goodchild). His father was a physician, whose roles had included medical officer of a school and education medical officer for Oxfordshire.

Joseph had two older brothers, Edwin Ralph Maddison (b. 1891 and known as Ralph) and John Edward Blackburn (b. 1893, known as Jack). Edwin and John also attended MCS, Edwin starting as a chorister in 1902 and John joining in 1907. John followed in his father's footsteps, qualifying as a physician in 1919. Ralph joined the Army, being gazetted Second Lieutenant in 1913. Joseph also had two younger sisters, Grace Emily (b. 1897) and Violet Stephanie (b. 1902).

The family lived for a number of years in Wolverhampton before moving to Oxford in about 1907.

Life at Magdalen College School (1909–1910) and beyond

Ralph, the eldest Morton brother, joined MCS as a Chorister in 1902. He was to stay at MCS for eight years, excelling as an athlete and sportsman, rowing for the 1st IV boat (1909–10), playing cricket for the 1st XI (1907–10, full colours 1908) and football for the 1st XI (1907–09, Full Colours 1909). Joseph initially attended St Edward's School from the summer term of 1905, while Jack joined his elder brother Ralph at MCS in January 1907, after the Morton family had moved to Oxford from Wolverhampton. It was not until January 1909, when Joseph moved from St Edward's to join his brothers, that the Morton trio at MCS was complete.

In his very first term at MCS, on 13 March 1909, Joseph Morton (at 6st 2lbs) coxed the 1st IV boat to a sixteen-length victory in the annual race versus Bath College on the home water of the Isis. Rowing at stroke was his eldest brother Ralph (at 9st 7lbs) and at no. 2 was Herbert Canton. In reward for his contribution, Joseph was awarded full rowing colours. On Sports Day 1909, Joseph tied for first place in the Junior High Jump with Donovan Leicester (both clearing 3ft 11ins) and also competed in the Junior 100 yard event. Later in the July of 1909 he swam the Long Pass. During the summer term Joseph had played cricket and during the autumn term had played football for the U15 XI teams. At the November Prize Day of 1909, in the presence of his proud mother and father, he capped his first year at MCS by being awarded the Repetition and Recitation prize for Form III. Joseph appeared set to emulate his older brothers, academically and on the sports field.

On Wednesday, 16 March 1910, at the landing stage on the river Cherwell and close to the White Bridges, Joseph Morton was requested by a Prefect, George C. Thompson, to assist getting his boat out of the water. When hit on the neck by a stone, thrown but not aimed at Morton by Sidney C.W. Disney (another Prefect), Morton let go of the boat and Thompson almost ended up in the river. This resulted in an angry exchange between Thompson and Morton. There is some confusion over whether Thompson immediately punished Morton by slapping his face, or whether Morton was chased, scared and ordered to report to the Prefects' Study. Whatever took place, Morton missed rowing that afternoon but did not report to the Prefects' Study; instead, he went home and reported the incident to his parents. Evidently Morton's face had been marked during the incident and he had ended up in the river. His father, Dr Morton (then the Education Medical Officer for Oxfordshire), wrote to Mr Brownrigg saying he thought his son had been punished sufficiently in the assault and should prefer for him not to be punished further. The following day Joseph was ordered by the Prefects to go the Prefects' Study after school. Morton duly reported to the study, finding all six prefects present. Before the caning, the head prefect (G.F. Newton) struck Joseph twice in the face, as hard as he could, causing him to flinch. He was then held down (by W.B. Broadbent) and again hit in the face with all Newton's force, between eight and ten times. Subsequently, Joseph was caned, twelve strokes by one boy, three by Newton and three by a third prefect. During the day,

Joseph's elder brother[1] sought retribution by hitting Thompson hard in the face during a Science lesson. For this the Headmaster punished the brother with a caning, and he was ordered to apologize to Thompson. The affair was becoming ugly and complicated. Upon returning home, Joseph was evidently in a poor condition so his father returned to school with him late in the evening to speak to the Headmaster. Dr Morton made efforts to get the school authorities to look at the matter of excessive punishment and illegal face-slapping, but an unsatisfactory response had been gained. Embarrassingly for the School, and the College, the case therefore ended up in the Oxford City Police Court on 19 July 1910, with the Senior Prefect (Giles Fendall Newton) as defendant.

Slapping was evidently regarded by the Prefects as a milder form of punishment than the cane, mid-way between the tiresome punishment of lines and the harsh punishment of caning. The punishment of slapping was concluded by the Court to be without the knowledge of the Headmaster, who strongly disapproved. The school was ordered to take measures to ensure that slapping did not take place at the school.[2] G.F. Newton was sentenced to one calendar month's imprisonment or required to pay a fine of 20s plus 14s costs. The case stands as one of the significant episodes that opened the debate on the inhumanity of and difficulty in controlling physical punishments for purpose of discipline in schools.[3] The event was a low point in Brownrigg's otherwise exemplary career as a Master and Headmaster at MCS, and both the College and School suffered significant embarrassment from the public airing of their procedures. Sadly, the episode meant that Joseph Morton moved schools, his family realizing that it was best if he continued his schooling elsewhere. His two older brothers also parted company with MCS at the end of that academic year, in July 1910. Ralph, then aged 18, was due to leave anyway, but Jack, then 17, should have stayed another year. The Morton boys had played a significant part in the life of the school for the previous eight years, and indeed the closeness of Ralph and Giles made the affair particularly sad and regrettable. Originally choristers together, both were excellent sportsmen. On the cricket field they had formed both a ball and bat partnership that is easily one of the best the school has ever produced, opening both the batting and bowling together for the School 1st XI for four years, often in the presence of Jack Morton, whose sporting skills were not far behind those of his elder brother.

There is an indication that MCS before and after the '1910 affair' was indeed a mild school with respect to its handing out of corporal punishment by either the Headmaster or his Prefects. Its small size would have helped, and indeed, after this date, pupil diary evidence portraits a very well controlled and happy school requiring only limited and relatively rare corporal punishment of its pupils.

Joseph joined Berkhamsted School in May 1910 and was a boarder at the school for two years. While there he sat junior local exams, obtained his Lifesaving Certificate and Medal and was awarded a Merit for singing. He left at the end of the Spring term of 1912. His intended profession, listed while at Berkhamsted, was a Lawyer.

For his final year of school education, from September 1912, Joseph Morton moved to board in the Sixth Form of the Perse School, Cambridge. After his previous experience at MCS it is interesting that in December 1912 he entered the Perse Boxing Competition, winning the over nine stone category. He went on to represent the Perse at the Public Schools Boxing Competition, only losing his contest narrowly by the casting vote of the referee. In 1913 Joseph tied for first place in the open High Jump (clearing 4ft 7ins) and was second in the open Long Jump. In the Hockey report of 1913 his critique reads that he 'Worked hard at left, but must make sure of hitting the ball, and of hitting harder.' In the summer of 1913 he played 1st XI cricket for the Perse. He also competed in the swimming sports of 15 July, held at the Town Bathing Sheds due to very inclement weather. Here he came second in the open 200 yard race after leading until the last 20 yards, but won both the Open Diving and the Object Diving competitions. He was awarded an Honorary Instructor's Certificate and a Teacher's Certificate from the Royal Life Saving Society and a Royal Humane Society Medal. Not surprisingly, he worked on the Swimming and Boxing Sub-Committees while at the Perse, and obtained House Colours for his efforts. Joseph Morton left the Perse in July 1913, going on to Christ Church, Oxford in 1914.

Morton's War

On 31 August 1914 Joseph Morton, in his first year at Oxford, applied for a temporary commission in the Army, submitting forms via the OTC at Oxford University. He was initially accepted into the Oxford University Officer Training Corp as a Cadet, and then in March 1915 he applied for an appointment to the Special Reserve of Officers, specifying his preference for service to be with the 3rd (Reserve) Battalion, South Staffordshire Regiment, for whom his brother Edwin was then serving as a Surgeon Lieutenant. Certifying his good moral character were John G.C. Anderson, then a Senior Student[4] and Tutor of Christ Church, but eventually an eminent professor of Ancient History; and Sir Robert Buckell, at that date previously four times, but eventually six times, Mayor of Oxford. Joseph Morton was gazetted Second Lieutenant (temporary) on 3 April 1915 and subsequently put his studies at Christ Church on hold. Soon after this, probably on its formation in September 1915, Morton was assigned to be Second Lieutenant (temporary) with the 27th (Reserve) Battalion, the Manchester Regiment. He was reassigned to the 22nd (Service) Battalion with the same regiment on 5 November.

The 22/Mancs set sail for France in early November 1915, joining the 91 Brigade, 7th Division, in December 1915.

In February the 22/Mancs moved to the Somme, and occupied trenches at Bray-sur-Somme, 4 miles south of the German-held and heavily fortified village of Mametz. Joseph Morton sailed from England to join the battalion in France in April 1916. On 2 June, after a substantial bombardment to soften up the German line, A-Coy successfully raided a German listening post despite encountering difficulties due to uncut enemy wire. On the last day of June 1916 the battalion

The Morton Family, c.1915.
From left to right: Ralph, Anne (mother), Edwin (father), Violet, Sarah Susannah Morton (grandmother), Jack (with bandage), Grace, Joseph (here as a Second Lieutenant).

moved up from camp at Bois des Tailles to the assembly trenches with a strength of 20 officers and 754 other ranks.

At 07.30 on 1 July, the first day of the Battle of the Somme, the 22/Mancs moved forward towards Fricourt from their trenches in two waves, D-Coy (on the left) and B-Coy (on the right) first, followed by A-Coy (on the left) and C-Coy (on the right). The leading companies took their first objective line of Bucket Trench to Dantzig Alley with heavy casualties. The supporting companies and remaining lead companies then pushed on to the final objective of Fritz Trench, but owing to further heavy casualties from machine gun and shell fire, they were unable to reach it. German soldiers emerging from dug-outs in Dantzig Alley meant that the battle was being fought on all sides, with the initially held objective line having to be cleared by 2/Queen's running bombing parties down the length of Dantzig Alley from the direction of Pomières Trench, taking about seventy-five prisoners. As night time came on 1 July the 22/Mancs dug in to hold Dantzig Alley, having suffered 490 casualties, including 10 officers killed and 8 wounded. Officer reinforcements were therefore immediately sent up. The remnants of the battalion stayed in these and nearby trenches consoli-

Joseph Morton.

dating their position until 5 July, when they were relieved and went to rest at billets and bivouac accommodation at Buire(-sur-l'Ancre). The battalion went to Mametz Wood and into Divisional Reserve on 14 July, while the remainder of the 91 Brigade attacked the German second line at Bazentin le Petit. Despite being in reserve, the 22/Mancs continued to supply companies to swell the numbers of the attacking battalions, again receiving many casualties. They evacuated their position at High Wood on 16 July and withdrew to bivouac locations in reserve, initially 8 miles back from the front at Méaulte and Dernancourt; then after entraining at Méricourt-sur-Somme they relocated a further 24 miles east to Frémont on 22 July.

On 23 July 1916, Morton was promoted to Lieutenant (temporary) and reassigned to the 23/Mancs, a bantam battalion[5] in the 104 Brigade 35th Division, who were also fighting on the Somme. Then, on 29 July the 23/Mancs were lent to the 90 Brigade and supported their attack on Guillemont, carrying SAA and bombs to supply the attack. For the next three weeks they were in training and at rest, billeted around Sailly-le-Sec and Corbie. The 23/Mancs were back in the front line on 19 August in newly captured trenches on the extreme right of the British line, with the French on their right. During the night of 20 August the Royal Engineers dug a new sap trench (and called it Bantam Trench) to allow the battalion a safe route to another recently captured trench (Lonely Trench) in advance of the 23/Mancs position. The following night the battalion raided German dug-outs and captured an enemy machine gun, suffering no casualties themselves. During this period there were many dead bodies still to be buried from earlier stages of the battle in August and the trenches were 'in [a] filthy state and [the] place [is] beginning to smell very badly'. They were relieved on 22 August and spent the rest of the month at rest and in support. At the start of September 1916 the battalion moved 30 miles north to Arras and, after a few days, went into the front line trenches around the city. The British released gas from the 23/Mancs' front line sector during the night of 8 October and followed this up with small raids on the German trenches. The enemy was found to be in good strength and bombs were exchanged before the parties returned. Thirty-three men had to be treated for the effects of the 'friendly' gas, which had remained in the British trenches after its discharge. During November and December the 23/Mancs continued to rotate in and out of the trenches around Arras during a period of persistent and considerable hostile exchanges. On 11 December 1916 the battalion received a draft of 171 men of average height or over and the following week 166 men of the battalion were marked down and eventually moved out as unfit. The average height of the battalion was increasing and the status of the 23/Mancs as a bantam battalion was beginning to be lost. In January 1917 the 23/Mancs moved to Beaufort-Blavincourt, for a period of training. Here the scheme of 'De-Bantamigation'[6] was continued, with many more men above the average height drafted into the 23/Mancs, with battle-weary men now passed as unfit sent to labour companies and base depots near the coast.

At the beginning of February 1917 the battalion relocated south via Amplier, Naours and Flesselles, eventually to near Chaulnes (40 miles) on 20 February where they relieved a French regiment in trenches deep in water and mud, south of the River Somme. On 26 February the battalion moved back to Rosières(-en-Santerre), then into Divisional Reserve until 6 March. During their next tour at the front they were commended for their numerous successful patrols of the enemy. This probably contributed to the Germans retiring from their lines near Chilly on 17 March. The retreat allowed the 23/Mancs to advance to Méharicourt where they occupied cellars rather than muddy trenches. The battalion then marched to Chilly and on to Fonches(-Fonchette)on 18 March before, on 19 March, moving to Parvillers(-le-Quesnoy) and ultimately to Voyennes, where they were attached to 32nd Division for road repair work in the local area. At the start of April the battalion moved on to Beauvois(-en-Vermandois), Étreillers and Vaux(-en-Vermandois), then to Villecholles and Maissemy, where two of the companies went into the front line on 11 April. A party of 160 men, commanded by 9 officers, raided the German-held village of Pontruet on 15 April but encountered no enemy opposition. The village was thoroughly searched and only freshly bloodstained bandages were found. The battalion was witnessing the strategic withdrawal of the Germans known as Operation Alberich. The Germans destroyed everything on the ground as they withdrew, flattening villages, poisoning wells, cutting down trees, blowing craters on roads, booby-trapping ruins and dug-outs. The withdrawal was to a stronger and shorter line called the 'Hindenburg Line', positioned to take tactical advantage of more easily defensible ground. For the remainder of April and into May the battalion proceeded in cautious pursuit of the Germans via Tetry, Bihécourt and Vermand. From Vadencourt, east of Saint Quentin, at 02.30 on 5 May, 5 officers and 159 other ranks raided and captured Somerville Copse under the cover of a heavy artillery barrage and a diversionary Lewis Gun and Rifle Grenade attack. They cleared out the dug-outs and shelters in the wood, driving the enemy out and capturing four prisoners. Sixty dead Germans were found in the wood, whereas just nine men of the 23/Mancs were wounded. Six days later on 11 May, an officer was wounded while on reconnaissance in front of the battalion outpost line near Vedencourt, before, on 15 May, the battalion moved into reserve around Péronne, Templeux-la-Fosse and Heudicourt. In June the battalion was again rotating in and out of the front line, with five men being killed by shell fire on 27 June. Three days later an enemy raid on the battalion's trench was repulsed, but not before the Germans captured a Sergeant who had only joined the battalion the night before. A badly wounded German soldier left behind in the British trench later died of his wounds.

At the start of July 1917 the 23/Mancs were in the front line at Villers-Guislain, south of Cambrai, before being relieved on 2 July and going into Divisional Reserve at Templeux-la-Fosse, 8 miles behind the lines. Here they trained and rested for two weeks before returning to the front lines at Épehy on 15 July, only a few miles from their previous front line sector. Eight days later they rotated into support trenches. On 26 July the front line to the right was raided by the Germans after an intense bombardment; the 23/Mancs stood in wait. Two days later the 23/Mancs raided the German trenches with four groups of fifteen men, each led by an officer. After a heavy artillery barrage two raiding groups entered the enemy trenches at 02.50, with their right flank covered by the third group, while the fourth group opened fire against the German trench. At 03.15 the four parties returned to their own lines, having captured two machine guns and inflicted several casualties on the enemy. Nine men of the 23/Mancs were wounded and one man was missing.

Two days later the battalion was relieved by the 17/Lancashire Fusiliers. Before the end of the month Joseph Morton became acting Captain in the 23/Mancs, gazetted on 20 July 1917. During the following month, August, the battalion spent all but ten days (8 to 18 August) in reserve at Gurlu Wood in the front line trenches at Épehy. During the night of 21 August they again made a raid on the German trenches. This time 14 officers and 259 other ranks, in four groups,

Joseph Morton in France (1915–1917).

under the cover of a heavy artillery and machine gun barrage, cut through formidable wire entanglements and entered the enemy trenches at 04.30, bombing dugouts and inflicting severe casualties on the enemy. They withdrew to their lines at 04.55 after suffering eight men killed or missing, and forty-eight wounded, including four officers.

During September the battalion rotated through a familiar Western Front cycle of front line (at Épehy), reserve (at Templeux-la-Fosse, then Villers-Faucon), billets (St Emilie), front line (Guillemont, where on 25 September one officer and three other ranks were wounded), camp (Aizecourt-le-Bas) and billets at Doingt.

Finally, on 2 October the battalion left the Somme area and relocated by train from Peronne, 35 miles north to Hauteville, west of Arras. There they stayed in billets and trained until 13 October, when they again relocated by train a further 40 miles north to Zegerscappel, just 12 miles from Dunkirk. After two nights in billets at Zegerscappel the battalion moved by train (from Bollezeele) 14 miles east to Proven, near Poperinge. The next day, 16 October, the battalion entrained again at Proven and detrained and went into the front line at Boesinghe, 3 miles north of Ypres. The battalion war diary entry for 17 October reports that one officer and seven other men were wounded in the front line, and one man was missing. They were relieved on 18 October and went to camp 4 miles back at De Wippe. On 20 October they went back into the front line trenches north-east of Langemarck. It is believed that Morton had only just returned to the battalion at this point after previously being wounded, reportedly several times, possibly at one of the above mentioned actions. The following passage is an adaption of the Battalion War diary of the 23/Mancs from 22 October:

> At 05.35 the battalion attacked [the area of Houthulst Forest] in conjunction with another battalion on our left and the 34th Division on the right. The first objective line was reached with slight casualties. From this point, however, the resistance was more stubborn and very heavy rifle fire and machine gun fire was experienced from both flanks. All the officers, with the exception of one who was acting as liaison officer with 34th Division on the right and a very large proportion of NCOs and men were either killed or wounded and the battalion was unable to make any further progress. The survivors that could be collected, that is about fifty other ranks under a Company Sergeant Major, withdrew to our original line, and later in the morning were relieved by the companies of the 20/LF who had been in reserve, and withdrew to the vicinity of Egypt House. That evening the battalion moved back to Pascal Farm and the following day were withdrawn from the line.

It was reported elsewhere that the division were attacked at an early stage of this action by German planes. The right flank of the 23/Mancs lost touch with the 16th Battalion, Royal Scots, and the 17th Battalion, Lancashire Fusiliers on their left flank drifted to further left and also lost contact. The consequence was that German strong points were left untouched on both sides and to their rear. Enemy machine gun fire from both sides caused enormous casualties and Morton was

Captain Joseph L. Morton depicted as the Good Shepherd with scenes from the life of the biblical Joseph (1955). St James' Church, Aston.

hit twice leading his own company to an advanced position. When he tried to rally the members of a neighbouring company who had lost all its officers he was hit again and killed, aged 22. Joseph Morton has no known grave. He is commemorated on the memorial wall of Tyne Cot.

His Colonel wrote, 'His death will be a tremendous blow to the battalion, as he had been with us [the Regiment] so long, and was loved, and respected, and honoured by all his ranks.'

A brother officer wrote, 'He was always perfectly fair, and would never let a man be done down. He died worthily, and was as nice and straight a man as you could have met. That is the character his men gave him, and they are good judges.'

A stained glass window memorial to Joseph Morton, and his parents, from their family exists in the Chancel (south window) of St James' Church, Aston (Oxfordshire).[7]

1. It is unsure whether this was Ralph or Jack.
2. Commonplace in most if not all public schools at the time was a system whereby prefects were given authority to maintain and keep discipline and order in the school. Thus, according to Law, a schoolmaster was entitled to delegate his powers of non-excessive corporal punishment to a monitor or prefect as long as it was under the direction of the headmaster.
3. The court case was reported by local press, including the *Oxford Chronicle*, 22 July 1910, the *Derby Daily Telegraph* and the *Nottingham Evening Post*, 20 July 1910.
4. Senior Students at Christ Church are equivalent of Fellows at other colleges.
5. The 23/Mancs at this stage was still classed as a bantam battalion, but eventually lost this status at the beginning of 1917. Bantam battalions recruited men who were below the normal minimum height requirement for army enlistment of 5 feet 3 inches, but above 5 feet, although officers tended to be well above average height. This allowed small but otherwise healthy young men to enlist, especially from industrial and coal mining areas where short stature was no sign of weakness. The much taller and thus easily identified officers of the bantam battalions provided obvious targets for the German rifles.
6. 'De-Bantamigation' is the phrase used in the war diary by the Lieutenant Colonel Commanding the 23/Mancs.
7. Joseph Morton's, along with two other boys' names, did not appear on the original MCS War Memorial that hangs in the school chapel, and over the years his story and sacrifice had been lost by the school. In 2013 his name and association with the school was rediscovered and at the Remembrance Service that year his sacrifice was acknowledged for the first time by the school. Plans are in hand to include his name on an additional memorial in Chapel alongside the original.

Wilfrid Hearne PEARSON

18 April 1888 – 29 September 1918

Rank and regiment: Private (10909), Inns of Court OTC; Second Lieutenant, 2/1st Battalion, The Northern Cyclist Battalion attached to 57th Battalion, Machine Gun Corps. **Medals awarded:** Victory, British War. **Theatre of War:** Western Front. **Memorial:** Anneux British Cemetery, France.

Wilfrid Hearne Pearson was born at 3 Winchester Road, St Giles, Oxford, on 18 April 1888, the third son of Arthur Pearson and Eunice Mary Pearson (*née* Hearne). He had two older brothers, Arthur Hearne (b. 1884) and Cyril Hearne (b. 1886), and two younger sisters, Bertha Irene Hearne (b. 1890) and Maud Cecilia Hearne (b. 1894).

Wilfrid's father, Arthur, was somewhat of an entrepreneur. He was a hardware merchant running the ironmongers at 31 Cornmarket, Oxford, from 1882 until 1912, when he moved his premises to George Street. By 1889 he also owned the Oxford Drug Company, on the corner of Broad Street, and in 1890 had become a portmanteau manufacturer after acquiring Boswells. Arthur was also a Wesleyan minister and in later life decided to take up a more academic existence, studying for a degree in Oxford. This meant that Wilfrid's brother Arthur had to take over the running of the businesses.[1] The Oxford Drug Company and Boswells are still owned by members of the Pearson family today.

Cyril did not follow in the family business, but became a schoolmaster, teaching in Wales in 1911. Bertha moved to Canada as a secondary school teacher but regularly returned to visit her family in England, where in 1985 she died. Maud died in Oxford in 1961, and like her sister never married.

Life at Magdalen College School (1903–1905) and beyond

Wilfrid initially attended the City of Oxford High School for boys from 1897 to 1902 and was a contemporary of T.E. Lawrence (better known as Lawrence of Arabia) for five years. He then joined MCS in January 1903, aged 14. In 1904 he played in the 1st XI Football team, at full back. *The Lily* described his style thus: 'Pearson, who is new to the side, at left-back is distinctly promising: he has a fair amount of dash and is a strong kick: occasionally he is wild.' He received full colours for his efforts receiving the comment, 'Has been very useful to the side.'

In each Hilary Term Pearson did not play hockey but concentrated on rowing. In 1904 he competed in the Form Four races; then in 1905 he made the school 1st IV crew for the prestigious 'Bath Race'. Despite racing on the opposition water of the Avon, losing the toss and not having the favoured bend, the lighter MCS boat held off the Bath College boat to win by a length. It was a major achievement for the crew and Pearson, who weighed 9st 6½lbs and rowed at no. 3. It was reported in *The Lily* that the crew 'travelled well between the strokes, and were much faster than they appeared to be' and that '[Pearson] has fought steadily against his natural tendencies to be late and slow'. These faults were not quite overcome till the actual day of the race, but he was then at his best, and backed stroke up well throughout the course.

When it came to sports days Pearson seemed to excel. In his first Sports Day of 1903 he came joint first in the Senior Long Jump, with a leap of 4 feet 9 inches. Uniquely in 1903 (and the following year) the school included a bicycle event in Sports Day, the 2 mile Handicap Bicycle Race. In an exciting finish the first and second placed bicycles collided with 30 yards to go, resulting in Pearson crossing the line second. However, the jury's verdict awarded second place to the felled cyclist and Pearson was given a prize for third place. The following year in 1904 Pearson made good use of his first bicycle race experience and won the event in a time of 5 minutes and 46 seconds. He also won the High Jump event, with a clearance of 4 feet 11½ inches. In 1905, in his last week at the school, Pearson went one better. He won four events and collected the coveted 'Ladies Plate' Trophy, for the person accumulating most points on Sports Day.[2] He won the 440 yard Sprint in 58.2 seconds; the High Jump with a clearance of 4 feet 11 inches; the Long Jump with a leap of 17 feet 5½ inches; and the 150 yard Sprint in 16.8 seconds; finally even in the 'fun' race, the Blindfolded 100 yard Walking Race, where 'remarkably few competitors finished between the posts',

Pearson managed a second place to complete a happy day, which he would surely never forget.

In 1905 he also played cricket for the School 1st XI team, which included Harold Dawes and Francis Pitts. At the end of the season *The Lily* reported that Pearson was 'Very useful in the field [works hard and throws well]. As a bat was converted from vigorous "mowing" and now gets himself out steadily by gentle strokes.' He finished the season with 35 runs from 11 innings. *The Lily* explained that it seems 'by much net practice he has acquired a capacity to play a ball to the off, but in the process seems temporarily to have lost the vigour which was associated with his natural style.' Possibly an example of early twentieth century over-coaching taking the fun out of his game! It would have been lovely to have seen his 11 innings in his natural style; one would like to predict that he might have ended up totalling more than 35 runs.

In 1905 Wilfrid, when aged 17, moved to the Leys School in Cambridge, where he was in North B House. While at the Leys he achieved 1st XI football colours and was introduced to the sport of Rugby, playing three-quarter for the

1906.—F. C. Pyman (3-*quarter*), B. H. Holloway (*half*), S. S. Mallinson (*back*), J. Brown, J. C. Boot, W. M. Fiddian (3-*quarter*), C. H. Reid, W. H. Pearson (3-*quarter*), L. B. Smith (*half*), E. A. Salter, A. H. Holman, J. P. Oliver, G. E. Toulmin, E. S. Ayre (3-*quarter*). Won 14, lost 1.

The Leys School Rugby 1st XV, 1906.

Wilfrid Pearson, is in the seated row, second from left, to the left of the boy with the ball.[3]

School's 1st XV in 1906 (see picture). He also continued his Long Jump success by winning the Leys Long Jump Open 1st Prize in 1906.[4] Wilfrid left the Leys after completing one year in 1906, then went on to qualify as a pharmacist before returning to Oxford to help run the pharmacy part of the family business. On returning to his home town he continued to play rugby, playing three-quarter for the Oxfordshire Nomads RUFC and captaining their side in 1909. Sitting on the committee of the Oxfordshire Nomads at that time was Basil Blackwell.

Before the war the Oxford Drug Company was running three chemist shops, with the main shop, which Wilfrid's father had rebuilt in 1912, moving to 31 Cornmarket in 1915.[5] Wilfrid was the pharmacist in charge of one of these shops.

Pearson's War

Wilfrid married Daisy Beatrice Turrill in 1915 and attested for the Army in December 1915, initially joining the Army Reserve because his position as a pharmacist was considered an exempt occupation.[6] As the war progressed, more and more exempt occupations were reconsidered by the War Office, and Wilfrid's exemption was withdrawn in January 1917. On 15 March 1917, Wilfrid and Daisy's daughter Margaret was born.[7]

On 26 March 1917 Wilfrid joined No. 14 Officer Cadet Battalion (Inns of Court Officers Training Corps) based at Berkhamsted. Eight months later, on 26 November, he was discharged from the Inns of Court OTC to take up a commission of Second Lieutenant in the 2/1 Northern Cyclist Battalion based in Skegness. Some time after this he became attached to the 57 Machine Gun Corp (a Divisional Machine Gun Battalion), who were formed on 1 March 1918.

At the beginning of July 1918 the 57/MGC were in the Bapaume area when they were placed in Reserve and sent for a period of rest and training at Bois de Warnimont. Pearson's B-Coy went to Orville on 5 July for three days' training, being repositioned on 14 July to Chateau de la Haie to provide reserve for the front line near Sailly. On 14 July the battalion held its sports day in preparation for the Divisional sports on 22 and 23 July. On 29 July the battalion moved from Corps Reserve and proceeded to Beaudricourt, then on to Gouves near Arras the following day.

The A- and D-Coys took over a section of the front line east of Arras on 1 August 1918, while Pearson's B-Coy remained in reserve and moved to battalion headquarters at Duisans. The war diary of the 57/MGC described the front line on 9 August as 'extremely quiet', but at the same time says that the British 'artillery fired continuously with the Germans only retaliating with harassing fire by night largely by using Yellow Cross gas shells'.[8] Twelve men were gassed when a shell went into the mouth of their dug-out. After seven days, B-Coy relieved D-Coy in the Fampoux South Sector (east of Arras) on the night of 9 August. B-Coy remained in the firing trenches for eight days until relieved on 17 August, when they returned to rest at the HQ at Duisans. The battalion remained in the rear at Duisans until 23 August, but due to a full moon providing visibility at

Wilfrid with his daughter Margaret in 1918.

night were bombed by enemy aircraft. Eventually the whole battalion, joined by A-Coy who had stayed in the front line and had gone over the top during an attack south of the Scarpe on 18 August, moved west to Sombrin. The battalion moved on to Bavincourt on 25 August. At this time the whole 57th Division began to be involved with the general advance forward from the Scarpe southwards. On the night of 26 August the battalion (less C-Coy, who were attached to the 172 Infantry Brigade) marched 9 miles to Blairville. The following night, the 57/MGC relieved the 52/MGC in the firing line at Henin (south-east of Arras). C- and D-Coy were both involved with an attack on the German lines at Riencourt on 28 August, then on the following morning and during continued fierce fighting in and around the village, Pearson's B-Coy was sent to relieve pressure on C- and D-Coys. Fierce counter-attacks were held off by the battalion, then on the night of 30 August B-Coy moved into position to support the next British attack. Fierce fighting resumed around Riencourt on 1 September, but eventually B-Coy were able to advance and reach their objectives. The following day, with the support of tanks, the 57 Brigade advanced south on the Drocourt-Quéant line, successfully taking all objectives (part of the Battle of Drocourt-Quéant line, a phase in the Battle of Arras).

The battalion concentrated at Hendecourt-lès-Cagnicourt on 3 September 1918 and spent the next five days reorganizing and refitting, albeit under heavy shell fire for much of the time. D-Coy had seven officers killed when a shell pitched into their mess on the 6 September. During the night of 8 September the battalion relieved the 63/MGC in the trenches in the Inchy-en-Artois sector (10 miles east of Cambrai). B-Coy on the left consisted of eight pairs of Vickers guns, with each gun manned by six men, and each gun pair positioned at a pre-calculated location so that total coverage of any attack was achieved. The Company headquarters was again separate. This separation between the machine gun pairs and the HQ was important to limit reduction in fire power caused by any one single enemy action.[9] The distance between the British and the German trenches at this point was only 200 yards, so any movement was carried out at night. Casualties taken during the daylight hours therefore had to wait until dark to be evacuated, because communication trenches in these now rapidly shifting front lines were non-existent. On 11 September the 57th Division attacked the line of the Canal du Nord, with the objective of taking the village of Moevres. Fierce fighting followed over the next four days, with the British achieving a foothold in the village on several occasions, only to be repelled again. The British machine guns laid down constant harassing fire, day and night, both on the communication headquarters of the Germans and on centres of activity on the Canal du Nord. The British withstood intense shell fire from the Germans during this time, including both Blue and Yellow Cross shells. During the night of the 15 September B-Coy was relieved from the firing line and went into reserve. The battalion concentrated at Noreuil (west of Cambrai) over the next two days, 8 miles behind the front line. They were then moved by train 30 miles

Wilfrid Pearson.

north-west to the relative sanctuary of Monchiet, west of Arras. Between 18 and 25 September they had a welcome rest from the intense fighting and spent time reorganizing and training and in recreation. Route marches were carried out and an inter-section football competition was started. Orders had already been received that they were to soon resume the attack, and on 25 September the battalion moved by train to Vraucourt, then marched the 2 miles to billet again at Noreuil. Orders were given to the Company Commanders on 26 September and the following morning at 01.45 the battalion marched to their assembly area via Lagnicourt and the track south of Quéant and Pronville. The battalion was in position by 05.20, and at 06.15 the companies were ordered to move forward. At 07.00 when the order '57th Division Move' was given the whole division moved forward. By 10.00 it was evident that crossing the canal to reach their objectives was not possible because the initial objectives of the attack had not been taken and the bridge crossings were not possible. The 57/MGC therefore had to re-group on the sunken road. B-Coy attempted to move forward but received six casualties through heavy shelling. Finally, by 11.45, the 172 Infantry Brigade were pushing forward to the Hindenburg Support line and enemy machine gun positions were being mopped up. Artillery was moved forward and despite the congestion B- and D-Coys transferred their weapons to pack animals and crossed the Canal with speed at midday. By 14.30 B-Coy were advancing across the Hindenburg Support Line in support of the 171/IB; and C- and D-Coy advanced in support of the 172/IB. The Germans' hold on the villages of Graincourt and Anneux, the gateway to Cambrai, started to crumble. German counter-attacks during the evening were repelled by artillery barrages. On the following morning, 28 September, the attack continued, with the 171/IB supported by B-Coy and 172/IB supported by D-Coy clearing the ground beyond Anneux and eventually linking up with the Canadian advance at Fontaine. As the day progressed, the infantry advance on the Marcoing Line started to suffer heavy casualties. Defensive positions were therefore taken up before nightfall. The following day, their positions were consolidated and counter-attacks were held off, eventually allowing an attack by the 171/IB supported by B-Coy 57/MGC on the left. Two sections of B-Coy advanced across the canal at the Lock Bridge at dusk, and a third section crossed and moved forward to the Marcoing Line and covered the canal crossing. The fourth section stayed in reserve in the sunken road. It was during the action on 29 September 1918 that Wilfrid Pearson of B-Coy 57/MGC was killed, aged 30. The Battle of the Canal du Nord continued for another two days, by which time the British had penetrated a majority of the defences of the Hindenburg Line, allowing the next attack (the Battle of Cambrai) to fully penetrate and start the advance beyond the Hindenburg Line.

News of Wilfrid's death reached the family in Oxford on the morning of Friday 4 October. Like many fathers and mothers who lost sons in the war, Wilfrid's father had a comforting apparition of Wilfrid some days after his death saying not to worry, for he was now all right. His father contributed to the

A tribute to Wilfrid Pearson exists in the City of Oxford Church of St Michael at the North Gate, close by where Wilfrid had worked

purchase of the school war memorial. It was great comfort to the family that Wilfrid's batman took the time to visit the Pearsons in Oxford when he returned to England in December 1918.

1. Old advertisement pages for Pearson & Co. from this early period of the company are reproduced in the book *Oxford Shops and Shopping, A Pictorial Survey from Victorian and Edwardian Times* by Michael L. Turner and David Vaisy.
2. The same 'Ladies Plate' trophy is still competed for and presented at every Sports Day.
3. With Pearson in the Leys 1st XV of 1906, and pictured in this photograph were: John C. Boot (2nd Baron Trent and son of Jesse Boot, who turned the Boots Company into a major national company), standing at back (right, tall player); and Bernard H. Holloway (the Sussex and MCC cricketer who toured the West Indies with the MCC in 1911) seated on the floor (left).

4. His family still possess the winning trophy, a cut glass and silver plated biscuit barrel, with the inscription 'Long Jump Open 1st Prize 1906'.
5. One of the Oxford Drug Company shops was in the Arcade, off Cornmarket, and its adverts were a regular feature in the local newspaper, declaring that it had an immense stock of sponges, imported before the war closed the fisheries of the Italian, Grecian and Turkish waters.
6. Under the Pharmacy Act of 1868 every pharmacy company was obliged to keep a qualified manager in every shop that it owned, to preserve the safety of the public.
7. Margaret E.H. Pearson, died 1993.
8. The Germans marked their shells with a yellow cross for mustard gas, a green cross for chlorine and phosgene gas, and a blue cross for diphenylchloroarsine (a solid released upon detonation to create a fine dust which could penetrate a respirator filter and cause irritation and pain, forcing the man to remove his mask).
9. By 1918 machine gun tactics had developed to be more akin to those of the artillery than the infantry. As well as using calculated positions for the machine gun sites to produce interlocking fields of fire, the guns were employed to produce a creeping barrage with fire falling ahead of the artillery barrage to target troops moving to the rear. A machine gun team in 1918 consisted of six men: two to carry the gun equipment (a water-cooled Vickers machine gun and tripod), two to carry the ammunition and two spare men. The No. 1 was a Lance Corporal who was in charge and fired the gun. The No. 2 fed the round belts into the gun. No. 3 supplied the ammunition to the gun. The others were ready with spare parts and acted as observers.

Francis Burton PITTS

9 January 1890 – 17 May 1917

Rank and regiment: Private (3098), 21st Royal Fusiliers; Second Lieutenant, 3rd Battalion (att. 8th) Leicestershire Regiment. **Medals awarded:** Victory, British War, 1914–1915 Star. **Theatre of War:** Western Front. **Memorial:** Cabaret-Rouge British Cemetery, France.

Francis Burton Pitts was born in Loughborough, the second son of Thomas Pitts and Honor Thursby Pitts (*née* Vale). His father was the Rector of Loughborough, Leicestershire. Francis had two brothers, Bernard Thursby (b. 1888) and Hugh Creighton Martindale (b. 1896). He also had a younger sister, Honor Mary Theodora (b. 1899). Bernard, like his father and grandfather, entered the Church. Hugh followed Frank into the Army, serving in the Machine Gun Corps during the war. The year 1917 was to be a tragic one for the family: one month after Frank's death, his uncle Octavius Vale died, and Frank's mother herself died a few months later, aged only 55.

Life at Magdalen College School (1904 – 1906) and beyond

Francis Pitts joined MCS in September 1904, having initially attended Loughborough Grammar School. Known as Frank, he was a good sportsman, gaining a place in the School 1st XI Football and Cricket teams in his first year at MCS. He was also a talented golfer, eventually representing Leicestershire. Francis Pitts played inside-left (forward) for the 1st XI Football team in the 1904, 1905 and 1906 seasons. At the end of the 1904 season he was awarded half colours, and his Football Profile in *The Lily* reads, 'Has a good idea of the game, and fed his wing man well. Is very small and timid, but must learn that a small nippy forward is very difficult to stop.' By 1905 Pitts had 'improved immensely on his last year's play, is faster, more foot-clever, and is not so easily knocked off the ball'. Sadly, his 1906 season never lived up to the promise of the previous season as he hurt himself at the beginning of the Michaelmas term; but it was acknowledged that he 'knows when to pass and when to "go on his own" and is quite a good shot'. During his three seasons at MCS he scored many goals, even scoring four in one game when, in November 1906, MCS beat their sister school, Magdalen College School of Brackley, 11–0. During his three years at MCS, Pitts played in teams that included Harold Dawes, Basil Blackwell, Leslie Hoyne-Fox and Wilfrid Pearson. He was awarded full colours in 1906. During his two summers at MCS, 1905 and 1906, Pitts kept wicket for the MCS 1st XI under the captaincy of the MCS cricketing legend Harold Dawes. His *Lily* profile of 1905 read: 'Gives promise as a wicket keeper and is sometimes quite smart but often misses an easy catch. As a batsman has wrists and a good eye and will be useful hereafter.' Batting in the middle order, he contributed many useful scores and was awarded half colours for his efforts.

Pitts successfully swam the Short Pass in the summer of 1905, and also showed himself to be a good gymnast during the School Competition at the University Gymnasium in the same term. In 1905 he won the Form IV French prize and in 1906 he gained a Junior School Certificate before leaving MCS at the Christmas of 1906, only two years and a term after starting.

It is uncertain what Pitts did upon leaving MCS, but it is probable that he was home-taught during this period until May 1909, when he joined the Royal College of Music, studying the organ and piano. He left the RCM in December 1912, aged 22.

Pitts' War

Francis Pitts signed up for the Army at Derby on 16 September 1914 when aged 24. His army attestation papers record his occupation as 'Gentleman'. Pitts, grey-eyed and 5 feet 6 inches tall, joined the 21st (Service) Battalion (4th Public Schools Battalion), Royal Fusiliers as a Private. The 21/RF were based at Ashstead, Surrey from October 1914 until March 1915, then at Clipstone Camp, Nottinghamshire (joining the 98 Brigade, 33rd Division), and finally at Tidworth Camp, Wiltshire, before sailing from Folkestone aboard the SS *Princess Victoria* for Calais on 14 November 1915. The 21/RF then travelled via Boulogne, east to Thiennes and on to the Béthune area, where they were to remain for the next four months. Pitts' battalion rotated in and out of the front line trenches and reserve line billets at Beuvry, Annequin, Les Harisoirs, Epinette, Festubert, Hingete, and L'Eclème. Francis Pitts' own 2-Coy 21/RF, and the rest of the battalion, experienced much heavy fire and conducted important fatigue work and training during this time before, on 28 February 1916, the 21/RF were transferred to GHQ troops and finally disbanded on 24 April.[1] On 28 February the battalion left Béthune and entrained for Saint Omer, then marched on to billets at Wardrecques, from where, on 3 March, Pitts was sent to hospital suffering from

Francis Pitts.

scabies.[2] He stayed in hospital for a week before returning to Wardrecques on 10 March. Two weeks later, on 24 March, he was posted back to No. 1 Officer Cadet Battalion, Denham, England to work towards a commission. After four months officer training, on 4 August, he was discharged from the Royal Fusiliers and granted a commission as a Second Lieutenant in the 3rd Battalion (attached 8th Battalion) Leicestershire Regiment, then based at Winestead Camp, Patrington Camp, Yorkshire.

Second Lieutenant Francis Pitts joined his new battalion on 9 August while they were in Divisional Reserve at Agnez-lès-Duisans, 6 miles west of Arras. On 11 August the newly joined officers were paraded under the direction of the CO of the battalion. The battalion went back into the trenches near Roclincourt, just north of Arras, on 18 August for a fourteen-day stint at the front. Work on strengthening and improving the trenches went on throughout this time. The battalion was treated to the sight of three German observation balloons opposite their trenches on the first day of their tour and experienced considerable artillery activity, from both sides, for much of the rest of the tour. After a three-day targeted bombardment by the British, the 8/Leics carried out a carefully prepared raid on the German lines on 23 August. The German front line was found to be deserted but useful tactical information was gained by the venture. The battalion war diary describes other German observation balloons going up on 25 August, but being quickly drawn down when British planes approached. At 01.15 on 27 August a German patrol was heard approaching the British lines by a sentry. They were only 20 yards from the battalion front line and on the edge of a sap trench filled in with wire due to German mining operations. A bomb was thrown at the patrol, seriously wounding one man. After the Lewis gunners and reliefs took up positions at either end of the sap a flare was sent up, revealing six Germans lying in the grass. The Lewis gun opened fire and groans were heard. An officer and another man went out to investigate but had a bomb thrown at them, which luckily failed to explode. The officer captured the German (of the 93rd [Anhalt] Infantry Regiment) who threw the dud bomb and brought him back in to the trench. Two other men went out to fetch the German who had been hit by the Lewis Gun fire, but he was found to be dead. The battalion left the trenches and marched 16 miles to rest billets at Lignereuil on 3 September, going via Agnez-lès-Duisans, Montenescourt and Avesnes-le-Comte, where they stopped for dinner. The next day was spent bathing a few miles away at the mill at Berlencourt. The Brigade held sports after the parade service on 9 September, with the Divisional Band in attendance. The Divisional Concert Party gave a performance and dinners and teas were served. The remainder of the time at rest camp was spent in training and route marching. On 13 September the battalion marched 9 miles to Frévent station, knowing they were heading for the Somme area. At midnight they entrained for Dernancourt, near Albert, 30 miles south, arriving fourteen hours later on 14 September. The next day they marched to bivouac between Méaulte and Fricourt, where they rested for two days before moving up through Mametz and Montauban(-de-Picardie) to a position half a mile east of Trones Wood. The next seven days were spent in reserve, supplying working parties for the front line and consolidating the positions that had been won. At 21.00 on 24 September the battalion marched up to their start position for an attack the next day. During the march they were heavily shelled, causing several casualties. At 12.30 the following day they launched their attack from a position on the right of Flers. The first objective of the attack was the first German line, a distance of about 1,000 yards. The attack was made in waves, each platoon forming a wave, and two waves going over the top at a time. The war diary says, 'The attack was launched with splendid heroism', with the first objective being gained after three quarters of an hour. The men then stopped a short time to consolidate their gain and to allow the artillery barrage to lift. They then pressed on to their second objective of the village of Gueudecourt. 'By the time they had reached the village they were sadly thinned by the tremendous artillery barrage the enemy put up and by machine guns which brought terrible havoc. Nonetheless with dauntless gallantry they pressed on, reaching the village and engaging the enemy in hand to hand fighting, which took place all the night.' In the morning the battalion was relieved in the village by the 7/Leics, who finally drove the Germans out. Dropping back to the second line, they were further relieved by the 6/Leics on 28 September, withdrawing further to Swiss Trench. Finally, on 1 October they were withdrawn into reserve and bivouacked at Bernafry Wood. On 2 October they marched for five hours to Dernacourt on the west side of Albert. The next day they entrained at the station for a 32-mile, seven-hour journey west to Longpré(-les-Corps-Saints), then after tea at the station they marched 7 miles to camp at Pont-Remy, near Abbeville. The next two days were spent like most days in rest camp doing 'interior economy and bathing'.[3]

On 7 October 1916 the battalion left the Somme region, entraining at Pont-Remy and journeying 50 miles north-east to Béthune, before marching a short distance to billet at Fouquereuil. After three day's rest they marched via Fouquières-lès-Béthune and Sailly-Labourse to trenches near Vermelles and took over the reserve line from the 2nd Rifle Brigade. During their time here the battalion was given permission for 25 per cent of each company to visit the Divisional Concert Party at Sailly-Labourse, and on 14 October the baths at Vermelles were opened from 10.00 to 12.00 for the benefit of the battalion. The battalion was moved up to the front line for five days on 17 October and soon found themselves again in the middle of heavy shelling and taking part in patrols that brought close encounters with the enemy. When back in the support trenches, 10 per cent of the men were allowed to go to the Divisional Cinema at Sailly-Labourse each day. On 26 October, those men who had completed two years' service were granted a Good Conduct badge by the CO. Francis Pitts would have been one of the 180 men to collect a badge, having served for twenty-five months by this stage.

November and December were spent rotating between the front, support and reserve lines approximately every six days. During the time in reserve their time was mostly filled doing fatigue duties, but permission for 25 per cent of the men per day to visit Béthune or the neighbouring villages was granted. The trenches during these two months were in a dreadfully wet and muddy state; add to this the psychological effect of the intense and constant mortar activity and machine gun strafing of the parapet at that time, and it is easy to see why allowing the men the freedom to spend some time in the local area when in reserve was crucial. Ironically, on 10 December a church service for the battalion was held in the brewery at Vermelles, before on 15 December, the battalion at last went to rest billets at the candle factory in Béthune. They moved 9 miles west of Béthune to Auchel, in the Reserve Division Area, on 20 December. On Christmas Day A-, C- and D-Coys had Christmas dinner in the school and B-Coy in their billet, while the officers and senior NCOs waited on the men, 'who seemed to thoroughly enjoy themselves'. For Boxing Day a football match between the Officers and the Sergeants was played on the nearby Royal Flying Corps ground; the Sergeants won 4–3. The Divisional Concert Party then gave a concert to the whole brigade in the gymnasium at Auchel. As further treats on 28 December, the battalion were entertained by the 'Lena Ashwell' Concert Party[4] in the gymnasium, and on New Year's Eve the Divisional Band 'played the Old Year out and the New Year in on the square at Auchel'.

The new year of 1917 saw the battalion at rest in Auchel until 26 January. During this time the men competed in brigade sports, consisting of boxing, cross country running, football, bayonet fighting and rapid wiring races. On 29 January the battalion entrained at Lillers and travelled 28 miles north to Proven, north of Poperinge, then marched 7 miles to billets near Winnezeele, where they began training again. They moved to Béthune on 13 February, then to Sailly-Labourse on 14 February. The following day they were back in the nearby trenches again, relieving the 1/KSLI, for a six-day stint. The remainder of February and all of March were again spent rotating between the front or support line trenches and reserve (at Noyelles) approximately every six days. At the end of March they finally moved away to rest, initially in billets at Mazinegarbe on 27 March, then on 29 March they travelled 23 miles south-west by motor bus to billet at La Herlière, south-west of Arras, to carry out field training. On 2 April the battalion moved 9 miles east and bivouacked at Adinfer, moving 5 miles east the following day to Hamelincourt. They went back to the front on 5 April for seven days, in the front outpost line at the Hénin(-sur-Cojeul) to Croisilles road. During this tour they sent out patrols continuously at night to make contact with and harass the enemy. D-Coy carried out a minor enterprise in conjugation with the 6/Leics and the 6 (Infantry) Brigade on 12 April which resulted in the loss of many lives. After this stint in the firing line they went to billets at Moyenneville (13 April) then Adinfer (14 April). From 15 to 23 April they were in divisional reserve at billets 12 miles back from the front in Bailleulmont. On 23 April the battalion was ordered to march 9 miles east to Boiry-Saint-Martin and remain there for two days. Then, on 25 April the battalion went into the support trenches at Saint-Léger for four days, before finding themselves returned to Divisional Reserve and bivouacked in the north of the village of Boyelles. In two days' time they were to attack the strongly defended village of Fontaine-les-Croisilles, 5 miles to the east. The three objectives for the attack were to secure La Sensée River in front of the village, the junction of the La Sensée River and the sunken road, and the enemy boundary around the village. During the night of 1 May the 110 (Infantry) Brigade took over the positions of the 64 (Infantry) Brigade north of the Hindenburg Support Line. The 8/Leics formed the right assaulting battalion and the 9/Leics formed the left assaulting battalion. The 6/Leics and the 7/Leics were in support and reserve respectively.

On the morning of 3 May at 03.45 the 8/Leics attacked the village of Fontaine-les-Croisilles under a creeping artillery barrage. The battalion was dispersed in two waves (60 yards between each wave) of two lines each (10 yards between lines), with a wave of 'moppers up' behind. A-, B-and C-Coy formed the front line of attack, from left to right, each company having a two-platoon frontage. D-Coy was drawn up in two lines, 60 yards in the rear 'mopping up'. Two tanks were to support the attack. The morning was incredibly dark, as sunrise was not until 05.23. The dust and smoke from the British barrage and the immediate barrage response from the Germans meant that it was impossible to see more than a few yards ahead. Direction was lost early and the line swung over to the right. By 06.00 it became evident that the attack had failed. No progress had been made by the 64 (Infantry) Brigade who were supposed to bomb south-eastwards down the Hindenburg Line, and the front of the 8/Leics was outflanked in parts, almost surrounded, with the prospect of being cut off. C-Coy had been held up by excessive machine gun fire which had necessitated taking up a defensive position in the sunken road. No assistance was given by the two tanks in the attack; both of them had broken down. The remainder of the battalion were still only advanced to a line roughly 300 yards short of their objective. Here the battalion remained until it was reinforced by the 6/Leics at 11.30. The line was held throughout the day and consolidated. From the 8/Leics 11 officers and 291 other ranks were killed, wounded or missing in the attack on the Hindenberg Line stronghold of Fontaine-les-Croisilles. Francis Burton Pitts was seen to be wounded during the attack and taken prisoner by the Germans. The Germans took him to a field hospital 20 miles behind their front lines at Bouchain. There, sadly, he died of his wounds two weeks later on 17 May, aged 27.

The MCS school magazine, *The Lily*, for November 1917 read:

> He had a great gift for games, especially golf and Association football, and created almost a record by getting into the football team in his first season. He also gained a Junior Certificate in 1906. We had lost sight of him when a Field Service Postcard arrived from France where he was serving in the ranks in the Leicestershire Regt., but his sterling qualities won a commission for

him. He was 'wounded and missing' in the Somme offensive on May 3rd, and it was not until quite recently that Canon Pitts heard that he had died in German hands on Ascension Day.

1. Transferred to GHQ troops means units at the disposal of the GHQ of the British Expeditionary Force in France, rather than under the command of a subordinate formation.
2. Scabies is a contagious skin condition caused by tiny mites which burrow into the skin.
3. General cleaning, domestic work and washing.
4. Lena Ashwell was an actress and entertainments manager who was an enthusiastic supporter of the British war aims. From 1915 she organized companies of actors, singers and entertainers to travel to France and perform for the troops close to the front line.

James Leslie ROBERTON

7 September 1894 – 6 September 1916

Rank and regiment: Second Lieutenant, 4th Battalion, Alexandra, Princess of Wales's Own (Yorkshire Regiment); Second Lieutenant, 25 Squadron, Royal Flying Corps. **Medals awarded:** Victory, British War. **Theatre of War:** Western Front. **Memorial:** Arras Flying Memorial, France.

James Leslie Roberton was the youngest son of Robert Hopkins Roberton and Mary Louisa Roberton (*née* Parren). He was born at Stoke Golding Lodge, Nuneaton, Leicestershire, on 7 September 1894. James' father was originally from Scotland and was a magistrate in Leicestershire.

James' older brother, William Parren (b. 1890) attended MCS and was a Captain in the Hampshire Regiment during the First World War. His older cousin, J.E. Roberton, also attended MCS and left straight from school to become a trooper for the Oxford Yeomanry in the Boer War and later took a commission with the Cameron Highlanders.

Life at Magdalen College School (1905–1913) and beyond

When James Leslie Roberton joined MCS in the Michaelmas Term of 1905 his brother William had already been at the school for five years. Often referred to by his second name Leslie or by his nickname Tag (as all the Robertons at the school were affectionately known), Leslie Roberton was to follow in many of his brother's footsteps as he progressed through the school. William left MCS in July 1909 (going on to Wadham College).

In March 1910 Leslie Roberton, along with nine other boys including Edward Andrews, were confirmed by the Master of Pembroke in the school chapel. Later that year he won the senior maths prize. In the Michaelmas Term of 1912 Leslie Roberton, along with Donovan Leicester, was appointed a House Prefect (William Roberton had been a House Prefect in 1908/09). In December 1912 Leslie was elected to be the Gentleman Usher for the Debating Society (a post his brother had held in 1908), when the motion was proposed that 'Military Conscription for Great Britain is desirable'. After completion of the well attended debate the voting was tied at an incredible twenty-three votes each. The president, Mr Brownrigg, had the casting vote. 'Brigger' voted for the motion. The topic of the debates, the attendance and the closeness of vote all indicate how prominent and important the topic of conscription was to the schools' community at that time.

Leslie Roberton was very involved with the sporting life of the school, never a star but always competing. He took part in several sports days at MCS. In July 1909 he came second in the junior 100 yard Sprint final, then in both 1910 and 1911 he competed in the 100 yard and 150 yard Sprints, winning through to the final of each event but not gaining a place. Both years he did, however, have the satisfaction of winning the traditional 200 yard 'Consolation Race' at the end of the day, ensuring that his brother (then at Wadham College), who won the old boy race in 1910, did not completely upstage him. In 1910, when the swimming sports had to be held in the Merton Street Baths due to inclement weather, Roberton won the two lengths race comfortably. On the tennis courts he competed in the doubles tennis tournament in the summer of 1910. However, it was on the football field and particularly on the river where he competed most notably.

Leslie Roberton played at right-half for the 1st XI football team for three consecutive seasons, 1910, 1911 (half colours) and 1912. The captain during his first year in the 1st XI was the inspirational Frank Wilkinson, who was in his final year at the school. During his three years in the 1st XI an ever present team mate was Victor Jessel.

Leslie Roberton started rowing for the 2nd IV boat in 1910 in a crew that included John Bellamy. He then progressed to the 1st IV the following year, receiving full colours. He was elected Captain of Rowing for 1912 and 1913 (his brother had been Captain of Rowing in 1908 and 1909) and continued to row as part of the 1st IV until he left in 1913. In the 1911 season the 1st IV was developing nicely and the date for the annual King's Worcester race was set when Roberton came down with measles. A few days later the stroke, Disney, also came down with measles so the Worcester race had to be called off. In the 1913 season, although Roberton's rowing was interrupted by absence, he did return to MCS to take the crew, which included Victor Jessel, to Worcester and supervise them in the absence of Mr Sherwood. In January 1913 Leslie Roberton proposed a resolution at the games committee that the design of the 1st IV cap should be changed. Many old boys objected to the resolution so the old cap design was kept again for 1913.

Leslie Roberton eventually left MCS after eight years in 1913 and went out to Rhodesia to learn farming. In 1914 he wrote to the school describing his adventures and experiences. On returning to England he entered the London Hospital to start his medical studies. Here he joined the London University, Senior Division, OTC, before eventually being gazetted to the Yorkshire Regiment.

In 1914, the year after Roberton left MCS, the launch of a new MCS boat made it to the front page of the local newspaper (see section on V.A.V.Z. Jessel).

Fittingly, 100 years later the new MCS quad boat, purchased in 2013, was christened *James Leslie Roberton* in his honour.

Roberton's War

Leslie Roberton was gazetted Second Lieutenant in the 3/4th Battalion, Alexandra, Princess of Wales's Own (Yorkshire Regiment) on 12 August 1915. This reserve battalion had been formed at Northallerton only four months prior to Roberton joining. He spent some time as a machine gun instructor with his battalion before transferring to the Royal Flying Corps in April 1916.

James Leslie Roberton.

On 6 May 1916, Roberton was transferred to 12 (Training) Squadron for instruction in aviation. On 23 May 1916, he passed the test for his aviator's certificate at the Military School, Thetford, in a Maurice Farman bi-plane. He continued his training with a transfer to 9 (Training) Squadron on 6 June 1916 and graduated from the Central Flying School on 11 August 1916. Five days later he was posted to the British Expeditionary Force and joined 25 Squadron in France on 17 August 1916, the day after the accidental death of Archibald Stanley Butler. This Squadron, under the command of Major R.G. Cherry, was part of the 10th Wing, 1 Brigade, First Army and based at Auchel (Lozingham) aerodrome.

It is possible that Roberton took part in the bombing raid on the German-held French town of Carvin on 22 August. Twelve FE2b, two-seater reconnaissance and bomber bi-planes from 25 Squadron attacked the town at 18.30 dropping thirty-three 20lb and twenty-eight incendiary bombs on the town. Some fifteen minutes later 2 Squadron dropped sixteen 112lb bombs. The town suffered considerable damage and many fires were left burning. Two days later Roberton was admitted to the 14th General Hospital, which was based at Wimereux, France. He was fit again on 2 September 1916 and left hospital for the No. 1 Aircraft Depot based near Saint Omer, before being reposted to 25 Squadron on 3 September.

The day before his twenty-second birthday, at 15.30 on 6 September 1916, James Roberton and his observer, Lieutenant Ernest Charles Kemp (also previously of the Yorkshire Regiment), left Auchel aerodrome in their FE2b/5238 aeroplane to conduct a patrol over the German lines between Hulluch and Lens, near Loos-en-Gohelle. They crossed over the lines to engage an enemy aircraft, a Fokker, and were shot down during aerial combat. Both Roberton and Kemp were seen to fall out of the plane after it burst into flames, probably due to the petrol tank blowing up.[1] The aircraft crashed 1,000 yards west of the lines, but no bodies were recovered. Both men are commemorated on the Arras Flying Memorial. The victory was credited to the German Ace, Oberleutnant Hans-Joachim Buddecke[2] and was the eighth of his eventual thirteen kills. The previous October, Buddecke had shot down and killed Oxford High School's Lieutenant William Lawrence (brother of T.E. Lawrence, 'Lawrence of Arabia').

The Roberton family links to MCS continued after the war, with his mother contributing to the school war memorial.

1. First World War pilots were not given the luxury of parachutes, despite balloon observation crews having them. The type of parachute used by balloon observers was a fixed container type, completely unsuitable for aircraft use. However, free-fall parachutes deployed by rip cord were known. Their use in aircraft was not sanctioned for development until September 1918. Previous to this, many excuses within the senior ranks of the RFC had been made to avoid having to divert time and money to a project that was deemed unnecessary. Most of these decision makers had not seen combat and the effects of being in a burning aircraft. Several stories exist of pilots choosing to jump to their death rather than be burnt alive in their machine.
2. Buddecke himself was eventually killed during aerial combat above Lens on 10 March 1918.

Francis Bernard ROBERTS

20 May 1882 – 8 February1916

Rank and regiment: Captain, 9th Rifle Brigade (The Prince Consort's Own). **Medals awarded:** Victory, British War, 1914–1915 Star. **Theatre of War:** Western Front. **Memorial:** Talana Farm Cemetery, Belgium.

Francis Bernard Roberts was born at Anjini Hill, Nasik in India on 20 May 1882. He was one of five sons of the Reverend Wilson Aylesbury Roberts and Ellen Roberts (*née* Nolan). His father had been born in Hereford, England, moved to India as a missionary in 1869 and returned to England by 1906, when the family lived at Viney Hill Vicarage, Gloucestershire. Francis' brothers were all born in India: Edward (b. 1872), Arthur Wilson (b. 1874), Reginald Aylesbury (b. 1876), Ernest Basil (b. 1879) and Herbert Cecil (b. 1888). Their father died in 1911.

Life at Magdalen College School (1894–1898) and beyond

Francis Roberts initially went to St John's School before attending MCS. After arriving at MCS he soon showed his athletic potential. On 7 November 1894 School Field was under flood and so routine games were not possible. The usual alternative activity was a Paper Chase, whereby three boys were chosen as Hares. The Hares, each provided with a bag full of pieces of paper, had to lay a paper trail while reaching a specific location then returning, cross-country style, to school. In the meantime the rest of the school, the 'Hounds', set off ten minutes later in pursuit. It was customary for the Hares to employ tactics of laying false trails, and the aim was for the Hares to return to school without being caught. For this chase Francis Roberts was chosen as one of the Hares and set off at 2.15pm. After reaching Shotover (approximately 3 miles away) and Cowley Marsh, torrential rain forced the Hares to return to school by road. They made it back to school without being caught, giving them the right to choose the Hares the next time. In pursuit, the last hound didn't return to the 'Kennels' until 6.45pm. Essentially, a four-hour cross-country run!

Roberts is first recorded playing cricket for the School in 1895 in the 'Junior team', but as early as spring 1896 it was recorded in *The Lily* that he 'should make [a] useful change bowler' and 'of our younger cricketers, perhaps the most promising, but if he is to earn his place in the eleven he must remember that it is no good making runs with the bat if you give away more in the field'. He did gain a place in the 1st XI in 1896 and in one match versus the Old Boys XI, on May Day 1896, Roberts came in for the school at no. 5. He joined the then Usher, Mr Brownrigg, who had opened the batting and was 'playing splendid cricket'. Roberts was out for a duck but Brownrigg went on to score 126. Despite this setback, Roberts was recognized at the end of the season as, 'A very neat bat, but owing to an injury at the beginning of the term has not been able to play in all the matches. A useful bowler and a smart fielder at point.' The following season, Roberts' third and final season at MCS, he was awarded full colours despite having 'greatly disappointed our expectations in batting, but at the end of the

Magdalen College School Cricket 1st XI, 1896.
Not in order: E.B. Carter, P.W. Shelford, F.C. Burgess, P.C. Brockenbury (wicketkeeper), W.G. Warren, C. Forward, E. St G. Causton (Captain), E.B. Roberts, F.B. Roberts, R.H. Alexander, C.H. Johnston.

season played better. Is, in fact, a smart bat, but is too impatient at the beginning of his innings to make runs. He fields quite smartly at point and cover point.'

In 1895 Roberts appeared in the school's football teams for the first time, soon making his way into the 1st XI. At the end of the following season, 1896, he received half colours and was reported to have played with considerable success as outside right: 'Is the best dribbler in the team, but too much inclined to pass back. Is somewhat slow'.

Roberts does not appear to have rowed competitively at school, however he competed in the school's Scratch Fours races of June 1895, finishing the competition in second place. Roberts rowed at bow in the Four stroked by the Reverend W.E. Sherwood. The following year, in June 1896, Roberts coxed the School's 1st IV boat in their win against Bath College.

During Sports Day in the summer of 1895, despite winning through to the 150 yard Handicap Final, Roberts did not achieve a place. However, in the

Magdalen College School Football 1st XI, 1896.

following event, the 300 yard Handicap, Roberts ran a well-judged final race and held off the favourite to win in 41 seconds after a 20-yard handicap start.

In his four years at MCS Roberts is not recorded doing any science subject, so must have just concentrated on the Humanities. In 1896 and 1897 Roberts obtained his Certificates in the Oxford and Cambridge Public Schools Examination. The following year he left MCS to take up a Senior Scholarship at Rossall School, at Fleetwood in Lancashire. He was the leading wicket-taker during all three years at Rossall School and was first in the batting averages in 1899 and second in the two subsequent years.

In 1901 he obtained a Scholarship at Jesus College, attending Cambridge at the same time as MCS old boy Leonard D. Cane. Roberts obtained a Cricket and a Hockey Blue while at Cambridge (*The Lily* also predicted he would obtain a Football Blue), and also played minor counties cricket for Oxfordshire in 1901, 1902 and 1903 while studying at Cambridge. Ironically, his minor counties debut, on 5 August 1901, was against Cambridgeshire at Fenners Cricket Ground. He was also a brilliant amateur golfer.

Magdalen College School Football 1st XI, 1896 (including staff players).
Boys who played for the Football 1st XI during the 1896 season included (not in picture order): F.C. Burgess, A. Campbell (goalkeeper), E. St G. Causton, A.H. Curtis, W.K. Page, E.B. Roberts, F.B. Roberts, E.S.K. Robinson, A.M. Walker, W.G. de G. Warren (captain), H.B. Williams. (Three other boys also appeared for the team that year: C.M. Johnson, M. Drewitt and W.B. Higgs). Masters who played versus adult opposition were: C.E. Brownrigg Esq (middle row, left) and E. Edgington Esq (middle row, right).

In November 1902 Roberts returned to Oxford to play in the Old Boys XI versus MCS football match. Leading 3–0 at the interval, the Old Boys XI dominated the first half, before the School 'played up well' in the second half and scored three goals to level the game. After the great fight back by the School, Roberts then asserted himself to score the winner for the old boys.

In the 1903 Varsity cricket match versus Oxford at Lords Roberts made a duck in the first innings and only managed to score 1 in the second. With his fast bowling he managed to take 6 for 153, but Oxford duly won by 268 runs. This did not stop him from going on to play for Gloucestershire from 1906 to 1914; indeed, in the 1909 County Championship season after ten innings he was top of the Gloucestershire batting averages with 40.6. In his first season for Gloucestershire, when playing versus Essex at the Ashley Down Ground in Bristol (6 and

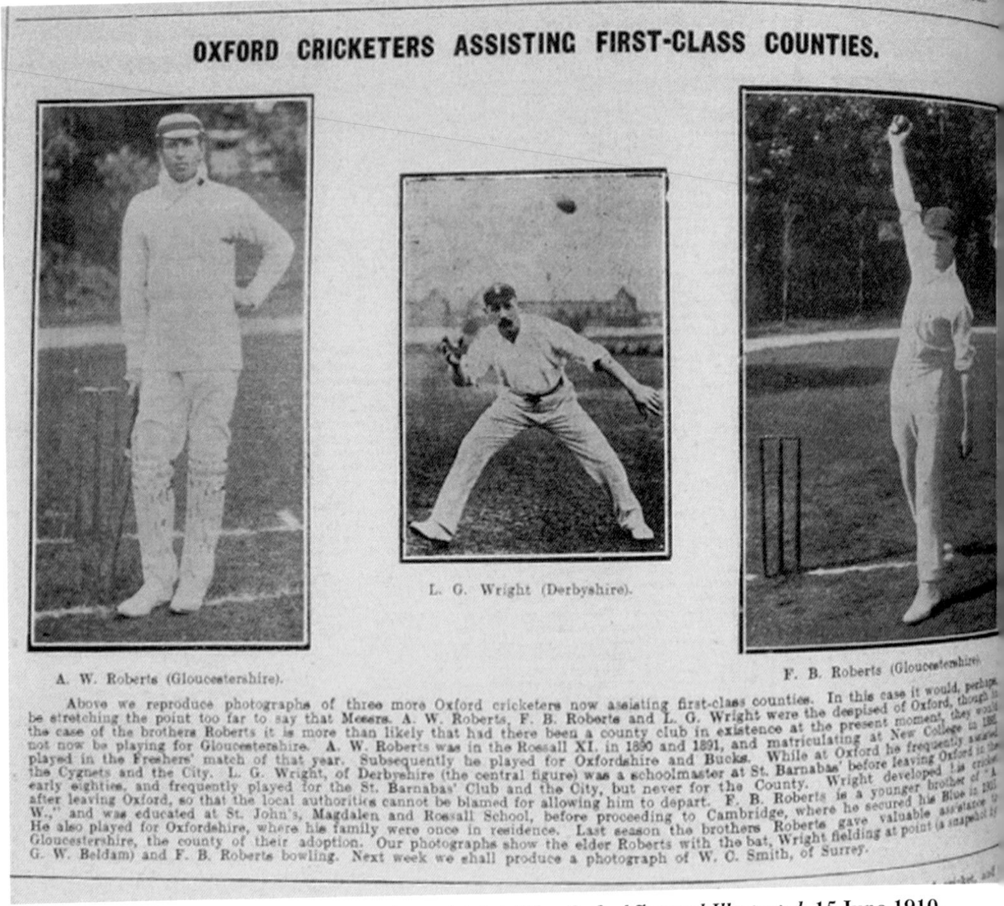

OXFORD CRICKETERS ASSISTING FIRST-CLASS COUNTIES.

L. G. Wright (Derbyshire).

A. W. Roberts (Gloucestershire).

F. B. Roberts (Gloucestershire).

Above we reproduce photographs of three more Oxford cricketers now assisting first-class counties. In this case it would, perhaps, be stretching the point too far to say that Messrs. A. W. Roberts, F. B. Roberts and L. G. Wright were the despised of Oxford, though in the case of the brothers Roberts it is more than likely that had there been a county club in existence at the present moment, they would not now be playing for Gloucestershire. A. W. Roberts was in the Rossall XI. in 1890 and 1891, and matriculating at New College in 189[illegible] played in the Freshers' match of that year. Subsequently he played for Oxfordshire and Bucks. While at Oxford he frequently assisted the Cygnets and the City. L. G. Wright, of Derbyshire (the central figure) was a schoolmaster at St. Barnabas' before leaving Oxford in the early eighties, and frequently played for the St. Barnabas' Club and the City, but never for the County. Wright developed his cricket after leaving Oxford, so that the local authorities cannot be blamed for allowing him to depart. F. B. Roberts is a younger brother of "A. W.," and was educated at St. John's, Magdalen and Rossall School, before proceeding to Cambridge, where he secured his Blue in 190[illegible]. He also played for Oxfordshire, where his family were once in residence. Last season the brothers Roberts gave valuable assistance to Gloucestershire, the county of their adoption. Our photographs show the elder Roberts with the bat, Wright fielding at point (a snapshot by G. W. Beldam) and F. B. Roberts bowling. Next week we shall produce a photograph of W. C. Smith, of Surrey.

A.W. Roberts (left) and F.B. Roberts (right). The *Oxford Journal Illustrated*, 15 June 1910.

7 August 1906), he and George Dennett (a left arm spinner) bowled unchanged throughout the entirety of the Championship match. Dennett took 10 wickets for 40 runs in the first innings and in the second innings they took 5 wickets each, Roberts taking 5–69 off 30.2 overs. Gloucestershire won the match by 9 wickets. It is reported that he played throughout his career wearing glasses. His brother, A.W. Roberts, was also a good cricketer and played twenty-nine first class matches for Gloucestershire from 1908 to 1913.

In 1910 Francis Roberts went to teach at Wellington College, becoming Tutor of the Beresford Dormitory. He was committed to his teaching and was therefore classed as an 'Amateur Player' and only able to play for Gloucestershire outside school term time. Sixty-four of his sixty-seven appearances for Gloucestershire were therefore in the month of August; his other three appearances were in the last weekend of July. In a First Class career that spanned eleven years and eighty matches (1903 to 1914) and included an innings of 80 runs versus Victor Trumper's Australians in 1909, Roberts' career records read:

Batting:

Innings	Not outs	Runs	Highest score	Average	100s	50s	Catches
138	12	2,566	157	20.36	5	6	66

Bowling:

Balls	Maidens	Runs	Wickets	Best	Average	5 wicket matches	10 wicket matches	Strike rate	Economy
5,835	224	3,005	88	5–69	34.14	1	0	66.30	3.08

When war was declared on Tuesday, 4 August 1914 Roberts was playing a Championship match against Somerset at Bristol. He was out for 0 in the second innings on that fateful day, but Gloucestershire hung on to win by 1 wicket. He was to play for Gloucestershire five more times that August. His last match was played on 24 and 25 August against a Yorkshire side that included the England legend Wilfred Rhodes. Roberts had by now progressed up the order and had a regular position in the top five. When he passed 9 runs in the first innings of this game he passed the landmark of 2,000 runs in Championship matches. Yorkshire won by an innings and 263 runs. Roberts returned to Wellington at the start of September, applied for a temporary commission in the army in November and was given temporary leave from Wellington to take up the commission in the December of 1914. He had played his last First Class match.

Roberts' War

Francis Roberts was commissioned as a Second Lieutenant in 9 Rifle Brigade (42 Brigade, 14th Division) in December 1914, his moral character and education being confirmed on his officer's application by the Master of Wellington College, William W. Vaughan. Roberts and the 9/RB were in England for the following six months, initially based at Petworth, then at Aldershot from February, where field manoeuvres and final training for war were undertaken. In May 1915 the 9/RB sailed from Southampton for Le Havre, France. Initially concentrating around Watten (north-west of Saint Omer), the 14th Division soon moved into the Ypres area.

After a short stay in St Silvestre the brigade moved on to billet at Zevencoten from 31 May to 5 June. Each day they went off to dig trenches, via an 11-mile round march. This is where Roberts first encountered enemy rifle fire sporadically flying by as they engineered the new trench systems. Over the next few days this would change to experiencing shrapnel shells and the first casualties. It was tiring work as digging was done throughout the day and night. From 6 to 10 June the 9/RB took up positions in established trenches at Bailleul then were relieved and went into billets between 11 and 15 June, carrying out reserve duties. On 16 June they took over trenches near the railway embankment at Ypres for the day, before returning to their billet huts when relieved. Before they had marched

Francis Roberts.

out of range of the German guns they were caught in an open field and bombarded with shrapnel shell fire. They had no other option but to return to the trenches, but found them full. Under fire they therefore had to dig more trenches in order to achieve cover. They eventually returned to their billet huts on 17 June and then dug precautionary trenches as German shells were starting to hit deeper into British territory. They spent the next two days at rest in their bivouac huts, then on 19 June relieved the 1 Gordon Highlanders in the Menin Gate trenches. Later that day, Roberts and his battalion were subjected to gas shells, but being fully equipped with the latest gas helmets they found they were completely protected. From 20 June and for the following three months the battalion were relentlessly rotated from the front line to support to reserve positions. When in the trenches they were routinely under heavy bombardments and sniper fire, but still required to do trench work, building and rebuilding defences and trench systems. Although during the day it was often quiet, dusk and dawn were often full with heavy shelling. Casualties slowly mounted, until on 22 June the 9/RB along with the rest of the brigade attacked the German trenches. On 23 June retaliatory gas shells were fired on their trenches and heightened enfilade sniping came from Hill 60. During this period of consolidation, enemy observation balloons and low flying aircraft were very active, attempting to locate and map the British positions and to report accuracy of artillery fire. A respite at billets in Poperinge on 27 June was welcomed, but still gun, sandbag and bomb training had to be carried out. The battalion returned to Ypres railway station on 30 June for fatigue work and for the next eight days did much cable-laying and trench work in the area, under constant observation from enemy balloons and aeroplanes and persistent artillery bombardments. It is little wonder that on Sunday, 4 July, the church parade saw a 60 per cent turnout of various denominations. On 12 July the battalion received three telescopic rifles which lifted moral and helped them retaliate against the German snipers. At 03.15 on 30 July the Commanding Officer of the battalion reported an 'enormous column of fire works' in the direction of the enemy redoubt. What he had seen was the German Liquid Fire attack at Hooge near the Menin Road. The British replied with a two-hour heavy artillery bombardment. Troops, including the 9/RB, were sent forward to hold the line and to counter-attack. Although only six '*Flammenwerfers*' were used on a limited front, the effect on the troops was dramatic, despite relatively few casualties from burns. The Germans captured whole trenches, and a general sense of demoralization was reported by the British. During the month of July the 9/RB had received 242 casualties. There was no relief and it is reported on 2 August 1915 that the men of the 9/RB had been in the trenches for eight continuous days, and were exhausted from want of sleep. Gradually, though, new drafts were received by the battalion. On 22 September a morale-boosting visit and inspection by Lord Kitchener was received by the 9/RB, but it was back to normal soon after, and on 25 September an attack on the Bellewaarde trenches by the Germans led to a desperate fight which saw the 9/RB reduced to just four officers and 140 other ranks. The encounter had been such a close-run struggle that the following day the VI Corps Commanding Officer delivered a congratulatory speech to the battalion for their defence and counter-attacks the previous day. This appears to have been a last effort in the region for a while and the 9/RB were able to go into reserve and rest from 26 September to 12 October.

Trench life for the 9/RB was resumed again on 13 October, but the relentless summer fighting appeared to abate. In October 1915 Francis Roberts was promoted to the rank of Captain. Rest and training became more frequent, indeed for the entire period of 1 to 17 November the battalion were away from trenches at Houtkerque, although fatigues were always a necessary part of the routine. Upon returning to the Ypres trenches between 18 and 30 November the weather turned very bad, alternating between rain and hard frost. The bad weather weakened the parapet, resulting in many collapses of these top protective parts of the trench. During the first two weeks of December the battalion rotated between rest in huts at Brandhoek and fire trench duty in Ypres. During the Christmas period (16 to 29 December) the battalion were fortunate to be in billets at Houtkerque rather than trenches, then on 30 December they moved to farm billets and the chateau at Elverdinghe (close to Ypres), from where on 4 January 1916 they had only a short way to their trenches at Elverdinghe. Here they stayed, rotating between trenches and billets at Elverdinghe, for the remainder of January. The first three days of February were again spent at rest in Elverdinghe Chateau. Then, on 4 February, the battalion relieved the 5th Battalion, the King's (Shropshire Light Infantry) in the left sector of the Elverdinghe trenches, for a five-day stint in the fire trench. On the fifth day Captain Francis Roberts was killed, aged 33. He had been in the Ypres area for his entire war and survived nine months. A telegram informing his family of Francis' death was received at the Cam Vicarage, Dursley, Gloucestershire the following day. Francis Bernard Roberts, Gloucestershire cricketer, is buried at Talana Farm Cemetery close to where he fell.

Clement Perronet SELLS

6 September 1889 – 4 July 1919

Rank and regiment: Lance Corporal (202), 2nd City of London Field Ambulance; Captain, Royal Army Medical Corps, attached 1/8th Battalion, Middlesex Regiment and RAF. **Medals awarded:** Victory, British War, 1914–1915 Star, Military Cross. **Theatre of War:** Western Front. **Memorial:** Northbrook Cemetery, Swanage, Dorset.

Clement Perronet Sells was the only son of Vincent Perronet Sells and Annie Bertha Sells (*née* Clements) of Highfield, Headington. He had one older sister, Muriel Annie Perronet (b. 1887). His father graduated from New College, Oxford and stayed on at the University as a Teacher in Chemistry. By the time Clement was 11 his father was the Secretary of Oxford University Appointments Committee. Clement married Mary Annie Jones at St Anselm's Church, Davies Street, London, on 18 December 1918.

Life at Magdalen College School (1900–1908) and beyond

Clement Sells joined MCS in the Michaelmas term of 1900 as a day boy, eventually becoming a Day Boy Prefect in his final year at school, 1907/08. He was accepted to the school as an Exhibitioner, a status he was to justify by gaining academic prizes and awards and eventually an Exhibition at Merton College. In 1902 he received the Form IV English prize and the Lower School Set 1 science prize. In 1904 he passed the Junior Certificate at the same time as Harold Dawes and Charles Maltby, collecting his certificate from Lord Halsbury, who was the Lord Chancellor at the time and a good friend of Charles Brownrigg. Sells' father Vincent is listed as a guest for this Prize Giving. In 1907 Sells showed his gift for memory when he won a prize in the repetition competition. Later that summer at prize giving he was awarded the Daubeny medal for Natural Sciences. At Easter 1908 he received the news that he had been given an Exhibition at Merton

College, Oxford, for Natural Sciences. In his final year at the school Clement played 1st XI Hockey, having the character profile, 'A rather clumsy outside-right but goes pretty straight and always tries hard'. Although he was not a member of the school cricket team, as an old boy he contributed towards the building of the cricket pavilion.

After Clement gained Honours in Natural Science at Merton he then went on to read medicine at Middlesex Hospital.

Sells' War

Upon the declaration of war in 1914, Clement Sells interrupted his medical studies and enlisted in the 2nd London Field Ambulance, Royal Army Medical Corps at Chelsea on 3 September 1914. Sells, whose eyesight was reported as 'good with glasses', sailed for France on 15 January 1915 on SS *Tintiretto* with the 28th Division. The division initially concentrated between Bailleul and Hazebrouck before advancing to Ypres, taking over a sector of the salient from the French army. During this, his first stint in France, Sells wrote a diary from 15 January to 28 April 1915. An entry for 11 February reads: 'At 7.30pm ordered to new hospital nearer cathedral. Just as arriving town shelled. One burst by gymnasium, a bit hitting the roof; two burst by hospital, hitting one of our ambulances and ADMS car ... Other shells burst in the street, one killing three horses and two men in [a] wagon. One killed some Life Guards in their billet.' Soon after, he experienced the devastating mine warfare that allowed the British to remove the Germans from Hill 60 at Zillebeke, and the ferocious counter-attacks carried out by the Germans. Within days the situation unfolded into what became known as the Battles of Ypres.

Sells returned to England on 26 April and was discharged from the army on 4 May 1915 in order to resume his medical studies at Middlesex Hospital, ultimately obtaining his conjoint diploma of MRCS and LRCP in 1916.[1] After completing his studies he was commissioned into the RAMC as Lieutenant and went back to France in January 1916, joining the 2/2nd LFA upon its move to the 56th Division in February 1916. The division was involved in the Battle of the Somme, from July to October 1916.

A letter to his sister Muriel, written on the Somme on 27 July 1916, describes how shells but not bullets can reach the Casualty Clearing Station he was based at. He writes that everything is 'so knocked about' and when a shell is arriving 'you hear a screaming whistle. If you hear it is plainly going over. The ones you do not hear are the ones that come near you.' He goes on to say:

> The bearers of the section fetch me wounded from [the] chateau about a mile behind the trenches to our motor wagons which bump them down to us to redress or if necessary and unavoidable to operate on: we have few ops. I have given chloroform about six times. We only keep the chaps one night and send them on in the morning to a clearing hospital [base hospital] by BRCS [British Red Cross Society] motor convoy ... I have had a parcel from Auntie Jenie containing sweets and a ginger bread made by Esther which is

Clement Sells (right) showing off his new fur coat that was issued in France during the winter of 1914/15.

lovely. Thanks for the offer of a torch but it would not be much use thanks very much. The weekly *Times* has been coming quite all right thanks . . . Next time you send a parcel you might include ¼lb cocoa. But I have plenty of grub to go with it so you need not send anything more for a few days . . . Well goodnight now. Best Love. CPS

Clement sketched a drawing of the CCS, viewed from the bottom of its garden, and sent it to his sister. The bottom room under the veranda was the combined kitchen, operating, sitting and dining room for the station. Clement had a bed-

A sketch by Clement Sells of his Casualty Clearing Station, some miles behind the front line, on the Somme in July 1916. The picture clearly shows damage from shells that could reach this far back.

room behind and above it. The devastation, even at this relatively safe distance from the front (approximately 2 miles back), is easy to see.

In October 1916 Sells returned home for a short period, suffering from 'trench fever'.[2] Returning to the front in December 1916, he was attached to the 1/8th Battalion Middlesex Regiment (167 Brigade, 56th Division). On 7 April 1917 while at the Madrillet Camp (near Rouen) he received an order to proceed to the front and rejoin the 1/8/MR and to take two 'smoke helmets' (gas masks) with him. He rejoined the 1/8/MR near Vimy Ridge, where he saw much action during the Battles of Arras in April and May.

After a period of time further north in August taking part in the Battle of Ypres, the 56th Division returned south, and in November 1917 during the fighting around Cambrai Sells was awarded the Military Cross for his bravery under fire. His MC citation reads: 'During the period 22 September 1917 to 24 February 1918, this Officer has been untiring in performing his duties and tending the wounded especially during fighting west of Cambrai, 20 November to 3 December

1917, when he organized his stretcher bearers and personally superintended the evacuation of wounded under an extremely heavy bombardment.'

He was later attached, in 1918, to the 83rd Wing of the RAF, in which he remained until he was invalided home in January 1919 suffering from endocarditis.[3] On 17 March 1919 Sells was admitted to hospital with a 'severe' condition and four days later was taken to the RAF Officers Hospital in Eaton Square, London, before being sent to convalesce at the Central RAF Hospital,

Clement Sells.

Finchley. Clement Sells passed away at the Royal Air Force Auxiliary Hospital (Grand Hotel), Swanage, Dorset, on 4 July 1919, aged 29.

In June 1919 it is acknowledged in *The Lily* magazine that Clement has made a contribution to the School War Memorial Fund and that a month later he died as a result 'of the after effects of trench fever' from active service in France. Emotionally connected to the school, he had paid a subscription to receive *The Lily* without further charge until 1922. Despite his sacrifice and devotion to the school his name does not appear on the original memorial that hangs in the School Chapel, and for ninety-three years he was not acknowledged by name during the School Remembrance Service. Nor does his name appear in the Roll of Honour in the School Hymn Book prior to 2015. In November 2012 acknowledgement of his sacrifice began, his name was read out in Chapel for the first time and plans are in hand to include his name on an additional memorial in Chapel alongside the original memorial and to include his name in subsequent editions of the School Hymn Book.

1. War Office letter No. 9/Infantry/9535 (AG2B) dated 11 March 1915 gave Sells permission to be released from military service to resume his medical studies.
2. Trench fever is a moderately serious disease transmitted by body lice. The disease is caused by the bacterium *Bartonella quintana* found in the stomach walls of the body louse. Chief symptoms of the disease were headaches, skin rashes, inflamed eyes and leg pains (resembling typhoid and influenza), with patients recovering after some five or six days, although prolonged hospitalization amounting to several weeks was common.
3. Endocarditis is a rare and potentially fatal type of heart infection. It is specifically an infection of the inner lining of the heart (the endocardium), most commonly caused by bacteria entering the blood and travelling to the heart.

Arthur Amyot STEWARD

14 July 1882 – 6 October 1917

Rank and regiment: Second Lieutenant, 168 Brigade, Royal Field Artillery; Lieutenant, 6 then 11 Balloon Company, Royal Flying Corps.
Medals awarded: Victory, British War. **Theatre of War:** Western Front.
Memorial: Duhallow ADS Cemetery, Belgium.

Arthur Amyot Steward was the youngest son of Reverend Canon Edward Steward (Rector of Boyton, Wiltshire) and Margaret Knyvett Steward (*née* Wilson), and was born at Salisbury. His father had studied at Magdalen College (1870–1874) and was a vicar and schoolmaster. Arthur had an older brother, Edward Merivale (b. 1881) and two sisters, Margaret Joan (b. 1880) and Muriel Knyvet (b. 1883). His brother Edward was a professional soldier and served in the Boer War and with the Indian Army during the First World War. Edward was awarded the OBE and CB for his services to the Army.

Arthur married Miriam Agnes Carver at Salisbury on 18 June 1912 and they had three daughters, Lavinia Margaret (b. 1913), Miriam Joan (b. 1915) and Aveluy Knyvett (b. 1916). The family lived at The Moot, Downton in Wiltshire.

Life at Magdalen College School (1892–1896) and beyond

Steward joined MCS as a chorister in April 1892, before his tenth birthday, and was reportedly a very popular boy with both his schoolmasters and peers. Arthur's maternal uncle, Herbert Amyot Brereton Wilson, was a chorister at MCS from 1867 to 1873. For three consecutive years, 1894 to 1896, Arthur rowed at stroke for boats competing in the Form Four races. In 1894 and 1895 he rowed for the Form III 2nd boat, and in 1896 he rowed for the Form IVb 2nd boat. In 1885 there was some doubt whether the Form Four races would be able to go ahead due to the river being ice-bound for the early part of the Hilary Term; however, when the thaw came, after much practice, each Form was able to contribute two boats and the event took place. Later in the Hilary Term of 1885, Steward coxed one of the Scratch Four boats that competed in the final day of term races, coming third in the final behind two boats that included schoolmasters at stroke (C. Edgington and Rev. W.E. Sherwood). He played football for the MCS chorister team from 1894. In the Hilary and Michaelmas Terms of 1896 he played a series of five football matches versus Haseley Manor School and Christ Church Choristers, scoring five goals. Steward also played cricket for the MCS junior side in 1894 and 1895 and progressed to play for the School 2nd XI in 1896. At Sports Day in July 1894 Steward won the under 12 quarter-mile race in a time of 75 seconds. He was said to have 'ran pluckily, but was somewhat distressed at the finish'. After his voice broke, Steward left MCS aged 14 at the Christmas of 1896, and went on to Wellington College.

He continued to subscribe to *The Lily* for many years after leaving MCS. After finishing his education at Wellington College in 1899 he volunteered to serve in the Boer War. Initially joining the OTC back in Oxford, he then joined the 3rd (Militia) Battalion, Norfolk Regiment on 30 March 1900. After six weeks training he was commissioned Second Lieutenant and a year later promoted to Lieutenant on 11 April 1901. Steward fought with the battalion in the Boer War and remained in South Africa until 1902. Unable to decide whether he wanted to be a soldier or a priest, Steward returned to England in March 1902, passed Responsions and matriculated at Magdalen College on 20 October, following in his father's footsteps. He resigned his commission on 13 December. Steward, who became a friend of Cosmo Lang (eventually Archbishop of Canterbury) while at Magdalen, rowed at no. 2 for the College Torpid boat of 1903, finishing fourth on the river. After taking his first university examinations in the summer of 1903 he decided to return to South Africa, where he worked in the South African Civil Service until 1905. In 1909 he returned to Magdalen to complete the final two years of his degree. Initially repeating his first exams, Steward then read for a degree involving a mix of classics, religion and French. In 1910 he rowed in the Magdalen College 2nd IV boat with MCS old boy F.G. Sherwood. In July 1911 he eventually received his BA degree. During these two years back at Magdalen, Arthur was a Gunner in the Artillery section of the Oxford University Officer Training Corps, passing his Certificate A and riding school qualification in 1911. He then attended Wells Theological College for a year and was ordained Deacon on 9 June 1912. Nine days later, on 18 June 1912, he married Miriam.[1] After spending a year as a School Chaplain of St Paul's, Sculcoate (Hull) he was ordained Priest in May 1913. Both his ordinations were carried out by his old friend Cosmo Lang (then Archbishop of York). On 3 April 1913 his first daughter, Lavinia, was born in Salisbury, and the following year, in July 1914, he returned to work in South Africa, at St Mary's Church in Johannesburg. While in South Africa his second daughter was born, on 25 March 1915. However, still undecided about his vocation, he returned to England on 17 September 1915 to volunteer for the army and received a commission in the Special Reserve of Officers of the RFA on 15 October 1915. He thus became one of the few combatant priests in the British Army.

Steward's War

When war broke out Steward believed that the call for soldiers in the fighting line was a call to him. Against the desire of the bishops, but with the approval of his father, he returned to England in September 1915 and applied to become an officer in the Royal Field Artillery on 6 October, being gazetted Second Lieutenant in the Special Reserve of the RFA on 13 October 1915 and going out to France in April 1916.

Steward joined D-Battery of the 168 Brigade, RFA on 17 September 1916. In August the 168/RFA had relocated north from the Somme to near Béthune, after having taken part in the bombardment on the Somme in the lead up to and for eighteen days following the 1 July 1916 offensive. When Steward joined them they were covering the Cambrin sector of the front, with the Brigade HQ north of Annequin. During the next month the brigade carried out routine wire-cutting bombardments, front line bombardments, creeping barrage bombardments for raids on the enemy trenches on the Cambrin sector, with the enemy being very quiet and only firing in retaliation. On 11 October Steward went on leave to England, giving him the opportunity to visit his home in Downton, Wiltshire, and see his third new baby daughter, Aveluy, born on 7 October 1916. Steward returned to the brigade on 20 October to find they had relocated 36 miles south, back to the Somme, placing their HQ at Mailly-Maillet. Some 5 miles south from here, and just north of Albert, is the village of Aveluy, from where Steward's daughter's name is taken. For the remainder of October the brigade bombarded selected German targets of front line, reserve line and communication trench positions. When November dawned the focus was bombarding strategic positions and approaches to the German-held strong point of Beaumont-Hamel. Finally, on 13 November the brigade provided the moving barrage to cover the advance by the 51st (Highland) Division towards this strategic village. By the evening Beaumont-Hamel was in British hands, one small victory as the Battle of the Somme was coming to a close.

Despite the history books drawing an end to the Battle of the Somme on 18 November 1916, the War Diary of the 168 Brigade shows how intense bombardments still continued throughout the remainder of November and beyond.

Arthur Steward.

On 3 December the 168 Brigade began to withdraw east, marching via Louvencourt (5 miles, 4 December) and Amplier (6 miles, 5 December) to Saint-Ouen (16 miles, 6 December) 14 miles north of Amien, where they stayed at rest and in training until the New Year.

On 2 January 1917 the brigade marched 16 miles from Saint-Ouen to Amplier, then progressed on via Louvencourt (3 January) 11 miles to their previous HQ at Mailly-Maillet (4 January). Throughout January the brigade was engaged in continuous artillery bombardments on the Somme, within sight of Thiepval. From 1 to 19 February the brigade was based at Courcelles(-le-Comte) and then marched to Wargnies on 21 February, from where Steward went on another ten days' leave back to England. While away he contracted laryngitis and was given permission to extend his leave by another week. He returned to the brigade on 28 February.

When Steward rejoined the brigade, they had moved 30 miles south, over the River Somme, to the area of Warvillers (20 miles south-east of Amien). In early March 1917 the 168/RFA were engaged in wire-cutting bombardments, and were twice shelled themselves with gas shells. On 11 March systematic bombardment of the German trenches paved the way for the first raids into enemy trenches on 12 March. Wire cutting and intensive bombardments of the front lines continued, allowing the French 35th Division to launch a full attack on 17 March. They encountered very little opposition so the 168/RFA advanced to within 1,000 yards of the German front line. The British Infantry advance found their sector of the German front line unoccupied, so the 168/RFA moved up further to Liancourt (-Fosse), then Nesle and Rouy-le-Petit, trying to keep up with, and cover the advance of, the British 14th Infantry Division. The Brigade HQ moved up to Mesnil-Saint-Nicaise, then Voyennes. When the brigade came into the town of Nesle they found many of the civilian occupants still there, witnessing the destructive path of battle cross their town. The majority of the horses had to be sent back to Warvillers on 23 March due to the lack of forage. They returned to Rouy-le-Petit four days later. The 168/RFA then moved 2 miles further east across the Canal de la Somme to Buny on 29 March, while the Brigade HQ went to Germaine. A, C and Steward's D-Battery moved on to Vaux(-en-Vermandois) while B-Battery went to Beauvois(-en-Vermandois). After two days 'registering' (finding the range of) the village of German-held village of Savy, D-Battery, using its Howitzers, bombarded the village from their position 2½ miles away. During 1 April the infantry successfully attacked the village of Savy and its wood, just to the north. The Brigade HQ moved to Fluquières, while the gun batteries moved on east to cover the attack on Francilly-Selency (3 miles further east), which was again successful. The Allies were encircling the town of Saint Quentin. By 4 April, it is reported in the war diary that, due to the relentless work carried out by the horses moving the guns and the equipment, many of the brigade's horses died from fatigue about this time. The battle continued, and as the brigade turned its firepower on the next German stronghold of Fresnoy-le-Petit and closed in on the town of Saint Quentin, on 6 April 1917 Steward was sent to the 4th Army Artillery School for a gunnery course at the at Vaux-en-Amiénois, 50 miles west to the north of Amien. Since February the Allies had advanced over ground purposefully laid to waste by the Germans, who fought small rearguard actions as they retreated to a new, shorter tactical line called the Siegfried Stellung (or the Hindenburg Line, as the British called it). The Germans had removed the salient they had been protecting in the area, shortened their lines by 30 miles and consolidated their positions behind new defences closer to supply routes. The Allies had progressed many miles in the area, but now occupied a devastated land that was without established supply lines.

At the start of May the 168/RFA was withdrawn to Attilly for rest (for general overhauling and cleaning up) until 6 May. Returning to action over 7 and 8 May, D-Battery and C-Battery were heavily shelled on 10 May, with their positions being damaged but suffering no casualties. On the night of 12 and 13 May the

168/RFA supported the 4th Battalion, Gloucestershire Regiment in their attack on Cepy Farm, with the accuracy of fire being praised by the Gloucesters. Over the next few days the brigade was relieved by the French and left the Somme. Marching east from Attilly to Languevoisin-Quiquery (14 miles, 18 May), Bouchoir (14 miles, 19 May), Ignaucourt (8 miles, 20 May), and finally to entrain at Guillaucourt (4 miles, 23 May). From Guillaucourt they journeyed by train 70 miles north to Bailleul, south of Ypres, arriving on 24 May. Here they immediately took up positions supporting the 36th Division. On 7 June the 168/RFA supported the successful attacks by the 36th Division on the Messines–Wytschaete ridge and the attack by the 11th Division on Oosttaverneline. Over the three days of this offensive action (6 to 9 June) the 168/RFA alone fired almost 20,000 shells. The brigade was then withdrawn and relocated, marching north to Steenvoorde (11 miles, 1 June), Wormhoudt (7miles, 14 June), Cappelle-la-Grande (10 miles, 16 June), then Leffrinckoucke (6 miles, 17 June). The brigade had arrived at the North Sea coast. Over the next two days the brigade gradually deployed into action, taking over from the French, bombarding the German positions at Lombartzyde, Nieuwpoort,[2] the most northerly point of the Western Front and only 60 miles across the sea from Dover. During the rest of June and July the brigade was involved with constant shelling of the German lines in the Nieuwpoort area, countering constant action from the German lines. The brigade was responsible for driving back several German attacks on the British lines, during a period of fighting seemingly as intense as any part of the Western Front. During 10 July alone, the 168/RFA expended 8,000 shells fending off an attack from the Germans.

On 29 July 1917 Steward left the 168/RFA on attachment to the Royal Flying Corps to become an Observation Ballooning Officer. He joined the 9th Balloon Section, 6th Balloon Company of the 2nd Balloon Wing. The 9th Balloon Section consisted of six Drachen type balloons, each with a mobile, petrol-powered winch that could work raise and lower at 600 feet per minute. The wing was located near Nieppe, 10 miles south of Ypres, until 28 September, and then moved north towards the Passchendaele sector during the intense period of fighting in the Ypres area that had been raging since the last day of July (the Third Battle of Ypres). By the end of September, Steward had accumulated nine dual ascents (his first on 12 August) with an officer-trainer, and six solo ascents (his first solo on 22 August). After his first solo ascent Steward had logged more than eight hours in the air and started to act as an officer-trainer himself. The Drachen balloons operated at a height of up to 3,500 feet, and the job of the observers was to liaise by radio-telephone with the Artillery, especially long-range batteries whose gunners could not see the targets at which they were firing. When attacked by hostile aircraft, the observers, unlike the pilots of fixed-wing aircraft, were trained to parachute down from the balloon baskets, and it was not unknown for individual wings to log as many as twenty such descents in one week. By 9 September, Steward had logged a further nine hours and twenty minutes in the air, before being transferred to 11-Coy, near Ypres, with whom he logged a further two hours and twenty minutes in September. On 5 October Steward was awarded the title of Balloon Officer. At about midnight the following day, on 6 October 1917 (the eve of his daughter Aveluy's first birthday), and after logging another hour in the air, Steward and two other officers were hit by a shell while asleep in their dug-out. Arthur Steward, aged 35, and Lieutenant George Harold Knight, aged 25, were killed instantly. They were buried next to each other at Duhallow Advanced Dressing Station Cemetery, near Ypres. The third man, Lieutenant Rosaire Henri Olivier, a Canadian, aged 29, died on 11 October 1917 at a hospital in Boulogne.

Extracts from four letters to members of Arthur's family after his death further reveal his story and indicate the esteem in which he was held by his friends and comrades:

> The four officers of the Section were sleeping in a big dug-out, which would have been proof against anything except a direct hit. Early this morning there was some desultory shelling around the Camp, and one of them came right through the roof of the dug-out, exploding on the floor ... Of the four officers inside, one beside your son was killed: and like him – painlessly and instantaneously: another seriously wounded. While the fourth escaped with a very bad shaking ... They are being buried today.
>
> (Lieutenant Colonel W.F. MacNeece, to Canon Edward Steward. 6 October 1917.)

> I cannot forget how he instigated a little visit from G. and myself to his rooms to climb the Magdalen Tower with him on May Day, 1911. It was the most beautiful one of the past thirty years and a 'vision' to think over.
>
> (From a very old friend, the widow of a former headmaster of Haileybury who had known the family for many years.)

> Being as I was in the same battery with him for a year, I knew him pretty well and had a great admiration for him. He was always cheerful in the worst circumstances and whenever there was a nasty bit of work on he would volunteer for it. He was a great favourite with us all. I had recommended him to be captain of the battery, and if I had not left it I might have persuaded him not to go to R.F.C. ... No one could help liking him. He was my favourite of all the many officers I have had under me in this war.
>
> (Major D.K. Tweedie DSO, 336/RFA (previously 168/RFA), 19 October 1917.)

> I saw so much of the four children during those happy visits to Sarum. You know how I loved their mother. I have a letter she wrote to me after she and Muriel had been to Oxford, which I call a 'Magdalen Rhapsody' – telling of Arthur plunging into the river after a football, and then singing most beautifully for the Christmas practice.
>
> (From an old friend.)

1. Their engagement had been announced in *The Times* seven months earlier on 13 November 1911.
2. The two alternative spellings Nieuwpoort and Nieuport were, and still are, both in common usage. Each time the town is referred to in this book, the specific source spelling for that section is used.

Edmund Alec TARBET

11 December 1890 – 21 August 1915

Rank and regiment: Private (2131), Ceylon Planters Rifle Corps; Second Lieutenant, 1st Battalion, Royal Inniskilling Fusiliers.
Medals awarded: Victory, British War, 1914–1915 Star.
Theatre of War: Egypt and Gallipoli. **Memorial:** Helles Memorial, Turkey.

Tarbet's father, Lieutenant Colonel Alexander Francis Tarbet (from Liverpool) and mother, Flora Elsie Maud Hooper (from Albury, Surrey) married in early 1890. Alec, as he was known, was born later that year and was to be their only child. Alec's father served with the 3rd Battalion South Lancashire Regiment and saw active service in Africa. He resigned his commission in 1907, only to rejoin the 3/S. Lancs (a reserve battalion, based in the north-west of England) in October 1914 and served until his retirement in June 1919. Before joining Magdalen College School in Oxford in 1903, Alec was a boarder at Eaton House School, now known as Orwell Park School in Suffolk.

Life at Magdalen College School (1903–1906) and beyond

Tarbet was a boarder at the school for four years (1903–1906) and according to Brownrigg 'his cheery ways and good spirits made him a favourite with all'. Indeed, it appears to be characteristic of him that once having got into Mr Etty's bad books on a day which coincided with both his birthday and a visit from his father, he made no defence or appeal until his punishment was over, then politely asked leave to go out with his father who had been quietly waiting for him.

Tarbet was academically strong, winning a school science prize in 1905. The following year he showed himself to be an able and confident speaker in the December debate on 'This House views the motor car with favour'. He was the only junior boy to stand and offer support for the motion. Quoting the complaints which were to be seen in the *Daily Telegraph* at the time against motor cars ('One man could not even go out of his gate without looking up the road'), Tarbet said that if a certain car by mischance had fallen into an area, 'was it the car's fault'? He then proceeded to defend the motor car for its more usual merits. Thanks to Tarbet's contribution the motion was eventually carried by twenty-seven votes to twenty.

Tarbet was a keen sportsman. During the wet summer term of 1903 he won the junior (handicap) walking race, over a distance of 6 miles. Swimming lessons were done in the River Cherwell and Tarbet is reported to have 'swum the short-pass' in the summer of 1904. Boys who became good enough to swim the 'long pass' were awarded the swimming certificate. Indeed, Tarbet completed the 'long-pass' the following year when he swam the required distance, along with Herbert Canton, Charles Maltby and seven others.

In the summer of 1905, at the age of 14, Tarbet's athleticism was really starting to show when he competed in the school sports day. He came second, by 2 yards, in the final of the 100 yard flat race, but had achieved the same time (12secs) as the winner (L.F. Tebbutt) in his semi-final race. In the high jump Tarbet 'was in a different class to the others'; he won with a height of 4 feet 2 inches (1.27m). In the long jump he achieved a jump of 16 feet 3 inches (4.95m) beating his rival Tebbutt by one inch. The rivalry between this pair continued into the more light hearted races, and in the sack race it is reported that Tarbet 'would have been a good second [place] if he had not sat down'. He finished third, with Tebbutt winning.

His ability was not restricted to track and field events, for in the following year he came fourth in the junior gymnasium competition, only three points behind the winner (C.L. Roberton), but importantly two points ahead of his ever present rival and friend Tebbutt. The competition had encompassed six disciplines, the rings, bars, high bars, ropes, horse and the ladder.

In the Michaelmas term of 1905, aged 15, Tarbet showed considerable promise on the football field, hardworking and fast; it is stated in *The Lily* that he 'should come on as a wing-forward or as a half-back'. It should be remembered that school reports of the day were very short and to the point and no punches were pulled. *The Lily* reports were the same. If a player was not up to scratch his faults and weaknesses were written for all to read. For Tarbet to get a relatively glowing report indicates his overall sporting ability. However, the following year when his performance dropped below the high standards that were being instilled in the boys, his player profile read: 'Began the season well on the outside right; has considerable pace and can centre at times. Late in the season seemed easily hurt.' Playing alongside Tarbet in the team of 1906 were Francis Pitts, Lesley Hoyne-Fox, and Harold Dawes, all of whom lost their lives during the First World War. Also in the 1906 team was Basil H. Blackwell (son of the founder of Blackwell's Bookshop and eventually the Blackwell's Group). Interestingly, Blackwell's player profile reads: 'At right half runs about a good deal, tries hard and often kicks the ball in the right direction. As a rule doesn't use his head.' After leaving MCS in 1907, Blackwell continually returned to school, working tirelessly as a rowing coach in his spare time. Later to become Sir Basil Blackwell, his name is still prominent in MCS, having served as chairman of the school, and in 2005 the new MCS library was named after this brilliant servant of Oxford and MCS.

Tarbet also represented MCS at cricket in the 'mumps-required game' of 1905 versus Oxford High School. Only players previously having had mumps were allowed to play. MCS were 121 all out with Tarbet coming in at no. 9 and being bowled for nought. Oxford High School were 81 for 3 in reply before rain resulted in the abandonment of the game.

Although there are no reports of Tarbet playing hockey for the school, records indicate that after leaving he played the sport seriously, representing mid-Surrey in 1908; by 1910 he was playing regularly for Ealing Hockey Club.

On leaving school in 1906 Tarbet became an engineer's apprentice and lived with his parents in Ealing, but his association with MCS did not end. He became a subscriber to *The Lily*, enabling him to keep up to date with school news, and in March 1907 he donated a book, *The White Plooms of Navarre*, to the school library.

Tarbet's War

Initially joining the Ceylon Planters Rifle Corps on 27 September 1914, within seven weeks Private (Rifleman) Tarbet found himself serving his country in the heat of Egypt, defending the Suez Canal and preventing ships of hostile nations using the passage. His cousin, Arthur Kenneth Tarbet, also joined the Ceylon Planters Rifle Corps at the same time. They were to share all their war experiences, obtaining their commissions together with the 1st Battalion, Royal Inniskilling Fusiliers and sadly both dying in the same action on the same day in 1915 during the Gallipoli campaign.

Tarbet applied for a temporary commission in the regular army towards the end of 1914, submitting that he could ride a horse but his preference was to join the infantry. Major Hall-Brown, recommending him for a commission, stated, 'He is of good moral character and to my personal knowledge has attained a good standard of education.' He was passed fit for his commission on 25 January 1915 and with his cousin together undertook officer training with the Officer Training Corps in Egypt.

Tarbet and his cousin received their temporary commissions as Second Lieutenants in the 1st Battalion, Royal Inniskilling Fusiliers on 19 April 1915. It is possible they were already part of the regiment on board the *Andania* when she set sail from Alexandria, Egypt on 10 April 1915, arriving in Mundros Bay, Gallipoli two days later. The 1/R.Innis.F. (as part of the 87 Brigade, 29th Division) landed unopposed at X beach in Gallipoli on 25 April. About an hour after landing the Turks counter-attacked, but the British forces held them off. The 1/R.Innis.F. took up a position on the right, with the Royal Fusiliers extending the line still further right (towards W beach) and the Border Regiment on the left. The advance from the beach, in what was to become known as the First Battle of Krithia, started on 28 April, and by the end of the day the 87 Brigade had advanced 3 miles to be 1¼ miles short of their initial target of Krithia.

During the night of 1 May between 16,000 and 20,000 Turks made a determined attack along the line. At daybreak, the French forces and the 87 Brigade counter-attacked. One and a half companies of the 1/R.Innis.F. charged a trench, capturing about 124 Turks, before taking up a line about 500 yards forward on one side of the *nullah* (a steep narrow valley). The rest of the 1/R.Innis.F. pushed forward to join the advance detachment. They came under heavy shell fire and due to the withdrawal of the 86 Brigade were also forced to withdraw back to the positions held the previous night. At 05.00 on 6 May orders were received for an attack to begin at 11.00, with the 87 Brigade being held in reserve until the third phase. This action was to become known as the Second Battle of Krithia and lasted until 8 May 1915.

The 87 Brigade moved into reserve on 10 May and were on fatigue duty on the 12 and 13 May at Lancashire Landing. The Turks, after moving in more howitzers, shelled the area of Lancashire Landing during 13 May, killing about sixty horses. That evening, the 1/R.Innis.F. were temporarily transferred to the 29 Indian Infantry Brigade (still the 29th Division).

On 22 May the 1/R.Innis.F., in an uncompleted advanced trench, were rushed by the Turks and had to temporarily abandon the trench, leaving behind a machine gun. The 1/R.Innis.F. counter-attacked, retaking the gun, killing about 180 Turks and taking about 15 prisoners in the process, whilst suffering approximately 100 casualties themselves.

On 4 June the entire 29th Division attacked the Turkish lines (the Third Battle of Krithia). The next day, the1/R.Innis.F. rejoined the 87 Brigade. The conditions that Tarbet experienced in the trenches at this time were not pleasant. Some of our trenches still contained dead Turks, some whole and some in bits; in some places they were stacked in heaps. Slowly the bodies were put in the worst trenches and filled in. In front of the trenches a large number of Allied and Turkish dead had lain in the open for several days, and the smell became vile. For most of June work continued to improve the trenches, interrupted by sporadic attacks from the Turks.

At the end of June the 87 Brigade took part in the action known as the Battle for Gully Ravine. Starting on 28 June, it lasted for four days. Eventually, the 87 Brigade was given some respite and by 12 July the whole 87 Brigade had moved by sea to Mudros, a small Greek port on the island of Lemnos, for some much needed rest. Sports were organized but the rest did not last long. The brigade returned to the peninsula on 22 July (disembarking at V, W and X beaches) to reoccupy the trenches at Gully Ravine and participate in the offensive beginning on the 6 August, the Battle of Krithia Vineyard.

On 16 August Tarbet's brigade embarked for Suvla in the north of the peninsula. Upon arriving the following day they were immediately placed under orders to be ready at short notice for the front line. On 20 August, in preparation for the Allied attack on Hill 70 the following day, the 87 Brigade took up the firing line on the north side of Chocolate Hill, with the 1/R.Innis.F. having to occupy only partially dug support trenches. The whole brigade was in position by midnight, ready to take part in the last great British attack of the Gallipoli campaign, the Battle of Scimitar Hill.

At 15.05 the following afternoon, the 1/R.Innis.F. pushed forward the firing line by about 400 yards to reach the foot of Hill 70 with minimal casualties. The whole battalion moved forward as one in an all-out assault on the hill at 15.30. The war diary records that the attack was pushed home with the greatest gallantry. On nearing the top of the hill, they came under heavy shrapnel and machine gun fire from a rise on the left. They reached a trench and jumped in but were swept by shrapnel from the right and rifle and machine gun fire from the left. The position was untenable and the survivors dropped back to get some cover. The Border Regiment were ordered forward to support the 1/R.Innis.F. and take the hill, but were again thwarted by rifle fire from the left and failed to take the summit. While the South Wales Borderers continued the attack, Captain Pike, the officer in charge of the 1/R.Innis.F., organized to eliminate the Turks' machine gun emplacements on the left rise. Despite some men being seen pushing over the skyline, deteriorating light and smoke from the burning heather meant that the progress and results of the attack were not observable. When the fighting eventually died down it was evident that the line had not been appreciably advanced and the losses sustained were heavy. Very few of the officers who took part in these attacks returned. The attack was abandoned on 22 August 1915 as the bush fires that ensued cremated many of the men who lay wounded in the undergrowth.[1]

Edmund Tarbet was last seen wounded during the assault on Hill 70. He was initially reported as missing in action, and it took a year before he was officially presumed to have died during the attacks on 21 August 1915, aged 24. His medals, plaque and scroll were sent to his father, Lieutenant Colonel Francis Tarbet, who retained an association with the School after Alec's death and donated £1.1s to the cost of the War Memorial.

1. The MCS old boy Reverend A.G. Parham, Precentor of Christ Church, Chaplain to the Forces (attached to 2nd South Midland Mounted Brigade) landed with the troops at Suvla Bay on 18 August and was awarded the MC in recognition for his work rescuing wounded and dying men from Chocolate Hill and the surrounding burning scrub of the Anafarta Plain on 21 August and the days that followed. He remained in the field for ten weeks under incessant fire, burying the dead and attending the wounded.

Thomas THOMAS

12 July 1897 – 3 November1916

Rank and regiment: Private (3021), 9th Battalion, Oxfordshire and Buckinghamshire Light Infantry; Lieutenant, 51st Company, Machine Gun Corps. **Medals awarded:** Victory, British War, 1914–15 Star. **Theatre of War:** Western Front. **Memorial:** Guards' Cemetery, Lesboeufs, France.

Thomas Thomas was the third son of David Robert Thomas and Margaret Thomas (*née* Jenkins). His parents, originally from Wales (Tan Yr Allt, Talybont), moved to Oxford, where Thomas and his three siblings were born. His father was a chemist (pharmacist) and had moved to Oxford by 1891 where he had his own chemist's business (Cousins, Thomas and Co.) at 20 Magdalen Street. David's cousin moved to Oxford with him to become first his housekeeper and then his wife. The business and family home had moved to 63 Banbury Road by 1901.

Thomas had two brothers, David Robert (b. 1894) and Jenkin (b. 1895), and one sister Margaret (b. 1898). All three brothers were day boys at MCS. His brothers also saw active service in the war, and were at the front when Thomas died. David served with the Welsh Regiment and Jenkin with the Gloucestershire Regiment. His sister Margaret married Jesse Wheatland Clinch in 1918, and moved to Australia a few years later.

Life at Magdalen College School (1909–1911) and beyond

Thomas briefly attended Oxford High School, then All Saints' School, Bloxham (1908–09) before joining MCS as a day boy in September 1909. His two brothers, David (January 1909 to July 1910) and Jenkin (January 1909 to July 1910) were already at the school. After two terms at MCS, at Easter 1910, Thomas won the Set V mathematics prize and the Form I and II classics prize. He rowed for the Form I and II boat in the Form Four races of March 1911, although he was then in Form III. In July of the same year he won the Junior 300 yard race, taking the lead straight from the gun and managing not to be passed.

After Thomas had left MCS in 1911 he returned to play an Old Boys XI cricket match on 19 June 1914, which included in the old boys' team, John Bellamy. The School 1st XI included Roger Field, Gordon Bradley and Victor Jessel. The School 1st XI was too strong for the old boys, and in front of the new Pavilion the school bowled out the old boys for just 59 runs. As with many matches in those days, the school then batted, amassing runs until stumps were drawn at a designated time. The School XI reached 127 for 5.

Thomas' War

Set to go on and study at Jesus College, Thomas joined the 9th (Reserve) Battalion, Oxfordshire and Buckinghamshire Light Infantry 'quite early and was for some time in Oxford'. His brother Jenkin, also in the OBLI and later the Gloucester Regiment, was wounded and taken prisoner by the Germans during the war. His other brother, David, was in the Royal Welsh Regiment after initially joining the Queen's Own Oxfordshire Hussars. Thomas was gazetted Second Lieutenant on 26 January 1915, aged 17, and on 10 April 1915 his battalion became part of the 8 (Reserve) Brigade based at Wareham. Thomas went out to France in August 1916 and was attached to the 51 Machine Gun Company (51 Brigade, 17th Division) on the Somme, becoming a temporary Lieutenant. On 4 August, in extremely hot weather, the 51/MGC arrived at Delville Wood, near Mametz, taking up defensive positions. The route into the wood was heavily shelled day and night, so gun teams went into the wood with rations and water for forty-eight hours, and were then relieved. The corps was relieved and withdrew to Buire(-Courcelles) on 12 August, before entraining for Gézaincourt four days later. During August and September the corps rotated between the front line and billets, spending approximately a week at each, but always changing location. Front line positions included Bienvillers (20 August), Hannescamps (1 September) and Hébuterne (16 September). Between 20 and 24 September the corps marched 30 miles west to Maison-Ponthieu, where they spent a week in training and on the final day prepared themselves for an attack south of Gommercourt, close to where they had previously been in the front line. The 51/MGC took over the line again at Hébuterne on 5 October, for a nine-day spell at the front, eventually being relieved by the 50/MGC on 14 October. They then moved north-west, billeting initially at Souastre and then at Lucheux. On 22 October they travelled south by motor lorry 20 miles further to Treux (west of

Thomas Thomas.

Albert), then on 27 October they marched north-east to Le Transloy, 4 miles south of Bapaume. They relieved the 25/MGC in the front line on 31 October; three days later the Germans heavily bombarded the 51 Brigade front line and their infantry attacked the right section of the line. Four of the corps machine guns fired effectively on the enemy and the attack was beaten off. During the action Thomas Thomas was killed, aged 19. He was buried nearby at Lesbœufs. On his grave his parents had inscribed in Welsh 'Gwellangauna Chywilydd' (Death rather than Dishonour).

A letter from the Colonel of the MGC to his parents read:

> I expect by now that you will have received news of your son's death. It was a great blow to us all to lose him, and although he had only been with us a short time we had got very fond of him. He always did his work well and cheerfully, and it was in carrying out his duty in taking up his section with ammunition to the front line that he met his death. I questioned the guide who was just behind him and who was blown a good distance by the same shell. He told me that after he recovered himself he ran to see what had happened to your son and found him badly hit in the head. He lived for two

or three minutes, as far as the guide could tell, but did not speak. I am sorry to say it was impossible to have a burial service owing to conditions which I know you will understand. We buried your son just outside our company headquarters at eight a.m. this morning, November 4th, and are having a cross made for his grave. My sincere sympathies are with you in your great loss. Your son died as every officer would wish to die; and although the loss be great you must feel as I do, proud of the way in which he met his death. I am, yours sincerely, Maurice Pasteur.

Dennis Henry WEBB

14 September 1893 – 10 November 1917

Rank and regiment: Private (5908), 20th Battalion, Royal Fusiliers; Second Lieutenant, 11th Battalion, Devonshire Regiment; Lieutenant, 2nd Company, Machine Gun Corps. **Medals awarded:** Victory, British War. **Theatre of War:** Western Front. **Memorial:** Duhallow ADS Cemetery, Belgium.

Dennis Henry Webb was born in London on 14 September 1893. He was the son of Thomas Henry Webb, a Professor of Music, and Alice Clarabelle Webb (*née* Gomez), a well-known vocalist. He had an older sister Dorothy (b. 1891). His mother was born in India and studied music under Dennis' father at Calcutta Cathedral. She was of Eurasian descent and it was probably from her that Dennis inherited his dark complexion and black hair. She moved to England in about 1885 and married Dennis' father in 1891. As she travelled widely giving concerts, not only in the UK but also in India and Singapore, she must have been somewhat of an absent figure in Dennis' young life. It is not clear if his mother and father formally separated but, when not at school, Dennis and his sister seem to have lived with his father and aunt (Frances Lucinda Webb) in Torquay, Devon, rather than with his mother at her apartment in London. Their father died in 1914, and Dorothy was then listed as Dennis' next of kin when he joined the Army.

Life at Magdalen College School (1904–1912) and beyond

Inheriting his mother's gift as a singer, Dennis Webb came to MCS as a chorister in January 1904, aged 10. Affectionately known to the school community as 'the dog', he was gifted academically and received many Prizes and an Exhibition; including the Form Vb Prize in 1908, a Modern Language Prize in 1909, the Ellerton Exhibition (a Prize awarded for the best performance by a Chorister in school examinations) in 1909, the Form Va Prize in 1910 and the Form VI and Va Repetition prize in 1912. In 1911 he attained a Senior Certificate in the Joint Board exams, but was absent for his second set of Senior Certificate exams in 1912 as he was in London taking alternative exams.

In 1910 he was appointed as a House Prefect, at the same time as Frank Wilkinson. In the same year he also became a committee member of the

Dennis Webb, MCS chorister, 1907.

Debating Society, and then in 1911 became the Vice-President. In 1911 he also became a Senior Prefect and had the responsibilities of Librarian and *ex officio* editor of *The Lily*. In 1911 and 1912 he was part of the organizing committee for the Sports Day.

Webb's only ever win in a Sports Day event was as an 11-year-old in the 440 yard flat race, winning in 75.4 seconds. In subsequent years he religiously entered most of the flat sprint races, but never achieved a place. In one last attempt to win on Sports Day he returned as an old boy in 1914, taking part in the Old Boy's 150 yard handicap race. Starting with a 15 yard advantage he finished second, being pipped to the post by R.H. 'Bertie' Clapperton (who started from scratch) in a remarkable time of 15.6 seconds for a person running in his 'Sunday best'.

In 1911 Dennis Webb competed in the Form Four rowing competition, rowing at bow for the Form Va 2nd boat. The boat, which included Frank Wilkinson (at no. 3) and Richard Christie (at no. 2), was described in *The Lily* as 'the most wonderful boat of the lot, and considering that two of its members had never touched an oar in their lives before, they have come on splendidly. With three days practice they practically gave up "deep sea fishing" altogether, and although none of them have any idea of watermanship, they get on a tremendous amount

Sports Day, 20 June 1914, The Old Boys race.
1st place R.H. Clapperton, 2nd place D.H. Webb (third from left, in dark trousers and white shirt plus tie). The new Pavilion can be made out in the background on the left.

of leg work, and drive the boat along at quite a fast pace. Bow improves in every race.' The following year, in 1912, Webb rowed at bow in the school's 2nd IV boat.

A keen tennis player, Webb competed in the Doubles Tennis tournament in three consecutive years from 1909 to 1911, winning and coming runner-up in the latter two years. Webb is also recorded playing in 1908 for the school Hockey team and in 1910 for the school 2nd XI Football team.

Dennis Webb left MCS in July 1912 and had intended to go on to University, but instead spent some time in France, where he became proficient in French. He then returned to England and became an assistant master at a school in Yorkshire, before moving to a school in Croydon owned and run by R.H. Alexander, an old boy from MCS.

Webb's War

Dennis Webb enlisted as a private in the 20th Battalion, Royal Fusiliers on 14 September 1914, the day of his twenty-first birthday. He spent the next few months training, probably at Leatherhead with his battalion. On 25 January 1915 he was granted a commission as a Second Lieutenant in the 11th Battalion, Devonshire Regiment. At that time, his new battalion was based in Torquay, so Webb was lucky enough to be billeted near to home for a while. Then on 10 April 1915 the 11/Devons changed status from a service battalion to a reserve battalion and in May 1915 moved to Wareham as part of the 10 (Reserve) Brigade.

In December 1915 Dennis attained the rank of Lieutenant and by May 1916 had transferred to the Machine Gun Corps and went out to France. The Machine Gun Corps was only formed in October 1915 and volunteers for what would later become unofficially known as the 'suicide squad' came from all parts of the Army. Webb sailed from Southampton, arriving in Le Havre on 17 May 1916. He probably spent the next three months training at the Machine Gun Base Depot at Camiers, north of Le Havre on the French coast. On 25 August he was posted to the 2nd Company Machine Gun Corps and joined his company the following day at Maxse Redoubt, just east of Albert, where the company was in Reserve.

Webb did not have much time to get to know his new company or surroundings as on 27 August 1916 the company relieved the 1st Company MGC in support near Mametz Wood. They moved into the front line on 31 August 1916 near Bazentin-Le-Grand. After three days in the front line the company moved back into reserve at Maxse Redoubt. The company were back in the same line by 5 September 1916 and on 9 September the company attacked the intermediate line with four guns attached to the 2 Royal Sussex Regiment, and two guns each to the 1st Battalion, Northamptonshire Regiment and 2nd Battalion, Kings Royal Rifle Corps. The attack was partially successful, with the loss of only three lives. The 2nd Company Machine Gun Corps moved back into reserve at Baizieux, west of Albert on 11 September 1916, where they spent the next week in training.

The company was soon back in action, spending a week in the reserve and support line near Mametz Wood before moving into the front line near Bazentin-Le-Grand on 26 September 1916. The following day, two guns supported a successful attack by the 2/R.Suss., before moving into reserve back to the west of Albert at Millencourt.

In October the company was attached to the X Corps at Tours and spent the rest of the month in training. On 26 October 1916 Webb was granted ten days leave to the UK. He rejoined his company on 9 November 1916 at Albert where they had become attached to the III Corps. The company moved back into the trenches at Bazentin-Le-Grand and Mametz Wood for the rest of November, but by the end of the month one gun had been put out of action by a direct hit from enemy fire.

December 1916 saw Webb take over the task of recording the daily events of the company in the War Diary. He records the movement of the company from Mametz Wood to High Wood during the month. By the beginning of January 1917 the company were back at Millencourt for training, before moving a few miles to Bresle on 24 January.

Nearly half the hospital admissions of soldiers in the field during the war were as a result of the poor living conditions, scabies being one of the most common conditions reported. Webb, like many other soldiers, was not immune and on 26 January 1917 was admitted to hospital suffering from scabies, passing through the 1 Field Ambulance and the 29 and 38 Casualty Clearing Stations before rejoining his Company on 28 January 1917.

February 1917 saw the company in Mericourt(-sur-Somme) before moving initially to Peronne and then to Chuignolles, where, by the middle of the month they were engaged in anti-aircraft work. Interspersed with days of training, firing on the German wires and lines was the order of the month for March 1917. By end of March 1917, the company began work on improving the Estrées to Villers-Carbonnel road and took up anti-aircraft positions at Brie to guard the Somme Bridge.

In April 1917 Webb, now as Adjutant, took up again the duty of recording the daily events in the War Diary. He records in detail the inspection of the company by Lieutenant Colonel Abadie; it was passed as satisfactory with only a few deficiencies in small kit, notably that the clothing could have been cleaner! The company spent the April in Chuignes and Morcourt, just south of Albert in a beautiful area right on the River Somme. Here they underwent training on use of cover, selection of gun positions, concealment from aircraft and range firing, as well as tactical training and communication. Brigade sports took place on 28 April and Webb's company came third in the Brigade Cup, winning the cross country race and coming second in the tug of war.

The company remained in Morcourt during May 1917, and at the same time that a company tailor was appointed a new standing order was issued forbidding the taking in of trousers! The company continued in training, but still found time for some bathing in the River Somme. On 18 May 1917 Webb was again granted ten days leave to the UK. When he rejoined his company on 29 May 1917 they had moved 60 miles north to a new sector, Meteren, to the south-west of Ypres. Webb had seen the last of the Somme.

By the middle of June the company had relocated to billets in Saint-Marie Cappel, west of Poperinge, before moving further north to Wormhoudt, then ultimately to the Channel coastline and Malo (Dunkirk) and Camp Zeepanne (6 miles along the coast from Nieuwpoort, where the front line met the North Sea). After two and half months' respite the company was back in trenches by 19 June 1917, and two sections of the company took over coastal defence duties, whilst others were engaged in anti-aircraft and camp improvement activities. On 10 July the enemy shelled the trenches at Nieuwpoort-Bains very heavily from 08.00 to 19.00, destroying the three bridges over the River Yser and cutting off British communication lines and reinforcement/retreat routes. At 19.00 the enemy attacked and captured the first and second line on a 1,400-yard front, with the MGC losing sixteen of their guns in the process. Cut off and with no communication link, Private F. Holloway volunteered to carry a communication to company HQ by swimming the river. This he successfully did under heavy shelling and machine gun fire. He was awarded the Military Cross for his actions and went on to survive the war. The British were able to reorganize and hold the remainder of the defensive systems and were resupplied over the next four days. On 15 July the company were relieved and marched 12 miles to Ghyvelde Camp, then on in the following days to billets and then to camps in the Saint Pol-sur-Mer area of Dunkirk (ultimately at Le Clipon camp). Here they went into special training for the remainder of July and all through August and September, negotiating obstacle courses and scaling the sea wall time and time again while carrying extra full loads. The 2nd Company MGC took part in the brigade boxing tournament on 15 August, then competed and won the brigade competition over the obstacle course on 18 August, only to be disqualified for carrying machine gunner's instead of infantry loads. Webb was given a five-day pass for leave in Paris on 10 September 1917, rejoining the company on 15 September 1917.

The 2nd Company MGC moved away from the coast on 22 October, 11 miles south to new billets in Eringhem, and Webb took his final leave on 24 October, returning to the UK for ten days. Meanwhile, the company had marched further south to billets in Herzeele, then continued their journey east to a training camp in the St Janster-Biezen area. Webb rejoined his company on 4 November, in time for their move to Poperinge on 6 November and their entrainment to the Ypres area the following day. The company spent the day cleaning out their new billets on 8 November before moving to their battery positions at 01.10 the following morning. One battery position was commanded by Dennis Webb. Each battery spent their time preparing their lines of fire. They had joined the final throes of the action that was to become known as the Second Battle of Passchendaele. On 10 November the 3 Brigade attacked the German lines, in cooperation with a British barrage on the German Lines. Each of the company's machine guns fired about 5,000 rounds during the attack and continued firing during the afternoon to protect the British infantry, who were pinned down in the furthest line of attack. During the day Dennis Webb was killed, aged 24, while commanding his machine-gun battery, just six days after returning from England. At night the guns were withdrawn and Webb's section was relieved by another section of the company. Four other ranks from the company were also killed on the same day. Dennis Webb was buried at Duhallow Advanced Dressing Station, just twenty paces away from MCS old boy Arthur Steward, who had died the previous month.

Francis Dudley WILKINSON

17 June 1893 – 19 April 1920

Rank and regiment: Private (2238), 18th (Service) Battalion (1st Public Schools), Royal Fusiliers (City of London Regiment); Lieutenant, 3rd (att. 8th and 10th) Battalion, The Buffs (East Kent Regiment).
Medals awarded: Victory, British War, 1914–1915 Star, Military Cross.
Theatre of War: Palestine, Western Front. **Memorial:** Buried at sea, off Port Sudan, Sudan.

Francis (Frank) Dudley Wilkinson was born at 'Glenlyn', Droitwich Road, Worcester, on 17 June 1893. He was the eldest child and only son of Reverend Arthur Dudley Wilkinson and Isabel Agnes Wilkinson (*née* Howat). His father graduated from Magdalene College, Cambridge, and entered the church. At the time of Frank's birth he was a second master at Queen Elizabeth Grammar School in Worcester and curate at the Church of Barbourne. The family moved to Oxford in 1903 when Arthur became the Vicar of Cumnor. Frank had two younger sisters, Doris Ruth (b. 1895) and Phyllis Mary (b. 1896). At the time of his death, Wilkinson's youngest sister, Phyllis, was living with her husband on the Derby Tea Estate, at Cachar in India.

Life at Magdalen College School (1905–1911) and beyond

Frank Wilkinson joined MCS in the Trinity term of 1905, and despite living locally in the village of Cumnor he was a boarder. Wilkinson was to become a stalwart of the school, regarded very highly by both his peers and masters alike. Renowned for his efforts on the sports field, he was also academically sound, winning the 1909 Form IV Prize and gaining his Junior Certificate in 1910. In his penultimate year at the school, from the Michaelmas term of 1910, Wilkinson became a House Prefect along with his contemporary Dennis Webb. After leaving MCS in July 1911 Wilkinson did not go on to University but would eventually go to work in London. It is interesting that after leaving MCS, the book that this all-action MCS sporting hero donated to the school library was a romance novel, *The Mistress of Shenstone*, by F.L. Barclay.

By the time he was 15 Wilkinson was playing football for the school 1st XI, initially playing at the back in 1908 then swapping to goalkeeper in 1909. In 1909

Francis Wilkinson.

his *Lily* Character Profile read: 'As a rule has kept goal, where he fields well the straight shots at him but is slow in moving to the others, and is weak at ground shots. Was also tried at half.' In front of him in defence was the ever present John Bellamy. In 1910 Wilkinson captained the team and changed position to play out of goal in the centre of defence 'tackling and kicking nicely, but needs more certainty'. The year 1910 saw his final football season at MCS; playing in the same team were Leslie Roberton and Victor Jessel. In 1912 Wilkinson was back on the MCS football field playing for the Old Boys XI against the School (which still contained six of the 1910 side he had captained), but losing 7–0. The following year, in 1913, Wilkinson again played in the Old Boys football match and gained revenge by beating the School by nine goals to two.

Seemingly a born defender, Wilkinson also played half-back for the school Hockey XI. In 1909 *The Lily* writes that Wilkinson 'Has proved a useful left-back. Has some pace and, though occasionally wild, works hard.' In the 1909 hockey side alongside Wilkinson were Hugh Canton, John Callender and Mr Brownrigg. In 1910 he played alongside Edward Andrews and Victor Jessel as well as the irrepressible Mr Brownrigg. Wilkinson's own development on the hockey pitch is questionable however: 'As right-half is rather inclined to miss the ball, but can hit hard, and though not a quick turner, has fair pace.' In his final season on the hockey field for MCS in 1911 Wilkinson was awarded full colours and given the role of Honorary Secretary. His play also became more solid: 'As right back is generally very sure and does a great deal of work: occasionally hits rather recklessly.'

Frank Wilkinson's favoured and best sport was cricket. He is described in *The Lily* as 'One of the finest free scoring bats we have produced'. Although his scores and averages do not reflect that he was an all-conquering sportsman, he was obviously rated very highly with regard to the adventurous way he approached the game, eventually becoming captain of cricket in his final year. In his first year playing for the school First XI in 1908, aged 14, he received half colours for his contribution, but only finished with a batting average of 6.2. The following season, in 1909, he did not live up to his initial promising start and was given the following profile in *The Lily*: 'Wilkinson has no defence and tries to cut everything, legitimate or not – at straight ones he hits wildly with a very crooked bat.' With the editor later adding that he 'could improve a great deal if he would learn patience and take more trouble at net practice'. All young MCS cricketers please take note! His batting average was only marginally better, with an average of 7 and highest score of 22 not out. Notably in 1909 he played against Noel Chavasse when Noel returned to MCS to play in the annual Old Boy versus School fixture that year. In 1910 he made significant progress, hitting his first 50 for the school and amassing 315 runs in 12 innings, at an average of 28.6, finishing top of the batting averages. He also added slow bowling to his cricketing credentials, bowling 16 overs and taking 2 wickets for 61 runs. *The Lily* rewarded his efforts with the following profile: 'Probably the most improved bat in the side and has played a succession of useful innings. Has a good reach and is much more patient in defence though he still might play straighter. A fair field and can throw.' He was awarded full colours. In 1911 Wilkinson was elected Captain of Cricket and became one of the main bowlers in the side, bowling a total of 64 overs and taking 17 wickets for 288 runs at an average of 16.9. He did not score as many runs with the bat, possibly due to a too cautious approach during his captaincy year. *The Lily* reported: 'Though he has played some good innings, has not been so successful with the bat this year, largely owing to his "stance" at the wickets which prevents him playing square at the ball. Has been useful as a slow bowler and can generally catch.'

Over his entire school career in the 1st XI Wilkinson played 43 innings and amassed 619 runs at an average of 15.5, his highest score being 81 not out. In 1912 Wilkinson returned to MCS to play cricket for the Old Boys XI in the annual fixture versus the school. Wilkinson made 90 before being caught, and the Old Boys posted a formidable total of 230 that the School failed to get. Wilkinson was also a keen cricketer outside school, playing for his home village of Cumnor. Famously, in 1912 both Frank and his father played in the Cumnor side that beat Cowley CC in the Oxford District League II Challenge Cup Final. In the game played at the Lincoln College Ground, Cumnor batted first and scored a total of 121, with Reverend Arthur Wilkinson (the President) contributing a valuable 14. Frank (the Honorary Secretary), batting at no. 6, failed to score. In reply, the favourites, Cowley CC, were bowled out for 86. The *Oxford Illustrated* newspaper printed the victorious team's picture and told the story of the success. To celebrate their victory a dinner was held for the team and the supporters at the Vine Inn, Cumnor.

In 1913 Frank's father, Reverend Arthur D. Wilkinson, was invited by Mr Brownrigg to play for his Masters' XI side versus the School XI on 28 May 1913. The Masters' XI were too strong for the School XI and won by 137 runs. Two weeks later Frank himself returned to play his last game for the Old Boys versus the school. In an exciting match the School, chasing a total of 142, eventually levelled the scores with 9 wickets down. With the School needing 1 run to win Wilkinson had Martin caught by Robert Foster (Arthur Foster's elder brother) for 25. The game was tied.

Wilkinson was also a strong athlete, being particularly good at the High Jump and competing in the Public Schools Sports Event of 1911 at Stamford Bridge. Prior to the event the quartet of Jessel, Clapperton, Thomson and Wilkinson had been given permission by the University to train at their athletics facility at Iffley Road. On the day of the event, 6 May, Mr Brownrigg escorted them to Fulham and entertained them to lunch at his club. Wilkinson, however, was unable to reproduce his school High Jump form (his personal best being 5ft 3ins) and he was beaten by the eventual winner, who cleared 5 feet 2 inches. Maybe Mr Brownrigg's club lunch had been a little too heavy for Wilkinson.

Frank Wilkinson's participation in Sports Days makes impressive reading. In 1907 he won the Junior Half Mile race (in 2min 33.4secs). In the 1908 Junior events he was first in the High Jump (4ft 7ins), first in the 330 yard Handicap

Cumnor CC, 1912: Oxford District League II Challenge Cup Winners.
This photograph proudly hangs in the Cumnor CC Pavilion, with the 19-year-old Frank Wilkinson (middle row far right) and Rev A.D. Wilkinson (middle row second from left), a permanent reminder of Cumnor's connection with Magdalen College School [Wilkinson being one of the MCS House names].

Final and second in the 100 yard Final. In the 1909 Senior events that took place on two gloriously hot days he was second in the Half Mile Handicap race to John Bellamy; second in the High Jump (4ft 11ins); and competed in the 100 yard race and 150 yard handicap race. In the 1910 Senior events he was joint first in the High Jump (5ft 3ins); first in the Half Mile Handicap race (2mins 14.4secs, the closest race of the day, falling over the line a foot and a half ahead of Newton in second place); third in the Half Mile race; and part of the winning 400 yard team (relay) race in a time of 48secs. In 1911 he was on the Sports Day organizing committee and competed in the Senior events. He competed in the 100 yard race; came third in the 150 yard Handicap Final where he pressed second-placed Jessel hard; came first in High Jump (5ft); came first in the Half Mile Handicap race (he was content to remain last until the second lap, then started going through the field until at the start of the straight he was in first place and finished very strongly in a time of 2 minutes 10.4 seconds, only 0.4 seconds outside the school record at the time); came second in both the Quarter Mile and the Mile races. Wilkinson gained fifteen Sports Day points in 1911, only one point behind the winner of the Ladies Plate. Wilkinson had acquitted himself well at his last Sports Day, an amazing day of competition, with the spectators again entertained by the band of the 4 Battalion OBLI, as they had been for the previous few years.

Wilkinson was also fond of playing tennis and in 1908 he entered the singles tennis competition at school, playing Charles Maltby in the first round. Maltby won the tie to progress to the next round.[1] Wilkinson also entered the tournament in 1910 and 1911, reaching the final in 1911 against Dennis Webb. In 1911 he also took part in the doubles competition.

In 1911 Wilkinson competed in the Form Four rowing competition, rowing at no. 3 for the Form Va 2nd boat. The boat, which included Dennis Webb (at bow) and Richard Christie (at 2), was described in *The Lily* as 'the most wonderful boat of the lot, and considering that two of its members had never touched an oar in their lives before, they have come on splendidly. With three days practice they practically gave up "deep sea fishing" altogether, and although none of them have any idea of watermanship, they get on a tremendous amount of leg work, and drive the boat along at quite a fast pace. [Wilkinson at] 3 does an enormous amount of work, but is slow with his hands, and is apt to hurry stroke.'

After leaving MCS Frank Wilkinson gained employment as a clerk in the London office of the High Commissioner of the Union of South Africa.

Wilkinson's War

Four weeks after the declaration of war with Germany, on 4 September 1914, the 6 feet 2 inches tall Wilkinson (34-inch chest, and green eyes) volunteered to serve his country and signed his attestation papers at the Westminster recruiting office, committing himself to three years' service in the army. Wilkinson was posted to Epsom on 15 September as a Private in the 18th (Service) Battalion, Royal Fusiliers, which had been formed only four days earlier. In the battalion at the same time as Frank Wilkinson were two other MCS old boys, Arthur Foster (MCS 1906–1908) and Horace Amon (MCS 1911–1913), linked in friendship not only because they had attended the same school (both overlapped with Wilkinson at MCS) but because all three were aged 21, with Wilkinson and Foster remarkably sharing the same birthday, 17 June 1893. They spent the next two years together, training in England, fighting in France and finally attending officer training together back in Oxford before going their own way and into different regiments and adventures.

The 18/RF, known as the 1st Public Schools Corps, was trained as part of the Public Schools and University Men's Force, until mid-summer 1915, when they then moved to Clipstone Camp, Nottinghamshire in June 1915 and transferred to the 98 Brigade, 33rd Division and were taken over by the War Office on 1 July

1915. Wilkinson was transferred on 27 July 1915 to the 33rd Division Cyclist Company, still in Nottingham, but six weeks later was transferred back to his original battalion, the 18/RF, on 14 September, then at Tidworth Camp in Wiltshire. Two months later, on 14 November 1915, the 18/RF sailed for France aboard the SS *Princess Victoria*. Soon after their arrival in France the battalion was transferred to the 19 Brigade of the same Division (27 November) and based in the Béthune area for the winter. Here, Wilkinson (in B-Coy) saw much action, rotating between the front and support lines at Annequin, Beuvry, Cambrin, Essars, Fouquereuil, Fontes and Givenchy. The battalion was transferred to GHQ Troops on 26 February 1916, moving away from the front line by train to Saint Omer then on to Campagne(-lès-Wardrecques) by foot. Over the next two months the majority of the men of the 18/RF were commissioned into other battalions, before it was finally disbanded on 24 April 1916. The MCS trio of Wilkinson, Amon and Foster (who was wounded in early March 1916) were all sent back to Oxford in late March 1916 for officer training with No. 4 Officer Cadet Corps,[2] on the recommendation of their Colonel, Lord Henry Scott.

After officer training they were gazetted into new regiments, with Frank Wilkinson joining the 3rd (Reserve) Battalion, the Buffs (East Kent Regiment) at Dover, as a Second Lieutenant on 4 August 1916.[3] The 3/Buffs remained in the UK throughout the war as the Dover Garrison, but after less than a month Wilkinson was attached to the 8/Buffs and posted to France.

Wilkinson joined the 8/Buffs (17 Brigade, 24th Division) on 17 September 1916, along with seven other officers, at the end of a ten-day rest period for the battalion at Yaucourt(-Bussus), near Abbeville. The following day, in very heavy rain, the battalion packed up and prepared to move back to the front lines. On 19 September they marched 5 miles to Pont Remy and from there moved by train 40 miles north-east to Pernes-Camblain. The advanced parties of the brigade had not had time to arrange billets, so accommodation for that night was difficult as the summer's harvest had just been collected and all the local barns around Floringhem were now full of wheat. After a pause here for three days the battalion moved closer to the front line, marching 5 miles east to billets at Haillicourt, then on 24 September they moved into the reserve line area, 7 miles further south at Gouy-Servins, billeting in the chateau and its outbuildings. They moved into front line trenches on 25 September just south of Souchez which, after a few days of 'perfect weather', were in a relatively decent state of repair. Over the next month the battalion spent periods of a week in the front line, then in support and then in reserve. Much tunnelling and underground mining warfare took place in the area of Carency and Souchez during this period, the front lines of the two opposing armies being in close proximity to each other and the soil in the sector being very good for tunnelling. The men on the front line were therefore under constant threat of mines being exploded beneath them. On several occasions camouflets were blown in order to destroy nearby enemy mines.

At the end of October the battalion moved to Mazingarbe, via Noeux-les-Mines, where the officers billeted in the town and the other ranks billeted in huts with electric lights. The battalion went into the front line on 2 November in the Loos(-en-Gohelle) area, where the trenches were in a very poor state. The trenches had not been revetted during the summer, so when the heavy rain of the autumn arrived the trenches began to collapse at an alarming rate. At times, every available man in the front line had to work to stop the trenches from falling in on themselves and the men losing their cover. The battalion continued to man the front line in this sector throughout November and December, spending time in the firing, the support and reserve line.

An interesting incident in the 8/Buffs' trenches gives an insight into how confusing the front line trench systems were at night, and how easy it was to become disorientated, especially after patrolling and probing the enemy trenches beyond no-man's land in the dark. On the morning of 4 December 1916, at about 10.00, in a quiet area of the British trenches, a German soldier was found sitting on the duckboards, smoking a pipe. Upon seeing a British soldier, the German fled down the trench, eventually running into the neighbouring Royal Fusiliers. The Royal Fusiliers kept the German, the 8/Buffs kept his rifle and equipment. The 8/Buffs returned to their billets at Mazingarbe on 16 December for a period of rest and Christmas festivities. The morning of 20 December, sports were played while the 12th Battalion, the Sherwood Foresters' band entertained. In the afternoon the officers served the men of the battalion Christmas dinner in the Brewery at Mazingarbe, while the divisional band performed. Later in the afternoon the 8/Buffs played 'the 1/Buffs at Rugger with the assistance of both bands', losing by one try to nil. The 'weather was cold and frosty and the day was distinctly successful'. During the evening the officers dined together with guests from the rest of the brigade. On 22 December the battalion returned to the front line, with Christmas Day providing no respite from the shelling; the war diary reported that 'This being the season of goodwill to all men, a nice programme of artillery strafe has been worked out'. The Germans welcomed in the New Year of 1917 with gas and lachrymatory shells all along the brigade's line of trenches, but seemingly worst of all for the officers was that 'A rumour is spreading that whisky can no longer be got'. The next day it was reported that 'The rumour is true. We are expected to go on with the war drinking lime juice.' At 04.30 on 5 January 1917, the battalion was holding the line with only two companies when a large enemy raiding party entered their trenches, avoided the sentry groups and progressed all the way to the support line, bombing dugouts and taking prisoners. The battalion suffered three men killed, three wounded and forty-two missing. Referred to as a 'disaster' in the war diary, the battalion's CO blamed 'higher authorities' for sending away experienced NCOs, leaving only inexperienced NCOs to take charge of important posts. The rest of January was spent in the same sector fitting revetting and new duckboards to the collapsing trenches and supplying raiding parties.

On 29 January the successful raiding party from two days previous, who had worn white smocks as camouflage against the snow, were treated to dinner at the Mazingarbe Brewery by the Major. The battalion moved back from the front line on 13 February a short distance for a period of rest and training at Nœux-les-Mines. They played football against the 1/RF on 22 February, but 'at the outset it was seen that they were slightly our superiors, there being apparently several professionals' and the 8/Buffs lost 0–3. Part of their training during this period involved practising infantry movements on the ground under the guidance of aeroplane support and intelligence from the air. The battalion went back into the front line near Bully(-les-Mines) and Grenay on 3 March. After a week they were relieved and went in to support, supplying working parties but enjoying the local cinema in the evening. Relief of the front line troops (i.e. swapping battalions) was usually carried out at night time and it is during March 1917 that the 8/Buffs reported their fastest time for completing the relief, four hours. The battalion war diary records that a German aeroplane dropped a 'dud' bomb on the town of Bully-Grenay on 11 March, killing a child and wounding two others plus a soldier. At the beginning of April, during a period out of the front line, the battalion was entertained by the Regimental Concert Party, 'The Buffellows'. Being out of the front line did not automatically mean safety, and in early April the battalion billets at Bully-Grenay were shelled and the town was targeted with a large number of gas shells. The battalion was reorganized and dispersed to alternative billets. During the first week of April 1917 the battalion witnessed the increased artillery fire on Vimy Ridge, just a few miles away. As the Canadians attacked the ridge on 9 April the 8/Buffs watched from their vantage point of the front line trenches at Angres as the barrage on the ridge crept forward and the Canadians gained their objectives. Several Germans in trenches opposite the 8/Buffs, taken by surprise at the suddenness of the happenings on Vimy Ridge, stood up in their trenches 'the better to see the show – and three of them were promptly knocked out by our sniping officer'. During 14 April the trenches opposite the 8/Buffs were reported to have been vacated by the Germans; the battalion therefore progressed forward unopposed and secured the old German trench system. The battalion advanced against the new enemy positions on 17 April, after a 'feeble artillery preparation', only to have to halt the advance due to heavy machine gun and artillery fire. Two days later the battalion was relieved and, despite being very tired and with sore feet, in high spirits they marched back 10 miles to Hesdigneul(-lès-Béthune), then a further 10 miles to Bourecq. Arriving on 22 April, they cleaned up and refitted. Moving a further 10 miles east to Erny-Saint-Julien on the 25 April, the battalion met many Portuguese, 'who take a great interest in the doings of the British Tommy'. While away from the front line the battalion played football every evening, with the CO noting, 'The French civilians cannot yet understand the Englishman's love of games.' At the end of April the battalion moved on via Bourecq to Labourse, where they enjoyed a welcome bath. Over the two days of 9 and 10 May the battalion moved with the rest of the brigade, marching 26 miles via Hazebrouck to Steenvoorde. Here they continued to rest and train until moving east to the Poperinge area at the end of May 1917. The brigade was preparing to attack the Messines Ridge near Ypres, and during the beginning of June the battalion, together with the rest of the brigade, practised the attack on model trenches in the Steenvoorde area. The battalion proceeded into Belgium and on to Heksken on 4 June, then on 6 June they moved on via Dickebusch to their 'assaulting positions' at English Wood and Scottish Wood, waiting in two deep dug-outs. Ammunition was drawn and issued. At 03.10 on 7 June the battalion was awakened by a series of terrific mines exploding and at the same time an artillery barrage opening up. In the afternoon the battalion moved up in support and to relieve the 41st Division, who had earlier taken the German positions. The 8/Buffs endured a heavy artillery bombardment for the remainder of the day. Wilkinson's C-Coy went into the front line of the offensive on 9 June, alongside A-Coy, while B- and D-Coy stayed in support. During the relief of the Warwickshire Regiment on 10 June the German artillery caused many casualties to the battalion. The exhausted battalion rested and slept all day on 11 June. The following day, the officers of the battalion left early in the morning to reconnoitre the next sector they were being asked to attack. In the late afternoon of 13 June the battalion moved up to Battle Wood, near Hollebeke, taking over the line from the 3rd Battalion, Rifle Brigade. The following day at 19.30, the battalion attacked the opposing German position on a two-company front, with each company on a two-platoon front, under cover of a lifting barrage. Keeping close to the lifting barrage, the battalion managed to move far enough forward so that the German artillery response was falling behind them. Little resistance was met until the battalion reached the first objective, the 'Spoil Bank', where a great deal of hand-to-hand fighting occurred and a German machine gun in a concrete emplacement was rushed and captured. By this time, C-Coy, having been subjected to enfilade artillery fire, had lost all its officers apart from the wounded Second Lieutenant Frank Wilkinson, who with the remainder of his company managed to continue forward and take their objective of the tram line. Sergeant Shute of C-Coy then took his platoon and cleared a system of dug-outs just ahead of the tram line. After consolidating their positions, at midnight Wilkinson withdrew to have his wounds dressed, leaving Sergeant Pells in sole charge of C-Coy. The following morning, all the companies were well dug in and camouflaged from the aerial reconnaissance of the Germans. The battalion was relieved that night by the 2nd Battalion the Leinster Regiment.

Wilkinson had received a bullet wound in his left thigh. Luckily the bullet did not damage any bone, but it did pass through his leg causing entrance and exit wounds. It was for his actions near Battle Wood on 14 June 1917 that Wilkinson won the Military Cross, for 'Conspicuous gallantry and devotion to duty. Although wounded early in the attack, he took charge of his company, and organized and led a raid against an enemy strong point, showing great dash and determination.' On 21 June 1917 he returned to the UK, sailing via Calais and Dover aboard the SS *Princess Elizabeth*, for further treatment and to convalesce. He was initially sent to Yorkhill Hospital, Glasgow, for treatment and was told he would require two months before being fit enough to be back at duty. Some time after, he returned to convalesce at home in Oxford.

When recovered from his leg wound, in October 1917, Wilkinson was sent out to Palestine and attached to the 10/Buffs (230 Brigade, 74th Division). He arrived in Palestine as the Third Battle of Gaza was being concluded, with the capture of the town of Beersheba and the position at Sheria finally being achieved. The British had been defeated at the first and second battles of Gaza, but finally the stalemate in Southern Palestine was broken and the British now had the Turkish army in retreat. Wilkinson had arrived just in time to take part in the advance and capture of Jerusalem and the resulting defence of the Holy City. Between 24 and 30 November the battalion advanced 55 miles on foot, and then proceeded to prepare roadways to allow transport support. On 8 December at 08.15 the attack on Jerusalem began. The city fell into British hands on 9 December during very wet weather, with 'casualties ... considerably light in view of the strength of individual positions taken'. Permission was granted on 21 December for forward parties to visit the historic sites of Jerusalem, and 'this privilege was greatly appreciated by all ranks'. Frank Wilkinson spent Christmas Day in bivouacs on the outskirts of Jerusalem in torrential rain. The day after Boxing Day, the brigade began to advance again and on 29 December Ramallah was taken without serious opposition. Frank Wilkinson spent the first two days of the New Year in the army hospital, but no record of his ailment was given. At the start of the following month, on 5 February, Wilkinson was gazetted Lieutenant. From 8 to 12 March the battalion cleared areas around Yebrud (Yabrud), in the face of heavy opposition, during the seizure of the Tell 'Asur area. The 74th Division was relieved and withdrew from the front line on 7 April, concentrating at Lydda (Lod). By 14 April they had journeyed 250 miles back to Qantara (Al Qantarah El Sharqiyya), Egypt, by train. Two weeks later, on 28 April they covered another 150 miles by train to Alexandria. The following day, Wilkinson and the rest of the 10/Buffs sailed from Alexandria on board SS *Malwa*, eventually disembarking at Marseilles, France on 7 May 1918.

Since late March the German Army had made great gains with its massive Spring offensive on the Western Front. Although the advance had not ultimately achieved its objective of getting behind the British line and taking the channel ports, it had taken more ground than all the advances of the previous years of the war combined and left the Allied army in desperate need of reinforcement and reorganization. The 74th Division had been withdrawn from Palestine to be part of the transformation of the ruined Fifth Army into the new Fourth Army. The 10/Buffs entrained at Marseilles on 9 May and journeyed almost 600 miles north in two days to Noyelles-sur-Mer, then marched on to billet at Forest-l'Abbaye. Here they stayed until 22 May, when they began to advance east, moving 30 miles to Buneville; then on 25 May they marched a further 9 miles to billets at Izel-lès-Hameau. During this time the battalion underwent intense training with Lewis guns, sniper scouting, signalling and bayonet fighting. The battalion moved by rail and road 25 miles north to Enquin-les-Mines on 25 June. They then relocated further north and into divisional reserve (Ham-en-Artois) on 10 July; the following day, they went into brigade reserve at La Pierrière. Here they formed working parties carrying out fatigue work at the front. They were relieved on 23 July and again went into divisional reserve a short distance away at La Miquellerie. After further training and preparation, the battalion went into the front line near Saint-Floris on 4 August. The following day, the British line to the right of the 10/Buffs began to push forward, and on 6 August the 10/Buffs attempted to keep in line with this advance despite initially encountering considerable opposition. By 8 August the battalion reached the west bank of the Lys Canal, but could not cross because the bridges had been blown up. By the following day, however, the Royal Engineers had constructed three bridges so that the advance could continue. By 11/12 August the line had pushed forward approximately 2,000 yards, but a German counter-attack forced the battalion to withdraw to their previous line at the Lys. The battalion was relieved and went into support on 14 August until 24 August, when they went into divisional reserve at La Pierrière, where they refitted before their march to Lillers on 28 August. Here they entrained south for the battlefields of the Somme. The 50-mile train journey delivered them to Heilly, south-west of Albert, from where they proceeded east 15 miles to Maurepas and took over at the front line on the last day of August. Heavily shelled all day on 2 September with high explosive and gas shells, three days later the battalion attacked and captured Midinette trench, then continued their advance, but had to withdraw to their originally won positions due to heavy machine gun fire. The following day, the battalion managed to push forward and take their objective points. They held this line under considerable artillery fire and sniping for six days until relieved by the 24/WR on 14 September. After a day refitting they took over at a front line section 3 miles north-west of Bellicourt on 16 September. On 18 September, covered by a creeping barrage, they advanced at 08.30, taking new objective lines. In the evening they had to withdraw because of their own artillery dropping on their new positions. At 05.40 on 21 September they advanced again behind a creeping barrage, till the enemy wire was reached. The battalion managed to penetrate beyond the first belt of wire but 'tremendous' machine gun fire from the strongly fortified machine gun post at Guillemont Farm was met when they were tackling the second belt. The 10/Buffs' advance was halted in the open of no-man's land. The battalion began to withdraw, but Wilkinson had been shot in the ankle and lay exposed. Unable to find cover he was shot again, this time in his abdomen. Although stretcher bearers tended him soon after he was shot they were unable to remove him from the exposed position. Wilkinson lay in the open all day, and then as dark approached he was shot a third time, tragically this time in the head. After dark his runner, searching for the wounded, found Wilkinson still alive. He attempted to carry him back, but had to go for help. When he returned, Wilkinson could not be found. During the early morning, any surviving men from the front companies returned to the safety of the British trenches, but Wilkinson was not amongst them. He had been taken captive by the Germans during the night.

Wilkinson's family was informed by telegram that he had been wounded and was a prisoner in the hands of the Germans. His father wrote to the War Office in November and requested that his possessions be released by the shipping agency company and sent home.

No more news was forthcoming until during the final advance of the war he was found in a piteous condition, abandoned in a shed, badly wounded in the head, untended and half starved. Repatriated on Armistice Day, 11 November 1918, Wilkinson had been in German hands for seven weeks. He was immediately taken to the 3rd Casualty Clearing Station, then after five days was passed on to the 2nd British Red Cross Hospital, Rouen. After two weeks he was transferred by the 3rd Ambulance Train, sailing aboard SS *St Patrick*, to England on 2 December. The following day, he arrived at the Prince of Wales' Hospital for Officers at Tottenham in London.

The gunshot wound to his head had produced bone fractures that were depressed and had resulted in facial paralysis. Although the paralysis passed after two months, his experiences, wounds and neglect had not only left him with physical and physiological scars but also with nocturnal bladder and bowel incontinence, mental lethargy and slow speech. The severe pressure sores, due to his neglect during his captivity, remained a problem for a long time, and metallic debris in his chest was evident on X-ray.

On 4 January 1919 he underwent an operation to produce a trephine opening at the site of his head wound (right frontal). Several bone pieces were removed from his brain tissue and the large cerebral 'abscess' underneath was opened, evacuated and drained. The skin flap was then replaced. In July he was operated on again, the wound was reopened and drained. Eleven months later, on 30 November 1919, he underwent an operation at the Empire Hospital[4] to close the trephine opening in his skull. For this a bone graft was taken from Wilkinson's shin. The result was seemingly completely satisfactory, with no gross neurological defect as a result of the operation and an improvement of his previously 'abnormal' psychological condition.

After the war, during his convalescence, Wilkinson was required to write a statement regarding the circumstances of his capture. All POWs were investigated after repatriation, to record the circumstances of capture and to potentially attach blame for the capture. On 31 July 1919 Wilkinson wrote:

> I was O.C [Officer Commanding] 'D' Coy on Sept 21st 1918 under the following circumstances. We were attacking Guillemont Farm and went over about 3 a.m. About ½ an hour after zero I was hit in the ankle, and almost immediately hit again in the right side. I was attended by S.B's [stretcher bearers] and remained lying in the open for the remainder of the day. Before dark I was again severely wounded in the head, right frontal region. After dark I was found by my runner, who tried to assist myself and my batman, also wounded, back to our lines, as we had failed to gain our objective earlier in the day. He however was unable to get us in, and I sent him to the nearest

Coy Headquarters to get assistance. After he had gone I fell into the hands of the Germans, but of this I have no definite recollection.

In August 1919 the War Office sent Wilkinson a letter declaring that the Army Council considered he was not to blame for his capture.

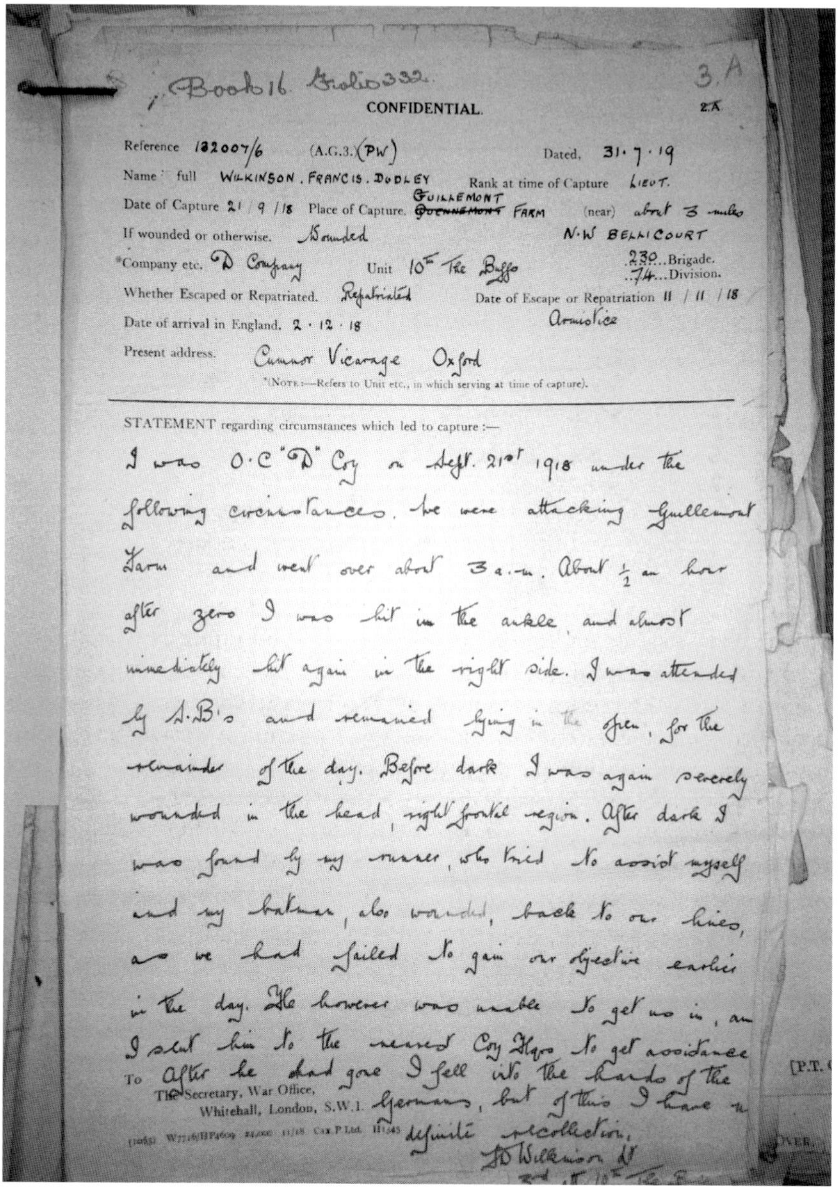
Book 16 Folio 332. 3.A

CONFIDENTIAL. 2.A

Reference 132007/6 (A.G.3.)(PW) Dated, 31·7·19

Name: full WILKINSON . FRANCIS . DUDLEY Rank at time of Capture LIEUT.

Date of Capture 21 / 9 / 18 Place of Capture. ~~QUENNEMONT~~ GUILLEMONT FARM (near) about 3 miles N·W BELLICOURT

If wounded or otherwise. Wounded

*Company etc. D Company Unit 10th The Buffs 230 Brigade. 74 Division.

Whether Escaped or Repatriated. Repatriated Date of Escape or Repatriation 11 / 11 / 18 Armistice

Date of arrival in England. 2 · 12 · 18

Present address. Cumnor Vicarage Oxford

*(NOTE:—Refers to Unit etc., in which serving at time of capture).

STATEMENT regarding circumstances which led to capture:—

I was O.C "D" Coy on Sept. 21st 1918 under the following circumstances. We were attacking Guillemont Farm and went over about 3 a.m. About ½ an hour after zero I was hit in the ankle, and almost immediately hit again in the right side. I was attended by S.B's and remained lying in the open, for the remainder of the day. Before dark I was again severely wounded in the head, right frontal region. After dark I was found by my runner, who tried to assist myself and my batman, also wounded, back to our lines, as we had failed to gain our objective earlier in the day. He however was unable to get us in, and I sent him to the nearest Coy Hqrs to get assistance. After he had gone I fell into the hands of the Germans, but of this I have no definite recollection.

F D Wilkinson Lt

To The Secretary, War Office, Whitehall, London, S.W.1.

Wilkinson's statement detailing his capture.

By 24 February 1920 his head wound had 'soundly healed', but he was still complaining of headaches and not being able to concentrate for any length of time. His memory was poor, he was easily fatigued and he was still suffering from 'foot drop' with the left foot. The large wound to the right side and rear of his abdomen wall was well healed, but along with significant muscle loss and loss of sensation, he also complained of pain from inside.

Wilkinson was gazetted on to the retired list on 31 March 1920, due to ill health caused by wounds. Recovery had initially seemed hopeless, but due to wonderful groundbreaking surgery of the day, Wilkinson slowly picked up his strength. When he was allowed out of hospital for a time, one of his first acts was to come to see his old school, still very weak and ill. After further periods in hospital and after further operations, he improved much more rapidly, and on his next visit to school was reported to be 'almost like his old self'.

In 1920 Wilkinson was given a grant of land in British East Africa, where some other officers were going to a 'Disabled Officers Colony' (BEADOC). He was passed fit by the doctors, and bade his family a cheery farewell as he set off to start a new life. On the way out, when the ship stopped at Port Sudan, he went ashore and suffered heat stroke. This was reported to have affected the old head wound and he died three days later on 19 April, aged 26. He was buried at sea the following day.

'To have suffered what he suffered for nearly two years and then to have died when on the road to health and a new life is a tragedy greater than tears' reported *The Lily*. Colonel Ponsonby, under whom he served in Palestine, wrote to his father:

> I remember so well his arrival in Palestine ... Different to many newly-joined officers, he fitted in with our complex plan at once. His modesty and silence pleased his officers, and his thoroughness and thoughtfulness for their comfort endeared him to the men, but it is not for me to tell you what an example his army life set to all of us of courage and thoughtfulness for others. I need only say that when we of the Battalion meet in the future we shall always speak tenderly and with happy memory of 'Wilkie'. I know that I am voicing the thoughts of all the Battalion when I send you their sympathy on the loss '*tam cari capitis*'.

1. Wilkinson versus Maltby battles continue to this day, as two of the six MCS houses are named after them.
2. No. 4 Officer Training Corps was based in central Oxford at 9 Alfred Street.
3. In August 1916 Arthur Foster was commissioned as a Second Lieutenant in the 3rd (Reserve) Battalion KOYLI (for the rest of Foster's story, see his biographical section in this chapter); Horace Amon was commissioned as a Second Lieutenant in the Royal Sussex Regiment (for more on Amon see biographical section on Foster).
4. Empire Hospital for Officers (For Injuries to the Nervous System), Vincent Square, Westminster, SW1.

William Humphrey WILLIAMS

18 June 1891 – 3 May 1918

Rank and regiment: Captain, 1/6th Battalion, Lancashire Fusiliers, attached 125th Machine Gun Corps; Captain and Flight Commander, 142 Squadron, Royal Air Force. **Medals awarded:** Victory, British War, 1914–1915 Star. **Theatre of War:** Gallipoli, Egypt and Palestine. **Memorial:** Ramleh War Cemetery, Israel.

William Humphrey Williams was born in Wales, the eldest son of John Williams and Sarah Ann Williams (*née* Griffith). His father was an organist and music teacher. He had three younger sisters: Kathleen Roberta (b. 1893), Millicent Margaret E. (b. 1897) and Eva Julian (b. 1899). He also had one younger brother, John Arthur Julian (b. 1902). His younger brother also attended MCS and was at school when news of Williams' death reached him on 10 May 1918.

Life at Magdalen College School (1902 – 1908) and beyond

William Williams joined MCS as a Chorister in 1902 and remained at the school as a boarder for several years after his voice broke. He finally left in 1908 at the age of 17, after taking the Oxford and Cambridge Junior Certificate Examination. He initially went to work in the slate quarry business, but then joined Turner Brothers Asbestos Company in Rochdale.

Williams' War

William Williams joined the army at the outbreak of war when he obtained a temporary commission as a Second Lieutenant on 1 September 1914; and three months later gained promotion to temporary Lieutenant with the 1/6th Battalion, Lancashire Fusiliers (a Territorial Force). After his initial training he joined his battalion as part of the 125 Brigade, 42nd Division on the Gallipoli peninsula on 22 July 1915.

At the beginning of August 1915 Williams and his battalion were in the firing line between the north-west corner of Krithia Vineyard and a small *nullah*, where they took part in the battle of Krithia Vineyard between 6 and 13 August 1915. This was essentially a diversionary attack on the Turkish lines to pin down Turkish reinforcements, while the IX Corps made new landings 20 miles north at Suvla Bay. The August attacks by the British and ANZAC forces in the north and the south both failed, and the British attack against Scimitar Hill on 21 August signified the last major British offensive of the Gallipoli campaign. On 24 August the 1/6 LF went into reserve.

By the beginning of September the battalion was back holding the firing line, this time between the sea and the east end of Fusiliers Bluff. The battalion were relieved by the 10th Battalion, Manchester Regiment on 18 September and moved to bivouacs on Gully Beach. Six days later, they were back in the line where they remained until the end of the month. October followed the same pattern of rotation for the battalion, in and out of the lines.

In October 1915 Williams applied and was recommended, by the Lieutenant Colonel commanding the Regiment, for a permanent commission in the regular army, desiring to join the Royal Field Artillery. He was described by his Commanding Officer as 'a capable and energetic officer who has shown much keenness in performance of his duties'; and after seeing Williams ride he was of the opinion that 'he has sufficient confidence and the necessary qualification to make an efficient horseman after due instruction'. However, due to there being no vacancies with the RFA he could not be considered for appointment and Williams remained with 1/6 Lancashire Fusiliers.

The battalion was split into three on 2 November, with seventy-five men being sent to Mudros and the remaining two thirds staying at Gully Beach or on Geoghegans Bluff, a wide, flattish area just above Gully Ravine. An attack on these trenches by the Turks on 22 November was successfully rebuffed. The battalion then moved to the Eski-Hissarlik line trenches four days later. Probably due to illness, Williams was 'taken off the strength of officers' on 12 December, but was fit enough to rejoin his battalion the following day.

Orders were received by the battalion on 19 December 1915 to attack the Turkish lines, as part of the diversionary tactics to allow the start of the secret evacuation of the entire Allied Force from the peninsula. The Turks responded to the attack by counter-attacking, but were repelled. On 24 December the battalion received orders to go into reserve at Gully Ravine, and on Christmas Day 1915 found themselves enjoying the luxury of being in dug-outs with corrugated iron roofs. Two days later, on 27 December, the battalion embarked on the SS *Ermine*, leaving Gallipoli behind, and sailed for Mudros, a port on the small Mediterranean Island of Lemnos. It is known that Williams suffered a 'poisoned arm' during his time on Gallipoli and was incapacitated for some time. The battalion war diary does not record when Williams left to convalesce, but it does record that he rejoined the battalion on 1 January 1916 in Mudros, where the battalion underwent training. Williams was the only original officer of his company to survive the campaign. By 8 January the entire Allied force had been evacuated from under the noses of the Turks, without a single loss of life during the operation – a small victory considering more than half of the 480,000 men who had gone ashore had become casualties during the eight-month campaign.

Less than two weeks later, on 12 January 1916, the battalion embarked for Alexandria in calm weather, setting sail at 03.00. The men were accommodated well on board but were tightly packed for the four days it took to reach their destination. From Alexandria the battalion moved by train to Cairo, arriving at their camp on 17 January. The battalion moved by train on 24 January to Tel-El-Kabir, which at that time was a training camp for the Australian Imperial Force. Five days later, the battalion entrained to Shallufa, one of the bases responsible for defence of the Suez Canal.

On 14 March 1916 Second Lieutenant Williams, plus one other officer and thirty-five other ranks of the 1/6 LF, were attached to the newly formed 125th Machine Gun Company. Williams held the rank of temporary Captain for a brief period at the end of August before being gazetted to the rank of Lieutenant on 7 September. In October he returned to England for five weeks, having been given an attachment to the Royal Flying Corps. It is likely that during this visit to England he became engaged to Edith Ormerod (of Fern Bank, Castleton, Lancashire; originally from Christchurch, New Zealand). After gaining his 'wings' as a pilot, he was appointed Flying Officer and made Captain on 5 February 1917, becoming a pilot instructor at Aboukir (Abu Qir) in Egypt. Less than five months later, on 24 June 1917, he was promoted to Flight Commander.

At Ismailia, Egypt, on 2 February 1918, 142 Squadron RFC was formed as an army co-operation squadron. Shortly afterwards, in the Spring of 1918, it moved to Ramleh in Palestine, where Captain Williams joined the squadron and immediately took an active part in operations. The Royal Air Force was officially formed on 1 April 1918 and Williams' squadron became 142 Squadron RAF. From this date onwards, flight records exist for 142 Squadron.

Williams' flight records for April and May 1918 are reproduced below:

Date (1918)	**Machine**	**Flight duration (mins)**	**Flight purpose**	**notes**
April				
4	Martinsyde (A3955)	55	Test	
5	"	160	Bombing	
6	BE12a (A6323)	5	Test	
7	"	15	test	
8	"	15	test	
11	Martinsyde (A3955)	15	test	
12	Martinsyde (A3945)	25	transferring plane from No. 1 Sq. AFC	
13	"	35	practice bomb drop	
"	"	25	"	
"	"	10	"	
14	RE8 (B6601)	20	test	Obs. Captain Bunton
16	"	25	practice formation flying	"
18	Martinsyde (A3998)	20	test	
19	Martinsyde (A3955)	25	test	
"	Martinsyde (A3845)	20	test	
23	RE8 (B6601)	20	test	Obs. Capt. Bunton
24	"	25	Ramleh to Mydel	Obs. Lt. Mills
"	"	20	Mydelto Ramleh	Obs. Rauosell
25	BE12a (A6323)	40	test	
26	"	10	flight to Junction Station	
28	"	40	test	
May				
1	"	130	bombing	
3	Martinsyde (A3945)	115	bombing	Accidentally killed

During the whole of the April the squadron did not lose a single flyer, so Williams' death during a bombing raid on Turkish lines on 3 May 1918, aged 26, was the first loss for this new RAF squadron. The flight log records 'Accidentally killed', although *The Lily* magazine for the school interpreted the news it received to be that Williams 'was shot down over Turkish lines and for some time it was hoped that he had reached ground safely and taken prisoner'. Six days after his death, his engagement of marriage to Edith Ormerod was announced in *Flight* magazine.

Leslie Farquhar YEO

13 Dec 1892 – 10 March 1915

Rank and regiment: Lieutenant, 2nd Battalion, South Staffordshire Regiment. **Medals awarded:** Victory, British War, 1914 Star. **Theatre of War:** Western Front. **Memorial:** Béthune Town Cemetery, France.

Leslie Farquhar Yeo was born at Hampstead on 13 December 1892, the youngest son of Thomas Webber Yeo (b. 1838) and Helen Margaret Yeo (*née* Farquhar, b. 1861 in Calcutta, India). His father was a solicitor and was already in his fifties when Leslie was born. Leslie had two older brothers, Thomas Farquhar (b. 1881) and Robert Arthur (b. 1883); and three older sisters, Helen Mary (b. 1880), Gladys (b. 1884) and Ivy Margaret (b. 1885). Sadly, his father died in 1905. His mother remarried, in 1909, George Pearson.

Although the family lived in Hampstead, London, for most of Leslie's life, at the time he went up to Cambridge in 1911 his residence is recorded as Dalau, Llanbadarn Fawr, Aberystwyth.

Life at Magdalen College School (1910–1911) and beyond

Leslie Yeo joined MCS as a boarder at a mature age of 17 in the Easter of 1910. He therefore only attended the School for the one year before reaching University age and leaving, in March 1911, to progress to Trinity College, Cambridge. Despite his age he appears to have joined a younger form (Form IV), and competed in the Junior section of the gymnastics competition. It is uncertain why he joined this Form, as other boys of the same age joining at the same time went into the Form higher, as did one boy who was a year younger. Soon after joining he won the repetition and recitation competition for Form IV. The following academic year, in October 1910, having progressed up to Form V, Yeo was the 'Mover' at the Debating Society and proposed the motion that 'The policy of the present Government as regards the Navy places the country in imminent danger of invasion'. The 'Opposer' was Andrew H. Herbertson (who was killed in action in May 1917). The motion was lost by twelve votes to nine. The Secretary and Gentleman Usher at the time was Frank Wilkinson, with Dennis Webb on the Committee. Charles Brownrigg, as ever, was the President.

Yeo played in goal for the school football teams, appearing in the same team as Wilkinson and Jessel that beat the Master's XI 2–1, and playing for the 2nd XI, captained by Dennis Webb, that beat All Saints' School 2–0 in the Michaelmas

Term of 1910. He also rowed at no. 3 for the Form V 3rd IV boat in the Form rowing races in the Hilary Term of 1911.

Upon leaving MCS he was admitted as a pensioner (a normal undergraduate) at Trinity College, Cambridge on 25 June 1911. His tutor was William Cecil Dampier Whetham, a Lecturer in Natural Sciences. Yeo passed Special Examinations in Law, Parts I and II (1912 and 1913), and in Military Subjects, Parts I and II (1913 and 1914), obtaining a second class pass in all except the last, in which he obtained a first. He was awarded his BA in 1914.

Yeo's War

Leslie Yeo immediately signed up for the army when the declaration of war with Germany was announced. He was commissioned as a full Lieutenant, and a letter dated 6 August 1914 instructed him to join his battalion, the 2nd Battalion, South Staffordshire Regiment, which had been mobilized on 4 August, as soon as possible. The battalion set sail from Southampton on 12 August aboard the SS *Irrawaddy*, disembarking at Le Havre the following day. On 15 August the 2/S.Staffs (now part of the 6 Brigade, 2nd Division) travelled 190 miles east by train to Wassingy, then marched 5 miles south to a place called Iron, arriving the following morning. Here they billeted for five days then marched 12 miles north to the town of Landrecies, stopped the night, then marched a further 13 miles to Hargnies. At 02.30 on 23 August the battalion marched 13 miles to Givry, then on towards Mons. After marching a further 2 miles they reached the village of Harmingies where at 11.00 they came under enemy fire for the first time. Moderate firing continued in the afternoon, then in the evening an artillery battle commenced and the battalion organized to defend the village. On the morning of 24 August, the 2/S.Staffs were ordered to retire south and cover the retreat of the brigade. Upon reaching Bavay, a distance of 14 miles, the troops dug all through the night to form a line of resistance. The following day, the Germans had advanced to the British defensive line but were held off while the remainder of the brigade had retreated. The 2/S.Staffs received no casualties on this day and in the afternoon they then retired themselves 14 miles to the village of Maroilles. There was no rest, however, as the Germans had immediately followed the retreat, and by 20.00 were outside the village. The British stood to arms throughout the night, but no attack came. At 05.30 the 2/S.Staffs quietly slipped away from the village and, predictably, marched another 'regulation' 14 miles to Venerolles. The retreat continued, covering and guarding in turn bridges and roads, and passing through Mont Doriginy, Aminigy and Ambleny. They billeted where possible, fighting exhaustion and the high temperatures of the hot August 1914 weather. Although they were supposedly only part of the General Reserve at this time, they were in the thick of the action, and on 1 September the Germans engaged the battalion once again with heavy artillery fire. The battalion continued retreating, via Thury-en-Valois, Trilbardou, Voisins (Quincy-Voisins), across the River Marne and eventually reached just south of Saint-Siméon. Bivouacking at Chaumes on 5 September, the brigade had reached the furthest

Leslie Yeo.

westerly point of the retirement from Belgium. After retreating over 130 miles (as the crow flies), and with the German supply lines now overstretched, on 6 September the British finally saw the opportunity to go on the offensive. It is noted by the Adjutant in the 2/S.Staffs war diary that 'between 21 August and 5 September inclusive, the 6 Brigade marched a distance of 236 miles in 16 days, with only one day's halt during this period. The average number of miles marched per day was 15.7.'

The 2/S.Staffs began advancing north again on 7 September; two days later the weather began to cool and the fitness of the 2/S.Staffs troops was reported as very good. On 10 September, after advancing 25 miles, the brigade surprised a German column south of Hautevesnes and after a two-and-a-half-hour fight the German unit surrendered and 430 German prisoners were taken. The race north continued, with the brigade encountering very strong German positions at Moussy and at Soupir on 14 September. The companies of the 2/S.Staffs were shuttled between these two places and rotated between the front line, support and reserve. Finally, on 15 September, the French relieved the British lines. The battalion marched to Fismes and entrained for an unknown destination. They passed through Amien, Boulogne and Calais and after thirty-six hours arrived at Strazelle at midnight on 17 October. They immediately marched 4 miles to billets at Hazebrouck (16 miles south-west of Ypres). The brigade was needed in the Pas-de-Calais region to help stop the Germans swinging north-west, outflanking the Allies and taking the Channel ports in the 'race to the sea'. Advancing west, on 20 October the 2/S.Staffs billeted in Ypres, then on 23 October they went to the assistance of the Queen's Regiment to regain advanced trenches at Pilkem (near Langemark), losing forty 'other ranks' in the process (part of the Battle of Langemark, 21 to 24 October). Advancing to the Becelaere–Moorsleede road on 27 October, the battalion occupied trenches in this area for the next two and a half weeks, withstanding heavy shelling and infantry attacks (part of the Battle of Gheluvelt, 29 to 31 October). During this time the Germans sapped to within 100 yards (even within 25 yards at points) of the British trenches producing much close-quarter fighting. The British fought desperately to hold on in the face of a German Fourth Army onslaught, knowing that a breakthrough to Ypres and beyond would spell disaster. Against the odds and in worsening weather they stopped a breakthrough and the town of Ypres remained in Allied hands. On 15 November the 139th French Regiment reinforcements finally relieved the 2/S.Staffs of their task and over the next three days they made their way back to Ypres and then marched 15 miles west into the relative safety of Caëstre. Here they received a much needed month in reserve and at rest in billets before returning to front line duty, even enjoying a brigade visit from the king on 3 December. The First Battle of Ypres effectively ended on 22 October, due to mutual exhaustion of the two armies.

On 22 December the battalion drove 20 miles south in motor buses of the London General Omnibus Company to Béthune, then marched the remaining 3 miles to take over trenches at Beuvry. Here they stayed for the next week and spent Christmas Day 1914 in the front line, only having to put up with sniping but no shelling. They were relieved and went to billets on 27 December, but were back in front line trenches at Le Touret, which were in a very bad state, on 2 January. In places they were waist-deep in water. The battalion rotated in and out of the front line trenches of the Le Touret, Festubert and Rue du Bois area for the whole of January. During this time many men of the battalion went sick from cold, rheumatism and swollen feet. In February they found themselves relocated not far away from the trenches at Givenchy. The first two months of the year in these trench systems was relatively quiet, but a policy of aggressive pressure had been decided by the Allied Command. In support of this policy a daylight raid was carried out by two parties of twenty men of the 2/S.Staffs on 20 February, after a short artillery bombardment. The reason given was to see if the Germans were carrying out any mining operations. The German trenches were rushed and entered, no mines were found and two men of the battalion were killed and four wounded in the process. The next British action was to be much more significant. On 10 March at 07.30 a thirty-five-minute bombardment of 2 miles of German trenches, by 300 artillery pieces, started. This was the first use of the tactic that was to form the basis of all major British operations on the Western Front for the next two years. After the bombardment men exited the trenches relatively quickly by way of previously engineered traverses to advance upon the enemy first and second lines whilst their occupants were taking shelter. However, as soon as the men left the shelter of the parapet they were subjected to severe cross-fire from German machine guns. The initial thirty-five-minute bombardment had had limited effect on the German defensive systems. Although some men managed to

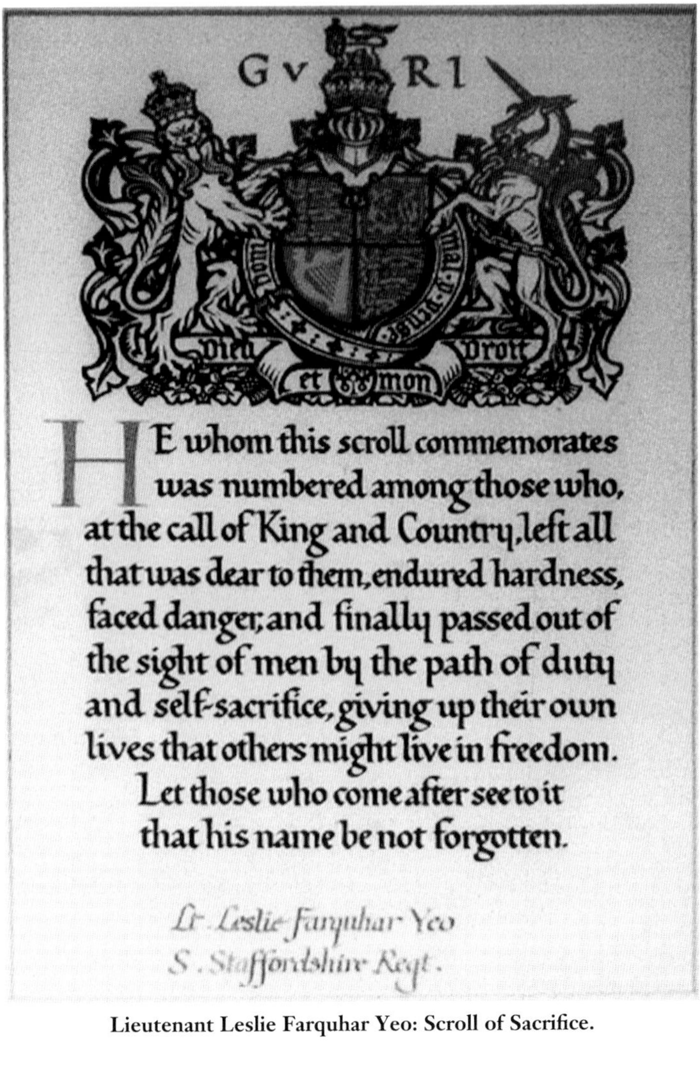
G V R I

Dieu et mon Droit

HE whom this scroll commemorates was numbered among those who, at the call of King and Country, left all that was dear to them, endured hardness, faced danger, and finally passed out of the sight of men by the path of duty and self-sacrifice, giving up their own lives that others might live in freedom.

Let those who come after see to it that his name be not forgotten.

Lt. Leslie Farquhar Yeo
S. Staffordshire Regt.

Lieutenant Leslie Farquhar Yeo: Scroll of Sacrifice.

survive the 80-yard distance and made it to the German trenches, no permanent lodgement could be achieved. Eventually the attack ceased. A new thirty-minute bombardment was commenced at 14.15 followed by a fresh assault, this time led by Yeo's C-Coy going over the top first in different locations to those initially used, aided by sand bag steps, as the German machine guns were now trained on the trench outlets used in the first assault. But still the leading sections, including C-Coy, advanced only to be mown down by machine gun fire soon after they had mounted the parapet. The British wire had not been cut in sufficient places to allow the sections of the advance to disperse sufficiently, and most of the German wire had not been affected at all by the preliminary bombardment. Communication trenches became blocked by sections rushing into them to find alternative exit routes, meaning supporting companies were no longer able to advance to their start points and support the lead sections. It was decided not to press the assault further. The troops set about repairing the trenches and collecting the wounded and their belongings. In this action on the first day of the Battle of Neuve Chapelle, the 2/S.Staffs suffered the following casualties: five officers and fifty-seven other ranks killed or missing; two officers and seventy-four other ranks wounded.[1] Hit in the stomach by a piece of shrapnel during this second charge, Yeo was taken to No. 4 Field Ambulance, then on to the French Military Hospital in Béthune, where he died of his wounds later that day, aged 22. While being treated, Yeo sent an orderly to deliver his effects (a cigarette case with some photos in it, a pocket note book with 25 francs, some papers and a card from his mother) to his company commander, Captain H.S. Blockey. Both Blockey and his previous company commander, Captain R.W. Morgan, wrote letters to Yeo's mother expressing their deepest sorrow on the loss of her son. Having commanded C-Coy before it was assigned a Captain to take command, Yeo was described as a 'brave, popular and gallant officer' who had 'stuck through the campaign magnificently'.

1. The battle continued through 10, 11 and 12 March. The German front line trench was taken by the end of the first day, but the trench system survived, enabling them to create a new line. Fierce fighting continued, Neuve Chapelle village was in British hands but nearly 13,000 men were killed or wounded.

Victor Albert Villiers ZACHARIAS JESSEL

24 January 1896 – 6 April 1917

Rank and regiment: Private (2713), Inns of Court OTC; Lieutenant, 7th Battalion (att. 15th) Durham Light Infantry. **Medals awarded:** Victory, British War, 1914–1915 Star. **Theatre of War:** Western Front. **Memorial:** Arras Memorial, France

Born Victor Albert Villiers Zacharias at 26 Cornmarket Street, Oxford, Victor was the third son of Joel and Rachel (*née* Frankenstein) Zacharias. His two brothers were George Jessel (b. 1883) and Arthur Reginald Frankenstein (b. 1890).

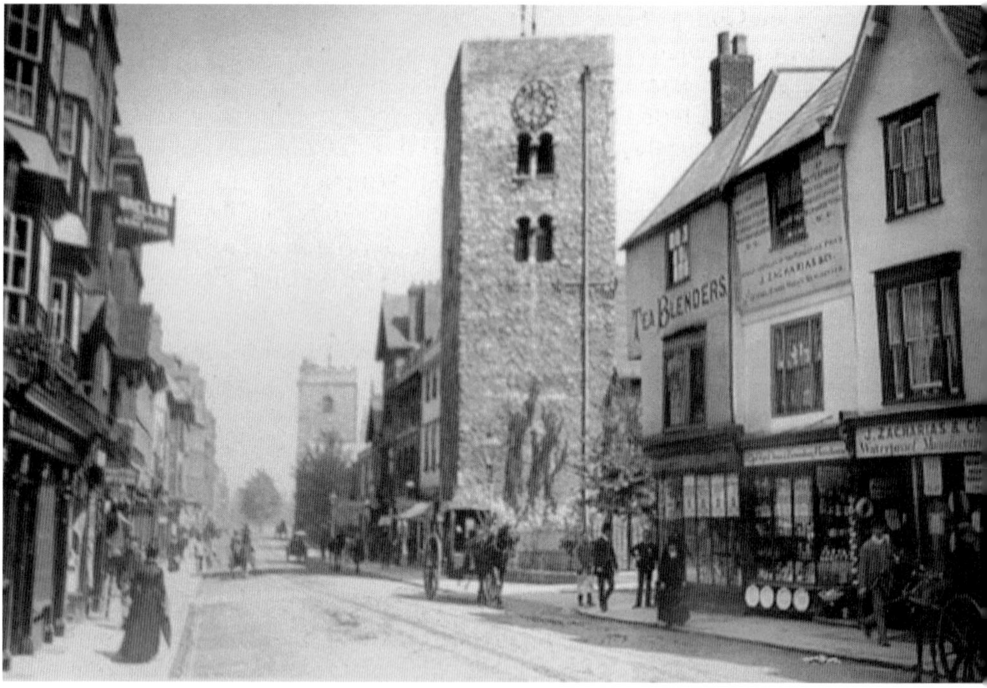

Cornmarket Street,Oxford, showing St Michael at the North Gate Church and the Zacharias & Co. shop on the right.

Joel was a waterproof manufacturer (Zacharias & Co.) in Oxford, with a shop and business at 26–27 Cornmarket Street, where currently Pret A Manger is based.

The family company grew in the 1880s out of an earlier china dealing concern but later specialized in waterproofed items, including chauffeurs' clothing, motorcycling suits, car, motorcycle and cart covers and the like. At the turn of the nineteenth century the company was meeting the growing need for protection from the weather for the new motoring public, in their wonderfully liberating but at that time very exposed and weather-susceptible contraptions. Zacharias became famous for their trench-style raincoats for both ladies and gentlemen, and their slogan 'Zacs for Macs' adorned the shop and Oxford buses for many years.[1] In 1902 the family changed their name by deed-poll to include Jessel in their surname – not an uncommon thing to do at the time because of the expression of anti-Semitism that an obviously Jewish name could then attract. Jessel's father died in August 1905, shortly before Victor started at MCS. Victor's youngest brother, Arthur, also attended MCS (1905–1907) before going up to Oxford. Arthur graduated with a degree in Civil Law and by 1911 was working as a solicitor's articled clerk in Oxford. His eldest brother, George, graduated from Oxford University in 1906 and became a doctor, qualifying from the London Hospital in 1909.

Life at Magdalen College School (1906–1914)

After briefly being educated at Oxford High School, Victor Jessel joined MCS as a day boy and School Exhibitioner in January 1906, joining his brother Arthur who had started at MCS the term before. In November 1908 Victor shared the Lower School History prize with Donovan Leicester and in 1909 he won the Form IV Classics prize. Ultimately, in 1912 he obtained exemption from Responsions.[2] Interestingly, in the December 1912 Debating Society meeting, Jessel seconded the Opposer to the motion, 'Military Conscription for Great Britain is desirable.' In Michaelmas 1913 he spoke against 'Home Rule for Ireland'. For two years, 1913 and 1914, he was the Vice-President of the Debating Society.

Jessel's all-round strength and maturity made him a well-respected member of the school and in Michaelmas term of 1913 he was made a Day Boy Prefect, at the same time that John Callender was made a House Prefect. Jessel kept in touch with the school after he left, subscribing to *The Lily* in 1915, 1916 and the year of his death, 1917. In 1915, the year after he left, it will interest all fans of Mr Darcy to know that he chose to donate a copy of Jane Austen's *Pride and Prejudice* to the School Library.

In the Athletics arena in 1908 he had started to show his prowess on the running track, coming second in the Junior half mile race on Sports Day. The following year, 1909, he won the same race (albeit in a slightly slower time of 2min 36.2secs). In 1910 he repeated his half mile win, taking the lead right from the start and winning by 70 yards in a time of 2 minutes 34.6 seconds. Middle distance events were ones in which he excelled, and in 1909 he won the 100 yard sprint in a time of 12 seconds. He repeated this win in the 100 yards in 1910, beating John Callender into second place, again with a time of 12 seconds. In 1910 he also won the High Jump event with a jump of 4 feet 4 inches.

In 1911 (6 May) a team, which included Jessel, was sent to compete in the Public School Athletics Sports Event held at London Athletics Club Stadium of Stamford Bridge.[3] In preparation for the events, Mr Brownrigg had obtained permission for the team to practise on the Iffley Road track (the four-man team also contained Frank Wilkinson). Clapperton achieved second place and a silver medal in the Long Jump, but the others underperformed. On the day, Mr Brownrigg journeyed with them and entertained them 'to lunch at his club'.

In 1912 the trio of Thomson, Clapperton and Jessel battled it out in the Senior 100 yard sprint and the Quarter Mile races on Sports Day, with Jessel narrowly missing out to his closest rivals in both events. In the 1913 Sports Day, despite Jessel competing in the 100 yards, Quarter Mile, High Jump and 150 yard handicap, another challenger, H. Amon, pipped Jessel to the coveted prize of the Ladies Plate (for best combined performances) by one point. As in previous years, the 1914 Sports Day events formed part of the Commemoration Day activities of the school. The events were actually split over two days, the Thursday and the Commemoration Day Saturday. It was Jessel's final Sports Day before leaving school and his last chance to win the Ladies Plate. He competed in and won the

8 OXFORD JOURNAL ILLUSTRATED, WEDNESDAY, JUNE 22, 1910.

MAGDALEN COLLEGE SCHOOL SPORTS.

A large number of people watched these sports, which were held under ideal conditions on the School ground on Saturday last. Our photographs show:—(1) Quarter W. B. Broadbent winning. (2) Junior High Jump, Jessel clearing 4ft. 4in. (3) 150 Yards (Seniors), Morton breaking the tape. (4) Senior Long Jump, Broadbent record with a magnificent jump of 21ft. 3in. (5) The Band Race, which caused much amusement, each man having to play his instrument whilst running. (6) Start of the Race. Note the positions of the competitors in this event.—(O.J.I. Photographs).

Victor A.V.Z. Jessel (top, centre) winning the High Jump event in 1910 on School Field.[4]

100 yard race in a time of exactly 11 seconds, beating amongst others Donovan Leicester and John Callender in the Final, despite a poor start. Jessel comfortably won the Quarter Mile race in a time of 58 seconds.

In the mile race Jessel led for two laps of the track, but the previous events had taken their toll and he dropped out during the third lap. Next came the Cricket Ball throwing event, where he came second with a throw of 75 yards. Then followed the 150 yard handicap sprint race; Jessel progressed through the heats but went out in the semi-final stages. The race was probably biased too much against the senior boy, with some boys starting 16 yards ahead of Jessel, who had to do the full 150 yards. Finally, the team race (4 × 400 yard relay) was won by a team made up of Searby *ma*, Beasley *mi*, Bell and Jessel, in a time of 50 seconds. There was a tie for the Ladies Plate, with Searby *ma* and Jessel both finishing on 12 points, but at last he had won the prize. The Trophy was presented by Lady Stainer[5] to the victors on the steps of the new Pavilion for the first time.[6]

Victor Jessel appears in the School Lawn Tennis Club competition in 1910, going out in the second round. In 1911 he partnered Dennis Webb in the doubles competition and came second at the end of the term.

Magdalen College School Sports Day, June 1914.
Left inset (2), Victor A.V.Z. Jessel winning the Quarter Mile race in 1914 on School Field.

Jessel first appears in the footballing records in Michaelmas 1908 at the age of 12, playing for the U15 side and the 2nd XI. By 1910 he was playing in the 1st XI. He continued to play 1st XI Football until he left school in December 1914. He was mostly in defence throughout his school days, usually at right back, *The Lily* write-ups tell us he was liable to be clumsy with his kicking. In 1913 he was made captain of the 1st XI side and his Football Character Report in *The Lily* reads: 'Is both fast and strong and has plenty of weight. Would have been more effective if he had decided on a definite place in the field and stuck to it. As full back works hard, but is apt to kick wildly.' Jessel received his full colours for Football as early as 1912, along with his athletics rival H. Amon. The teams that the school played against during this time were not only local teams but were schools such as Leighton Park (Reading) and even Clayesmore (Pangbourne). Distance appears not to have been a barrier to playing sport during Brownrigg's era.

The first entry in *The Lily* that records Victor Jessel playing cricket for a school team is in the summer of 1910 when he batted at no. 8 (15 not out) for the 2nd XI in their victory over Abingdon. In this game he helped J.V. Haseler to his bowling figures of 6–41 by also taking a catch. In the next game, versus All Saints' School, despite Haseler taking 2 wickets in the first over of the game, MCS lost when they were bowled out for 24 in reply to All Saints' 105. Once again Jessel helped Haseler take another 6 wickets (6–44) by taking a catch off his bowling. In Jessel's

The athletic sports in connection with Magdalen College School took place on Thursday and Saturday, and attracted a large number of parents and friends. There was an interesting programme, at the conclusion of which the prizes were presented by Lady Stainer. (1) Some of the competitors starting in the junior half-mile; (2) Jessel carries off the seniors' quarter-mile; (3) the old boys' race; (4) the seniors' 150 yards handicap, won by Searby; (5) finish of the junior 100 yards, won by Mason; (6) Mason wins the junior high jump at 4ft. 2½in.; (7)
makes his winning jump of 18ft. 3in.; (8) the sack race; (9) a good finish in the junior 300 yards, Kearton first.—(O.J.I. photos).

Magdalen College School Sports Day, School Field, June 1914.

next game, this time for the U15 side, Haseler once again took 6 wickets (6–41), but MCS lost again to Dragons CC. Jessel, promoted to bat no. 3, was out for a duck. He also bowled his only recorded over in this game (0–8). Interestingly, another Oxford shop owner's son, Edward Andrews, was also a member of these two 1910 MCS sides. The Cricket Prospect article written in March 1911, prior to the next season, states that Jessel would 'soon improve if he played with a straighter bat' – an adage still stated to modern-day MCS boys 100 years on. Quaintly, the article finished 'with a prayer that we may be spared of any more floods; for the "square" has every appearance of being in fine condition by next term.' The school still says the same prayer each year, but usually to no avail! During the 1911 season Jessel broke into the 1st XI side that was captained by Frank Wilkinson, playing in three of their games. He batted at no. 10 in each game and did not bowl, but at least he witnessed Wilkinson claiming the wicket of the Master, Mr Brownrigg, during the game against G.R. Wood Esq's XI. Jessel's Cricket Character write-up in *The Lily* that year was not entirely flattering: 'Has a remarkably ugly defence of his own and believes that to long leg is the only scoring stroke. As he has physique and a good reach [he] should cultivate the entirely opposite method.' It would take him until 1913 to make a double-figure score. By 1912 Jessel has adopted the role of wicket keeper and in one game against the Old Boys XI he finds himself competing against last year's school Captain, Frank Wilkinson. Jessel stood behind Wilkinson while he hit the ball very hard and did not give a chance, until he fell for 90. Jessel took one catch behind the stumps, but the Old Boys team scored a formidable 230 all out. In reply, helped by a last wicket stand of 50, the school managed a creditable 207 all out.

As the 1913 cricket season approached MCS feared it lacked depth in its bowling attack. Also, due to School Field having been under water at the start of the season, no early season practice was possible. *The Lily* does not report any wins during the entire season and Jessel is portrayed thus in *The Lily* of July 1913, Cricket Characters section: 'Has not made much advance as a bat and pays little attention to coaching. Could, with his long reach, make a useful bat but has no stroke between a wild hit and a very tame "stop" shot. Promises well as a wicket keep, but after sundry injuries lost his nerve.'After being hurt while keeping wicket in 1914 Jessel appears to have lost his nerve to keep, therefore swapped to fielding in the outfield and is reported taking some good catches. The season included a rare tied match, at home to Bloxham, but once again *The Lily* reports did not spare any blushes: 'Jessel would do better if he definitely made up his mind to stand firm and hit (he can hit the ball a shrewd blow) and not for three out of four balls to edge in front of his wicket and hang his bat motionless in the air ... [He] can hit hard, but generally gets out by excess caution.' Despite these shortcomings as a cricketer he received Half Colours for Cricket at the end of the 1914 season.

In 1911 and 1912 Jessel is reported as playing hockey for the school team. In 1912 he even gets on the score sheet in two of the games, despite being a defensive player. The hockey teams during these years featured Callender, Wilkinson, Andrews, Rev. Deuchar and Mr Brownrigg in their games. In the Hockey Highlights of *The Lily* of 1911 Jessel is recorded thus: 'Has played some good games at centre-half, and has pace and determination, but in a hard game may lose his head (or his temper) and hit wildly.' In his Valete of 1915 he is officially recorded as being a member of the 2nd XI 1911–1912 and the 1st XI 1913–1914, and being Captain of Hockey in 1914. The grounds utilized for the Hockey during these years included School Field, Lincoln College Ground and even the University Parks, but playing condition were often 'in a very bad condition, being little better than a morass'.

Jessel first appears in the Rowing reports for the House Fours in 1911, but as early as December 1912 it is reported in the Rowing Prospect that he is a 'rival' for Scattergood at the no. 2 position in the 1st IV boat. Indeed, in the following season of Hilary term 1913 Jessel rowed at no. 2 in the Worcester race. Traditionally the crew would travel and stay at the King's School the night before the race; however, because MCS was 'mumpy' they had to travel there and back in one day. The crew lunched in Worcester and changed in a barge close to the starting point. That day the River Severn was tremendously fast-flowing so the River Authorities shortened the course. Not having much time to practise, the crew did not get used to the stream. From the start they were behind and at best they came within ½ length of the Worcester boat, but eventually they lost by 5½ lengths in

No. 9,359 [New Series No. 229]. WEDNESDAY, FEBRUARY 18, 1914. ONE PENNY.

LAUNCH OF MAGDALEN SCHOOL NEW BOAT.

The launch and christening of Magdalen College School's new boat (the first for [illegible] years) took place in the school grounds on Monday. Before a gathering of the scholars, parents and old boys, the boat was christened by Mrs. Brownrigg, wife of the Headmaster, after which it was floated, and the crew went for a short row.—[illegible] photo.

The launch and christening of a new MCS boat in 1914.

OXFORD JOURNAL ILLUSTRATED, WEDNESDAY, FEBRUARY 18, 1914. 3

TRYING THE NEW MAGDALEN SCHOOL BOAT.

Some more photographs taken at the christening and launching. (1) The crew "in full swing" after the ceremony. (2) V. A. V. Jessel, captain of the crew.—(O.J.I. photos).

The crew 'in full swing' after the launch of the new MCS boat in 1914.
Right, V.A.V.Z. Jessel, Captain of Boats 1914, near the white bridges.

a time of 8 minutes 25 seconds. Jessel, aged 17 at the time, was 12st 3lb, the heaviest of the MCS crew and more than a stone heavier than any of the Worcester crew. His photos indicate that he is lean, so his stature was probably tall and athletic. No rowing report for 1914 is given in *The Lily*, but Jessel was the only non-leaver from the previous year, so would have been the senior rower of the IV and was made Captain of Boats for 1914.

Jessel was a 1st team player in all the major sports of the School at the time (Football, Hockey, Cricket), plus a 1st IV rower, competitive tennis player and supreme athlete in track and field, winning the Sports Day Ladies Plate. When he left MCS at Christmas in 1914, he was probably one of the finest all round sportsmen the school has produced.

During Jessel's final year at the school, in 1914, the launch and christening of a new MCS boat by Mrs Brownrigg made it to the front page of the local newspaper. The boat's first outing was watched by most of the school, and as Captain of Boats at the time, Jessel was photographed for posterity near to the symbolic white bridges.

V.A.V. Zacharias Jessel, Captain of Boats, 1914.

Jessel's War

After leaving MCS, Jessel (then 5ft 10½ins and weighing 172lbs) enlisted in the Army on 15 January 1915 in London, initially joining the Inns of Court Officers Training Corps. It is enlightening that he modified the oath on his attestation papers, from 'I swear by Almighty God that' to 'I do solemnly and sincerely

Victor Zacharias Jessel.

affirm that'. On 17 May 1915 he was discharged from the Inns of Court OTC at Berkhamsted to take up a commission of Second Lieutenant in the 7th Battalion, Durham Light Infantry. Recorded on his application papers for appointment to the commission it is C.E. Brownrigg, who confirms his good moral character and states that he has known Jessel for nine years. Two months later, on 10 July 1915, Jessel arrived in France and joined up with the rest of the 7/DLI (151 Brigade, 50th Division), who had been at the front since April. The 7/DLI were in the trenches from 10 to 15 July at Kemmel, where Jessel had a frightening introduction to life at the front; for on 14 July, after a heavy artillery bombardment the previous day, the Germans exploded a large mine only 100 feet to the left of the 7/DLI front line section. At the same time they opened rapid fire on the British trenches for ten minutes. The 7/DLI were relieved on 15 July, initially withdrawing to Locre then marching on further to billets at Pont de Nieppe. Two days later they marched to billets at Armentières, where they stayed in reserve until taking over in front line trenches in the area during a relatively quiet period from 24 July until 1 August. The battalion spent the next three and a half months in this area (Armentières and Houplines), during a relatively quiet period, rotating in and out of the front line trenches, spending approximately a week at a time in the trenches followed by roughly a week in reserve in nearby billets. While in the trenches the battalion was kept active, patrolling at night, gathering wire samples and information on the German defences and sniping continuously during the day. Intriguingly, on 13 September the Germans poured a liquid over their parapet which ignited the grass. The fire burned rapidly towards the British obstacles but before it reached them the wind direction veered south-west and the fire ceased to advance. When in reserve the battalion supplied working parties, which included officers, to reconstruct trench systems and improve drainage. Lieutenant General Sir Charles Ferguson,7th Baronet, in command of II Corps, visited the 7/DLI twice during this period, inspecting their trenches on 31 July and on 22 October; he was apparently 'pleased with everything'.

The battalion left the Houplines trenches on 13 November and marched 9 miles north 'in excellent style' to billets in Bailleul. On 22 November the battalion marched past General Sir Herbert C.O. Plumer, in command of the Second Army, as they took on the role of, and commenced their training as, the Pioneer Battalion for the 50th Division.[7]

In December the battalion continued to billet at Bailleul, carrying out route marches, practice attacks on dummy trenches and target practice on ranges. In mid-December they then moved 8 miles north-east to Dickebusch, from where they supplied working parties to the Ypres area, attached to and working on the trenches of 149, 150 and 151 Brigades. The work included revetting communication trenches and making special dug-outs for machine gunners. Time was spent working on the Sanctuary Wood trenches and also in starting a Repair Workshop in the front line at Canada Huts. Behind the front lines, they built a Grenade School, firing ranges for target practice and a cycle repair shop for the division's bicycles. During 22 January and 5, 14 February 1916 the battalion was heavily shelled, suffering five casualties on the later date. To lift the spirits of the men they were treated to the band playing a programme at the YMCA on 13 February, and Miss Lena Ashwell's Concert Party entertained the men at the same venue the following week.

On 25 February a German plane dropped two bombs on the battalion's Dickebusche Camp. This may have been the straw that broke the camel's back, for after seven months of active service and the relentless barrage of shells at the front, Jessel was finally disabled through shell shock on this day. Suffering from symptoms of neurasthesia and having had an epileptic fit, he was considered unfit for general service and sent away from the front line on 13 March, initially to Le Touquet, then, via Boulogne and Dover aboard the Hospital Ship *Cambria* on 15 March, back to England and to the 3rd London General Hospital, Wandsworth. In April he was moved on to his home town of Oxford to the 3rd Southern General Hospital (based at the Examination Schools), where he was still complaining of hearing shells. In May he was moved again to the 1st Northern General Hospital, Newcastle, where he was put on 'light duty', but reassessed and considered still unfit for general service. In July he was at the Brocton Camp on

Cannock Chase, where he was assessed as being fit and well, but still unfit for general service. Finally on 12 September 1916 at Blyth he was adjudged to have recovered from his shell shock and was passed fit for general service. One can only imagine the dread with which this news was received by Jessel, still not 21, but true to his duty he returned to the front.

Upon returning to front line duties in France Jessel was attached to 15/DLI (64th Bde., 21st Div.) in the Annequin area, close to Béthune. The November of his return saw the weather turn very cold in northern France, and the trenches were described by the Adjutant as 'bleak'. The 15/DLI rotated between the support line, the front line and the reserve. They returned to the front line on a cold and frosty 'but healthy' night of 16 November. The following night, a patrol resulted in the officer in charge of the party (Captain A. Sephton) being killed, shot through the head. Night time explorations into no-man's land were not for the faint hearted. During the same tour at the front, on the night of 19 November, Jessel led a small party into no-man's land to obtain identification of and information on the German troops opposing them; but although the party approached close to the German line and waited there, they had to return empty handed. Jessel went out again on the same night but was again unsuccessful. The routine of rotation in and out of the line continued, but even when in reserve regular duties of guarding, cleaning, drilling etc. were still carried out. 'Wacking out', the sharing and passing around of parcels and letters from home with friends, gave a welcome respite from duties. Back at the front line on the day of 28 November, Germans were seen opposite the DLI trenches. They shouted that they were Saxons and tried to enter into conversation, one of them calling out 'Somme No Bon!' They were fired upon and disappeared hurriedly.

At the start of December 1916 the battalion moved 3 miles west along the line to take up a section of the front line near Labourse. As the days crept closer to Christmas, shelling activity from both sides increased and it was suspected that the Germans were preparing for an assault, until on Christmas Eve there was a gas attack alert. The early hours of Christmas Day were marked by a heavy bombardment of the German lines and 20 miles south the British made a successful raid on the German front. Boxing Day saw no let up by the British, with the heavy shelling as the Germans were suspected of relieving their lines. On 27 December the Germans heavily shelled the Annequin area with gas shells. The wind was in the favour of the British and the attack was ineffective, with the British having to keep on guard in case of a change in the wind direction.

The battalion spent the period from 28 December 1916 to 28 January 1917 at Nœux-les-Mines in rest, playing sports matches and tournaments, with the scores of the inter-company and inter-battalion football matches recorded in the war diary in as much detail as the military manoeuvres. The rest period was punctuated with German shelling, including gas shells and low flying aircraft dropping bombs, as well as a heavy fall of snow and officers' tactical exercises. On 28 January the battalion left their rest camp and journeyed 30 miles north to snow-covered Wormout, where 'the people speak much Flemish'. The battalion billeted at Wormout until 11 February, then entrained from Esquelbecq and detrained 30 miles south at Fouquereuil near Béthune. A short route march saw them arrive at billets in Annezin. The next day they were inspected by the Commander-in-Chief as they route marched 5 miles to Sailly Labourse, an area the DLI had previously occupied in December. Their new front line sector was the 'Village Line' in the Cambrin Sector. The trenches were in a very bad condition owing to severe frosts being followed by thaws. These conditions resulted in much traffic 'on top' and, as a result, many casualties were suffered from sniper fire. The 15/DLI spent six days in these appalling conditions, from 19 to 25 February. When eventually they were relieved, the two companies that were relieved at night left over 'the top' to accelerate proceeding. The month of March was spent rotating around these trenches and in reserve and support in billets at Béthune. The first day of April, the battalion took up a position at a railway cutting, guarding a section of an outpost line. Over the few next days a severe snowstorm produced a strangely picturesque scene and all was quiet at the front where the 15/DLI relieved the Lincolnshire Regiment in their line of outposts. The changed scenery required the DLI to re-establish the location of the enemy positions. On Good Friday 1917, Victor Jessel, aged 21, leading the patrol to observe and acquire information about the German front line, was killed (one man with him was wounded) while in no-man's land. Jessel was the youngest Lieutenant in the battalion. He was the first Oxford Jew to die in the Great War. A month later, on 9 May 1917, Jessel's cousin Harry Mitchell Davidson (OBLI), the son of Victor's paternal Aunt Rosa, became the second Oxford Jew to be killed in the First World War. Jessel's body was never recovered. His name adorns the Arras Memorial wall, and an inscription in memory of Victor is seen on his parents' grave at Wolvercote Cemetery, Oxford.

In his will, Victor left his personal estate for the benefit of his mother, but upon her death it was to be divided amongst three hospitals (Chelsea Royal and Manchester and London Jewish Hospitals). He was certainly a charitable and socially responsible character. Victor's brother Arthur was wounded and invalided in 1916 but survived the war. Sadly, Arthur's wife, Barbara L. Jessel (*née* Murray, married 1915, St George Church, Hanover Square, London) died in 1919, and he himself died in 1922, aged only 29.

1. Old advertisement pages for Zacharias & Co., Waterproofers, from this era are reproduced in the book *Oxford Shops and Shopping, A Pictorial Survey from Victorian and Edwardian Times* by Michael L. Turner and David Vaisy.
2. Responsions was the first of the three examinations once required for an academic degree at Oxford University. Responsions were normally taken prior to Matriculation at a university, to verify the quality of a student with a standardized, but relatively simple test.
3. Until 1905 Stamford Bridge, Fulham (officially opened in 1877) was used almost exclusively by the London Athletics Club as an arena for athletics meetings. In 1905 the then newly formed Chelsea Football Club moved into a newly developed 10,000-seat stadium on the same site, but it continued to be used to host athletic meetings for several years afterwards.
4. In 1910 a marquee is seen in the background on School Field, where the pavilion now stands.

5. Lady Stainer, the wife of Sir John Stainer, the English composer (famously of *The Crucifixion*) and organist, was for many years a friend of MCS because of her husband's association with the college and its choir. She presented awards on many occasions. She died in 1916 and is buried along with her husband in Holywell Cemetery near St Cross Church, Oxford.
6. The Pavilion on School Field was begun in 1913 and completed in 1914.
7. On 16 November 1915 the 7/DLI became the Pioneer Battalion for the 50th Division. A Pioneer Battalion was devoted to various types of labouring work. Men in a Pioneer Battalion tended to be experienced in various construction industry trades and general labouring. They underwent basic military training, including firearms, but were also supplied with the necessary additional tools required for the work they were assigned to do in the field as Pioneers.

APPENDIX 1A

Magdalen College School Roll of Service 1914–1918

The ultimate sacrifice made by the fifty boys is only part of the story of the contribution made by those that served the country during the Great War. Of course, others served and many were unfortunate to receive horrific injuries both physical and mental. Behind every surviving name is once again a character, an original schoolboy and a story that would deserve a book itself. The list of those MCS old boys known to have served the country during the First World War is given here. The Roll totals 248 men. Of these, fifty lost their lives and are highlighted in **bold**.

Between 1917 and 1920 *The Lily* included pleas to hear from or of other old boys who had served but were not included in the list published in 1917 (then 228 men). The roll included here is a good representation of those from the school that served but will in all probability be incomplete.

Notes: w – wounded; inv – invalided; mid – mentioned in dispatches; s –master of the school; pow – prisoner of war; b – blinded; g – gassed.

Name	Title/Rank	Honour	Organization/Regiment	Notes
Allen, J.H.H.			OVR	s
Allistone, H.A.W.	2/Lt.		ASC	
Amon, H.	Capt.	MC & bar	Royal Sussex Regiment	
Andrews, E.R.L.	**Pte.**		**Royal Fusiliers**	
Archibald, G.K.	Maj./Temp. Lt.-Col.	DSO	ASC	mid
Austin, S.			Interned in Austria	
Bacon, R.L.			employed Munitions	
Badcock, W.J.	Rev.		CF	
Barratt, J.L.	**2/Lt.**		**King's (Liverpool) Regiment**	
Bartlett, H.W.	Lt.	MC	London Regiment	w
Bean, C.A.	Lt.		King's (Liverpool) Regiment	w
Beasley, F.R.	Lt.		Australian Infantry	w
Beaumont, G.E.	Lt.		RAMC	
Bell, A.C.	2/Lt.		OBLI	
Bell, A.P.	2/Lt.		RAMC	
Bell, H.C.	2/Lt.		Royal Dublin Fusiliers, Connaught Rangers, later employed Munitions	w, inv
Bellamy, J.H.	**2/Lt.**		**Sherwood Foresters**	

Name	Title/Rank	Honour	Organization/Regiment	Notes
Bickerton, G.T.	2/Lt.		RFC	
Bickerton, J.M.N.S.	Lt.		RAMC	
Blagdon, M.B.	**2/Lt.**		**Queen's (Royal West Surrey Regiment)**	
Bloxsome, H.E.			RAMC	
Bowen, H.G.	2/Lt.		ASC	
Boyer, G.W.B.	2/Lt.		RFA	
Bradley, G.	**2/Lt.**		**OBLI**	
Bradley, G.R.	2/Lt.		RFC	inv
Bradley, H.F.	Lt.		RFC	w
Brereton, H.	**Lt.**		**RFC**	
Brewis, G.R.			OVR	s
Broadbent, W.B.	2/Lt.		Lancashire Fusiliers	
Brown, P.W.	Cdt.		RAF	
Brownrigg, C.E.	2/Lt.		OVR	s
Burgess, F.C.	2/Lt.		Essex Regiment	
Burstall, F.C.	Capt.	MC	Devon Regiment	mid
Bushell, G.E.	Cdt.		OVR	
Butler, A.S.	**2/Lt.**		**RFC**	
Callender, J.C.	**Lt.**		**OBLI**	
Campbell, F.A.B.	2/Lt.		Wiltshire Regiment	
Cane, L.D.	**Capt. & Adjt.**		**Royal Fusiliers**	
Cannon, G.M.	Lt.		AOC	
Cannon, H.S.	**Cpl.**		**Royal Engineers**	
Canton, H.W.	**Capt.**		**East Lancashire Regiment**	
Capel, J.M.	Pte.		24 Battalion Royal Fusiliers (Sportsman's Battalion)	
Carter, B.A.	W/Op.		Indian Transport	
Carter, B.R.H.	**2/Lt.**		**RFC**	
Carter, G.C.	2/Lt.	MC	Gloucester Regiment	
Causton, E.P,G.	Capt.		RAMC (late Surgeon, RN)	
Chavasse, C.M.	Rev.	MC	CF	w
Chavasse, N.G.	**Capt.**	**MC, VC & bar**	**RAMC**	**w, mid**
Christie, R.C.	**2/Lt.**		**Royal Engineers**	
Clapperton, J.F.	Capt.		Devon Regiment	
Clapperton, R.H.	Capt.	MC	Devon Regiment	
Clarke, H.L.	Rev. 2/Lt.		Sherwood Foresters	
Clark-Turner, F.	2/Lt.		ASC	
Clements, W.D.	Rev.		Chaplain RN	
Cockell, G.B.	Capt.		Tanks Corps	mid
Cocker, N.	Sgt.		Worcester Regiment	
Cockram, G.H.H.	Cdt.		OVR	
Cooke, C.	Capt.		RAMC	
Cowan, D.J.	Lt.		Connaught Rangers	w, pow
Cox, P.H.	Lt.		Durham LI	
Cox, S.H.	2/Lt.		ASC	
Crofts, J.E.V.			RAMC	
Cunliffe, J.H.G.			employed Munitions	

Name	Title/Rank	Honour	Organization/Regiment	Notes
Curry, D.	Lt.		RN, HMS *Superb*	
Curry, H.F.	Lt.	DSC	RN, HMS *Oceon*	
Dams, K.L.	Lt.		Sherwood Foresters	
Darbishire, A.D.	**2/Lt.**		**Argyll and Sutherland Highlanders**	
David, T.W.E.	Lt.-Col.	KBE, DSO	Australian Mining Corps	inv
Davies, E.F.	Lce.-Cpl.		OVR	
Davies, I.D.	Sub-Lt.		RNAS Air Ministry (clerical)	
Dawes, H.H.	**2/Lt.**		**Artists' Rifles**	**w**
Deglatigny, P.	2/Lt.	Cr. de G.	French Artillery	
de la Hey, T.C.	Rev.	MC	CF	
Deuchar, G.L.	Lce.-Cpl., Rev.		OVR	s
Disney, S.C.W.	Maj.	MC	Lincolnshire Regiment	w
Ditton Newman, H.	Lce.-Br		Royal Garrison Artillery	
Dodds, H.R.	2/Lt.		Sherwood Foresters	
Donne, B.			Oxford University OTC	
Drayton, H.U.			RNAS	s
Drew, A.	2/Lt.		RFA	
Dyer, C.M.	**2/Lt.**		**Rifle Brigade**	
Elkington, C.	Cpl.		Royal Engineers	
Elliot, J.D.			King's Royal Rifle Corps	
Embling, H.J.	Rev.		RN	
Etty, J.L.	Lt.		OBLI	s
Farnell, R.L.	Lt.		West Kent. attd Royal Dublin Fusiliers	
Field, F.W.			Queen's Own Oxfordshire Hussars	
Field, R.G.	**Pte.**		**Royal Fusiliers**	
Filsell, A.E.			OVR	
FitzGerald, R.V.L.	2/Lt.		Royal Dublin Fusiliers	
Fletcher, R.G.T.	Cdt.		OVR	
Forrest, J.E.			OVR	
Foster, A.E.	**2/Lt.**		**King's Own Yorkshire Light Infantry**	
Foster, R.S.	Lt.		KSLI attd. K. Afr. Rifles	w
Fox Russell, J.	**Capt.**	**MC, VC**	**RAMC**	
Francis, T.W.M.	Lt.		MGC (Cavalry)	
Freeman, C.L.			OVR	s
Gadney, G.S.	**2/Lt.**		**Gloucester Regiment**	
Gale, A.E.M.	Cdt.		OVR	
Galpin, H.F.	2/Lt.		ASC	
Garnons Williams, R.D.	**Lt.-Col.**		**Royal Fusiliers**	
Gough, P.	Rev.		Chaplain RN	
Grundy, G.L.O.	Capt.		MGC	mid, w
Gwilliam, G.L.	Sub-Lt.		RNAS	
Hall, H.A.L.	Maj.	MC	Royal Engineers	
Hall, H.G.L.	Maj.		ASC	
Hanby, D.W.	Lt.		Railway Transport	
Hanby, E.W.	**2/Lt.**		**Middlesex Regiment**	

Name	Title/Rank	Honour	Organization/Regiment	Notes
Harries, G.H.	Rev.	MC	CF	
Haseler, J.V.	2/Lt.	DCM	Royal Warwickshire Regiment	w
Hemmerde, C.E.	**Capt.**	**MC**	**Royal West Kent Regiment**	**w**
Henderson, N.E.N.	**2/Lt.**		**KOSB**	**w**
Herbertson, A.H.	**Lt.**		**KRRC**	**w**
Hickey, B.G.L.	Lt.		Cheshire Regiment	w
Hickey, V.C.F.	2/Lt.		RGA	
Hicks, E.R.	Lt.		Lincolnshire Regiment	w, inv
Hoey, J.T.S.	Lt.	Cr. de G.	OBLI	mid
Houghton, C.G.	Lt.		Inns of Court OTC	
Houghton, F.M.C.	**Lt.**		**RFC**	
Hoyne-Fox, L.	**Lt.**		**Rajputanas**	
Hughes-Chamberlain, G.W.	2/Lt.		New Army	
Isaac, A.G.F.	Bt.-Maj.	MC	Royal Berkshire Regiment	mid
Jacks, G.V.	Cadet		OVR	
Jenner-Clarke, J.W.	**2/Lt.**		**MGC**	
Jones, F.B.	Capt.	MC	OBLI	
Jones, J.W.	2/Lt.		RFC	
Kidd, H.B.	2/Lt.		Leicestershire Regiment	
King, V.K.	**Lt.**		**RAF**	
Landon, F.W.B.	Maj.-Gen.	CB	ASC	mid
Lane, J.E.	Major		RAMC	
Lee, T.A.	Rev.		CF	
Lees, P.B.	**2/Lt.**		**Northants Regiment**	
Leicester, D.N.	**2/Lt.**		**Gloucester Regiment**	
Luget, F.B.	Lt.		RFC	
Maltby, C.R.C.	**Capt. & Adjt.**		**Rifle Brigade**	
Marks, A.K.	Capt.		ASC	
Marks, P.D.	Lt.-Col. & Paymaster		RN	
Marks, W.O.	Lt.-Col.	DSO	ASC (DAQMG)	mid
Marsh, G.H.	2/Lt.		Manchester Regiment	
Martin, G.N.	2/Lt.		Somerset Light Infantry	
Mason, A.C.	2/Lt.		Suffolk Regiment	
Masson, A.H.L.	Cdt.		OVR	
Masters, F.N.D.	2/Lt.		RFA	
Matheson, G.G.	**Cpl.**		**New Zealand Light Infantry**	
Mawson, G.H.	Lt.		Royal Engineers	w
Merriman, N.A.			Electrical Section, ACC	
Millard, W.M.	2/Lt.		OBLI	b
Miller, A.A.			OVR	
Mintoft, H.S.	**2/Lt.**		**East Yorkshire Regiment**	
Moore, H.T.	2/Lt.		RFA	
Morgan, B.E.	2/Lt.		Royal Engineers	
Morgan, H.B.T.	Capt.		RAMC	

Name	Title/Rank	Honour	Organization/Regiment	Notes
Morris, C.E.	Maj., acting Lt.-Col.	DSO	Queen Victoria Own Corps of Guides, attached 85th Burma Rifles, Indian Army	
Morris, H.R.			Pioneer Corps	
Morris, M.A.	**Lt.**		**Hampshire Regiment**	
Morton, E.R.M.	Capt.		ASC	
Morton, J.E.B.	2/Lt.		New army	
Morton, J.L.M.	**Capt.**		**Manchester Regiment**	
Moulding, W.	2/Lt.	Cr. Mil.	RFC	
Myrtle, J.Y.E.			OVR	
Napier, H.	2/Lt.		London Regiment	
Neill, E.M.	2/Lt.	MC	Household Battalion, Grenadier Guards	w
Newton, G.F.	Lt.		RFA (employed munitions)	g, inv
Ogle, N.	DAAG, Maj.	DSO	Punjabis	mid
Omond, J.S.	Capt.		Army Ordnance Corps	mid
Page, G.B.F.	Surg.		RN, RNAS	
Page, W.W.K.	Lt.	MC	attd. Indian Cavalry	
Palin, A.C.S.	Capt.		Leinster Regiment	w
Palin, G.T.			RMA, Woolwich	
Parham, A.G.	Rev.	MC	Chaplain to the Forces	mid
Pearson, W.H.	**2/Lt.**		**MGC**	
Phipps, K.C.G.			Friends' Ambulance Service	
Pickford, E.W.	2/Lt.		RFC	pow
Pilcher, K.R.			RGA	w
Pitts, F.B.	**2/Lt.**		**Leicestershire Regiment**	w, pow
Poole, A.L.	Lt.		Gloucester Regiment	w
Pullan, P.D.			OVR	s
Rambaut, A.E.	Lt.		Northumberland Fusiliers	
Rambaut, G.M.	Maj.	DSO	RFA	w
Ray, G.H. le P.	2/Lt.		RFC	
Read, H.S.H.	2/Lt.		RFC	
Read, W.D.B.	2/Lt.		Royal West Surrey Regiment	
Richardson, E.V.	Lt.		MGC	
Ricketts, W.A.L.	Lt.		ASC	
Ridgeway, E.H.	Lt.		RN	
Ridgeway, N.V.	2/Lt.		unattached, Tonbridge	
Roberton, J.L.	**2/Lt.**		**RFC**	
Roberton, L.	Ass. Paymaster		RNR	
Roberton, W.P.	Lt.		Hampshire Regiment	
Roberts, F.B.	**Capt.**		**Rifle Brigade**	
Rowley, W.H.	Maj.		RA	
Ryman-Hall, B.	2/Lt.		ASC	
Scattergood, T.A.	Lt.	Chevalier de l'Ordre Saint Sauveur	ASC	
Scott, H.R.			Oxford University OTC	
Scott-Tucker, J.R.C.	Maj.	Cr. de G.	Gloucester Regiment	w, mid
Searby, H.R.	Lt.		OBLI & South Lancashire Regiment	

Name	Title/Rank	Honour	Organization/Regiment	Notes
Searby, J.E.			OVR	
Sells, C.P.	**Capt.**		**RAMC**	
Seys, G.W.	2/Lt.		King's (Liverpool) Regiment	
Seys, R.C.	Capt.		RA	
Shakel, F.F.W.	Lt.		Queen's Westminster Cadet Corps	
Shepperd, C.B.	2/Lt.		Border Regiment	
Simmonds, D.G.	Lt. & Adjt.		SWB attd. Royal Welsh Fusiliers	w
Slater, O.R.			Oxford University OTC, Royal Engineers cadet Battalion	
Smith, H.J.F.			Oxford University OTC, Cadet Battalion Guards Regiment	
Sparks, L.	Lce.-Cpl.		Royal Fusiliers	
Squire, L.G.	2/Lt.		OBLI	
Steward, A.A.	**Lt.**		**RFA**	
St John, F.J.	Major		King's Own Yorkshire Light Infantry	
Tarbet, E.A.	**2/Lt.**		**Royal Inniskilling Fusiliers**	
Tattersall, P.R.	W/Op.		Merchant Service	
Thomas, D.R.	Capt.	MC	Royal Welsh Regiment	
Thomas, J.	2/Lt.		OBLI	w, pow
Thomas, T.	**2/Lt.**		**OBLI**	
Thomson, D.H.W.	Capt.		West Riding Regiment	
Thomson, G.G.	Capt.	MC	North Staffordshire Regiment, Tank Corps, attached Cheshire Regiment	w, mid
Tirbutt, C.D.	2/Lt.		Royal West Kent Regiment attd. Middlesex Regiment	
Turner, E.G.	Maj.	DSO	AVC	
Turner, F.	2/Lt.		DCLI	
Twiss, E.K.	Maj.	DSO	Jats. attd. Dorset Regiment	mid
Venables, E.M.	2/Lt., Rev.		unattached, Harrow	
Verney, L.M.	Maj.	DSO	AVC	mid
Vines, W.S.	Capt.		Highland Light Infantry	w
Vernon-Harcourt, B.F.	Maj.		RFC, School of Aeronautics	
Wallis, W.H. St J.	Lt.		RNVR	w
Ward, R.O.	Maj.	MC	HAC, attd RFA	
Webb, D.H.	**Lt.**		**MGC**	
Weir, P.	2/Lt.		ASC	
West, W.G.	Capt.		Sherwood Foresters	
Westaway, E.V.			Worcester Regiment	
Wiggins, C.A.	Maj.		RAMC	
Wiggins, H.B.	Rev.		CF	
Wiggins, R.V.N.			Inns of Court OTC	
Wilkinson, F.D.	**Lt.**	**MC**	**East Kent Regiment**	**2w, pow**
Williams, A.R.	2/Lt.		MGC	w

Williams, L.M.	2/Lt.	RFC	
Williams, T.S.B.	Major	Indian Medical Corps	
Williams, W.H.	**Flt. Cdr.**	**RFC (Lancashire Fusiliers)**	
Wills, R.G.	Capt.	RAMC	
Wilson, K.	Capt.	ASC	
Wood, G.R.	Lt.	OBLI	s
Woodhead, S.	WO	AOC	
Woodhead, L.	2/Lt.	RNR	
Woolmer, S.L.		HAC	
Wylie, C.E.F.	2/Lt.	OBLI	
Yeo, L.F.	**2/Lt.**	**South Staffordshire Regiment**	
Zacharias Jessel, A.R.	2/Lt.	Northants Regiment	w, inv
Zacharias Jessel, V.A.V.	**Lt.**	**Durham Light Infantry**	

APPENDIX 1B

Date analysis: when were the boys at MCS?

(The table indicates the academic years in which they attended MCS and academic year in which they died †)

Surname (age at death)	**Academic Year**	1889/90	1890/91	1891/92	1892/93	1893/94	1894/95	1895/96	1896/97	1897/98	1898/99	1899/1900	1900/01	1901/02	1902/03	1903/04	1904/05	1905/06	1906/07	1907/08	1908/09	1909/10	1910/11	1911/12	1912/13	1913/14	1914/15	1915/16	1916/17	1917/18	1918/19	1919/20
Andrews (21)																			■	■	■	■	■					†				
Barratt (19)																						■	■	■	■	■	■	■		†		
Bellamy (23)															■	■	■	■	■	■	■	■							†			
Blagden (19)																					■	■	■	■	■	■	■	■			†	
Bradley (19)																					■	■	■	■	■	■		†				
Brereton (22)																	■	■	■	■	■								†			
Butler (26)														■	■	■												†				
Callender (21)																			■	■	■	■	■	■	■	■	■		†			
Cane (32)								■	■	■	■	■	■															†				
Cannon (26)															■												†					
Canton (23)																■	■	■	■	■	■						†					
Carter (19)																					■	■	■	■						†		
Chavasse (32)										■	■	■	■																†			
Christie (22)																								■				†				
Darbishire (36)				■	■	■	■	■	■																			†				

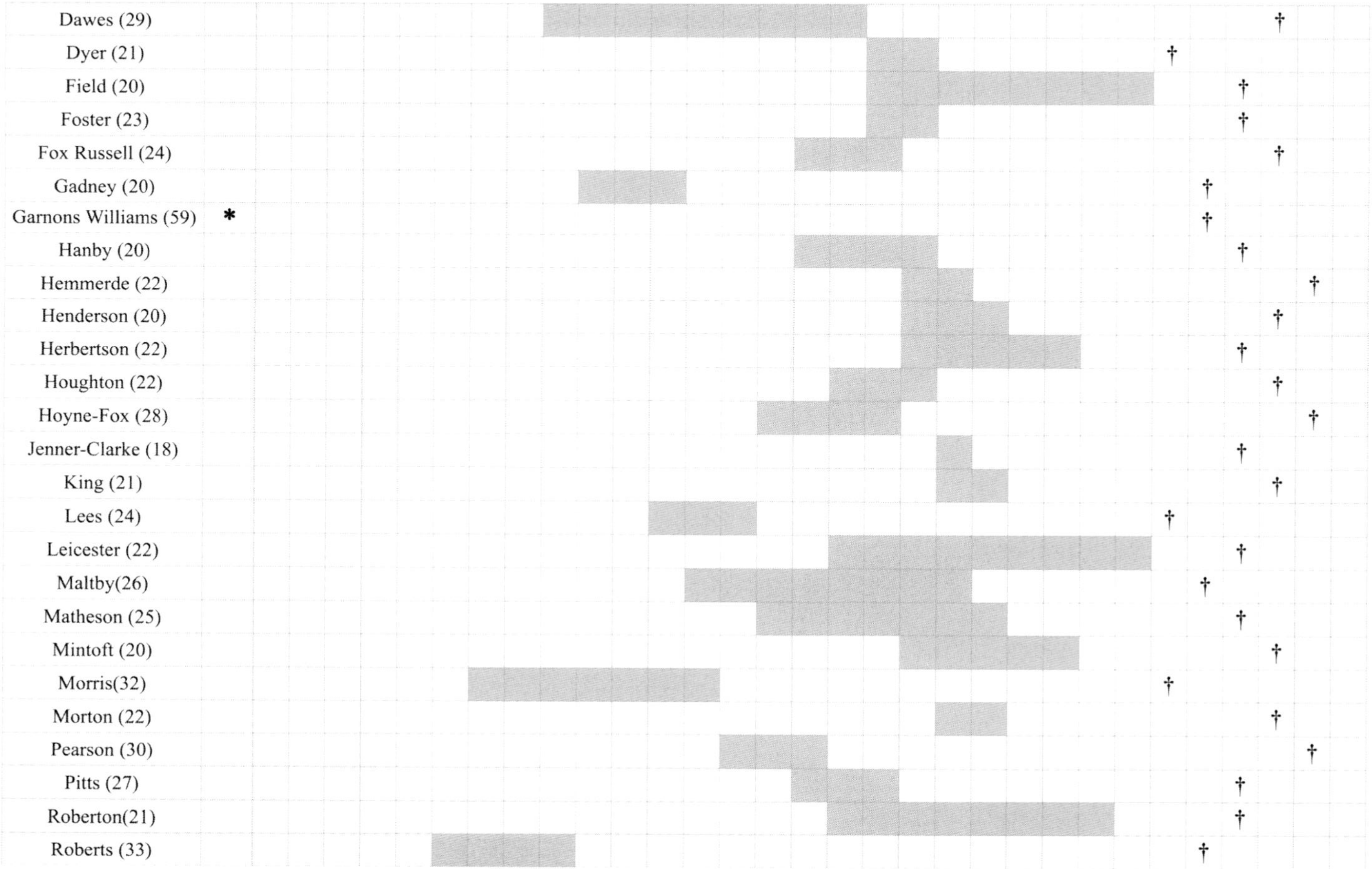
Dawes (29)
Dyer (21)
Field (20)
Foster (23)
Fox Russell (24)
Gadney (20)
Garnons Williams (59) *
Hanby (20)
Hemmerde (22)
Henderson (20)
Herbertson (22)
Houghton (22)
Hoyne-Fox (28)
Jenner-Clarke (18)
King (21)
Lees (24)
Leicester (22)
Maltby(26)
Matheson (25)
Mintoft (20)
Morris(32)
Morton (22)
Pearson (30)
Pitts (27)
Roberton(21)
Roberts (33)

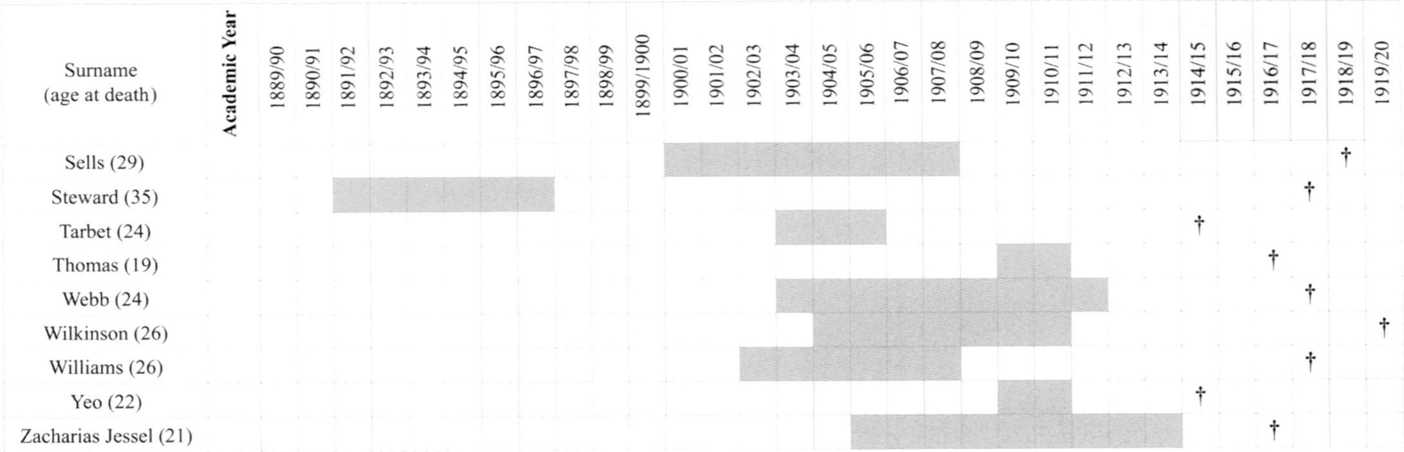

* Garnons Williams was present at MCS from January 1870 to July 1872.

The average age of the boys at death was 25. The oldest was R.D. Garnons Williams, aged 59. The youngest was J.W. Jenner-Clarke, 18 years and 10 months.

APPENDIX 2A

Structure of the Army

Enlistment for the army was initially voluntary, with the minimum age being 18. In March 1916 the Military Service Act came into effect and made enlistment for single men between the ages of 18 and 41 compulsory. The act was modified in May 1916 to include married men and by April 1918 the upper age limit had been increased to 51. In order to allow an appreciation of the structure of the army alluded to throughout this book a simplified overview using an organization chart and notes are given for the reader.

British Expeditionary Force (BEF): Global term for all the army units in France, Flanders and Italy during the First World War. Commanded by Field Marshal Sir John French until 19 December 1915, then by General (later Field Marshal) Sir Douglas Haig for the remainder of the war.

Regiments: A Regiment can be thought of as the parent body of its battalions.[1] Regiments never fought as whole bodies, but their battalions were dispersed across the divisions. Soldiers often show their primary military loyalty to their regiment. During the First World War regiments often raised battalions according to the region's ability to support them.[2]

Army: Identified for example, as 'First Army'. By March 1915 there were two armies in the BEF. By 1918 this had risen to five. Each army had two or more Corps.

Corps: Identified by Roman numerals, e.g. II Corps. Each Corps consisted of two or more Divisions.

Division: Identified for example, as 8th Division. Each Division consisted of three brigades. A Division was essentially a miniature army containing all the necessary combat and support units to enable it to fight independently. It is the Divisions that frequently moved during the war to be under the command of different Corps or Armies.

Brigade: Identified for example, as 92 Brigade. Each brigade consisted of four infantry battalions or three cavalry regiments. In March 1918 the brigades were reduced in strength from four to three battalions due to manpower shortages. It should be noted that the Rifle Brigade is a title of an infantry regiment and is not a separate brigade. Artillery Brigade (given Roman numerals) was roughly equivalent to a battalion and commanded by a Lieutenant Colonel.

Battalion: Identified for example, as 5th Battalion, or to accommodate men wishing to join territorial battalions rather than new army battalions, new 'old

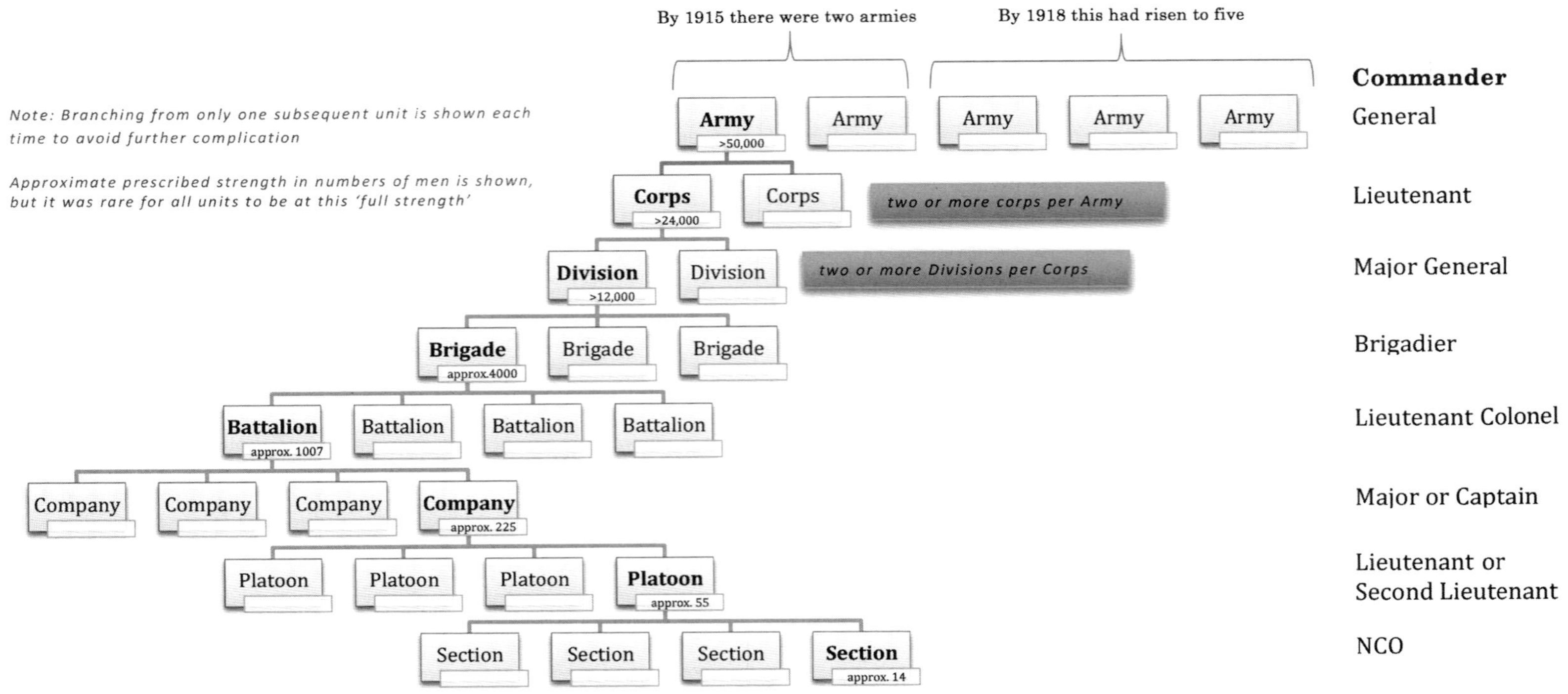
Note: Branching from only one subsequent unit is shown each time to avoid further complication
Approximate prescribed strength in numbers of men is shown, but it was rare for all units to be at this 'full strength'
By 1915 there were two armies
By 1918 this had risen to five
Commander
Army >50,000
Army
Army
Army
Army
General
Corps >24,000
Corps
two or more corps per Army
Lieutenant
Division >12,000
Division
two or more Divisions per Corps
Major General
Brigade approx.4000
Brigade
Brigade
Brigadier
Battalion approx. 1007
Battalion
Battalion
Battalion
Lieutenant Colonel
Company
Company
Company
Company approx. 225
Major or Captain
Platoon
Platoon
Platoon
Platoon approx. 55
Lieutenant or Second Lieutenant
Section
Section
Section
Section approx. 14
NCO

territorial battalions' were created and given the same number as the original but with the addition of a prefix e.g. 1/5th Battalion, 2/5th Battalion etc. A battalion consisted of thirty officers and 977 men. Battalions often went into battle fielding only a few hundred men. Each battalion was divided into four companies. The word 'Service' was added to new army battalions to distinguish them from original regular, reserve or territorial battalions.

Company: Identified for example as A-, B-, C- or D-Company, or alternatively W-, X-, Y- or Z-Company. A company was one quarter of the fighting arm of the battalion.

Platoon: A platoon was one quarter of a company. If the officer commanding the platoon was killed in battle an NCO (Corporal or Sergeant etc.) would assume control.

Section: A section was one quarter of a platoon.

Notes

1. The commanding officer of a Regiment was a Colonel.
2. Some battalions were known unofficially, or sometimes even officially, as Pals Battalions if they had been raised from one whole close knit community. Devastatingly if a Pals Battalion suffered heavy losses during a battle whole communities could lose their menfolk overnight. The appeal of the Pals was a good way to attract men to join up but not good for the structure of the community.

APPENDIX 2B

British Army Ranks during the First World War

In order to allow an appreciation of the relative levels of rank amongst the MCS boys a simplified overview of officer ranks and army 'ranks' in hierarchical order is given below. From its inception on 1 April 1918 until after the Great War, the Royal Air Force used the same rank names as the army. None of the MCS boys to die during the Great War were in the Royal Navy.

Officer ranks	**Army 'ranks'**[3,4]
Field Marshal	Warrant Officer
General	Sergeant
Lieutenant General	Corporal[5]
Major General	Lance Corporal[6]
Brigadier General	Private[7]
Colonel	
Lieutenant Colonel	
Major	
Captain	
Lieutenant[1]	
Second Lieutenant[2]	

Due to the casualty rates, temporary appointments to higher ranks were often made until Regular Army officers became available to fill the senior post on a permanent basis. Hence, it is common to see on war records the word 'Temporary' before an officer's rank.

Notes:

1. French *lieu* (place) *tenant* (holder), pronounced 'Leftenant'. The Lieutenant normally commands a small tactical unit such as a platoon. A Lieutenant often takes the place of a superior officer when that officer is absent.
2. The lowest rank of commissioned officer (CO). A graduate of a military academy or an officer training school. Subaltern is a term applied to any officer below the rank of captain, especially a Second Lieutenant (derivation from Latin, related to the word for alternate).
3. There were well over 100 different but comparable titles for men in the different army units.
4. Non-commissioned officers (NCOs) were all army 'ranks' above private. Warrant Officer (WO) is a rank between CO and NCO. Both WOs and NCOs usually held an appointment as well as a rank.
5. Bombardier is used instead of Corporal for Artillery Units.
6. Lance Bombardier is used instead of Lance Corporal for Artillery Units.
7. Sapper is used by the Royal Engineers. Gunner is used by Royal Artillery.

APPENDIX 2C

British Campaign Medals

A Guide to British Campaign Medals awarded amongst the fifty MCS boys during the First World War

All campaign medals are named to the recipient and also show his rank, number (unless to an officer, as Great War officers did not have a number) and regiment. Service medals were issued automatically to 'other ranks', but officers or their next of kin had to apply for them. When medals were sent to the next of kin of men who had been killed two further items were included: a bronze plaque[1] bearing the man's name and inscribed with the words '*He Died For Freedom And Honour*', and a scroll bearing the man's name, rank and regiment.

The 1914 Star

The bronze 1914 Star (affectionately known as 'Pip' or the 'Mons Star')[2] was awarded to those who served in France or Belgium between 5 August and 22 November 1914. A narrow horizontal bronze clasp sewn on to the ribbon was also awarded if the recipient had actually served under fire of the enemy. Recipients of this medal were responsible for assisting the French to hold back the German army in the first sixteen weeks of the war. This included the battle of Mons, the retreat to the Seine, the battles of Le Cateau, the Marne, the Aisne and the first battle of Ypres.

The 1914–15 Star

The bronze 1914–15 Star (also known as 'Pip') was awarded to all who served in any theatre of war against Germany between 5 August 1914 and 31 December 1915, except those eligible for the 1914 Star. Similarly, those who received the Africa General Service Medal or the Sudan 1910 Medal were not eligible for the award.

The British War Medal, 1914–18

This silver medal (affectionately known as 'Squeak') was awarded to officers and men of the British and Imperial Forces who either entered a theatre of war or entered service overseas between 5 August 1914 and 11 November 1918. This was later extended to as late as 1920 for men serving in ongoing theatres of war.

The Allied Victory Medal

Eligibility for this bronze medal (known affectionately as 'Wilfred') was more restricted and not everyone who received the British War Medal also received the Allied Victory Medal.[3]

The Silver War Badge

The badge (also known as 'Services Rendered Badge'or 'Silver Wound Badge') was originally issued to officers and men who were discharged or retired from the military forces as a result of sickness or injury caused by their war service. Wearing the badge enabled men no longer dressed in uniform to be distinguished from those who had never joined up.

Notes

1. Sometimes called 'A Dead Man's Penny'
2. When the Great War medals were issued in the 1920s it coincided with a popular comic strip published in the *Daily Mirror* newspaper. Written by Bertram J. Lamb, and drawn by the cartoonist Austin B. Payne, Pip was the dog, Squeak the penguin and Wilfred the rabbit. It is believed that Payne's batman during the war had been nicknamed 'Pip-squeak' and this is where the idea for the names of the dog and penguin came from. For some reason the three names of the characters became associated with the three campaign medals being issued at that time.
3. When only the British War Medal and Allied Victory Medal are on display together they are sometimes known as 'Mutt and Jeff'.

APPENDIX 2D

Gallantry Medals

A guide to gallantry medals received by MCS boys during the First World War

The First World War brought about many instances of gallantry, but in order for an award to be honoured the person usually had to survive the incident. The main exception to this is the award of a Victoria Cross which can be made posthumously, but still requires three witnesses to the act of valour. It is without doubt that many more acts of bravery were carried out which could have resulted in a gallantry award; but due to the man being killed or because there was no surviving witness, no award was made. One only has to read the biographies of the MCS boys in this book to see that other gallantry medals were possibly deserved among this small group alone.

The Victoria Cross (VC)

It is the premier award for supreme acts of gallantry in the face of the enemy. Made from the metal of guns captured from the Russians in the Crimean War, it is inscribed with the words 'For Valour'. Some 615 VCs were awarded during the First World War. Only one person in the First World War received both the Victoria Cross and bar (a second award of the Victoria Cross); he was MCS old boy Captain Noel Chavasse.[1]

Level 1 Gallantry Award

Companion of The Order of the Bath (CB)

CBs are awarded to an Officer of the rank of Lieutenant Commander, Major or Squadron Leader or above, who in addition must have been mentioned in dispatches for distinction in a command position in a combat situation.

Order – Third Class

Distinguished Service Order (DSO)

Awarded to Officers at a rank of, or one rank above or below, Major. Awarded for an act of meritorious or distinguished service in wartime, usually when in the presence of the enemy and from 1917 onwards restricted to this criterion. However, between 1914 and 1916 also awarded to some Staff Officers when they were not in contact with the enemy.

Level 2 Gallantry Award

Distinguished Conduct Medal (DCM)
The first official medal award to recognize an act of gallantry in the field in the face of the enemy by a member of the armed forces below the rank of officer. The 'other ranks' equivalent of the DSO. The reverse of the medal bears the inscription 'For Distinguished Conduct in the Field'

Level 2 Gallantry Award

The Military Cross (MC)
This silver cross was a decoration for gallantry during active operations in the presence of the enemy. Commissioned officers in the British Army with the rank of Captain or below were eligible for the award. It is the equivalent of the DSC (for valour at sea) and DFC (for valour in the air).

Level 3 Gallantry Award

Distinguished Service Cross (DSC)
Awarded to naval officers below the rank of Lieutenant Commander for gallantry at sea in the presence of the enemy. It is the equivalent of the MC (for valour on the land) and DFC (for valour in the air).

Level 3 Gallantry Award

Military Medal (MM)
Awarded to'other ranks' of the British Army for gallantry and devotion to duty when under fire in battle on land. On the reverse is inscribed 'For Bravery in the Field'.

Level 3 Gallantry Award

Mentioned in Despatches (MiD)[2]
This is not a medal award but a reward of being named and commended for a noteworthy act of gallantry in an official report (written by the senior commander of an army in the field). It is then published in the *London Gazette*. As for the VC, but unlike other awards, the MiD can be awarded posthumously. A bronze oak leaf was issued and could be worn on the ribbon of the Victory Medal.

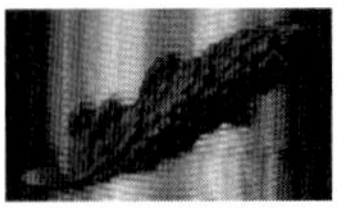

Level 4 Commendation

In addition, other allied powers commonly recognized acts of gallantry in collaborative action. These included three French awards received by MCS boys during the First World War: the Croix Militaire (Cr. Mil.); the Chevalier de l'Ordre Saint Sauveur; and most commonly, the Croix de Guerre (Cr. de G).

Croix de Guerre (Cr. de G)

'Cross of War'. Commonly bestowed on foreign military forces allied to France, it is awarded for acts of heroism involving combat with the enemy that have been mentioned in dispatches.

Notes

1. Only two other people in history have been awarded the VC and bar: Lieutenant Colonel Arthur Martin-Leake (May 1902 and November 1914) and Captain Charles Upham (May 1941 and July 1942).
2. The phrase 'Mentioned in Dispatches' was first used in a *Morning Post* newspaper article of 6 October 1898, written by Winston Churchill.

Abbreviations and Glossary

Adjutant – A staff officer who assists the commanding officer. This person often wrote the war diary entries for the battalion.
ADS – Advanced Dressing Station.
ADMS – Assistant Director Medical Services.
ASC – Army Service Corps.
Attestation (papers) – The attestation paper was an agreement to be in the army for the duration of the war and an oath of allegiance to the king.
ANZAC – Australian and New Zealand Army Corps.
Armistice – An official and arranged halt in hostilities to allow peace negotiations. The Armistice between the Allies and Germany which ended the war was signed on 11 November 1918 and was valid for thirty-six days; it was regularly renewed until peace treaties were signed.

BA – Bachelor of Arts.
Bantam – Term for members of battalions between 5ft 1in and 5ft 4in.
Barrage – Artillery bombardment.
Battels – The account of a member of a college for board, provisions and other college expenses.
Battery – A group of six guns or howitzers.
Bayonet – A knife-like blade attached to the point of a gun, used for close-quarter fighting.
BEADOC – British East Africa Disabled Officers Colony.
BEF – British Expeditionary Force.
Blue Cross shells – German shells marked with a blue cross during the First World War usually contained either diphenylchloroarsine or diphenylcyanoarsine, chemicals that affect the upper respiratory system and induce vomiting.
Buffs – The Buffs (East Kent Regiment).
BW – Black Watch (Royal Highlanders).

CCS – Casualty Clearing Station: main medical establishment immediately behind the front line.
CEF – Canadian Expeditionary Force.
Central Powers – Term used to describe the alliance bloc of Germany, Austria-Hungary, Bulgaria and the Ottoman Empire, due to their comparatively central location in Europe.
Commoner – A term for an undergraduate not having a scholarship or exhibition.

CCF – Combined Cadet Force.
CO – Commanding Officer.
Commem – The MCS Commemoration Service.
Communication trench – Small trenches usually built at right angles to regular trenches to allow 'protected' communication between them.
Cox's Corner – Local term for Parson's Pleasure, a location on the Cherwell River where MCS swimming events took place. Named after Charlie Cox, the proprietor of the bathing place.
Coy – Company.
Creeping barrage – Artillery bombardment whose range was extended at timed intervals so as to avoid hitting one's own advancing troops.

DAAG – Deputy Assistant Adjutant General.
DCLI – Duke of Cornwall's Light Infantry.
Detrain(ed) – Unload (troops) from a train.
Devons – Devonshire Regiment.
DLI – Durham Light Infantry.
Duckboard – Wooden planking used at the bottom of trenches or across muddy ground.
Dud – A shell which failed to explode.

EEF – Egyptian Expeditionary Force.
Eights Week – Eights week is a four-day regatta of bumps races between colleges of Oxford University. It usually takes place in May each year.
E. Lancs – East Lancashire Regiment.
Enfilade fire – Gunfire from the side along the line of troops.
Entente Powers – The alliance of the British, French and Russian Empires as well as Belgium.
Entrain(ed) – Load up a train (with troops).
ESR – East Surrey Regiment.
Essex – Essex Regiment.
E. Yorks – East Yorkshire Regiment.
Exhibition(er) – A financial award to an individual student, normally on grounds of merit.

Fatigue (duty) – Work assigned to military personnel that does not require the use of firearms.
FOEF – French Oriental Expeditionary Force.
Fire-step – A trench was normally deep enough for soldiers to walk along completely concealed. The fire-step ran along the forward wall and allowed soldiers to peer or fire over the top.
Firing line/trench – Front line trench.
Form Fours – Coxed-four rowing races between school forms.
Front line – The closest trench system to the enemy.

Gazetted – See *London Gazette*.
GHQ – General Headquarters (one was formed for each theatre of war).
Ploucs – Gloucestershire Regiment.
GOC – General Officer Commanding.
The Gut – A stretch of narrow water on the River Isis in Oxford.

Hants – Hampshire Regiment.
HB – Howitzer Brigade.
Hindenburg Line – A connected series of German defensive fortifications on the Western Front behind which German forces withdrew in the winter of 1916/17.
Home front – Civilian areas during wartime, particularly with regard to activities that support the war effort, such as production. Also used to describe armed service duties on British soil, such as training or home-defence.
Howitzer – An artillery gun characterized by a relatively short barrel.

IB – Infantry Brigade.

Jack Johnson shell – A 'Jack Johnson' was the British nickname used to describe the impact of a heavy, black German 15cm artillery shell. Jack Johnson was the world heavyweight boxing champion from 1908 to 1915.
Jumping up/off point – The starting position for an attack.

KBE – Knight Commander of the Most Excellent Order of the British Empire.
KSLI – The King's (Shropshire Light Infantry).
King's – The King's (Liverpool Regiment).
KOYLI – The King's Own Yorkshire Light Infantry.
KOSB – The King's Own Scottish Borderers.
KRRC – The King's Royal Rifle Corps.

Leics – Leicestershire Regiment.
Lewis Gun – An Allied light machine gun using a characteristic disc-shaped magazine.
The Lily – The MCS magazine.
LF – Lancashire Fusiliers.
LFA – London Field Ambulance.
London Gazette – The official journal of record of the British government, in which certain statutory notices are required to be published. In time of war, despatches from the conflict are published in the *London Gazette*. People referred to are said to have been 'mentioned in despatches'. When members of the armed forces are promoted, and these promotions are published here, the person is said to have been 'gazetted'.
LMSSA – Licentiate of Medicine & Surgery of the Society of Apothecaries.

Manch. – Manchester Regiment.
Matriculate – To enrol at a College or University.
Menin Gate – The Menin Gate Memorial to the Missing is a war memorial in Ypres, Belgium dedicated to the British and Commonwealth soldiers who were killed in the Ypres Salient and whose graves are unknown.
MGC – Machine Gun Corps.
MEF – Mediterranean Expeditionary Force.
MCS – Magdalen College School.
Middx. – The Duke of Cambridge's Own (Middlesex Regiment).
Mills Bomb – The standard British hand grenade.
Mortar – Short-muzzled, high trajectory, muzzle loading artillery pieces often used for close infantry support.
MRCS – Member of the Royal College of Surgeons.

NCO – Non-commissioned officer.
NZEF – New Zealand Expeditionary Force.
Nissen hut – A prefabricated steel structure, made from a half cylindrical skin of corrugated steel. Designed and patented in 1916 by Major Peter N. Nissen 29/RE, who received a DSO for his services to the war effort.
North'n – Northamptonshire Regiment.
No-man's land – The ground between opposing lines of trenches.
N.Staffs – North Staffordshire Regiment.
Nullah – A steep narrow valley.

OBLI – Oxfordshire and Buckinghamshire Light Infantry.
Old Boys – Past pupils of the school. After 1935 the term Old Waynfletes seems to have been adopted.
OVR – Oxford Volunteer Regiment.
Old Waynfletes (OWs) – Former pupils of MCS. Prior to 1935 old pupils from the school were simply referred to as Old Boys.
OTC – Officer Training Corps.
OUOTC – Oxford University Officer Training Corps.
Over the top – Climbing up out of a trench and attacking.
OVTC – Oxfordshire Volunteer Training Corps.

Parapet – The raised side of the trench facing the enemy.
Pavé – Stone roads.
Pioneers – Each Army Division was allotted a Pioneer battalion that was devoted to various types of labouring work. These battalions had military training but the men were also skilled or experienced in a trade or general labouring.
Push – A large-scale attack on enemy positions.

Queen's – The Queen's (Royal West Surrey Regiment).
QORWK – The Queen's Own (Royal West Kent Regiment).

RAF – Royal Air Force, the British air wing of the armed forces formed on 1 April 1918.
RAMC – Royal Army Medical Corps.
RAP – Regimental Aid Post.
RE – Royal Engineers.
Redoubt – Fortified strongpoint in a trench system.
Reserve (line) – An area some distance behind the front line, out of immediate danger from enemy action. Here troops would be housed in billets or tents and spend time at rest, in training and doing recreational activities. Troops in reserve were also used for fatigue duties in the surrounding area. The reserve areas usually had their own trench systems, designed to contain any break through the front line by the enemy.
RB – Rifle Brigade.
RF – Royal Fusiliers.
RFA – Royal Field Artillery.
RFC – Royal Flying Corps, the air arm of the British army until April 1918.
RHA – Royal Horse Artillery.
R. Innis. F. – Royal Inniskilling Fusiliers.
Rotation – The infantry troops were moved between front line, support line and reserve line duties. The time spent at each varied, but front line duty was usually restricted to less than a week.
RMA – Royal Military Academy (Woolwich provided officer training for Artillery and Engineers; Sandhurst for Infantry).
R. Suss – Royal Sussex Regiment.
RVC – Rifle Volunteer Corps.
RWF – Royal Welsh Fusiliers.

Salient – A 'bulge' or projection of the front line towards the enemy.
sap/sapping – The practice of digging small 'sap' trenches at roughly ninety degrees out from existing lines and then digging a new trench line at the front of the saps.
SAA – Small Arms Ammunition.
SLI – Somerset Light Infantry.
Shrapnel – Steel balls or fragments from an exploding artillery shell, which injure or kill nearby personnel.
Shell shock – A term which refers to several forms of war neurosis or psychological illness caused by noise and exposure to fighting; now known as 'combat stress reaction' or 'post-traumatic stress disorder'.
SIO – Signalling and Intelligence Officer.
SBR – Small box respirator (gas mask).
Sher. For. – Sherwood Foresters (Nottinghamshire and Derbyshire Regiment).
S. Lanc. – South Lancashire Regiment (The Prince of Wales's Volunteers).
SS – Steam Ship.
S. Staffs – South Staffordshire Regiment.

Stand To – Manning trenches to repel an attack, always done as precaution at dawn and dusk.

Support (line) – An area from where troops could reach the front line in a short time in order to quickly support or help with any defensive or attacking duties. Also troops in support were used for fatigue duties in the front line area.

TF – Territorial Force, volunteer reserve component of the British Army from 1908 to 1920, when it became the Territorial Army.

Thiepval – The Thiepval Memorial to the Missing of the Somme is a major war memorial to 72,191 missing British and South African men who died in the Battles of the Somme between 1915 and 1918 with no known grave. It is near the village of Thiepval, Picardy in France.

TMB – Trench Mortar Battery.

Torpids – Torpids is a bumping race, a type of rowing race that takes place between college crews of Oxford University each year in the Hilary Term.

Trench Fever – Illness similar to influenza, caused by lice.

Trench Foot – Fungal infection of the foot which could become gangrenous, caused by exposure to wet and cold.

Tyne Cot – A Commonwealth War Graves Commission (CWGC) burial ground near Passendale, Belgium. It is the largest cemetery for Commonwealth forces in the world, for any war. Its name is said to come from the Northumberland Fusiliers seeing a resemblance between the German concrete pill boxes, which still stand in the middle of the cemetery, and typical Tyneside workers' cottages – Tyne Cots.

VAD – Voluntary Aid Detachment.

Western Front – The line or area of conflict between Germany and the Entente Powers stretching from the Belgian coast, through northern France, to the Swiss border.

Wipers – British slang for the Belgium town of Ypres.

WIY – Warwickshire Imperial Yeomanry.

Worcs – Worcestershire Regiment.

WR – Welsh Regiment.

Yellow Cross shells – German shells marked with a yellow cross which usually contained a payload based on sulphur mustards (various chloroalkyl sulphides), cytotoxic blistering agents, which affected exposed surfaces of the body.

Y & L – Yorkshire and Lancaster Regiment.

YMCA – Young Men's Christian Association; ran canteens behind the front lines.

Zeppelin – A German airship.

Zero Hour – When an attack began.

Battalions to which the MCS boys belonged are initially introduced in full in the text (according to *British Regiments 1914–18*, Brig. E.A. James) but thereafter are written in abbreviated form (using standard abbreviations adopted in the reference text, *Order of Battle of Divisions*). Reference to battalions to which the MCS boys did not belong are immediately written in abbreviated form. Example:

Full Battalion details = 1st Battalion, King's Own Yorkshire Light Infantry
Abbreviated = 1/KOYLI

Some Regiments had a second and a third battalion of the same number; for example, 4th Battalion, King's Own Yorkshire Light Infantry had a first, second, and third of the fourth Battalion. They are abbreviated thus:

1/4/KOYLI
2/4/KOYLI
3/4/KOYLI.

Companies within battalions are abbreviated as follows:

B Company = B-Coy
Number 3 Company = No. 3-Coy *or* 3-Coy

Squadrons are abbreviated as follows:

Number 142 Squadron = 142 Squadron

Time. When discussing time in the military context the 24 hour clock is used. In the civilian context the 12 hour clock is used. In the following styles:

Military context (24 hour clock)	Civilian context (12 hour clock)
03.35	3.35am
15.35	3.35pm

Bibliography

The following sources were amongst those used in the research and writing of this book.

Published Sources:

Books

Bridger, Geoff; *The Great War Handbook*, Pen & Sword, 2009.
Brockliss, Laurence W.; *Magdalen College Oxford. A History*, Magdalen College, 2008.
Cannan, May W.; *Grey Ghosts and Voices*, Roundwood Press, 1976.
Clayton, Ann; *Chavasse Double VC*, Pen & Sword, 2008.
Clayton, Martin; Zon, Bennett; *Music and Orientalism in the British Empire, 1780s-1940s: Portrayal of the East*, Ashgate Publishing, 2007.
Coppard, George; *With a Machine Gun to Cambrai*, Cassell, 1999.
Cooper, Stephen; *The Final Whistle*, The History Press, 2012.
Darbishire, Arthur D.;*An Introduction to a Biology and Other Papers*, Cassell & Co. Ltd, 1917.
Darbishire, Arthur D.;*Breeding and the Mendelian Discovery*, Cassell & Co. Ltd, 1911.
van Emden, Richard; *The Last Fighting Tommy*, Bloomsbury, 2009.
Gunther, Robert; *The History of the Daubeny Laboratory*, Oxford University Press, 1904.
Hanson, Neil; *First Blitz*, Corgi, 2008.
Haynes, H.G.L.; Montgomery Smith, E.C.; *The 'Second–Seconds' in France, The Story of the 2/2nd City of London Field Ambulance*, Spottiswoode, Ballantyne and Co. Ltd, London, 1920.
Hey, Colin G.; *Magdalen Schooldays 1917–1924*, Senecio Press, 1977.
Holt, Tonie and Holt, Valmai; *Major and Mrs Holt's Battlefield Guide to the Ypres Salient and Passchendaele*, Pen & Sword, 2008.
Holt, Tonie and Holt, Valmai; *Major and Mrs Holt's Battlefield Guide to the Somme*, Pen & Sword, 2008.
Hutchins, Roger and Sheppard, Richard; *The Undone Years*, The Magdalen Society, 2004.
Molony, Charles V.; *Invicta: With the First Battalion, The Queen's Own Royal West Kent Regiment in the Great War*, London, Nisbet, 1923.
Keegan, John; *The First World War*, Vintage Books, 1999.
Lewis, Cecil; *Sagittarius Rising*, London, Peter Davies Ltd, 1936.
Lewis-Stempel, John; *Six Weeks*, Orion, 2010.
Nicolson, Juliet; *The Great Silence*, John Murray, 2010.
O'Connor, Mike; *Airfields and Airmen, Ypres*, Pen & Sword, 2004.
Pearson, Richard; *The Boys of Shakespeare's School*, The History Press, 2010.
Richmond, Lesley and Turton, Alison; *The Brewing Industry: A Guide to Historical Records*, Manchester University Press, 1990.
Seldon, Antony and Walsh, David; *Public Schools and The Great War, The Generation Lost*, Pen and Sword, 2014.
Sheffield, Gary; *The Chief. Douglas Haig and the British Army*, Aurum, 2012.
Simkins, Peter, Jukes, Geoffrey; and Hickey, Michael; *The First World War, The War to End all Wars*, Osprey, 2013.
Smith, L. Cecil; *Annals of Public School Rowing*, Blackwell, 1919.
Stanier, Robert; *Magdalen School. A History of Magdalen College School, Oxford*, Blackwell, Oxford, 1958.
Stevens, Philip;*The Great War Explained*, Pen & Sword, 2012.
Westwell, Ian; *The Complete Illustrated History of World War I*, Anness Publishing Ltd, 2011.
Willmott, Hedley P.; *World War I*, Dorling Kindersley, 2003.

Compact Discs

British Roll of Honour, 1914–1916, S&N Genealogy Supplies.
Bond of Sacrifice, Volume 2 January to June 1915, S&N Genealogy Supplies.

Reference Publications

Airmen Died in the Great War 1914–1918, Chris Hobson, J.B. Hayward and Son, 1995.
The Army List, London, monthly throughout the war.
Balliol College Roll of Honour 1914–1919.
Baker's Biographical Dictionary of Musicians, Slonimsky, Nicolas; Schirmer Books, 2001.
British Regiments 1914–1918, Brigadier E.A. James, 5th Ed., 1998, The Navy and Military Press.
The Central Council of Church Bell Ringers, Rolls of Honour.
Dulwich College Roll of Honour.
De Ruvigny's Roll of Honour, 1914–1924.
Indian Army Quarterly List.
Ireland, Casualties of World War I, 1914–1918.
John Wisden's Cricketers' Almanack for 1917, 54th Ed., London; Editor, Pardon, S.H.
London University Roll of Honour.
Magdalen College School Hymn Book, Gresham Books, 2005.
Magdalen College School, Oxford. Examination Lists, 1888–1895.
Magdalen College School, Oxford. Examination Lists, 1896–1900.
Magdalen College School, Oxford. Examination Lists, 1905–1910.
Order of Battle of Divisions, compiled by Major A.F. Beake, Index and Parts 1–4, 2008, The Navy and Military Press.
The Sky their Battlefield. Air Fighting and the Complete List of Allied Casualties from Enemy Action in the First War, Trevor Henshaw, Grub Street, 1995.
Soldiers Died in the Great War (via ancestry.co.uk).

Journals, Magazine and Individual Articles

The British Medical Journal
Flight Magazine, The British Air Services (via http://www.flightglobal.com/pdfarchive/index.html).
IBIS, The International Journal of Avian Science.
Journal of the Royal Army Medical Corps ('John Fox-Russell VC MC, RAMC (1893–1917) A Forgotten Hero of Military Medicine'; E. Dolev, 1996, 142, pp. 126–128).

Databases, Indexes and Directories

Articles of Clerkship 1756–1874.
British Officer Prisoners of War, 1914–1918.
Census records for England and Wales from 1841 to 1911.
Crockford's Clerical Directory.
England & Wales Birth, Marriage and Death Indexes 1837–2005.
England & Wales Christening Records 1530–1906.
Great Britain, Royal Aero Aviators' Certificates, 1910–1950.
Honolulu, Hawaii, Passenger and Crew Lists, 1900–1959.
Kelly's Directories.
London and Surrey Marriage Bonds and Allegations Index 1597–1921.
India Births and Baptisms, 1786–1947.
National Probate Calendar (Index of Wills and Administrations) for England & Wales.
New York, Passenger Lists, 1820–1957.
New Zealand Birth, Marriage and Death Indexes.
New Zealand Electoral Rolls, 1853–1981.
Parish Registers of Baptisms, Marriages, and Burials.
UK Medical Registers, 1859–1959.
UK Incoming Passenger List, 1878–1960.

UK Outward Passenger Lists, 1890–1960.
US Passport Applications, 1795–1925.

Newspapers and Periodicals
Aberdeen Journal; *Aberdeen Daily Journal*; *Cambrian News*; *Devizes and Wiltshire Gazette*; *Evening Telegraph*; *Gloucester Journal*; *Hastings and St Leonards Observer*; *Kent and Sussex Courier*; *Kilmarnock Standard*; *London Gazette*; *London Daily News*; *Manchester Courier and Lancashire General Advertiser*; *Newcastle Journal*; *Oxford Journal Illustrated*; *Oxford Chronicle*; *Oxford Journal*; *Oxford Times*; *Shrewsbury Chronicle*; *The Sphere*; *Sydney Morning Herald*; *The Times*; *The Times of India*; *Wellington Independent*; *Western Daily Press*; *The Wipers Times*, The Complete Series, Little Books Ltd, 2013.

School / College Magazines
The Blundellian (Blundell's School, for J.W. Jenner-Clarke); *The Clayesmorian* (Clayesmore School, for R.C. Christie); *The Denstonian* (Denstone College, for F.M. Houghton); *The Felstedian* (Felsted School, for E.W. Hanby); *The Magdalen College School Journal, 1870–1880* (for R.D. Garnons Williams and the origins of the Cadet Corps); *The Lily*, 1880 onwards (Magdalen College School, for all the boys and reformation of the Cadet Corps); *The Pauline* (St Paul's School, for H. Brereton); *The Pelican* (Perse School for J.L.M. Morton); *The Spike: or, Victoria College Review War Memorial Number* (Victoria University Students' Association for G.G. Matheson)

Websites
Often a most mistrusted source of information, many historians either 'put them down' or ignore their use, for good reason. For this project, the internet has unearthed countless leads and connections to pull stories together. If the URL changes over time, simply having the host name can lead you to find what you are looking for. For this reason included below, in full, are many of the website addresses that were useful in the writing of this book. Many will stay active for a long time, others will change, but knowing the information was in the public domain gives confidence that it can be found again. Listed before the web page is the subject, or boy, the site is relevant to.

Boer War:
www.angloboerwar.com

British Newspaper Archive:
http://www.britishnewspaperarchive.co.uk/

Commonwealth War Grave Commission:
http://www.cwgc.org/

80 Field Company, The Royal Engineers:
http://www.wartimememoriesproject.com/greatwar/allied/royalengineers80fldcoy-gw.php

The Long, Long Trail:
http://www.1914-1918.net/

The Plain:
http://www.headington.org.uk/oxon/streets/inscriptions/east/fountain.htm

The Sandhurst Collection – RMA Sandhurst and RMA Woolwich Registers:
http://archive.sandhurstcollection.co.uk/search/

The South African War Memorial:
http://www.oxfordhistory.org.uk/war/other_wars/the_plain.html

Western Front Association:
http://www.westernfrontassociation.com/

E.R.L. Andrews:
www.headington.org.uk/oxon/stmargaret/andrews_lawrence.html

J.H. Bellamy:
http://www.headington.org.uk/history/war/allsaints/bellamy_john.html

A.S. Butler:
http://churchrecords.irishgenealogy.ie/churchrecords/details/76bdd00017541

J.C. Callender:
http://oxfordshireandbuckinghamshirelightinfantry.wordpress.com/2010/01/08/lieutenant-john-clement-callender/

H.S. Cannon:
http://baph.org.uk/archive/q076.html

H.W. Canton:
http://www.isle-of-wight-memorials.org.uk/people_c/canton_hw.htm

N.G. Chavasse:
http://www.ramc-ww1.com/profile.php?cPath=647&profile_id=10085

R.C. Christie:
http://www.roll-of-honour.com/Sussex/Brighton_WW1_C.html
http://www.dnw.co.uk/auction-archive/catalogue-archive/lot.php?auction_id=62&lot_id=41567

A.D. Darbishire:
http://www.ngrm.org.uk/Collections/IndustrialRailways/PenmaenmawrAndWelshGraniteCompany
http://www.headington.org.uk/oxon/sunningwell/17_darbishire.html

C.M. Dyer:
http://en.wikipedia.org/wiki/Louis_Dyer

A.E. Foster:
http://en.wikipedia.org/wiki/Myles_Birket_Foster
http://benbeck.co.uk/fh/collaterals/4N13cousins.html

J. Fox Russell:
http://en.wikipedia.org/wiki/John_Russell_(VC)
http://www.stbees.org.uk/publications/wardead/sbsvcs.htm
http://www.rwfphotos.co.uk/page1485.html
http://www.bbc.co.uk/history/ww2peopleswar/stories/22/a8477922.shtml
http://www.scoutswales.org.uk/sites/default/files/centenary_history_full.pdf
http://www.ramc-ww1.com/profile.php?cPath=647&profile_id=11779
http://www.anglesey.info/holyhead-fox-russell-heroes.htm

G.S. Gadney:
http://www.oxfordhistory.org.uk/cornmarket/east/03_painted_room.html
http://www.headington.org.uk/oxon/stmargaret/gadney_gilbert.html
http://www.remembering.org.uk/glosregtofficers/glos_regt_offrs_8_battalion.htm

R.D. Garnons Williams:
http://www.penmon.org/page36.htm
http://en.wikipedia.org/wiki/Richard_Garnons_Williams
http://www.penmon.org/page36.htm
http://www.britishfuture.org/wp-content/uploads/2012/11/How-Should-Sport-Remember.pdf
http://www.alibris.co.uk/booksearch?qsort=&page=1&matches=0&browse=1&isbn=9781157520924&full=1
http://www.espn.co.uk/wales/rugby/player/558.html

E.W. Hanby:
http://www.aim25.ac.uk/cgi-bin/vcdf/detail?coll_id=19209&inst_id=118&nv1=browse&nv2=repos

C.E. Hemmerde:
http://janetandrichardsgenealogy.co.uk/Lieut%20C%20E%20Hemmerde.html

N.E.N. Henderson:
http://en.wikipedia.org/wiki/Nelson_Henderson
http://www.espn.co.uk/scotland/rugby/player/1049.html
http://ukcomics.wikia.com/wiki/James_Henderson_%26_Sons

A.H. Herbertson:
http://www.jstor.org/discover/10.2307/1792720?uid=3738032&uid=2&uid=4&sid=21103626252991
http://www.jstor.org/discover/10.2307/40565956?uid=3738032&uid=2&uid=4&sid=21103626252991
http://people.wku.edu/charles.smith/chronob/HERB1865.htm

L.V. Hoyne-Fox:
http://www.winkleighheroes.co.uk/level3/kutdeathmarch.htm

J.W. Jenner-Clarke:
http://www.blundells.org/archive/in-memoriam/jenner-clarke_jw.html

K.V. King:
http://www.hambo.org/lancing/view_man.php?id=305

D.N. Leicester:
http://glosters.tripod.com/1917off.html

C.R.C. Maltby:
http://1914-1918.invisionzone.com/forums/index.php?showtopic=53838

G.G. Matheson:
http://www.nzetc.org/tm/scholarly/tei-VUW1937_65Spik-t1-body-d49.html
http://www.uiowa.edu/~boosf/Matheson.pdf
http://www.nzwargraves.org.nz/
http://100nzmemorials.blogspot.co.uk/2012/09/killed-in-action-7-june-1917-eketahuna.html

H.S. Mintoft:
http://www.genuki.org.uk/big/eng/YKS/Photos/WMframes/NRY/AlneStMaryWMPlaque.html
http://archiver.rootsweb.ancestry.com/th/read/YORKSGEN/2004-01/1073693565

M.A. Morris:
http://www.headington.org.uk/oxon/stmargaret/morris_michael.html

J.L.M. Morton:
http://www.astonoxon.com/Pages/StJamesChurch.aspx
http://www.chch.ox.ac.uk/cathedral/memorials/WW1/Joseph-Morton
http://www.activehistory.co.uk/Miscellaneous/wulfsww1/obits/morton_jlm.htm
http://www.roll-of-honour.com/Cambridgeshire/CambridgePerseSchool.html
http://themanchesters.org/forum/index.php?action=printpage;topic=1572.0

W.H. Pearson:
http://www.roll-of-honour.com/Cambridgeshire/CambridgeLeysSchoolWW1.html
http://www.roll-of-honour.com/Cambridgeshire/CambridgeLeysSchoolWW1.html
http://www.headington.org.uk/oxon/broad/buildings/south/01,02,03.htm

F.B. Pitts:
http://www.lesgrammar.org/Archives/frameset.htm

J.L. Roberton:
http://1914-1918.invisionzone.com/forums/index.php?showtopic=13807
http://www.25squadron.org.uk/History.htm

F.B. Roberts:
http://www.jesus.cam.ac.uk/about-jesus-college/old-library-archives/exhibitions/first-world-war/
http://www.cricketarchive.com/Gloucestershire/Players/32/32406/32406.html
http://www.espncricinfo.com/wisdenalmanack/content/story/228033.html

C.P. Sells:
http://archiver.rootsweb.ancestry.com/th/read/GREATWAR/2001-10/1002778081

A.A. Steward:
https://sites.google.com/site/downtonremembers/world-war-i
http://www.epsomandewellhistoryexplorer.org.uk/WarMemorialsSurnamesS.html#StewardAA

E.A Tarbet:
http://www.angloboerwar.com/index.php?option=com_grid&gid=22_uw_0&p=51

T. Thomas:
http://www.wwwmp.co.uk/ceredigion-memorials/talybont-war-memorial/
http://www.oxfordhistory.org.uk/war/schools/oxfordboyshigh/index.html

W.H. Williams:
http://1914-1918.invisionzone.com/forums/index.php?showtopic=81398

L.F. Yeo:
http://www.yeosociety.com/resources/wills/Wills%20-1907-1917.htm
http://www.yeosociety.com/ourheroes/ww1.htm

V.A.V.Z. Jessel:
http://www.oxfordhistory.org.uk/war/schools/oxfordboyshigh/index.html
http://www.jewishgen.org/jcr-uk/community/oxford_articles/pte_Davidson.htm
http://www.cemeteryscribes.com/showmedia.php?mediaID=206

Unpublished Sources:

National Archives, London

War Diaries: WO 95/2423 (20/RF for E.R.L. Andrews); WO 95/1429 (13/King's for J.L. Barratt); WO 95/2187 (11/Sher. for. for J.H. Bellamy); WO 95/2423 (1/Queen's for M.B. Blagden); WO 95/1900 (5/OBLI G. Bradley); WO 95/1890 (11/King's H. Brereton); WO 95/3067 (2/4/OBLI for J.C. Callender); WO 95/2423 (20/RF for L.D. Cane); WO 95/1152 (6 Cavalry Brigade for H.S. Cannon); WO 95/1498 (1/E.Lanc. for H.W. Canton); WO 95/2027 (80 Field Company, RE, for R.C. Christie); WO 95/3119 and WO 95/128 (1/28/London for H.H. Dawes); WO 95/2262 (4/RB for C.M. Dyer); WO 95/2423 (20/RF for R.G. Field); WO 95/2127 (7/KOYLI for A.E. Foster); WO 95/2423 (18/RF for A.E. Foster and F.D Wilkinson); WO 95/4626 (1/6/RWF for J. Fox Russell); WO 95/2085 (8/Glouc. for G.S. Gadney); WO 95/2208 (12/RF for R.D. Garnons Williams); WO 95/2639 (23/Middx. for E.W. Hanby); WO 95/1861 (6/ QORWK for C.E. Hemmerde); WO 95/1555 (1/ QORWK for C.E. Hemmerde); WO 95/2304 (1/KOSB for N.E.N. Henderson); WO 95/1900 (9/KRRC for A.H. Herbertson); WO 95/2115 (10/KRRC for A.H. Herbertson); WO 95/1896 (7/KRRC for A.H. Herbertson); WO 95/1908 (6/DCLI for J.W. Jenner-Clarke); WO 95/1910 (14/TMB for J.W. Jenner-Clarke); WO 95/1722 (2/North'n. for P.B. Lees); WO 95/1580 (12/Glouc. for D.N. Leicester); WO 95/2121 (12/RB for C.R.C. Maltby); WO 95/3688 (1/Auckland for G.G. Matheson); WO 95/2161 (1/E.York. for H.S. Mintoft); WO 95/4312 (2/Hants for M.A. Morris); WO 95/1669 (22/Manch. for J.L.M. Morton); WO 95/2484 (23/Manch. for J.L.M. Morton); WO 95/2974 (57/MGC for W.H. Pearson); WO 95/2427/4 (21/RF for F.B. Pitts); WO 95/2165 (8/Leic. for F.B. Pitts); WO 95/1901 (9/RB for F.B. Roberts); WO 95/2381 (168/RFA for A.A. Steward); WO 95/4311 (1/R.Innis.F. for E.A. Tarbet); WO 95/2008 (51/MGC for T. Thomas); WO 95/1273 (2/MGC for D.H. Webb); WO 95/22071 (8/Buffs for F.D. Wilkinson); WO 95/3153 and WO 95/4678 (10/Buffs for F.D. Wilkinson); WO 95/4315 and WO 95/4594 (1/6/LF for W.H. Williams); WO 95/1362 (2/S.Staff. for L.F. Yeo); WO 95/2840 and WO 95/2823 (7/DLI for V.A.V.Z. Jessel); WO 95/2161 (15/DLI for V.A.V.Z. Jessel).

Service Records: WO 339/81850 (J.L. Barratt); WO 339/60307 (J.H. Bellamy); WO 339/88370 (M.B. Blagden); WO 339/32649 (G. Bradley); WO 339/10539 (H. Brereton); WO 374/11395 (A.S. Butler); WO 374/11819 (J.C. Callender); WO 339/147 (L.D. Cane); WO 339/8260 (H.S. Canton); WO 339/51913 (A.D. Darbishire); WO 363/D430 (H.H. Dawes); WO 339/16561 (C.M. Dyer); WO 339/58815 (A.E. Foster); WO 374/59795 (J. Fox Russell); WO 76/97/26 and

WO 76/398 (R.D. Garnons Williams); WO 339/56807 (E.W. Hanby); WO 339/53983 (C.E. Hemmerde); WO 339/78230 (N.E.N. Henderson); WO 339/2758 (A.H. Herbertson); WO 339/14689 (F.M.C. Houghton); WO 339/14459 (J.W. Jenner-Clarke); WO 339/101551 (K.V. King); WO 339/26383 (P.B. Lees); WO 339/17731 (D.N. Leicester); WO 339/34666 (C.R.C. Maltby); WO 374/48066 (H.S. Mintoft); WO 339/32152 (J.L.M. Morton); WO 374/53111 (W.H. Pearson); WO 339/60849 (F.B. Pitts); WO 339/3707 (F.B. Roberts); WO 339/44387 (A.A. Steward); WO 339/3079 (E.A. Tarbet); WO 339/32721 (D.H. Webb); WO 339/58966 (F.D. Wilkinson); WO 339/48002 (W.H. Williams); WO 339/11094 (L.F. Yeo); WO 374/77784 (V.A.V.Z. Jessel).

Note: Service records for H.H. Dawes (without a commision) and C.P. Sells (before his commision) were gained from the WO 363 series ('burnt records') and WO 364 series ('unburnt records') of service records for other ranks. No service records survive for Privates E.R.L. Andrews, H.S. Cannon, R.G. Field and D.H. Webb.

AIR Records: AIR 1/166/15/153/1 (History of the 15 Squadron); AIR 1/167/15/155/1 (History of the 19 Squadron); AIR 27/305/1 (History of the 25 Squadron); AIR 27/501 (52 Squadron Operations Record); AIR 1/2029/204/326/5 (142 Squadron); AIR 76/53 (H. Brereton); AIR 76/70/0/430 (A.S. Butler); AIR 76/78 (B.H. Carter); AIR 76/239 (F.M.C. Houghton); AIR 76/277/26 (K.V. King); AIR 76/429 (J.L. Roberton).

Medal Index Cards: WO 372 series (for all boys).

Campaign Medal Rolls: WO 329 series (for all boys).

Archives New Zealand

Personnel Records: New Zealand Defense Force, R21373674, AABK 18805 W5549 6 / 0079095 (for G.G. Matheson); War Diaries: 1 Auckland Infantry Battalion – 1 New Zealand Infantry Brigade, R 23804604 ACID 18388 WA 71/101/[71n] and R 23804612 ACID 18388 WA 71/101/[71v].

Auckland War Memorial Museum

Cenotaph Database and Personal collections.

British Library, London

India Office indexes (for L.V. Hoyne-Fox).

Imperial War Museum, London

Noel Chavasse documents.

Magdalen College Archive, Oxford

The school science class notebooks and register of John Manley, 1888–1918; MCS Confirmation Register; MCS, Oxford, Register 1862–1879, Choristers Entries (register) 1904–1930.

Magdalen College School Archive, Oxford

Numerous documents.

Oxfordshire History Centre

Audio recording: BBC Radio Oxford interview with Colin G. Hey, 1977.
Microfiched newspapers including *Oxford Journal Illustrated.*

Senate House Library, London

London University OTC list.

Other School / College / Organisation Archive or Registers

Abingdon School Archive, Balliol College Archive, Berkhamsted School Archive, Blundell's School Archive, Denstone College Archive, Dulwich College Archive, Framlingham School Archive, Lancing College Archive, Leicester Grammar School Archive, The Leys School Archive, Manchester University Archive, Merton College Archive, Oxford University Alumni Register, 1500–1886, Perse School Archive, Victoria University of Wellington Record Service and Library, Worcester College

Archive, University College London Archive, The Royal Indian Engineering College, Coopers Hill 1871–1906 Register, Douai and Woolhampton School Register

Acknowledgement for photographs
Every effort was made to trace the copyright owners for the images used throughout this book and I am indebted to the people and organizations mentioned in the acknowledgments for their kind permission to reproduce their photographic images.

In the few cases where copyright owners were not traceable, if they come to light in the future the relevant acknowledgement will be published in subsequent editions of the book.

Images of the Magdalen College School Brass War Memorials and of the portrait of C.E. Brownrigg was commissioned from and expertly taken by Rob Judges.

Index of People

General Index